John Forster, Walter Savage Landor, Charles George Crump

Imaginary Conversations

Vol. 2

John Forster, Walter Savage Landor, Charles George Crump

Imaginary Conversations
Vol. 2

ISBN/EAN: 9783744742634

Printed in Europe, USA, Canada, Australia, Japan

Cover: Foto ©Thomas Meinert / pixelio.de

More available books at **www.hansebooks.com**

Imaginary Conversations

By Walter Savage Landor

With Bibliographical and Explanatory Notes by Charles G. Crump

IN SIX VOLUMES

SECOND VOLUME

LONDON: PRINTED FOR J. M. DENT & CO.
AND PUBLISHED BY THEM AT ALDINE
HOUSE, 69 GREAT EASTERN STREET.
MDCCCXCI.

TABLE OF CONTENTS.

——:o:——

CLASSICAL DIALOGUES.

(ROMAN.)

(DIALOGUES OF SOVEREIGNS AND STATESMEN.)

CLASSICAL DIALOGUES.

(ROMAN.)

CLASSICAL DIALOGUES.

(ROMAN.)

————*————

IV. LUCULLUS AND CÆSAR.[1]

Cæsar. Lucius Lucullus, I come to you privately and un-
attended for reasons which you will know; confiding, I dare not
say in your friendship, since no service of mine toward you hath
deserved it, but in your generous and disinterested love of peace.
Hear me on. Cneius Pompeius, according to the report of my
connections in the city, had, on the instant of my leaving it for the
province, begun to solicit his dependants to strip me ignominiously
of authority. Neither vows nor affinity can bind him. He would
degrade the father of his wife; he would humiliate his own children,
the unoffending, the unborn; he would poison his own nascent love,
—at the suggestion of Ambition. Matters are now brought so
far, that either he or I must submit to a reverse of fortune; since
no concession can assuage his malice, divert his envy, or gratify
his cupidity. No sooner could I raise myself up, from the consternation and stupefaction into which the certainty of these reports

[1 It is difficult to gather from this Conversation the date at which it
is supposed to take place; probably it is not possible to do so. Cæsar
has come to visit Lucullus in secret, to ask him for his help against
Pompey. At no time would Cæsar have been likely to take such a step,
least of all during the full tide of his success in Gaul, when his alliance
for Pompey was still vigorous. But the history is unimportant. For
the splendours of the villa of Lucullus, see Plutarch's Life of Lucullus,
which has furnished Landor with the materials for his picture. (Imag.
Convers., iv., 1829. Works, i., 1846. Imag. Convers., Gks. and Rom.,
1853. Works, ii., 1876.)]

had thrown me, than I began to consider in what manner my own
private afflictions might become the least noxious to the republic.
Into whose arms, then, could I throw myself more naturally and
more securely, to whose bosom could I commit and consign more
sacredly the hopes and destinies of our beloved country, than his
who laid down power in the midst of its enjoyments, in the vigor
of youth, in the pride of triumph, when Dignity solicited, when
Friendship urged, entreated, supplicated, and when Liberty herself
invited and beckoned to him from the senatorial order and from
the curule chair? Betrayed and abandoned by those we had
confided in, our next friendship, if ever our hearts receive any,
or if any will venture in those places of desolation, flies forward
instinctively to what is most contrary and dissimilar. Cæsar is
hence the visitant of Lucullus.

Lucullus. I had always thought Pompeius more moderate and
more reserved than you represent him, Caius Julius; and yet I am
considered in general, and surely you also will consider me, but
little liable to be prepossessed by him.

Cæsar. Unless he may have ingratiated himself with you
recently, by the administration of that worthy whom last winter
his partisans dragged before the Senate, and forced to assert
publicly that you and Cato had instigated a party to circumvent
and murder him; and whose carcass, a few days afterward, when
it had been announced that he had died by a natural death, was
found covered with bruises, stabs, and dislocations.[2]

Lucullus. You bring much to my memory which had quite
slipped out of it, and I wonder that it could make such an impression on yours. A proof to me that the interest you take in my
behalf began earlier than your delicacy will permit you to acknowledge. You are fatigued, which I ought to have perceived before.

Cæsar. Not at all; the fresh air has given me life and
alertness: I feel it upon my cheek even in the room.

Lucullus. After our dinner and sleep, we will spend the remainder of the day on the subject of your visit.

Cæsar. Those Ethiopian slaves of yours shiver with cold upon

[2 See Plutarch. There can be no doubt that the informer Vettius was
instigated into making the charge by Vatinius, a creature of Cæsar's, who
had proposed the law giving him an extraordinary command in Gaul.
The charge drove Lucullus from Rome.]

the mountain here; and truly I myself was not insensible to the change of climate, in the way from Mutina.

What white bread! I never found such even at Naples or Capua. This Formian wine (which I prefer to the Chian), how exquisite!

Lucullus. Such is the urbanity of Cæsar, even while he bites his lip with displeasure. How! surely it bleeds! Permit me to examine the cup.

Cæsar. I believe a jewel has fallen out of the rim in the carriage: the gold is rough there.

Lucullus. Marcipor, let me never see that cup again! No answer, I desire. My guest pardons heavier faults. Mind that dinner be prepared for us shortly.

Cæsar. In the meantime, Lucullus, if your health permits it, shall we walk a few paces round the villa? for I have not seen any thing of the kind before.

Lucullus. The walls are double; the space between them two feet; the materials for the most part earth and straw. Two hundred slaves, and about as many mules and oxen, brought the beams and rafters up the mountain; my architects fixed them at once in their places: every part was ready, even the wooden nails. The roof is thatched, you see.

Cæsar. Is there no danger that so light a material should be carried off by the winds, on such an eminence?

Lucullus. None resists them equally well.

Cæsar. On this immensely high mountain, I should be apprehensive of the lightning, which the poets, and I think the philosophers too, have told us strikes the highest.

Lucullus. The poets are right; for whatever is received as truth is truth in poetry; and a fable may illustrate like a fact. But the philosophers are wrong, as they generally are, even in the commonest things; [3] because they seldom look beyond their own tenets, unless through captiousness, and because they argue more than they meditate, and display more than they examine. Archimedes and Euclid are, in my opinion, after our Epicurus,

[[3] First ed. reads: "things, because they write more attentively than they examine. Archimedes, in my opinion, is the only one worthy of the name, for he alone has kept," &c. Five lines below, from "I had" to "philosophers" added in 2nd ed.]

the worthiest of the name, having kept apart to the demonstrable, the practical, and the useful. Many of the rest are good writers and good disputants; but unfaithful suitors of simple science, boasters of their acquaintance with gods and goddesses, plagiarists and imposotrs. I had forgotten my roof, although it is composed of much the same materials as the philosophers'. Let the lightning fall : **one** handful of silver, or less, repairs the damage.

Cæsar. Impossible ! nor **indeed one** thousand nor twenty, if those tapestries* and pictures are consumned.

Lucullus. True ; but only the thatch would **burn.** For, before the baths were tessellated, I filled the area with alum and water, and soaked the timbers and laths **for** many **months,** and covered them afterward with **alum** in powder, by means of liquid glue. Mithridates[4] taught me **this.** Having in vain attacked with combustibles a wooden tower, I took it by stratagem, and found within it a mass of **alum, which,** if a great hurry had not been observed by **us among** the enemy **in** the attempt to conceal **it,** would have escaped **our** notice. I never scrupled to **extort** the truth from my prisoners ; but my instruments were purple robes and plate, and the only wheel in my **armory,** destined to such purposes, was the wheel of Fortune.

Cæsar. I wish, in my campaigns, I could have equalled your clemency and humanity ; but the Gauls are more uncertain, fierce, and perfidious **than** the wildest tribes of Caucasus ; **and our** policy cannot be carried with us, it must be formed upon the spot. They love you, not for abstaining **from** hurting them, but for ceasing ; and they embrace you only **at** two seasons,—when stripes are fresh, or when stripes are imminent. Elsewhere, I hope to become the rival of Lucullus in this admirable part of virtue.

I shall never build villas, because,—but what are your proportions ? Surely the edifice is extremely low.

Lucullus. There is only one floor ; the height of the apart-

* Cæsar would regard such things attentively. "In *expeditionibus* tessellata et sectitia pavimenta circumtulisse ; signa, tabulas, operis antiqui, semper animosissime comparâsse," says Suetonius.

[4 Mithridates, King of Pontus, whom Lucullus conquered, thus delivering Rome from a dangerous enemy. Pompey, however, gained the glory for himself by causing Lucullus to be deprived of his command just at the close of the war, and putting himself in his place.]

ments is twenty feet to the cornice, five above it ; the breadth is twenty-five, the length forty. The building, as you perceive, is quadrangular : three sides contain four rooms each ; the other has many partitions and two stories, for domestics and offices. Here is my salt-bath.

Cæsar. A bath indeed for all the Nereids named by Hesiod, with room enough for the Tritons and their herds and horses.

Lucullus.[5] Next to it, where yonder boys are carrying the myrrhine vases, is a tepid one of fresh water, ready for your reception.

Cæsar. I resign the higher pleasure for the inferior, as we all are apt to do ; and I will return to the enjoyment of your conversation when I have indulged a quarter of an hour in this refreshment.

Lucullus. Meanwhile, I will take refuge with some less elegant philosopher, whose society I shall quit again with less regret. (*Cæsar returning.*) It is useless, O Caius Julius, to inquire if there has been any negligence or any omission in the service of the bath ; for these are secrets which you never impart to the most favored of your friends.

Cæsar. I have often enjoyed the luxury much longer, but never more highly. Pardon my impatience to see the remainder of your Apennine villa.

Lucullus. Here stand my two cows. Their milk is brought to me with its warmth and froth ; for it loses its salubrity both by repose and by motion. Pardon me, Cæsar : I shall appear to you to have forgotten that I am not conducting Marcus Varro.

Cæsar. You would convert him into Cacus : he would drive them off. What beautiful beasts ! how sleek and white and cleanly ! I never saw any like them, excepting when we sacrifice to Jupiter the stately leader from the pastures of the Clitumnus.

Lucullus. Often do I make a visit to these quiet creatures, and with no less pleasure than in former days to my horses. Nor indeed can I much wonder that whole nations have been consentaneous in treating them as objects of devotion : the only thing wonderful is that gratitude seems to have acted as powerfully and extensively as fear ; indeed more extensively, for no object of worship whatever has attracted so many worshippers.

[5 From " *Lucullus* " to " villa " (16 lines) added in 2nd ed.]

Where Jupiter has one, the cow has ten : she was venerated before he was born, and will be when even the carvers have forgotten him.

Cæsar. Unwillingly should I see it ; for the character of our gods hath formed the character of our nation. Serapis and Isis have stolen in among them within our memory, and others will follow, until at last Saturn will not be the only one emasculated by his successor. What can be more august than our rites ? The first dignitaries of the republic are emulous to administer them : nothing of low or venal has any place in them ; nothing pusillanimous, nothing unsocial and austere. I speak of them as they were ; before Superstition woke up again from her slumber, and caught to her bosom with maternal love the alluvial monsters of the Nile. Philosophy, never fit for the people, had entered the best houses, and the image of Epicurus had taken the place of the Lemures. But men cannot bear to be deprived long together of any thing they are used to, not even of their fears ; and, by a reaction of the mind appertaining to our nature, new stimulants were looked for, not on the side of pleasure, where nothing new could be expected or imagined, but on the opposite. Irreligion is followed by fanaticism, and fanaticism by irreligion, alternately and perpetually.

Lucullus. The religion of our country, as you observe, is well adapted to its inhabitants. Our progenitor, Mars, hath Venus recumbent on his breast and looking up to him, teaching us that pleasure is to be sought in the bosom of valor and by the means of war. No great alteration, I think, will ever be made in our rites and ceremonies,—the best and most imposing that could be collected from all nations, and uniting them to us by our complacence in adopting them. The gods themselves may change names, to flatter new power : and, indeed, as we degenerate, Religion will accommodate herself to our propensities and desires. Our heaven is now popular : it will become monarchal ; not without a crowded court, as befits it, of apparitors and satellites and minions of both sexes, paid and caressed for carrying to their stern, dark-bearded master prayers and supplications. Altars must be strewn with broken minds, and incense rise amid abject aspirations. Gods will be found unfit for their places ; and it is not impossible that, in the ruin imminent from our contentions for power, and in the necessary extinction both of ancient families and of generous sentiments, our consular fasces may become the water-sprinklers of some upstart priesthood, and that my son may apply for lustration to the son of my groom. The interest of such men requires that the spirit of arms and of arts be extinguished. They will predicate peace, that the people may be tractable to them ; but a religion altogether pacific is the fomenter of wars and the nurse of crimes, alluring Sloth from within and Violence from afar. If ever it should prevail among the Romans, it must prevail alone : for nations more vigorous and energetic will invade them, close upon them, trample them under foot ; and the name of Roman, which is now the most glorious, will become the most opprobrious upon earth.

Cæsar. The time I hope may be distant ; for next to my own name I hold my country's.

Lucullus. Mine, not coming from Troy or Ida, is lower in my estimation : I place my country's first.

You are surveying the little lake beside us.[6] It contains no fish, birds never alight on it, the water is extremely pure and cold ; the walk round is pleasant, not only because there is always a gentle breeze from it, but because the turf is fine, and the surface of the mountain on this summit is perfectly on a level to a great extent in length,—not a trifling advantage to me, who walk often and am weak. I have no alley, no garden, no inclo-sure ; the park is in the vale below, where a brook supplies the ponds, and where my servants are lodged ; for here I have only twelve in attendance.

Cæsar. What is that so white, toward the Adriatic ?

Lucullus. The Adriatic itself. Turn round and you may descry the Tuscan Sea. Our situation is reported to be among the highest of the Apennines.—Marcipor has made the sign to me that dinner is ready. Pass this way.

Cæsar. What a library is here ![7] Ah, Marcus Tullius ! I

[6 " Beside us " added in 2nd ed.]

[7 Plutarch praises Lucullus for his learning. " He had applied himself to the sciences called *liberal*, and was deep in the study of *humanity* from his youth. . . . While he was but a youth, as he was jesting with Hortensius the orator and Gisenna the historian, he undertook to write a short history of the Marsi either in Greek or Latin verse as the lot should fall. They took him at his word, and, according to the lot, it was

salute thy image. Why frownest thou upon me,—collecting the consular robe, and uplifting the right arm, as when Rome stood firm again, and Catiline fled before thee?

Lucullus. Just so; such was the action the statuary chose, as adding a new endearment to the memory of my absent friend.

Cæsar. Sylla, who honoured you above all men, is not here.

Lucullus. I have his *Commentaries:* he inscribed them, as you know, to me. Something even of our benefactors may be forgotten, and gratitude be unreproved.

Cæsar. The impression on that couch, and the two fresh honeysuckles in the leaves of those two books, would show, even to a stranger, that this room is peculiarly the master's. Are they sacred?

Lucullus. To me and Cæsar.

Cæsar. I would have asked permission—

Lucullus. Caius Julius, you have nothing to ask of Polybius and Thucydides; nor of Xenophon, the next to them on the table.

Cæsar. Thucydides! the most generous,[8] the most unprejudiced, the most sagacious, of historians. Now, Lucullus, you whose judgment in style is more accurate than any other Roman's, do tell me whether a commander, desirous of writing his *Commentaries,* could take to himself a more perfect model than Thucydides?

Lucullus. Nothing is more perfect, nor ever will be: the scholar of Pericles, the master of Demosthenes, the equal of the one in military science, and of the other not the inferior in civil and forensic; the calm dispassionate judge of the general by whom he was defeated, his defender, his encomiast. To talk of such men is conducive not only to virtue but to health.

to be in Greek. That history of his is still extant." Plutarch also says that Sylla dedicated his commentaries to Lucullus "as a person who could reduce the acts and incidents to much better order, and compose a more agreeable history of them than himself." The wealth which Lucullus acquired in Asia in his campaigns against Mithridates and Tigranes was partly expended in collecting books. "His libraries," says Plutarch, "were open to all." At the date of this Conversation Cicero was in exile. Cæsar had been willing to save him the disgrace, and, with that intention, offered him a post in Gaul. Cicero's refusal obliged Cæsar to leave him to his fate, and he was exiled under a law, brought in by Clodius, condemning him for the measures he had taken against the associates of Catiline.]

[8 First ed. reads: "generous of military men; the most," &c.]

Cæsar. We have no writer who could keep up long together his severity and strength. I would follow him; but I shall be contented with my genius, if (Thucydides in sight) I come many paces behind, and attain by study and attention the graceful and secure mediocrity of Xenophon.

Lucullus. You will avoid, I think, Cæsar, one of his peculiarities, —his tendency to superstition.

Cæsar. I dare promise this; and even to write nothing so flat and idle as his introduction to the *Cyropædia.* The first sentence that follows it, I perceive, repeats the same word, with its substantive, four times. This is a trifle; but great writers and great painters do miracles or mischief by a single touch. Our authors are so addicted of late to imitate the Grecian, that a bad introduction is more classical than a good one. Not to mention any friend of yours, Crispus Sallustius, who is mine, brought me one recently of this description; together with some detached pieces of a history, which nothing in our prose or poetry hath surpassed in animation.

Lucullus. We ought to talk of these things by ourselves, not before the vulgar; by which expression I mean the unlearned and irreverent, in Forum and in Senate. Our Cicero has indeed avoided such inelegance as that of Xenophon; one perhaps less pardonable may be found repeatedly in his works: I would say an inelegance not arising from neglect, or obtusity of ear, but coming forth in the absence of reflection. He often says, "*mirari soleo.*" Now surely a wise man soon ceases to wonder at any thing; and, instead of indulging in the habitude of wonder at one object, brings it closer to him, makes it familiar, discusses, and dismisses it. He told me in his last letter of an incredible love and affection for me. Pardon me, Cæsar! pardon me, Genius of Rome, and Mercury! I exclaimed, "*the clown!*" laughing heartily. He would not that I should really have thought his regard *incredible;* on the contrary, that I should believe in it and confide in it to its full extent, and that I should flatter myself it was not only possible but reasonable. In vain will any one remark to me, "*Such phrases are common.*" In our ordinary language there are many beauties, more or less visible according to their place and season, which a judicious writer and forcible orator will subject to his arbitration and service: there are also many things which, if used at all, must be used cautiously. I may be much at my ease without being in tatters, and without treading on the feet of those I come forward to salute. I arrogate to myself no superiority in detecting a peculiar and latent mark upon that exalted luminary: his own effulgence showed me it. From Cicero down to me the distance is as great, as between the prince of the Senate and the lowest voter. I influenced the friends of order: he fulminated and exterminated the enemies. I have served my country: he hath saved it.

This other is my dining-room. You expect the dishes.

Cæsar. I misunderstood,—I fancied—

Lucullus. Repose yourself, and touch with the ebony wand, beside you, the sphynx on either of those obelisks, right or left.

Cæsar. Let me look at them first.

Lucullus. The contrivance was intended for one person, or two at most, desirous of privacy and quiet. The [9] blocks of jasper in my pair, and of porphyry in yours, easily yield in their grooves, each forming one partition. There are four, containing four platforms. The lower holds four dishes, such as sucking forest-boars, venison, hares, tunnies, sturgeons, which you will find within; the upper three, eight each, but diminutive. The confectionery is brought separately, for the steam would spoil it, if any should escape. The melons are in the snow, thirty feet under us: they came early this morning from a place in the vicinity of Luni,[10] so that I hope they may be crisp, independently of their coolness.

Cæsar. I wonder not at any thing of refined elegance in Lucullus; but really here Antiochia and Alexandria seem to have cooked for us, and magicians to be our attendants.

Lucullus. The absence of slaves from our repast is the luxury, for Marcipor alone enters, and he only when I press a spring with my foot or wand. When you desire his appearance, touch that chalcedony just before you.

Cæsar. I eat quick and rather plentifully; yet the valetudinarian (excuse my rusticity, for I rejoice at seeing it) appears to equal the traveller in appetite, and to be contented with one dish.

Lucullus. It is milk: such, with strawberries, which ripen

[9 First ed. reads: "The apparent blocks."]
[10 First ed. reads: "Luni, travelling by night. *Cæsar*," &c.]

on the Apennines many months in continuance, and some other berries [11] of sharp and grateful flavor, has been my only diet since my first residence here. The state of my health requires it ; and the habitude of nearly three months renders this food not only more commodious to my studies and more conducive to my sleep, but also more agreeable to my palate than any other.

Cæsar. Returning to Rome or Baiæ, you must domesticate and tame them. The cherries you introduced from Pontus are now growing in Cisalpine and Transalpine Gaul ; and the largest and best in the world, perhaps, are upon the more sterile side of Lake Larius.

Lucullus. There are some fruits, and some virtues, which require a harsh soil and bleak exposure for their perfection.

Cæsar. In such a profusion of viands, and so savory, I perceive no odor.

Lucullus. A flue conducts heat through the compartments of the obelisks ; and, if you look up, you may observe that those gilt roses, between the astragals in the cornice, are prominent from it half a span. Here is an aperture in the wall, between which and the outer is a perpetual current of air. We are now in the dog-days ; and I have never felt in the whole summer more heat than at Rome in many days of March.

Cæsar. Usually you are attended by troops of domestics and of dinner-friends, not to mention the learned and scientific, nor your own family, your attachment to which, from youth upward, is one of the higher graces in your character. Your brother was seldom absent from you.

Lucullus. Marcus was coming ; but the vehement heats along the Arno, in which valley he has a property he never saw before, inflamed his blood, and he now is resting for a few days at Fæsulæ,[12]

[11 Footnote in 1st ed. reads : "The raspberry and gooseberry are not cultivated in Italy, but grow plentifully on many parts of the Alps and Apennines. In one garden, belonging to a Florentine, are currants introduced by a French family. None of these fruits is known at Rome. Where the climate does much for fruit, the people do little."]

[12 Fiesole, Landor's home for many years. Lucullus was so much attached to his brother Marcus that as a young man he refused to accept any office without him. Lucullus died before his brother; "who," says Plutarch, "did not long survive him, . . . he was the best and most affectionate of brothers."]

a little town destroyed by Sylla within our memory, who left it only air and water, the best in Tuscany. The health of Marcus, like mine, has been declining for several months: we are running our last race against each other, and never was I, in youth along the Tiber, so anxious of first reaching the goal. I would not outlive him: I should reflect too painfully on earlier days, and look forward too despondently on future. As for friends, lampreys and turbots beget them, and they spawn not amid the solitude of the Apennines. To dine in company with more than two is a Gaulish and German thing. I can hardly bring myself to believe that I have eaten in concert with twenty; so barbarous and herdlike a practice does not now appear to me,—such an incentive to drink much and talk loosely; not to add, such a necessity to speak loud, which is clownish and odious in the extreme. On this mountain-summit I hear no noises, no voices, not even of salutation; we have no flies about us, and scarcely an insect or reptile.

Cæsar. Your amiable son is probably with his uncle: is he well?

Lucullus. Perfectly. He was indeed with my brother in his intended visit to me; but Marcus, unable to accompany him hither, or superintend his studies in the present state of his health, sent him directly to his Uncle Cato at Tusculum,—a man fitter than either of us to direct his education, and preferable to any, excepting yourself and Marcus Tullius, in eloquence and urbanity.

Cæsar. Cato is so great, that whoever is greater must be the happiest and first of men.

Lucullus. That any such be still existing, O Julius, ought to excite no groan from the breast of a Roman citizen. But perhaps I wrong you; perhaps your mind was forced reluctantly back again, on your past animosities and contests in the Senate.

Cæsar. I revere him, but cannot love him.

Lucullus. Then, Caius Julius, you groaned with reason, and I would pity rather than reprove you.

On the ceiling at which you are looking, there is no gilding, and little painting,—a mere trellis of vines bearing grapes, and the heads, shoulders, and arms, rising from the cornice only, of boys and girls climbing up to steal them, and scrambling for them: nothing over-head; no giants tumbling down, no Jupiter thundering, no Mars and Venus caught at Mid-day, no river-gods pouring out their urns upon us; for, as I think nothing so insipid as a flat ceiling, I think nothing so absurd as a storied one. Before I was aware, and without my participation, the painter had adorned that of my bed-chamber with a golden shower, bursting from varied and irradiated clouds. On my expostulation, his excuse was that he knew the Danaë of Scopas, in a recumbent posture, was to occupy the centre of the room. The walls, behind the tapestry and pictures, are quite rough. In forty-three days the whole fabric was put together and habitable.

The wine has probably lost its freshness: will you try some other?

Cæsar. Its temperature is exact; [13] its flavor exquisite. Latterly I have never sat long after dinner, and am curious to pass through the other apartments, if you will trust me.

Lucullus. I attend you.

Cæsar. Lucullus, who is here? What figure is that on the poop of the vessel? Can it be—

Lucullus. The subject was dictated by myself; you gave it. [14]

Cæsar. Oh how beautifully is the water painted! How vividly the sun strikes against the snows on Taurus! The gray temples and pier-head of Tarsus catch it differently, and the monumental mound on the left is half in shade. In the countenance of those pirates I did not observe such diversity, nor that any boy pulled his father back: I did not indeed mark them or notice them at all.

Lucullus. The painter in this fresco, the last work finished, had dissatisfied me in one particular. "That beautiful young face," said I, "appears not to threaten death."

"Lucius," he replied, "if one muscle were moved, it were not Cæsar's: beside, he said it jokingly, though resolved."

"I am contented with your apology, Antipho; but what are you doing now? for you never lay down or suspend your pencil,

[13 First ed. for "exact" reads "admirable," and for "exquisite" reads "incomparable."]

[14 See Plutarch's life of Cæsar for the story of this picture. When a youth Cæsar was captured and put to ransom by Cilician pirates. He paid them the ransom, promising at the same time to return and crucify them; a threat which he accomplished. Venus, the tutelary deity and ancestress of the Julian family looks on, and admires the threat.]

let who will talk and argue. The lines of that smaller face in the distance are the same."

"Not the same," replied he, "nor very different : it smiles, as surely the goddess must have done at the first heroic act of her descendant."

Cæsar. In her exultation and impatience to press forward, she seems to forget that she is standing at the extremity of the shell, which rises up behind out of the water ; and she takes no notice of the terror on the countenance of this Cupid who would detain her, nor of this who is flying off and looking back. The reflection of the shell has given a warmer hue below the knee ; a long streak of yellow light in the horizon is on the level of her bosom, some of her hair is almost lost in it ; above her head on every side is the pure azure of the heavens.[15]

Oh! and you would not have led me up to this? You, among whose primary studies is the most perfect satisfaction of your guests !

Lucullus. In the next apartment are seven or eight other pictures from our history.

There are no more : what do you look for ?

Cæsar. I find not among the rest any descriptive of your own exploits. Ah, Lucullus! there is no surer way of making them remembered.

This, I presume by the harps in the two corners, is the music-room.

Lucullus. No, indeed ; nor can I be said to have one here : for I love best the music of a single instrument, and listen to it willingly at all times, but most willingly while I am reading. At such seasons, a voice or even a whisper disturbs me ; but music refreshes my brain when I have read long, and strengthens it from the beginning. I find also that if I write any thing in poetry (a youthful propensity still remaining), it gives rapidity and variety and brightness to my ideas. On ceasing, I command a fresh measure and instrument, or another voice ; which is to the mind like a change of posture, or of air to the body. My health is

[15 First ed. reads : "heavens. I have read the picture ; and thus it ends. Oh! and you would not have shewn me this? You," &c. Two lines below, "*Lucullus.* This is the only one in fresco ; but in the next," &c. Five lines below, "remembered : the soul of them is here. This," &c.]

benefited by the gentle play thus opened to the most delicate of the fibres.

Cæsar. Let me augur that a disorder so tractable may be soon removed. What is it thought to be?

Lucullus. There are they who would surmise and signify, and my physician did not long attempt to persuade me of the contrary, that the ancient realms of Æætes have supplied me with some other plants than the cherry, and such as I should be sorry to see domesticated here in Italy. [16]

Cæsar. The gods forbid! Anticipate better things! The reason of Lucullus is stronger than the medicaments of Mithridates; but why not use them too? Let nothing be neglected. You may reasonably hope for many years of life: your mother still enjoys it.*

Lucullus. To stand upon one's guard against Death exasperates her malice and protracts our sufferings.

Cæsar. Rightly and gravely said: but your country at this time cannot do well without you.

Lucullus. The bowl of milk, which to-day is presented to me, will shortly be presented to my Manes.

Cæsar. Do you suspect the hand?

Lucullus. I will not suspect a Roman: let us converse no more about it.

Cæsar. It is the only subject on which I am resolved never to think, as relates to myself. Life may concern us, death not; for in death we neither can act nor reason, we neither can persuade nor command; and our statues are worth more than we are, let them be but wax. Lucius, I will not divine your thoughts; I will not penetrate into your suspicions, nor suggest mine. I am lost in admiration of your magnanimity and forbearance,—that your only dissimulation should be upon the guilt of your assassin; that you should leave him power, and create him virtues.

Lucullus. Caius Julius, if I can assist you in any thing you

[16 Cornelius Nepos attributes the imbecility and death of Lucullus to a potion given to him by his freedman Callisthenes, who wished to increase his master's affection for him. Landor supposes Pompey to have caused the poison to be administered.]

* Cicero relates that he went from his villa to attend her funeral a few years afterward.

meditate, needful or advantageous to our country, speak it unreservedly.

Cæsar. I really am ashamed of my association with Crassus and Pompeius: I would not have any thing in common with them, not even power itself. Unworthy and ignominious must it appear to you, as it does to me, to compromise with an auctioneer and a rope-dancer; for the meanness and venality of Crassus, the levity and tergiversation of Pompeius, leave them no better names. The bestiality of the one, the infidelity of the other, urge and inflame me with an inextinguishable desire of uniting my authority to yours for the salvation of the republic.

Lucullus. I foretold to Cicero, in the words of Lucretius on the dissolution of the world, —

> Tria talia texta
> Una dies dabit exitio.

Cæsar. Assist me in accomplishing your prophecy; or rather, accept my assistance: for I would more willingly hear a proposal from you than offer one. Reflections must strike you, Lucullus, no less forcibly than me, and perhaps more justly: you are calmer. Consider all the late actions of Cneius, and tell me who has ever committed any so indecorous with so grave a face? He abstained in great measure from the follies of youth, only to reserve them accumulated for maturer age. Human life, if I may venture to speak fancifully in your presence, hath its equinoxes.[17] In the vernal, its flowers open under violent tempests; in the autumnal, it is more exempt from gusts and storms, more regular, serene, and temperate, looks complacently on the fruits it has gathered, on the harvests it has reaped, and is not averse to the graces of order, to the avocations of literature, to the genial warmth of honest conviviality, and to the mild necessity of repose. Thrown out from the course of Nature, this man stood aside and solitary, and found every thing around him unattractive. And now, in the decline of life, he has recourse to those associates, of whom the best that can be said is that they would have less disgraced its outset. Repulsing you and Cicero and Cato, the leaders of his party and the propagators of his power, Pompeius the Great takes the arm of Clodius, and walks publicly with him in the Forum; who nevertheless the

[17 First ed reads: "its vernal equinox; it first flowers," &c. Six lines below, from "Thrown" to "outset" (5 lines) added in 2nd ed.]

other day headed a chorus (I am informed) of the most profligate and opprobrious youths in Rome, and sang responsively worse than Fescennine songs to his dishonor. Where was he? Before them?—in court?—defending a client? He came indeed with that intention; but sat mortified, speechless, and despondent. The Senate connived at the indignity. Even Gabinius, his flatterer and dependant, shuns him. The other consul is alienated from him totally, and favors me through Calpurnia, who watches over my security and interests at home. Julia, my daughter, was given in marriage to Pompeius for this purpose only : she fails to accomplish it; politically then, and morally, the marriage loses its validity by losing its intent. I go into Gaul, commander for five years; Crassus is preparing for an expedition against the Parthians; the Senate and people bend before Pompeius, but reluctantly and indignantly. Everything would be more tolerable to me, if I could permit him to boast that he had duped me ; but my glory requires that, letting him choose his own encampment, square the declivities, clear the ground about the eminence, foss and pale it, I should storm and keep it. Whatever he may boast of his eloquence and military skill, I fear nothing from the orator who tells us what he would have spoken, nor from the general who sees what he should have done. My first proposal for accommodation and concord shall be submitted to you (if indeed you will not frame it for me), and, should you deem it unfair, shall be suppressed. No successive step shall be made by me without your concurrence ; in short, I am inclined to take up any line of conduct, in conjunction with you, for the settling of the Commonwealth. Does the proposal seem to you so unimportant on the one hand, or so impracticable and unreasonable on the other, that you smile and shake your head ?

Lucullus. Cæsar! Cæsar! you write upon language and analogy; no man better. Tell me then, whether mud is not said to be settled when it sinks to the bottom ? and whether those who are about to sink a State do not in like manner talk of settling it?

Cæsar. I wish I had time to converse with you on language, or skill to parry your reproofs with equal wit ; for serious you cannot be. At present let us remove what is bad ; which must always be done before good of any kind can spring up.

The designs of Cneius are suspected by many in the Senate, and his pride is obnoxious to all. Your party would prevail against him; for he has enriched fewer adherents than you have, and even his best friends are for the most part in a greater degree yours.

Lucullus. I have enriched no adherents, Caius Julius. Many of my officers, it is true, are easy in their circumstances; they however gained their wealth, not from the plunder of our confederates, not from those who should enjoy with security their municipal rights and paternal farms in Italy, but from the enemy's camps and cities.

Cæsar. We two might appease the public mind, preparing the leaders of the Senate for our labors, and intimidating the factious.

Lucullus. Hilarity never forsakes you, Cæsar! and you are the happiest man upon earth in the facility with which you communicate it. Hear me, and believe me. I am about to mount higher than triumviral tribunal, or than triumphal car. They who are under me will turn their faces from me; such are the rites: but not a voice of reproach or of petulance shall be heard, when the trumpets tell our city that the funereal flames are surmounting the mortal spoils of Lucullus.

Cæsar. Mildest and most equitable of men! I have been much wronged; would you also wrong me? Lucius, you have forced from me a tear before the time. I weep at magnanimity; which no man does who wants it.

Lucullus. Why cannot you enjoy the command of your province, and the glory of having quelled so many nations?

Cæsar. I cannot bear the superiority of another.

Lucullus. The weakest of women feel so; but even the weakest of them are ashamed to acknowledge it: who hath ever heard any one? Have [18] you, who know them widely and well? Poetasters and mimes, laboring under such infirmity, put the mask on. You pursue glory: the pursuit is just and rational; but reflect that statuaries and painters have represented heroes calm and quiescent, not straining and panting like pugilists and gladiators.

From being for ever in action, for ever in contention, and

[18 First ed. reads: "not you."]

from excelling in them all other mortals, what advantage derive
we ?   I would not ask what satisfaction, what glory ?   The
insects have more activity than ourselves, the beasts more strength,
even inert matter more firmness and stability ; the gods alone
more goodness.   To the exercise of this every country lies open ;
and neither I eastward nor you westward have found any exhausted by contests for it.

Must we give men blows because they will not look at us ? or
chain them to make them hold the balance evener ?

Do not expect to be acknowledged for what you are, much
less for what you would be ; since no one can well measure
a great man but upon the bier.   There was a time when the
most ardent friend to Alexander of Macedon would have embraced the partisan for his enthusiasm, who should have compared
him with Alexander of Pheræ.   It must have been at a splendid
feast, and late at it, when Scipio should have been raised to an
equality with Romulus, or Cato [19] with Curius.   It has been
whispered in my ear, after a speech of Cicero, "If he goes on so,
he will tread down the sandal of Marcus Antonius in the long
run, and perhaps leave Hortensius behind."   Officers of mine,
speaking about you, have exclaimed with admiration, "He fights
like Cinna."   Think, Caius Julius (for you have been instructed
to think both as a poet and as a philosopher), that among the
hundred hands of Ambition, to whom we may attribute them
more properly than to Briareus, there is not one which holds
any thing firmly.   In the precipitancy of her course, what
appears great is small, and what appears small is great.   Our
estimate of men is apt to be as inaccurate and inexact as that of
things, or more.   Wishing to have all on our side, we often
leave those we should keep by us, run after those we should
avoid, and call importunately on others who sit quiet and will
not come.   We cannot at once catch the applause of the vulgar
and expect the approbation of the wise.   What are parties ?   Do
men really great ever enter into them ?   Are they not ball-
courts, where ragged adventurers strip and strive, and where
dissolute youths abuse one another, and challenge and game and
wager ?   If you and I cannot quite divest ourselves of infirmities

[19 First ed. reads: "the elder Cato with Curius, or the younger with
him."   Four lines below, from "and" to "behind" added in 2nd ed.]

and passions, let us think however that there is enough in us to be divided into two portions, and let us keep the upper undisturbed and pure. A part of Olympus itself lies in dreariness and in clouds, variable and stormy; but it is not the highest: there the gods govern. Your soul is large enough to embrace your country: all other affection is for less objects, and less men are capable of it. Abandon, O Cæsar! such thoughts and wishes as now agitate and propel you: leave them to mere men of the marsh, to fat hearts and miry intellects. Fortunate may we, call ourselves to have been born in an age so productive of eloquence, so rich in erudition. Neither of us would be excluded, or hooted at, on canvassing for these honors. He who can think dispassionately and deeply as I do, is great as I am; none other. But his opinions are at freedom to diverge from mine, as mine are from his; and indeed, on recollection, I never loved those most who thought with me, but those rather who deemed my sentiments worth discussion, and who corrected me with frankness and affability.

Cæsar. Lucullus, you perhaps have taken the wiser and better part, certainly the pleasanter. I cannot argue with you: I would gladly hear one who could, but you again more gladly. I should think unworthily of you if I thought you capable of yielding or receding. I do not even ask you to keep our conversation long a secret, so greatly does it preponderate in your favor; so much more of gentleness, of eloquence, and of argument. I came hither with one soldier, avoiding the cities, and sleeping at the villa of a confidential friend. To-night I sleep in yours, and, if your dinner does not disturb me, shall sleep soundly. You go early to rest I know.

Lucullus. Not, however, by daylight. Be assured, Caius Julius, that greatly as your discourse afflicts me, no part of it shall escape my lips. If you approach the city with arms, with arms I meet you; then your denouncer and enemy, at present your host and confidant.

Cæsar. I shall conquer you.

Lucullus. That smile would cease upon it: you sigh already.

Cæsar. Yes, Lucullus, if I am oppressed I shall overcome my oppressor: I know my army and myself. A sigh escaped me, and many more will follow; but one transport will rise

amid them, when, vanquisher of my enemies and avenger **of my**
dignity, I press again the hand of Lucullus, mindful **of this**
day.

V. MARCUS TULLIUS AND QUINCTUS CICERO.[1]

Marcus. The last calamities **of** our country, my brother
Quinctus, have again united us ; **and** something like the tenderness of earlier days appears to **have** returned, in the silence of
ambition and **in the** subsidence of hope. It **has** frequently
occurred to me how different we are from the moment when the
parental roof bursts asunder, as it were, and the inmates are
scattered abroad, **and** build up here and there new families.
Many, who before lived in amity and concord, are then in the
condition of those who, receiving intelligence of a shipwreck,[2]

[[1] In this Conversation Landor introduces Cicero and his brother
Quintus—not Quinctus as he spells the name—talking together **not long**
before the date at which they were both put to death. According to
Plutarch—Vit. Ciceronis—they were then at Cicero's villa at Tusculum,
but Landor supposes them to be at Formiæ. The Conversation is full of
allusions to the history of Rome, especially to that part of it included
in Cicero's life. For his **facts**, though **not** for his view of Cicero's
character, Landor seems to have made use of Middleton's Life of
Cicero; in Plutarch's life he **does** not **seem** to have found much that
could serve his purpose. Quintus Cicero was a less amiable man than
his brother, and his hot and unrestrained temper was in part the cause of
the disagreement between the brothers referred to early in the Conversation. Quintus had served Cæsar as one of his lieutenants in Gaul, and won
distinction there. But when Cæsar broke with the Senate and Pompey,
he was persuaded by his brother to adhere to Pompey ; and after
Pompey's defeat at Pharsalia, he expressed his annoyance at having deserted Cæsar in unmeasured language ; see, for instance, Cicero's letter
to Atticus (xi. 9). His son, the younger Quintus, did something to widen
the breach between his father and uncle. But during the rule of Cæsar
the brothers were reconciled, and after his murder they both remained
opponents of Antony, and were both put to death in the proscription
which followed the success of Octavius and Antony. (Imag. Convers.,
ii., 1824 ; ii., 1826. Works, i., 1846. Imag. Convers., Gks. and Rom.,
1853. Works, ii., 1876.)]
　[[2] First ed. reads : "shipwreck on the shore, collect," &c.]

collect at once for plunder, and quarrel on touching the first
fragment.

Quinctus. We never disagreed on the division of any property, unless indeed the State and its honors may be considered
as such; and although, in regard to Cæsar, our fortune drew us
different ways latterly,[3] and my gratitude made me, until your remonstrances and prayers prevailed, reluctant to abandon him, you
will remember my anxiety to procure you the consulate and the
triumph. You cannot and never could suppose me unmindful of
the signal benefits and high distinctions I have received from
Cæsar, or quite unreluctant to desert an army, for my services
in which he often praised me to you, while I was in Britain and
in Gaul. Such moreover was his generosity, he did not erase
my name from his *Commentaries* for having abandoned and
opposed his cause. My joy therefore ought not to be unmingled
at his violent death, to whom I am indebted not only for confidence and command, not only for advancement and glory, but
also for immortality. When you yourself had resolved on leaving
Italy to follow Cneius Pompeius, you were sensible, as you told
me, that my obligations to Cæsar should at least detain me in
Italy. Our disputes, which among men who reason will be
frequent, were always amicable; our political views have always been similar, and generally the same. You indeed were
somewhat more aristocratical and senatorial; and this prejudice
hath ruined both. As if the immortal gods took a pleasure in
confounding us by the difficulty of our choice, they placed the best
men at the head of the worst cause. Decimus Brutus and Porcius
Cato held up the train of Sylla; for the late civil wars were only
a continuation of those which the old dictator seemed, for a time,
to have extinguished in blood and ruins. His faction was in
authority when you first appeared at Rome; and although, among
your friends and sometimes in public, you have spoken as a Roman
should speak of Caius Marius, a respect for Pompeius (the most
insincere of mortals) made you silent on the merits of Sertorius,[4]

[3 From "latterly" to "him" (2 lines) and 3 lines below, from "You"
to "amicable" (15 lines) added in 2nd ed.]

[4 After the momentary triumph of the Democratic party under Marcus
and Cinna had been crushed at Rome by Sulla, Sertorius for some time
kept up the struggle in Spain. He made his camp into another Rome,

—than whom there never was a better man in private life, a magistrate more upright, a general more vigilant, a citizen more zealous for the prerogative of our republic.   Caius Cæsar, the later champion of the same party, overcame difficulties almost equally great, and, having acted upon a more splendid theatre, may perhaps appear a still greater character.

Marcus.   He will seem so to those only who place temperance and prudence, fidelity and patriotism, aside from the component parts of greatness.   Cæsar, of all men, knew best when to trust Fortune : Sertorius never trusted her at all, nor ever marched a step along a path he had not patiently and well explored.   The best of Romans slew the one, the worst the other. The death of Cæsar was that which the wise and virtuous would most deprecate for themselves and for their children ; that of Sertorius what they would most desire.   And since, Quinctus, we have seen the ruin of our country, and her enemies are intent on ours, let us be grateful that the last years of life have neither been useless nor inglorious, and that it is likely to close, not under the condemnation of such citizens as Cato and Brutus, but as Lepidus and Antonius.   It is with more sorrow than asperity that I reflect on Caius Cæsar.[5]   Oh ! had his heart been unambitious as his style, had he been as prompt to succor his country as to enslave her, how great, how incomparably great, were he !   Then perhaps at this hour, O Quinctus, and in this villa, we should have enjoyed his humorous and erudite discourse ;

surrounded himself with a fictitious senate, and in every way preserved an appearance of constitutional action.   His eminent military genius enabled him to resist the generals sent against him, and even Pompey could gain no victories over him.   His assassination by Perpenna alone put an end to the war.]

[5 Cicero's reflections in his letters upon the death of Cæsar do not express much regret.   In a letter to Cassius (Ad. Fam., xii. 4) he says— "I could wish you had invited me to your dinner on the Ides of March : there would then have been nothing left over."   Cicero only regretted that Antony had not been murdered as well as Cæsar.   The visit from Cæsar, referred to below, is described by Cicero (Ad. Att., xiii. 52). He seems relieved to have got the visit over so well.   "The guest," he says, "was not the sort of person to whom you would say—'I shall be most delighted if you will come here on your way back;' once is enough.   As to our conversation, it was mostly like that of two *savants*."—Jean's translation.]

for no man ever tempered so seasonably and so justly the materials
of conversation. How graceful was he! how unguarded! His
whole character was uncovered; as we represent the bodies of
heroes and of gods. Two[6] years ago, at this very season, on the
third of the Saturnalia, he came hither spontaneously and unexpectedly to dine with me; and although one of his attendants
read to him, as he desired while he was bathing, the verses on
him and Mamurra, he retained his usual good-humor, and discoursed after dinner on many points of literature, with admirable
ease and judgment. Him I shall see again; and, while he ac-
knowledges my justice, I shall acknowledge his virtues, and contemplate them unclouded. I shall see again our father, and
Mutius Scævola, and you, and our sons, and the ingenuous and
faithful Tyro. He alone has power over my life, if any has; for
to him I confide my writings. And our worthy Marcus Brutus
will meet me, whom I would embrace among the first; for, if I
have not done him an injury, I have caused him one. Had I
never lived, or had I never excited his envy, he might perhaps
have written as I have done; but for the sake of avoiding me he
caught both cold and fever. Let us pardon him; let us love
him. With a weakness that injured his eloquence, and with a
softness of soul that sapped the constitution of our State, he is no
unworthy branch of that family which will be remembered the
longest among men.

Oh happy day, when I shall meet my equals, and when my
inferiors shall trouble me no more!

Man thinks it miserable to be cut off in the midst of his projects: he should rather think it miserable to have formed them.
For the one is his own action, the other is not; the one was
subject from the beginning to disappointments and vexations, the
other ends them. And what truly is that period of life in which
we are not in the midst of our projects? They spring up only
the more rank and wild, year after year, from their extinction or
change of form, as herbage from the corruption and dying down
of herbage.

I will not dissemble that I upheld the senatorial cause for no

[6 From "Two" to "judgment" (7 lines) added in 2nd ed.]

other reason than that my dignity was to depend on it. My[7] first
enthusiasm was excited by Marius ; my first poem was written on
him. We were proud of him as a fellow-citizen of Arpinum.
Say no more of him. It is only the most generous nature that
grows more generous by age : Marius, like Pompeius, grew more
and more austere.   I praised his exploits in the enthusiasm of youth
and poetry, either of which is sufficient excuse for many errors ;
and both together may extort somewhat more than pardon, when
valor in a fellow-townsman is the exciter of our praise. But,
sitting now in calmer judgment, we see him stripped of his victorious arms and sevenfold consulship ; we see him in his native
rudeness, selfishness, and ferocity ; we see him the murderer of
his colleague in the consulship, of his comrade in the camp.
Scarcely can we admire even the severity of his morals, when its
principal use was to enforce the discipline needful to the accom-
plishment of his designs.

Quinctus. Marius is an example that a liberal education is
peculiarly necessary where power is almost unlimited.   Quiet,
social, philosophical intercourse can alone restrict that tendency
to arrogance which war encourages, and alone can inculcate that
abstinence from wrong and spoliation which we have lately seen
exercised more intemperately than even by Marius or by Sylla,
and carried into the farms and villas of ancient friends and close
connections.

Marcus. Had the party of our townsman been triumphant,
and the Senate (as it would have been) abolished, I should never
have had a Catilinarian conspiracy to quell, and few of my best
orations would have been delivered.

Quinctus. Do you believe that the Marian faction would have
annulled your Order ?

Marcus. I believe that their safety would have required its
ruin, and that their vengeance, not to say their equity, would have
accomplished it. The civil war was of the Senate against the

[7 From " My " to " *Marcus* " (24 lines) added in 3rd ed. First ed. reads:
" it. Had the opposite party been," &c.; and 4 lines below, " delivered.
Without a senate what Verres? . ... *Quinctus*," &c. The alterations
in this place have rather obscured the sense. As this and the following
speeches of Marcus now stand, they read like a defence of Marius and an
attack on the Senate.]

Equestrian Order and the people, and was maintained by the
wealth of the patricians, accumulated in the time of Sylla, from
the proscription of all whom violence made, or avarice called, its
adversaries.   It would have been necessary to confiscate the whole
property of the Order, and to banish its members from Italy.
Any measures short of these would have been inadequate to compensate the people for their losses ; nor would there have been a
sufficient pledge for the maintenance of tranquillity.   The exclusion
of three hundred families from their estates, which they had acquired in great part by rapine, and their expulsion from a country
which they had inundated with blood, would have prevented that
partition-treaty, whereby are placed in the hands of three men
the properties and lives of all.

There should in no government be a contrariety of interests.
Checks are useful ; but it is better to stand in no need of them.
Bolts and bars are good things ; but would you establish a college
of thieves and robbers to try how good they are ?   Misfortune
has taught me many truths, which a few years ago I should have
deemed suspicious and dangerous.   The fall of Rome and of
Carthage, the form of whose governments was almost the same,
has been occasioned by the divisions of the ambitious in their
Senates : for we Conscript Fathers call that ambition which
the lower ranks call avarice.   In fact, the only difference is that
the one wears fine linen, the other coarse ; one covets the government of Asia, the other a cask of vinegar.   The people were indifferent which side prevailed, until their houses in that country
were reduced to ashes ; in this, were delivered to murderers and
gamesters.

Quinctus.   Painful is it to reflect, that the greatness of most
men originates from what has been taken by fraud or violence out
of the common stock.   The greatness of States, on the contrary,
depends on the subdivision of property, chiefly of the landed, in
moderate portions ; on the frugal pay of functionaries, chiefly of
those who possess a property ; and on unity of interests and designs.
Where provinces are allotted, not for the public service, but for
the enrichment of private families ; where consuls wish one thing,
and tribunes wish another,—how can there be prosperity or safety ?
If Carthage, whose government (as you observe) much resembled
ours, had allowed the same rights generally to the inhabitants of

Africa; had she been as zealous in civilizing as in coercing them, —she would have ruined our Commonwealth and ruled the world. Rome found the rest of Italy more cultivated than herself, but corrupted for the greater part by luxury, ignorant of military science, and more patient of slavery than of toil. She conquered; and in process of time infused into them somewhat of her spirit, and imparted to them somewhat of her institutions. Nothing was then wanting to her policy, but only to grant voluntarily what she might have foreseen they would unite to enforce, and to have constituted a social body in Italy. This would have rendered her invincible. Ambition would not permit our senators to divide with others the wealth and aggrandizement arising from authority: and hence our worst citizens are become our rulers. The same error was committed by Sertorius, from purer principles, when he created a Senate in Spain, but admitted no Spaniard. The practice of disinterestedness, the force of virtue, in despite of so grievous an affront, united to him the bravest and most honorable of nations. If he had granted to them what was theirs by nature, and again due for benefits, he would have had nothing else to regret, than that they had so often broken our legions, and covered our commanders with shame.

What [8] could be expected in our country, where the aristocracy possessed in the time of Sylla more than half the land, and disposed of all the revenues and offices arising from our conquests? It would be idle to remark that the armies were paid out of them, when those armies were but the household of the rich, and necessary to their safety. On such reasoning there is no clear profit, no property, no possession; we cannot eat without a cook, without a husbandman, without a butcher: these take a part of our money. The armies were no less the armies of the aristocracy than the money that paid and the provinces that supplied them; no less, in short, than their beds and bolsters.

Why could not we have done from policy and equity what has been and often will be done, under another name, by favor and injustice? On the agrarian law we never were unanimous; yet Tiberius Gracchus had among the upholders of his plan the most prudent, the most equitable, and the most dignified in the republic, —Lælius, the friend of Scipio, whose wisdom and moderation you

[8 From "What" to "charcoal" (198 lines) added in 2nd ed.]

have lately extolled in your dialogue; Crassus, then **Pontifex** **Maximus**; and Appius Claudius, who resolved by this **virtuous** and patriotic deed to wipe away the stain left for **ages** on his family, by its licentiousness, pride, and tyranny. To these names another must **be** added; a **name** which we have been taught from our **youth** upward to hold in reverence,—the greatest of our jurists, **Mutius** Scævola. The adversaries of **the** measure cannot deny the **humanity** and liberality of its provisions, by which those who might be punished **for** violating **the** laws should be indemnified for the **loss of** the possessions they held illegally, and these possessions should be distributed among the poorer families; **not** for the purpose of corrupting their **votes,** but that they should **have** no temptation to sell them.

You smile, Marcus!

Marcus. For this very thing the Conscript Fathers were **inimical** to Tiberius Gracchus, **and** accused him of an attempt to **introduce** visionary **and impracticable** changes into the Commonwealth. Among **the elder of his** partisans some were called **ambitious,** some **prejudiced; among the** younger, some were **madmen,** the **rest traitors,—just as** they were protected or unprotected by **the** power **of their** families or the influence of their friends.

Quinctus. The most equitable and necessary law promulgated of latter times in our republic was that by Caius Gracchus, who, finding all our magistratures in the disposal of **the** Senate, and witnessing the acquittal of all criminals whose peculations and extortions had ruined our provinces and **shaken our** dominion, transferred the judicial power to the Equestrian **Order.** Cepio's [9] **law,** five-and-twenty years afterward, **was** an infringement of **this; and the** oration of Lucius Crassus in its favor, bearing with **it the force of** genius and the stamp of authority, formed in great measure, as you acknowledge, both your politics and your eloquence. The intimacy **of** Crassus with Aculeo, the husband of our maternal **aunt,** inclined **you** perhaps to follow the **more** readily his

[9 See Middleton's life **of** Cicero, pref. p. xxiii. Landor has taken **the** statement about Cepio's law direct from Middleton, and **has** forgotten that between the date of that law and the date of this Conversation the controversy had passed through other stages. That Sylla had transferred the judicial power back to the Senate, and that the Lex Aurelia had ordered the judges to be chosen from the Senators, the Knights, and the Tribuni Aerarii. See also Landor's note at end of Conversation.]

opinions, and to set a higher value than you might otherwise have done on his celebrated oration.

Marcus. You must remember, my brother, that I neither was nor professed myself to be adverse to every agrarian law, though I opposed with all my energy and authority that agitated by Rullus. On which occasion I represented the two Gracchi as most excellent men, inflamed by the purest love of the Roman people, in their proposal to divide among the citizens what was unquestionably their due. I mentioned them as those on whose wisdom and institutions many of the solider parts in our government were erected; and I opposed the particular law at that time laid before the people, as leading to the tyranny of a decemvirate. The projects of Cæsar and Pompeius on this business were unjust and pernicious; those of Gracchus I now acknowledge to have been equitable to the citizens and salutary to the State. Unless I made you this concession, how could I defend my own conduct, a few months ago, in persuading the Senate to distribute among the soldiers of the fourth legion and the legion of Mars, for their services to the republic, those lands in Campania which Cæsar and Pompeius would have allotted in favor of their partizans in usurpation! Caius Gracchus on the contrary would look aside to no advantage or utility; and lost the most powerful of his friends, adherents, and relatives, by his inflexible rectitude. Beside those letters of his which are published, I remember one in answer to his mother, which Scævola was fond of quoting, and of which he possessed the original.

Quinctus. Have we the transcript of it?

Marcus. The words of Cornelia,[10] as well as I can recollect them, are these :—

" I have received the determination of Lælius and Scipio, in which they agree, as usual. He tells me that he never shall cease to be the advocate of so righteous a cause, if you will consent that the soldiers, who subdued for our republic the cities of Carthage and Numantia, shall partake in the public benefit; that Scipio is well aware how adverse the proposal would render the Senate to him, and at the same time how unpopular he shall be among his fellow-citizens at Rome, which may excite a suspicion

[10 These letters are of course as imaginary as the Conversation; but they are based upon historical evidence.]

in bad and thoughtless men that he would gratify the army in
defiance of each authority. He requests you to consider that
these soldiers are for the greater part somewhat elderly; and
that granting them possessions, on which they may sit down and
rest, cannot be the means an ambitious man would take for his
aggrandizement. He wishes to render them inclined to peace,
not alert for disturbances, and as good citizens as they have been
good soldiers; and he entreats you, by the sanctity of your office,
not to deprive them of what they should possess in common with
others, for no better reason than because they defended by their
valor the property of all. If you assent to this proposal, it will
be unnecessary for him, he says, to undertake the settlement of
the Commonwealth referred to him by the Senate,—not without
danger, my dear Caius, though rather to his life than to his
dignity. So desirable a measure, he adds, ought never to be
carried into effect, nor supported too pertinaciously, by the
general of an army."

Quinctus. I never knew of this letter. Scævola, I imagine,
would not give it out of his hands for any one to read, in public
or at home. Do you remember as much of the answer?

Marcus. I think I may do; for the language of the Gracchi
was among my exercises, and I wonder that you have not heard
me rehearse both pieces, in the practice of declamation. Caius
answers his mother thus:—

"Mother, until you have exerted your own eloquence to
persuade me, if indeed you participate in the opinions of Lælius, never shall I agree that the soldiers of Scipio have an
allotment of land in Italy. When we withdraw our veterans
from Spain and Africa, barbarian kings will tread upon our
footsteps, efface the traces of our civilisation, and obliterate
the memorials of our glory. The countries will be useful to
us: even if they never were to be, we must provide against
their becoming injurious and pernicious, as they would be under
any other power. Either we should not fight an enemy, or we
should fight until we have overcome him. Afterward to throw
away what we have taken is the pettishness of a child; to drop
it is the imbecility of a suckling. Nothing of wantonness or
frowardness is compatible with warfare, or congenial with the
Roman character. To relinquish a conquest is an acknowledgment of injustice, or incapacity, or fear.

"Our soldiers under the command of Scipio have subdued two countries, of a soil more fertile than ours, and become by a series of battles, and by intestine discord, less populous: let them divide and enjoy it.   The beaten should always pay the expenses of the war, and the instigators should be deprived of their possessions and their lives.   Which, I pray you, is the more reasonable,—that the Roman people shall incur debts by having conquered, or that the weight of those debts shall fall totally on the vanquished?   Either the war was unjust against *them*, or the conditions of peace against *us*.   Our citizens are fined and imprisoned (since their debts begin with fine and end with imprisonment) for having hurt them.   What! shall we strike and run away?   Or shall our soldier, when he hath stripped the armor from his adversary, say, 'No, I will not take this: I will go to Rome, and suit myself with better'?

"Let the army be compensated for its toils and perils: let it enjoy the fruit of its triumph on the soil that bore them: for never will any new one keep the natives in such awe.   Those who fight for slavery should at all events have it: they should be sold as bondmen.   The calamities of Carthage and of Numantia strike the bosom even of the conqueror.   How many brave, how many free, how many wise and virtuous, perished within their walls!   But the petty princes and their satellites should be brought to market: not one of them should have a span of earth, or a vest, or a carcass of his own.   Spaniards and Africans, who prefer the domination of a tetrarch to the protection of the laws, ought to be sold for the benefit of our legionaries in Spain and Africa, whether by the gang or the dozen, whether for the mine or the arena.   While any such are in existence, and while their country, of which they are unworthy, opens regions unexplored before us and teeming with fertility, I will not permit that the victorious army partake in the distribution of our home domains.   Write this to Lælius ; and write it for Scipio's information, imploring him so to act as that he never may enfeeble the popular voice, nor deaden the world's applause. Remind him, O mother, for we both love him, how little it would become a good citizen and brave soldier, to raise up any cause, why he should have to guard himself against the suspicions and stratagems of the Senate."

Quinctius. **The** attempt to restore the sounder of our institutions was insolently and falsely called innovation. For, from the building of our city, a part of the conquered lands was sold by auction *under the spear,*—an expression which hath since been used to designate the same transaction within the walls; another part was holden in common; a third was leased out at an easy rate to the poorer citizens. So that formerly the lower and intermediate class possessed by right the exclusive benefit of *two-thirds,* and an equal chance (wherever there was industry and frugality) of the other. Latterly, by various kinds of vexation and oppression, they had been deprived of nearly the whole.

Cornelia was not a woman of a heart so sickly tender as to awaken its sympathies at all hours, and to excite and pamper in it a false appetite. Like the rest of her family, she cared little or nothing for the applauses and opinions of the people: she loved justice; and it was on justice that she wished her children to lay the foundation of their glory. This ardor was inextinguished in her by the blood of her eldest son. She saw his name placed where she wished it; and she pointed it out to Caius. Scandalous words may be written on the wall under it, by dealers in votes and traffickers in loyalty; but little is the worth of a name that perishes by chalk or charcoal.

Marcus. The moral, like the physical body, hath not always the same wants in the same degree. We put off or on a greater or less quantity of clothes according to the season; and it is to the season that we must accommodate ourselves in government, wherein there are only a few leading principles which are never to be disturbed. I now perceive that the laws of society in one thing resemble the laws of perspective: they require that what is below should rise gradually, and that what is above should descend in the same proportion, but not that they should touch. Still less do they inform us, what is echoed in our ears by new masters from camp and schoolroom, that the wisest and best should depend on the weakest and worst; and that when individuals, however ignorant of moral discipline and impatient of self-restraint, are deemed adequate to the management of their affairs at twenty years, a State should never be; that boys should come out of pupilage, that men should return to it; that people, in their actions and abilities so contemptible as the

triumvirate, should become by their own appointment our tutors
and guardians, and shake their scourges over Marcus Brutus,
Marcus Varro, Marcus Tullius. The Romans are hastening
back, I see, to the government of hereditary kings, whether by
that name or another is immaterial, which no virtuous and dignified
man, no philosopher of whatever sect, hath recommended, approved, or tolerated; and than which no moralist, no fabulist, no
visionary, no poet, satirical or comic, no Fescennine jester,
no dwarf or eunuch (the most privileged of privileged classes),
no runner at the side of a triumphal car, in the uttermost
extravagance of his licentiousness, has imagined any thing more
absurd, more indecorous, or more insulting. What else indeed
is the reason why a nation is called barbarous by the Greeks
and us? This alone stamps the character upon it, standing for
whatever is monstrous, for whatever is debased.

What a shocking sight should we consider an old father of a
family led in chains along the public street, with boys and prostitutes shouting after him!—and should we not retire from it
quickly and anxiously? A sight greatly more shocking now
presents itself: an ancient nation is reduced to slavery, by those
who vowed before the people and before the altars to defend her.
And is it hard for us, O Quinctus, to turn away our eyes from
this abomination? Or is it necessary for a Gaul or an Illyrian
to command us that we close them on it?

Quinctus.[11] No, Marcus, no! Let us think upon it as our
forefathers always thought, and our friends lately.

Marcus. I am your host, my brother, and must recall you
awhile to pleasanter ideas. How beautiful is this Formian coast!
how airy this villa! Ah, whither have I beckoned your reflections!—it is the last of ours perhaps we may ever see. Do you
remember the races of our children along the sands, and their consternation when Tyro [12] cried "*The Læstrygons! the Læstrygons!*"

[11 From "*Quinctus*" to "*Marcus*" (3 lines) added in 3rd ed.]
[12 "Tiro was trained up in Cicero's family, among the rest of his young
slaves, in every kind of useful and polite learning, and being a youth of
singular parts and industry, soon became an eminent scholar, and
extremely serviceable to his master in all his affairs both civil and
domestic. . . . We are indebted to him for preserving and transmitting
to posterity the precious collection of Cicero's letters." Middleton's Life
of Cicero, ed. Moxon, p. 169. Cicero gave Tiro his liberty. For the

He little thought he prophesied in his mirth, and all that poetry has feigned of these monsters should in so few years be accomplished. The other evening, an hour or two before sunset, I sailed quietly along the coast, for there was little wind, and the stillness on shore made my heart faint within me. I remembered how short a time ago I had conversed with Cato around the villa of Lucullus, whose son, such was the modesty of the youth, followed rather than accompanied us. O [13] gods! how little then did I foresee or apprehend that the guardianship of this young man, and also of Cato's son, would within one year have devolved on me, by the deplorable death of their natural protector! A fading purple invested by degrees the whole promontory: I looked up at Misenus, and at those solitary and silent walks, enlivened so lately by friendship and philosophy. The last indeed of the thoughts we communicated were sorrowful and despondent; but, heavy as they were, they did not pain me like those which were now coming over me in my loneliness on the sea. For there only is the sense of solitude where every thing we behold is unlike us, and where we have been accustomed to meet our friends and equals.

Quinctus. There is something of softness, not unallied to sorrow, in these mild winter days and their humid sunshine.

Marcus. I know not, Quinctus, by what train or connection of ideas they lead me rather to the past than to the future; unless it be that, when the fibres of our bodies are relaxed, as they must be in such weather, the spirits fall back easily upon reflection, and are slowly incited to expectation. The memory of those great men who consolidated our republic by their wisdom, exalted it by their valor, and protected and defended it by their constancy, stands not alone nor idly; they draw us after them, they place us with them. O Quinctus! I wish I could impart to you my firm per-

---

Læstrygons, see Odyssey, **x.** "Then he raised the war cry through the town and the valiant Læstrygons, at the sound thereof, flocked together from every side, a host past number, not like men but like the giants. They cast at us from the cliffs with great rocks, each of them a man's burden, and anon there arose from the fleet an evil din of men dying and ships shattered withal. And like folk spearing fishes they bare home their hideous meal." Butcher and Lang's Odyssey, **p. 157.**]

[13 From "O" to "protector!" added in 2nd ed.; from "A" to "*Quinctus*" added in 3rd ed. First ed. reads: "us. There is something . . . sunshine. I," &c.]

suasion, that after death we shall enter into their society; and what matter if the place of our reunion be not the Capitol or the Forum, be not Elysian meadows or Atlantic islands? Locality has nothing to do with mind once free. Carry this thought perpetually with you; and Death, whether you believe it terminates our whole existence or otherwise, will lose, I will not say its terrors, for the brave and wise have none, but its anxieties and inquietudes.

Quinctus. Brother, when I see that many dogmas in religion have been invented to keep the intellect in subjection, I may fairly doubt the rest.

Marcus. Yes, if any emolument be derived from them to the colleges of priests. But surely he deserves the dignity and the worship of a god, who first instructed men that by their own volition they may enjoy eternal happiness; that the road to it is most easy and most beautiful, such as any one would follow by preference, even if nothing desirable were at the end of it. Neither to give nor to take offence, are surely the two things most delightful in human life; and it is by these two things that eternal happiness may be attained. We shall enjoy a future state accordingly as we have employed our intellect and our affections. Perfect bliss can be expected by few; but fewer will be so miserable as they have been here.

Quinctus. A belief to the contrary, if we admit a future life, would place the gods beneath us in their best properties,—justice and beneficence.

Marcus. Belief in a future life is the appetite of reason: and I see not why we should not gratify it as unreluctantly as the baser. Religion does not call upon us to believe the fables of the vulgar, but on the contrary to correct them.

Quinctus. Otherwise, overrun as we are in Rome by foreigners of every nation, and ready to receive, as we have been, the buffooneries of Syrian and Egyptian priests, our citizens may within a few years become not only the dupes, but the tributaries, of these impostors. The Syrian may scourge us until we join him in his lamentation of Adonis; and the Egyptian may tell us that it is unholy to eat a chicken, and holy to eat an egg; while a sly rogue of Judæa whispers in our ear, "That is superstition; you go to heaven if you pay me a tenth of your harvests." This, I have heard Cneius Pompeius relate, is done in Judæa.

Marcus. **True, but the tenth paid all the expenses both of** civil government and religious ; for the magistracy was (if **such** an expression can be repeated with seriousness) *theocratical.* **In** time of peace, a decimation of property would **be** intolerable.[*] Pisistratus [14] and Hiero did exact it ; but they were usurpers, and the exercise of their power was no more legitimate than the assumption. ᛫ Among us, likewise, the tribunes of the people have **complained,** in former times, that taxes levied on the commons went to abase and ruin them. Certainly the Senate did not contribute in the same proportion ; **but the** commons were taxed out **of the** produce of what had been allotted to them **in the** partition **of** conquered lands ; and it was only **the** stipend **of the** soldier for preserving by arms the property that **his arms had won.** The **Jews have** been always at war ; **natives of a sterile country and** borderers of a fertile one, **acute,** meditative, melancholy, morose. I know **not** whether we ourselves have performed such **actions as** they have, or whether any nation has fought with **such resolution** and **pertinacity. We laugh** at their worship : **they abominate ours. In this I think we are the** wiser ; **for** surely **on** speculative points **it is better to** laugh than to abominate. But whence have you **brought your** eggs and **chickens ?** I have heard our Varro tell many **stories about the** Egyptian ordinances, but I do not remember this among **them ; nor** indeed **did** his friend Turranius who resided long in that country, and was intimately versed in its antiquities, nor his son Manius, a **young man** of **much pleasantry,** **ever** relate it in conversation when **we met at Varro's.**

Quinctus. Indeed the distinction seems a **little** too absurd, **even** for the worshippers **of** cats and crocodiles. Perhaps I may **have** wronged them ; the **nation I may** indeed have forgotten, but I am certain of the fact : I **place it in** the archives of superstition, you **may** deposit **it in its right** cell. Among the Athenians, the priestess of Minerva **was** entitled to a measure of

---

[*] The Spaniards **had been a** refractory and rebellious people, and **there-**fore were treated, we may presume, with little lenity ; yet T. Livius **tells** **us** that a part of Spain paid a *tenth*, another part a *twentieth.* Lib. xliii. See also Tacitus on the subject of taxation, *Ann.* **xiii.**; and Burmann *De Vectigali.*

[[14] From " Pisistratus " **to** " won " (9 lines) added in 3rd ed. **11 lines** below, from " among " to " Varro's " (4 lines) added in 3rd ed.]

barley, a measure of wheat, and an obol, **on every birth and death.***
Some **eastern** nations are so totally subjected **to the priesthood, that**
a member of it is requisite **at** birth, at death, and, **by Thalassius !**
at marriage itself. He **can even** inflict pains **and** penalties **; he can**
oblige **you to** tell him **all** the **secrets** of the heart **; he can call**
your **wife to** him, your **daughter to** him, your **blooming and in-**
nocent **son ;** he can absolve **from** sin **; he** can exclude from
pardon.

Marcus. Now, Quinctus, **egg and** chicken, **cat and** crocodile,
disappear and vanish : **you repeat impossibilities ; mankind,** in its
lowest degradation, **has never been** depressed so low. **The savage**
would strangle **the** impostor that **attempted it ;** the **civilized man**
would scourge **him** and hiss **him from** society. **Come, come,**
brother ! we may **expect such a state of things, whenever we find**
united the genius **of** the Cimmerian **and the courage of the Trog-**
lodyte. Religions **wear out, cover them with gold or case them**
with iron as you **will.** Jupiter is now **less powerful in Crete than**
when he was in his cradle **there, and spreads fewer terrors at**
Dodona than a shepherd's cur. Proconsuls have removed **from**
Greece, from Asia, from Sicily, **the most celebrated statues ; and**
it is doubted at last **whether** those deities **are in heaven, whom a**
cart and a yoke **of oxen have carried away on earth. When the**
civil wars are over, and the **minds of men become indolent and**
inactive, as is always **the** case after **great excitement, it is not**
improbable that some novelties **may** be **attempted in religion ; but,**
as my prophecies in the **whole course of the late events have been**
accomplished, so you may **believe me when I prognosticate that**
our religion, although it **should** be **disfigured and deteriorated,**
will continue in many of its **features, in** many of its **pomps and**
ceremonies, the same. **Sibylline** books will **never** be wanting
while fear and curiosity are **inherent in the** composition of **man.**
And there is something consolatory **in** this idea of duration and
identity ; for whatever be your philosophy, you **must** acknowledge
that it is pleasant to **think, although you** know **not wherefore, that,**
when we go **away, things visible, like things intellectual,** will
remain in great **measure as we left them. A slight** displeasure
would be felt by **us, if we were certain** that **after our** death our
houses would be taken down, though not only **no longer** inhabited

* Aristot. *Œconom.* 1. 2.

by us, but probably not destined to remain in the possession of our
children; and that even these vineyards, fields, and gardens, were
about to assume another aspect.

Quinctus. The sea and the barren rocks will remain for ever
as they are; whatever is lovely changes. Misrule and slavery
may convert our fertile plains into pestilential marshes; and whoever shall exclaim against the authors and causes of any such
devastation may be proscribed, slain, or exiled. Enlightened and
virtuous men (painfullest of thoughts!) may condemn him; for
a love of security accompanies a love of study, and that by degrees
is adulation which was acquiescence. Cruel men have always at
their elbow the supporters of arbitrary power; and although the
cruel are seldom solicitous in what manner they may be represented
to posterity, yet, if any one among them be rather more so than
is customary, some projector will whisper in his ear an advice like
this: "Oppress, fine, imprison, and torture those who (you have
reason to suspect) are or may be philosophers or historians; so
that, if they mention you at all, they will mention you with indignation and abhorrence. Your object is attained: few will
implicitly believe them; almost every one will acknowledge that
their faith should be suspected, as there are proofs that they wrote
in irritation. This is better than if they spoke of you slightingly,
or cursorily, or evasively. By employing a hangman extraordinary,
you purchase in perpetuity the title of a clement prince."

Marcus. Quinctus, you make me smile, by bringing to my
recollection that, among the marauders of Pindenissus,[15] was a
fellow called by the Romans Fœdirupa, from a certain resemblance
no less to his name than to his character. He commanded in a
desert and sandy district, which his father and grandfather had
enlarged by violence; for the family were, from time immemorial,
robbers and assassins. Several schools had once been established
in those parts, remote from luxury and seduction; and several
good and learned men taught in them, having fled from Mithridates.

[15 For an account of Cicero's warfare against the inhabitants of
Pindenissus, a mountain fortress in Cilicia, see letter to Atticus v., 20.
Fœdirupa is not mentioned by Cicero. What particular antipathies of
Landor's are concealed under the names Fœdirupa (? treaty-breaker) and
Gentius, the editor has not been able to discover with certainty; but the
passage is evidently meant to have a modern application.]

Fœdirupa assumed on a sudden the air and demeanor of a patriot, and hired one Gentius to compose his rhapsodies on the love of our country, with liberty to promise what he pleased. Gentius put two hundred pieces of silver on his mule, rode to the schools, exhibited his money, and promised the same gratuity to every scholar who would arm and march forth against the enemy. The teachers breathed a free and pure spirit, and, although they well knew the knavery of Gentius, seconded him in his mission. Gentius, as was ordered, wrote down the names of those who repeated the most frequently that of country, and the least so that of Fœdirupa. Even rogues are restless for celebrity. The scholars performed great services against the enemy. On their return they were disarmed; the promises of Fœdirupa were disavowed; the teachers were thrown into prison, accused of violating the ancient laws, of perverting the moral and religious principles, and finally of abusing the simplicity of youth by illusory and empty promises. Gentius drew up against them the bills of indictment, and offered to take care of their libraries and cellars while they remained in prison. Fœdirupa cast them into dungeons; but drawing a line of distinction much finer than the most subtle of them had ever done, "I will not kill them," said he; "I will only frighten them to death." He became at last somewhat less cruel, and starved them. Only one was sentenced to lose his head. Gentius comforted him upon the scaffold, by reminding him how much worse he would have fared under Mithridates, who would not only have commanded his head to be cut off, but also to be fixed on a pike; and by assuring him that, instead of such wanton barbarity, he himself would carry it to the widow and her children, within an hour after their conference. The former words moved him little; he hardly heard them: but his heart and his brain throbbed in agony at the sound of children, of widow. He threw his head back; tears rolled over his temples, and dripped from his gray hair. "Ah, my dear friend," said Gentius, "have I unwittingly touched a tender part? Be manful; dry your eyes; the children are yours no longer; why be concerned for what you can never see again? My good old friend," added he, "how many kind letters to me has this ring of yours sealed formerly!" Then, lifting up the hand, he drew it slowly off, overcome by excess of grief. It fell into his bosom, and to

moderate his grief he was forced to run away, looking through the
corner of his eye at the executioner. The rogue was stoned to
death by those he had betrayed, not long before my arrival in
the province ; and an arrow from an unseen hand did justice on
Fœdirupa.[16]

Quinctus. I have seen in my life-time several rogues upon
their crosses, although few, if any, so deserving of the punishment
as Gentius and his colleague. Spectacles of higher interest are
nearer and more attractive. It would please me greatly, if either
the decline of evening or the windings of the coast would allow
me a view of Misenus ; and I envy you, Marcus, the hour or
two before sunset, which enabled you to contemplate it from the
unruffled sea at your leisure. Has no violence been offered to the
retirement of Cornelia ? Are there any traces of her residence
left amid our devastations, as there surely ought to be, so few
years after her decease ?

Marcus. On that promontory her mansion is yet standing ;
the same which Marius bought afterward, and which our friend
Lucullus last inhabited ; and, whether from reverence of her
virtues and exalted name, or that the gods preserve it as a monument of womanhood, its exterior is unchanged. Here she resided
many years,[17] and never would be induced to revisit Rome after the
murder of her younger son. She cultivated a variety of flowers,
naturalized exotic plants, and brought together trees from vale and
mountain : trees unproductive of fruit, but affording her, in their
superintendence and management, a tranquil expectant pleasure.
"There [18] is no amusement," said she, "so lasting and varied, so
healthy and peaceful, as horticulture." We read that the Babylonians and Persians were formerly much addicted to similar

[[16] First ed. reads : " Fœdirupa. I return amidst these home scenes.
On the promontory of Misenus is yet standing the mansion of Cornelia,
mother of the Gracchi ; and, whether," &c.]

[[17] See Mr Forster's Life of Landor, p. 282, for a characteristic stanza
where Landor promises to come back and tell his children :—
    "Severing the bridge behind, how Clelia
    Saved the whole host to fight again.
    And, loftier Virtue ! how Cornelia
    Lived when her two brave sons were slain."
For Clelia read Horatius.]

[[18] From " There " to " horticulture " (2 lines) added in 3rd ed.]

places of recreation. I have scarcely any knowledge in these matters ; * and the first time I went thither I asked many questions of the gardener's boy, a child about nine years old. He thought me even more ignorant than I was, and said, among other such remarks, "I do not know what they call this plant at Rome, or whether they have it there ; but it is among the commonest here, beautiful as it is, and we call it cytisus." "Thank you, child !" said I, smiling ; "and," pointing toward two cypresses, "pray what do you call those high and gloomy trees at the extremity of the avenue, just above the precipice ?" "Others like them," replied he, "are called cypresses ; but these, I know not why, have always been called Tiberius and Caius."

Quinctus. Of all studies, the most delightful and the most useful is biography. The seeds of great events lie near the surface ; historians delve too deep for them. No history was ever true : lives I have read which, if they were not, had the appearance, the interest, and the utility of truth.

Marcus. I have collected facts about Cornelia, worth recording ; and I would commemorate them the rather, as, while the Greeks have had among them no few women of abilities, we can hardly mention two.

Quinctus. Yet ours have advantages which theirs had not. Did Cornelia die unrepining and contented ?

Marcus. She was firmly convinced to the last that an agrarian law would have been just and beneficial, and was consoled that her illustrious sons had discharged at once the debt of nature and of patriotism. Glory is a light that shines from us on others, and not from others on us. Assured that future ages would render justice to the memory of her children, Cornelia thought they had already received the highest approbation, when they had received their own.

Quinctus.[19] If any thing was wanting, their mother gave it.

Marcus. No stranger of distinction left Italy without a visit to her. You would imagine that they, and that she particularly,

---

* "De hortis quod me admones, nec fui unquam valde cupidus, et nunc domus suppeditat mihi hortorum amœnitatem." Ad Q. Fratr. 1. 3. ep. 4.

[19 1st ed. reads: "own. If," &c. From "*Marcus*" to "Gracchi" (20 lines) added in 2nd ed. From "Gracchi" to "abated" (12 lines) added in 3rd ed.]

would avoid the mention of her sons : it was however the subject
on which she most delighted to converse, and which she never
failed to introduce on finding a worthy auditor.   I have heard
from our father and from Scævola, both of whom in their
adolescence had been present on such occasions, that she mentioned her children, no longer indeed with the calm complacency
and full content with which she showed them to the lady of
Campania as her gems and ornaments, but with such an exultation
of delight at their glory, as she would the heroes of antiquity.
So little of what is painful in emotion did she exhibit at the
recital, those who could not comprehend her magnanimity at first
believed her maddened by her misfortunes ; but so many signs of
wisdom soon displayed themselves, such staidness and sedateness
of demeanor, such serene majestic suavity, they felt as if some
deity were present ; and when wonder and admiration and awe
permitted them to lift up their eyes again toward her, they
discovered from hers that the fondest of mothers had been speaking,—the mother of the Gracchi.

Quinctus.   I wish you would write her life.

Marcus.   Titus Pomponius [20] may undertake it ; and Titus may
live to accomplish it.   All times are quiet times with him ; the
antagonist, the competitor of none,—the true philosopher !   He
knows the worth of men and the weight of factions, and how
little they merit the disturbance of our repose.   Ah, Quinctus !
that I never looked back until I came upon the very brink of the
whirlpool ! that, drawing all my glory from my lungs, I find all
my peace in exhaustion !   Our Atticus never did thus ; and he
therefore may live to do what you propose for me, not indeed too
late in the day, but with broken rest, and with zeal (I must
acknowledge it) abated.   Your remark on biography is just ;
yet how far below the truth is even the best representation of
those [21] whose minds the gods have illuminated !   How much
greater would the greatest man appear, if any one about him could
perceive those innumerable filaments of thought which break as
they rise from the brain, and the slenderest of which is worth all
the wisdom of many at whose discretion lies the felicity of

[20 Titus Pomponius Atticus.]
[21 First ed. reads : "those on whose minds the Gods or Muses vouchsafe to descend.   How," &c.]

nations! This in itself. is impossible ; but there are fewer who mark what appears on a sudden and disappears again (such is the conversation of the wise), than there are who calculate those stars that are now coming forth above us : scarcely one in several millions can apportion, to what is exalted in mind, its magnitude, place, and distance. We must be contented to be judged by that which people can discern and handle : that which they can have among them, most at leisure, is most likely to be well examined and duly estimated. Whence I am led to believe that my writings, and those principally which instruct men in their rights and duties, will obtain me a solider and more extensive reputation than I could have acquired in public life, by busier, harder, and more anxious labors. Public men appear to me to live in that delusion which Socrates, in the *Phædo*,[22] would persuade us is common to all our species. "We live in holes," says he, "and fancy that we are living in the highest parts of the earth." What he says physically I would say morally. Judge whether my observation is not at least as reasonable as his hypothesis ; and indeed, to speak ingenuously, whether I have not converted what is physically false and absurd into what is morally true and important.

Quinctus. True, beyond a question, and important as those whom it concerns will let it be. They who stand in high stations wish for higher ; but they who have occupied the highest of all often think with regret of some one pleasanter they left below. The [23] most wonderful thing in human nature is the variance of knowledge and will, where no passion is the stimulant : whence that system of life is often chosen and persevered in, which a man is well convinced is neither the best for him nor the easiest. Few can see clearly where their happiness lies ; and, in those who see it, you will scarcely find one who has the courage to pursue it. Every action must have its motive ; but weak motives are sufficient for weak minds ; and whenever we see one, which we believed to be a stronger, moved habitually by what appears inadequate, we may be certain that there is (to bring a metaphor from the forest) more top than root. Servius Tullius,

[22 Phædo, 189.]
[23 In 1st ed. from "The " to "root " (11 lines) is printed as part of the footnote †.]

a prudent man, dedicated to fortune what we call the narrow temple, with a statue in proportion, expressing his idea that Fortune in the condition of mediocrity is more reasonably than in any other the object of our vows. He could have given her as magnificent a name, and as magnificent a residence, as any she possesses ; and you know she has many of both ; but he wished perhaps to try whether for once she would be as favorable to wisdom as to enterprise.*

Marcus. If life allows us time for the experiment, let us also try it. †

Sleep,[24] which the Epicureans and others have represented as the image of death, is, we know, the repairer of activity and strength. If they spoke reasonably and consistently, they might argue from their own principles, or at least take the illustration from their own fancy, that death like sleep may also restore our powers, and in proportion to its universality and absoluteness. Pursuers as they are of pleasure, their unsettled and restless imagination loves rather to brood over an abyss, than to expatiate on places of amenity and composure. Just as sleep is the renovator of corporeal vigor, so, with their permission, I would believe death to be of the mind's ; that the body, to which it is attached rather from habitude than from reason, is little else than a disease to our immortal spirit ; and that, like the remora, of which mariners tell marvels, it counteracts, as it were, both oar and sail, in the most strenuous advances we can make toward felicity. Shall we

* Plutarch, in his *Problems*, offers several reasons, each different from this.

† That Cicero began to think a private life preferable to a public, and that his philosophical no less than his political opinions were unstable, is shown nowhere so evidently as in the eighth book of his *Epistles*. "Nam omnem nostram de republicâ curam, cogitationem, de dicendâ in senatu sententiâ, &c., abjecimus, et in Epicuri nos, adversarii nostri, castra conjecimus." Several years before the date of this, he writes to Atticus, "Malo in illâ tuâ sediculâ quam habes sub imagine Aristotelis sedere, quam in istorum sellâ curuli, tecumque apud te ambulari quam cum eo quocum video esse ambulandum : sed de ista ambulatione sors viderit, aut siquis est qui curet deus." L. iv. E. ix.

Demosthenes, in his later days, entertained the opinion that if there were two roads, the one leading to government, the other to death, a prudent man would choose the latter.

[24 From "Sleep" to "called upon" (185 lines) added in 2nd ed.]

lament to feel this reptile drop off? Or shall we not, on the contrary, leap with alacrity on shore, and offer up in gratitude to the gods whatever is left about us uncorroded and unshattered? A broken and abject mind is the thing least worthy of their acceptance.

Quinctus. Brother, you talk as if there were a plurality of gods.

Marcus. I know not and care not how many there may be of them. Philosophy points to unity; but while we are here, we speak as those do who are around us, and employ in these matters the language of our country. Italy is not so fertile in hemlock as Greece; yet a wise man will dissemble half his wisdom on such a topic; and I, as you remember, adopting the means of dialogue, have often delivered my opinions in the voice of others, and speak now as custom not as reason leads me.

Quinctus. Marcus, I still observe in you somewhat of aversion to Epicurus, a few of whose least important positions you have controverted in your dialogues; and I wish that, even there, you had been less irrisory, less of a pleader; that you had been, in dispassionate urbanity, his follower. Such was also the opinion of two men the most opposite in other things, Brutus and Cæsar. Religions may fight in the street, or over the grave: Philosophy never should. We ought to forego the manners of the Forum in our disquisitions, which, if they continue to be agitated as they have been, will be designated at last not only by foul epithets drawn from that unsober tub, but, as violence is apt to increase in fury until it falls from exhaustion, by those derived from war and bloodshed. I should not be surprised, if they who write and reason on our calm domestic duties, on our best and highest interests, should hereafter be designated by some such terms as *polemical* and *sarcastic*. As horses start aside from objects they see imperfectly, so do men. Enmities are excited by an indistinct view; they would be allayed by conference. Look at any long avenue of trees, by which the traveller on our principal highways is protected from the sun. Those at the beginning are wide apart; but those at the end almost meet. Thus happens it frequently in opinions. Men, who were far asunder, come nearer and nearer in the course of life, if they have strength enough to quell, or good sense enough to temper and assuage, their earlier

animosities.   Were it possible for you to have spent an hour with
Epicurus, you would have been delighted with him; for his
nature was like the better part of yours.   Zeno set out from
an opposite direction, yet they meet at last and shake hands.   He
who shows us how Fear may be reasoned with and pacified, how
Death may be disarmed of terrors, how Pleasure may be united
with Innocence and with Constancy; he who persuades us that
Vice is painful and vindictive, and that Ambition, deemed the
most manly of our desires, is the most childish and illusory,—
deserves our gratitude.   Children would fall asleep before they
had trifled so long as grave men do.   If you must quarrel with
Epicurus on the principal good,[25] take my idea.   The happy man
is he who distinguishes the boundary between desire and delight,
and stands firmly on the higher ground; he who knows that pleasure
not only is not possession, but is often to be lost and always to be
endangered by it.   In life, as in those prospects which if the sun
were above the horizon we should see from hence, the objects
covered with the softest light, and offering the most beautiful
forms in the distance, are wearisome to attain and barren.

In one of your last letters, you told me that you had come over
into the camp of your old adversary.

Marcus.   I could not rest with him.   As we pardon those
reluctantly who destroy our family tombs, is it likely or reasonable that he should be forgiven who levels to the ground the
fabric to which they lead, and to which they are only a rude and
temporary vestibule?

Quinctus.   Socrates was heard with more attention, Pythagoras had more authority in his lifetime; but no philosopher
hath excited so much enthusiasm in those who never frequented,
never heard nor saw him; and yet his doctrines are not such
in themselves as would excite it.   How then can it be, otherwise
than partly from the innocence of his life, and partly from the
relief his followers experienced in abstraction from unquiet and
insatiable desires?   Many, it is true, have spoken of him with

[25] Epicurus' speculations on the "principal good" were contained in
his work entitled "Περὶ τελοῦς." Cicero in the Tusculan Disputations,
iii., 18. 42, speaks of it as "a book to be thrown away, filled with talk
about pleasure." There are more attacks upon it in the "De finibus"
and elsewhere.]

hatred; but among his haters are none who knew him: which is remarkable, singular, wonderful; for hatred seems as natural to men as hunger is, and excited like hunger by the presence of its food; and the more exquisite the food, the more excitable is the hunger.

Marcus. I do not remember to have met anywhere before with the thought you have just expressed. Certain it is, however, that men in general have a propensity to hatred, profitless as it is and painful. We say proverbially, after Ennius or some other old poet, the descent to Avernus is easy: not less easily are we carried down to the more pestiferous pool whereinto we would drag our superiors and submerge them. It is the destiny of the obscure to be despised; it is the privilege of the illustrious to be hated. Whoever hates me proves and feels himself to be less than I am. If in argument we can make a man angry with us, we have drawn him from his vantage-ground and overcome him. For he, who in order to attack a little man (and every one calls his adversary so) ceases to defend the truth, shows that truth is less his object than the little man. I profess the tenets of the New Academy, because it teaches us modesty in the midst of wisdom, and leads through doubt to inquiry. Hence it appears to me that it must render us quieter and more studious, without doing what Epicurus would do; that is, without singing us to sleep in groves and meadows, while our country is calling on us loudly to defend her. Nevertheless, I have lived in the most familiar way with Epicureans,[26] as you know, and have loved them affectionately. There is no more certain sign of a narrow mind, of stupidity, and of arrogance, than to stand aloof from those who think differently from ourselves. If they have weighed the matter in dispute as carefully, it is equitable to suppose that they have the same chance as we have of being in the right; if they have not, we may as reasonably be out of humor with our footman or chairman: he is more ignorant and more careless of it still.

I have seen reason to change the greater part of my opinions. Let me confess to you, Quinctus, we oftener say things because we can say them well, than because they are sound and reasonable.

[26 In Cicero's Lucullus, c. 36. 115, he speaks of "the Epicureans, among whom I have so many friends, good men, so affectionate to one another."]

One would imagine that every man in society knows the nature of friendship. Similarity in the disposition, identity in the objects liked and disliked, have been stated (and stated by myself) as the essence of it; nothing is untruer. Titus Pomponius and I are different in our sentiments, our manners, our habits of life, our ideas of men and things, our topics of study, our sects of philosophy; added to which our country and companions have these many years been wide apart: yet we are friends, and always were, and, if man can promise any thing beyond the morrow, always shall be.

Quinctus. Your "*idem velle atque idem nolle,*" [27] of which you now perceive the futility, has never been suspected; not even by those who have seen Marius and Sylla, Cæsar and Pompeius, at variance and at war, for no other reason than because they sought and shunned the same thing,—shunning privacy and seeking supremacy. Young men quote the sentence daily; those very young men perhaps who court the same mistress, and whose friendship not only has not been corroborated, but has been shattered and torn up by it. Few authors have examined any one thing well, scarcely one many things. Your Dialogues are wiser, I think, than those of the Greeks; certainly more animated and more diversified; but I doubt whether you have bestowed so much time and labor on any question of general interest to mankind, as on pursuing a thief like Verres, or scourging a drunkard like Piso, or drawing the nets of Vulcan over the couch of Clodius. For which reason I should not wonder if your Orations were valued by posterity more highly than your Dialogues; although the best oration can only show the clever man, while Philosophy shows the great one.

Marcus. I approve of the Dialogue for the reason you have given me just now: the fewness of settled truths, and the facility of turning the cycle of our thoughts to what aspect we wish, as geometers and astronomers the globe. A book was lately on the point of publication, I hear, to demonstrate the childishness

---

[27 "Idem velle atque idem nolle"—"to seek and shun the same thing"—a proverbial Latin phrase for to be of one mind, to be friends. It is used by Catiline in his address to the conspirators in Sallust Cataline; also by Cicero in his Oration pro Plancio, and elsewhere. Landor's use of it here is odd.]

of the Dialogue;[28] and the man upon the bench a litttle way below
the Middle Janus, who had already paid the writer thirty denars
for it, gave it back to him on reading the word *childish*.　For
Menander or Sophocles or Euripides had caught his eye, all of
whom, he heard, wrote in dialogue, as did Homer in the better
parts of his two poems; and he doubted whether a young man
ignorant of these authors could ever have known that the same
method had been employed by Plato on all occasions, and by
Xenophon in much of his *Recollections*, and that the conversations
of Socrates would have lost their form and force, delivered in
any other manner.　He might perhaps have set up himself
against the others; but his modesty would not let him stand
before the world opposed to Socrates under the Shield of Apollo.
Morus, the man below the Middle Janus,* is very liberal, and
left him in possession of the thirty denars, on condition that he
should write as acrimoniously against as eloquent and judicious
an author, whenever called upon.

Quinctus.[29]　Speaking of Plato in the earlier series of your
philosophical disquisitions, you more highly praised his language
than you appear to have done lately.

Marcus.　There is indeed much to admire in it; but even his
language has fewer charms for me now than it had in youth.
Plato will always be an object of admiration and reverence to
men who would rather see vast images of uncertain objects
reflected from illuminated clouds, than representations of things
in their just proportions, measurable, tangible, and convertible
to household use.　Therefore, in speaking on the levity of the
Greeks, I turned my eyes toward him; that none, whatever
commendations I bestowed upon his diction, might mistake me

[28] See Introduction, p. xvii. "Morus, the man below the Middle
Janus," is John Murray, the publisher of the *Quarterly Review*.　One
result of Hare's article was "that the criticism already sent to press by
the editor of the *Quarterly* had been recalled and returned to its author,
in order that he might omit sundry passages anticipated in the parody,
especially a long diatribe on the childishness of dialogues." Forster,
Life, 267, and preceding pages.]

* The *Middle Janus* is mentioned by Horace.　It has usually been
considered as a temple, and the remains of it are pointed out as such;
but in fact it was only the *central arch* of a market-place.

[29] From "Quinctus" to "predicament" (37 lines) added in 2nd ed.;
from "Quinctus" to "Morus" (60 lines) added in 3rd ed.]

in describing the qualities of his mind.   Politics will gain nothing
of the practical from him, Philosophy nothing of what is applicable to morals, to science, to the arts, or the conduct of life.
Unswathe his Egyptian mummy; and from the folds of fine
linen, bestrewn and impregnated with aromatics, you disclose
the grave features and gracile bones of a goodly and venerable
cat.   Little then can you wonder if I have taken him as one of
small authority, when I composed my works on *Government*, on
the *Social Duties*, or on the *Nature of the Gods.*

Quinctus.   You have forborne to imitate his style, although
you cite the words of a Greek enthusiast, who says that if
Jupiter had spoken in Greek he would have spoken in the
language of Plato.

Marcus.   Jupiter had no occasion for Philosophy; we have.

Quinctus.   I prefer your method of conducting the Dialogue,
although I wish you had given us a greater variety both of topics
and of characters.

Marcus.   If time and health are granted me, perhaps I may
do somewhat more than I or others have accomplished in this
department.

Quinctus.   Why do you smile?—at your confidence of
succeeding?

Marcus.   No, indeed; but because all strong and generous
wine must deposit its crust before it gratifies the palate; and are
not all such writings in the same predicament?

Quinctus.   Various pieces of such criticism have been brought
to me.   One writer says of you, "He would pretend to an equality
in style and wisdom with Theophrastus."   Another, "We
remember his late invectives, which he had the assurance to call
Philippics, fancying himself another Demosthenes!"   A third,
"He knows so little of the Dialogue, that many of his speakers
talk for a quarter of an hour uninterruptedly; in fact, until they
can talk no longer, and have nothing more to say upon the
subject."

Marcus.   Rare objection!   As if the dialogue of statesmen
and philosophers, which appertains by its nature to dissertation,
should resemble the dialogue of comedians, and Lælius and
Scævola be turned into Davus and Syrus!   Although I have
derived my ideas of excellence from Greece, out of which there

is nothing elegant, nothing chaste and temperate, nothing not barbarous, nevertheless I have a mind of my own equal in capacity and in order to any there, indebted as I acknowledge it to be to Grecian exercises and Grecian institutions. Neither my time of life nor my rank in it, nor indeed my temper and disposition, would allow me to twitch the sleeves of sophists, and to banter them on the idleness of their disputations with trivial and tiny and petulant interrogatories. I introduce grave men, and they talk gravely; important subjects, and I treat them worthily. Lighter, if my spirits had the elasticity to give them play, I should touch more delicately and finely, letting them fly off in more fantastic forms and more vapory particles. But who indeed can hope to excel in two manners so widely different? Who hath ever done it, Greek or Roman? If wiser men than those who appear at present to have spoken against my dialogues should undertake the same business, I would inform them that the most severe way of judging these works, with any plea or appearance of fairness, is to select the best passages from the best writers I may have introduced, and to place my pages in opposition to theirs in equal quantities. Suppose me introducing Solon or Phocion, Æschines or Demosthenes; that is, whatever is most wise, whatever is most eloquent; should it appear that I have equalled them where so little space is allowed me, I have done greatly more than has ever been done hitherto. Style I consider as nothing, if what it covers be unsound: wisdom in union with harmony is oracular. On this idea, the wiser of ancient days venerated in the same person the deity of oracles and of music: and it must have been the most malicious and the most ingenious of satirists, who transferred the gift of eloquence to the god of thieves.

Quinctus. I am not certain that you have claimed for yourself the fair trial you would have demanded for a client. One of the interlocutors may sustain a small portion of a thesis.

Marcus. In that case, take the whole Conversation; examine the quality, the quantity, the variety, the intensity, of mental power exerted. I myself would arm my adversaries, and teach them how to fight me; and I promise you, the first blow I receive from one of them I will cheer him heartily: it will augur well for our country. At present I can do nothing more liberal

than in sending thirty other denars to the mortified bondman of
Morus.

I have performed one action; I have composed some few
things, which posterity, I would fain believe, will not suffer to be
quite forgotten. Fame, they tell you, is air; but without air
there is no life for any: without fame there is none for the best.
And yet, who knows whether all our labors and vigils may not at
last be involved in oblivion? What treasures of learning must
have perished, which existed long before the time of Homer!
For it is utterly out of the nature of things, that the first attempt
in any art of science should be the most perfect. Such is the
Iliad: I look upon it as the sole fragment of a lost world.
Grieved indeed I should be to think, as you have heard me say
before, that an enemy may possess our city five thousand years
hence: yet when I consider that soldiers of all nations are in the
armies of the triumvirate, and that all are more zealous for her
ruin than our citizens are for her defence, this event is not unlikely
the very next. The worst of barbarism is that which emanates,
not from the absence of laws, but from their corruption. So
long as virtue stands merely on the same level with vice, nothing[30]
is desperate, nothing is irreparable; few governments in their easy
decrepitude care for more. But when rectitude is dangerous
and depravity secure, then eloquence and courage, the natural
pride and safeguard of States, become the strongest and most
active instruments in their overthrow.

Quinctus. I see the servants have lighted the lamps in the
house earlier than usual, hoping, I suppose, we shall retire to
rest in good time, that to-morrow they may prepare the festivities
for your birthday.

Marcus.[31] They are bringing out of the dining-room, I apprehend, the busts our Atticus lately sent me. Let us hasten to
prevent it, or they may place Homer and Solon with the others,
instead of inserting them in the niches opposite my bed, where I
wish to contemplate them by the first light of morning, the first
objects opening on my eyes. For, without the one, not only

[30 First ed. reads: "Nothing is amiss; few," &c.]
[31 From "*Marcus*" to "*Quinctus*" (14 lines) added in 3rd ed. Six
lines below, 1st ed. reads: "The Circean hills, and the island of
Parthenope, and even the white rocks," &c.]

poetry but eloquence too, and every high species of literary composition, might have remained until this day, in all quarters of the
globe, incondite and indigested; and without the other even
Athens herself might have explored her way in darkness, and
never have exhibited to us Romans the prototype of those laws
on which our glory hath arisen, and the loss of which we are
destined to lament as our last and greatest.

Quinctus. Within how few minutes has the night closed in
upon us!   Nothing is left discernible of the promontories, or the
long irregular breakers under them.   We have before us only a
faint glimmering from the shells in our path, and from the
blossoms of the arbutus.

Marcus.   The little solitary Circean hill, and even the nearer,
loftier, and whiter rocks of Anxur, are become indistinguishable.
We leave our Cato and our Lucullus; we leave Cornelia and her
children, the scenes of friendship and the recollections of greatness, for Lepidus and Octavius and Antonius: and who knows
whether this birthday, between which and us so [32] few days in-
tervene, may not be, as it certainly will be the least pleasurable,
the last!

Quinctus. Do not despond, my brother!

Marcus.   I am as far from despondency and dejection as from
joy and cheerfulness.   Death has two aspects: dreary and
sorrowful to those of prosperous, mild and almost genial to those
of adverse, fortune.   Her countenance is old to the young, and
youthful to the aged : to the former her voice is importunate, her
gait terrific; the latter she approaches like a bedside friend, and
calls in a whisper that invites to rest.   To us, my Quinctus,
advanced as we are on our way, weary from its perplexities and
dizzy from its precipices, she gives a calm welcome : let her
receive a cordial one.

If life is a present which any one foreknowing its contents
would have willingly declined, does it not follow that any one
would as willingly give it up, having well tried what they are?   I
speak of the reasonable, the firm, the virtuous; not of those who,
like bad governors, are afraid of laying down the powers and

[[32] First ed. reads: "only one other day intervenes," &c. Two lines
below, from "*Quinctus*" to "cheerfulness" (3 lines) added in 3rd ed.
From "Death" to "one" (9 lines) added in 2nd ed.]

privileges they have been proved unworthy of holding.   Were it
certain that the longer we live the wiser we become and the
happier, then indeed a long life would be desirable ; but since on
the contrary our mental strength decays, and our enjoyments of
every kind not only sink and cease, but diseases and sorrows come
in place of them, if any wish is rational, it is surely the wish that
we should go away unshaken by years, undepressed by griefs, and
undespoiled of our better faculties.   Life and death appear more
certainly ours than whatsoever else : and yet hardly can that be
called ours, which comes without our knowledge, and goes without it ; or that which we cannot put aside if we would, and
indeed can anticipate but little.   There are few who can regulate
life to any extent ; none who can order the things it shall receive
or exclude.   What value then should be placed upon it by the
prudent man, when duty or necessity calls him away ?   Or what
reluctance should he feel on passing into a state where at least he
must be conscious of fewer checks and inabilities ?   Such, my
brother, as the brave commander, when from the secret and dark
passages of some fortress wherein implacable enemies besieged him,
having performed all his duties and exhausted all his munition, he
issues at a distance into open day.

Every thing has its use : life to teach us the contempt of death,
and death the contempt of life.   Glory, which among all things
between stands eminently the principal, although it has been considered by some philosophers as mere vanity and deception, moves
those great intellects which nothing else could have stirred, and
places them where they can best and most advantageously serve
the Commonwealth.   Glory [33] can be safely despised by those only
who have fairly won it : a low, ignorant, or vicious man should
dispute on other topics.   The philosopher who contemns it has
every rogue in his sect, and may reckon that it will outlive all
others.   Occasion may have been wanting to some ; I grant it.
They may have remained their whole lifetime like dials in the
shade, always fit for use and always useless ; but this must occur
either in monarchal governments, or where persons occupy the
first station who ought hardly to have been admitted to the
secondary, and whom jealousy has guided more frequently than
justice.

[33 From " Glory " to " others " (5 lines) added in 2nd ed.]

It is true there is much inequality, much inconsiderateness, in the distribution of fame; and the principles according to which honor ought to be conferred are not only violated, but often inverted. Whoever wishes to be thought great among men must do them some great mischief; and the longer he continues in doing things of this sort, the more he will be admired. The features of Fortune are so like those of Genius as to be mistaken by almost all the world. We whose names and works are honorable to our country, and destined to survive her, are less esteemed than those who have accelerated her decay; yet even here the sense of injury rises from and is accompanied by a sense of merit, the tone of which is deeper and predominant.

When we have spoken of life, death, and glory, we have spoken of all important things, except friendship; for eloquence and philosophy, and other inferior attainments, are either means conducible to life and glory, or antidotes against the bitterness of death. We cannot conquer fate and necessity, yet we can yield to them in such a manner as to be greater than if we could. I have observed your impatience: you were about to appeal in behalf of virtue. But virtue is presupposed in friendship, as I have mentioned in my *Lælius*; nor have I ever separated it from philosophy or from glory. I [34] discussed the subject most at large and most methodically in my treatise on our *Duties*, and I find no reason to alter my definition or deductions. On friendship, in the present condition of our affairs, I would say but little. Could I begin my existence again, and, what is equally impossible, could I see before me all I have seen, I would choose few acquaintances, fewer friendships, no familiarities. This rubbish, for such it generally is, collecting at the base of an elevated mind, lessens its height and impairs its character. What requires to be sustained, if it is greater, falls; if it is smaller, is lost to view by the intervention of its supporters.*

---

[34] From "I" to "deductions" (3 lines) added in 3rd ed.]

* These are the ideas of a man deceived and betrayed by almost every one he trusted. But if Cicero had considered that there never was an elevated soul or warm heart which has not been ungenerously and unjustly dealt with, and that ingratitude has usually been in proportion to desert, his vanity if not his philosophy would have buoyed up and supported him. He himself is redundant in such instances. To set Pompeius aside, as a man ungrateful to all, he had spared Julius Cæsar in his consulate

In [35] literature, great men suffer more from their little friends
than from their potent enemies.   It is not by our adversaries that
our early shoots of glory are nipped and broken off, or our later
pestilentially blighted ; it is by those who lie at our feet, and look
up to us with a solicitous and fixed regard until our shadow
grows thicker and makes them colder.   Then they begin to praise
us as worthy men indeed, and good citizens, but rather vain, and
what (to speak the truth) in others they should call presumptuous.
They entertain no doubt of our merit in literature ; yet justice
forces them to declare that several have risen up lately who
promise to surpass us.   Should it be asked of them who these are,
they look modest, and tell you softly and submissively it would ill
become them to repeat the eulogies of their acquaintance, and
that no man pronounces his own name so distinctly as another's.
I had something of oratory once about me, and was borne on high
by the spirit of the better Greeks.   Thus they thought of me ;
and they thought of me, Quinctus, no more than thus.   They
had reached the straits, and saw before them the boundary, the
impassible Atlantic, of the intellectual world.   But now I am a

when he was implicated in the onspiracy of Cataline.   Clodius, Lepidus,
and Antonius had been admitted to his friendship and confidence ;
Octavius owed to him his popularity and estimation ; Philologus, †
whom he had fed and instructed, pointed out to his pursuers the secret
path he had taken to avoid them ; and Popilius, their leader, had by his
eloquence been saved from the punishment of one parricide that he might
commit another.

It were well if Cicero had been so sincere in his friendship as perhaps
he thought he was.   The worst action of his life may be narrated in his
own words : "Qualis futura sit Cæsaris Vituperatio contra Laudationem
meam perspexi ex eo libro quem Hirtius ad me misit, in quo colligit vitia
Catonis, sed cum maximis Laudibus meis : itaque misi librum ad Muscam,
ut tuis librariis daret, *volo enim eum divulgari*." Ad Attic. xii. 40.   An
honest man would be little gratified by the divulgation of his praises
accompanied by calumnies on his friend, or even by the exposure of his
faults and weaknesses.

[35 From "In" to "them" (102 lines) added in 2nd ed.   In the 2nd
ed. the allegory is related by Quinctus.]

---

† So his name is written by Plutarch, who calls him ἀπελεύθερος
Κοΐντου.   We may doubt whether it should not be Philogonus, for a
freed-man of Quinctus with that name is mentioned in the *Epistles* (ad
Q. F. 1. 3).

bad citizen and a worse **writer :** I want **the** exercise and effusion of my own breath to warm **me ;** I must **be** chafed by an **adver-** sary ; **I must** be supported **by a crowd ;** I require the Forum, the Rostra, **the** Senate : **in my** individuality **I am** nothing.

Quinctus. I remember **the** time when, **instead** of smiling, you **would** have been offended **and** angry at such levity and impudence.

Marcus. **The** misfortunes **of our** country **cover** ours, and I am imperceptible to myself in the **dark** gulf that is absorbing her. Should I be angry ? Anger, always irrational, is **most** so here. These men **see** those above them **as they** see the **stars :** one is almost as large as another, almost **as** bright ; small distance **between** them. They cannot quite touch us with the forefinger ; **but they can almost.** And what matters it ? They can utter as **many** things against us, and as fiercely, as Polyphemus did against **the** heavens. Since my Dialogues are certainly the last **things I** shall **compose,** and since we, my brother, shall perhaps, **for the** little time that is remaining of our lives, be soon divided, **we may** talk about these matters **as among** the wisest and most interesting : **and the rather,** if **there is** any thing in **them** displaying the character **of our** country **and** the phasis of our **times.**

Aquilius [36] Cimber, who lives somewhere **under** the Alps, was patronized by Caius Cæsar **for his** assiduities, **and by** Antonius for his admirable talent in telling **a story and** sitting up late. **He**

[36] Aquilius Cimber is rather **a** mysterious person. **He is to all** appearance an Edinburgh Reviewer, **but** it is difficult **to say exactly** which of **the band.** Hazlitt wrote the article **to** which this passage **is** intended as a **retort ;** but Aquilius Cimber is not Hazlitt, **nor is** he Jeffrey, though some part of the description might seem intended for him. It is almost impossible **to help** a suspicion **that** there was in Landor's mind some grievance against a greater writer, **and** that he is here aiming **some** satire at Scott. Of course much **of the passage** is utterly inapplicable to Scott. But there are clear allusions **to his study** of old Scotch History, **to** the Waverley Novels, **to** his work on **Demonology, to his** association with the firm of Constable, and **to his tenderness towards** the Young Pretender. It is even possible that Landor may have heard that Scott had **dined** with the Prince Regent, **who** would readily be transmuted **by** Landor into Antonius. There is one strong argument against the **identification.** In his later life Landor certainly felt, and expressed, strong **admiration for** Scott. But among all the alterations which he made in **this Conversation,** he left this passage uncancelled.]

bears on his shoulders the whole tablet of his nation, reconciling its incongruities. Apparently very frank, but intrinsically very insincere; a warm friend while drinking; cold, vapid, limber, on the morrow, as the festal coronet he had worn the night before.

Quinctus. Such a person, I can well suppose, may nevertheless have acquired the friendship of Antonius.

Marcus. His popularity in those parts rendered him also an object of attention to Octavius, who told me he was prodigiously charmed with his stories of departed spirits, which Aquilius firmly believes are not altogether departed from his country. He hath several old books relating to the history, true and fabulous, of the earlier Cimbri. Such is the impression they made upon him in his youth, he soon composed others on the same model, and better (I have heard) than the originals. His opinion is now much regarded in his province on matters of literature in general; although you would as soon think of sending for a smith to select an ostrich feather at the milliner's. He neglects no means of money-getting, and has entered into an association for this purpose with the booksellers of the principal Transpadane cities. On the first appearance of my Dialogues, he, not having read them, nor having heard of their tendency, praised them; moderately indeed and reservedly; but finding the people in power ready to persecute and oppress me, he sent his excuse to Antonius, that he was drunk when he did it; and to Octavius, that the fiercest of the Lemures [37] held him by the throat until he had written what his heart revolted at. And he ordered his friends and relatives to excuse him by one or other of these apologies, according to the temper and credulity of the person they addressed.

Quinctus. I never heard the story of Aquilius, no less amusing than the well-known one of him, that he went several miles out of his road to visit the tomb of the Scipios, only to lift up his tunic against it in contempt. He boasted of the feat and of the motive.

Marcus. Until the worthies of our time shone forth, he venerated no Roman since the exiled kings, in which his favorite is the son of the last; and there are certain men in high authority who assure him they know how to appreciate and compensate so heroic and sublime an affection. The Catos and Brutuses are

[37 Videlicet, "a bogy."]

wretches with him, and particularly since Cato pardoned him for
having hired a fellow (as was proved) to turn some swine into his
turnip-field at Tusculum. Looking at him or hearing of him,
unless from those who know his real character, you would imagine
him generous, self-dependent, self-devoted ; but this upright
and staunch thistle bears a yielding and palpable down for
adulation.

Quinctus. Better *that* than malice. Whatever he may think
or say of you, I hope he never speaks maliciously of those whose
livelihood, like his own, depends upon their writings,—the studious, the enthusiastic, the unhardened in politics, the uncrossed in
literature.

Marcus. I wish I could confirm or encourage you in your
hopes ; report, as it reaches me, by no means favors them.

Quinctus. This hurts me ; for Aquilius, although the Graces
in none of their attributions are benignant to him, is a man of industry and genius.

Marcus. Alas, Quinctus ! to pass Aquilius by, as not concerned in the reflection, the noblest elevations of the human mind
have in appurtenance their sands and swamps : hardness at top,
putridity at bottom. Friends themselves—and not only the little
ones you have spoken of, not only the thoughtless and injudicious,
but graver and more constant—will occasionally gratify a superficial feeling, which soon grows deeper, by irritating an orator or
writer. You remember the apologue of Critobulus?

Quinctus. No, I do not.

Marcus. It was sent to me by Pomponius Atticus soon after
my marriage : I must surely have shown it to you.

Quinctus. Not you, indeed ; and I should wonder that so
valuable a present, so rare an accession to Rome as a new Greek
volume, could have come into your hands and not out of them
into mine, if you had not mentioned that it was about the time of
your nuptials. Let me hear the story.

Marcus. " I was wandering," says Critobulus, " in the midst
of a forest, and came suddenly to a small round fountain or pool,
with several white flowers (I remember) and broad leaves in the
centre of it, but clear of them at the sides, and of a water the
most pellucid. Suddenly a very beautiful figure came from
behind me, and stood between me and the fountain. I was

amazed. I could not distinguish the sex, the form being youthful and the face toward the water, on which it was gazing and bending over its reflection, like another Hylas or Narcissus. It then stooped and adorned itself with a few of the simplest flowers, and seemed the fonder and tenderer of those which had borne the impression of its graceful feet; and, having done so, it turned round and looked upon me with an air of indifference and unconcern. The longer I fixed my eyes on her—for I now discovered it was a female—the more ardent I became and the more embarrassed. She perceived it, and smiled. Her eyes were large and serene; not very thoughtful as if perplexed, not very playful as if easily to be won; and her countenance was tinged with so delightful a color, that it appeared an effluence from an irradiated cloud passing over it in the heavens. She gave me the idea, from her graceful attitude, that, although adapted to the perfection of activity, she felt rather an inclination for repose. I would have taken her hand: 'You shall presently,' said she; and never fell on mortal a diviner glance than on me. I told her so. She replied, 'You speak well.' I then fancied she was simple and weak, and fond of flattery, and began to flatter her. She turned her face away from me, and answered nothing. I declared my excessive love: she went some paces off. I swore it was impossible for one who had ever seen her to live without her: she went several paces farther. 'By the immortal gods!' I cried, 'you shall not leave me!' She turned round and looked benignly; but shook her head. 'You are another's then! Say it! say it! utter the word once from your lips—and let me die!' She smiled, more melancholy than before, and replied, 'O Critobulus! I am indeed another's: I am a god's.' The air of the interior heavens seemed to pierce me as she spoke; and I trembled as impassioned men may tremble once. After a pause, 'I might have thought it!' cried I: 'why then come before me and torment me?' She began to play and trifle with me, as became her age (I fancied) rather than her engagement, and she placed my hand upon the flowers in her lap without a blush. The whole fountain would not at that moment have assuaged my thirst. The sound of the breezes and of the birds around us, even the sound of her own voice, were all confounded in my ear, as colors are in the fulness and intensity of light. She said many pleasing things to me, to the earlier and greater part of which I was insensible ; but in the midst of those which I could hear and was listening to attentively, she began to pluck out the gray hairs from my head, and to tell me that the others too were of a hue not very agreeable.   My heart sank within me.   Presently there was hardly a limb or feature without its imperfection.   'Oh ! ' cried I in despair, ' you have been used to the gods ; you must think so : but among men I do not believe I am considered as ill-made or unseemly.'   She paid little attention to my words or my vexation ; and when she had gone on with my defects for some time longer, in the same calm tone and with the same sweet countenance, she began to declare that she had much affection for me, and was desirous of inspiring it in return.   I was about to answer her with rapture, when on a sudden, in her girlish humor, she stuck a thorn, wherewith she had been playing, into that part of the body which supports us when we sit.   I know not whether it went deeper than she intended, but, catching at it, I leaped up in shame and anger, and at the same moment felt something upon my shoulder.   It was an armlet inscribed with letters of bossy adamant, ' Jove to his daughter Truth.'

" She stood again before me at a distance, and said gracefully, ' Critobulus !   I am too young and simple for you ; but you will love me still, and not be made unhappy by it in the end.   Farewell.' "

Quinctus.   Why did you not insert this allegory in some part of your works, as you have often many pages from the Greek ?

Marcus.   I might have done it, but I know not whether the state of our literature is any longer fit for its reception.

Quinctus.   Confess, if it is not, that the fault is in some sort yours, who might have directed the higher minds, and have carried the lower with them.

Marcus.   I regard with satisfaction the efforts I have made to serve my country ; but the same eloquence, the merit of which not even the most barbarous of my adversaries can detract from me, would have enabled me to elucidate large fields of philosophy, hitherto untrodden by our countrymen, and in which the Greeks have wandered widely or worked unprofitably.

Quinctus.   Excuse my interruption.   I heard a few days ago a pleasant thing reported of Asinius Pollio : he said, at supper, your language is that of an Allobrox.[38]

Marcus. After supper, I should rather think, and with Antonius. Asinius, urged by the strength of instinct, picks from amid the freshest herbage the dead dry stalk, and dozes and dreams about it where he cannot find it. Acquired, it is true, I have a certain portion of my knowledge, and consequently of my language, from the Allobroges : I cannot well point out the place, —the wall of Romulus, the habitations of Janus and of Saturn, and the temple of Capitoline Jove, which the confessions I extorted from their ambassadors gave me in my consulate the means of saving, stand at too great a distance from this terrace.

Quinctus. Certainly [39] you have much to look back upon, of what is most proper and efficacious to console you. Consciousness of desert protects the mind against obloquy, exalts it above calamity, and scatters into utter invisibility the shadowy fears of death. Nevertheless, O Marcus! to leave behind us our children, if indeed it will be permitted them to stay behind, is painful.

Marcus. Among the contingencies of life, it is that for which we ought to be best prepared, as the most regular and ordinary in the course of Nature. In dying, and leaving our friends, and saying, "I shall see you no more," which is thought by the generous man the painfullest thing in the change he undergoes, we speak as if we shall continue to feel the same desire and want of seeing them,—an inconsistency so common as never to have been noticed : and my remark, which you would think too trivial, startles by its novelty before it conciliates by its truth. We bequeath to our children a field illuminated by our glory and enriched by our example : a noble patrimony, and beyond the jurisdiction of prætor or proscriber. Nor indeed is

[38] After the flight of Catiline from Rome, Lentulus, Cethegus, and some others of his associates remained behind in Rome planning an outbreak in the city. Their plots were, however, revealed to Cicero by the ambassadors of the Allobroges, a Gallic tribe, who were at that time in Rome. The conspirators, believing that that tribe resented certain oppressions they had experienced from the Romans, endeavoured to persuade them to support Catiline, but the ambassadors revealed the negotiations to Cicero.]

[39] From "Certainly" to "you" (2 lines) added in 2nd ed. Five lines below, from "In" to "truth" (8 lines) added in 3rd ed.]

our fall itself without its fruit to them : for violence is the cause
why that is often called a calamity which is not, and repairs in
some measure its injuries by exciting to commiseration and tenderness. The pleasure a man receives from his children resembles
that which, with more propriety than any other, we may attribute
to the divinity : for to suppose that his chief satisfaction and
delight should arise from the contemplation of what he has done
or can do, is to place him on a level with a runner or a wrestler.
The formation of a world, or of a thousand worlds, is as easy to
him as the formation of an atom. Virtue and intellect are equally
his production ; yet he subjects them in no slight degree to our
volition. His benevolence is gratified at seeing us conquer our
wills and rise superior to our infirmities, and at tracing day after
day a nearer resemblance in our moral features to his. We can
derive no pleasure but from exertion ; he can derive none from it :
since exertion, as we understand the word, is incompatible with
omnipotence.

Quinctus. Proceed, my brother ! for in every depression of
mind, in every excitement of feeling, my spirits are equalized by
your discourse ; and that which you said with too much brevity
of our children soothes me greatly.

Marcus. I am persuaded of the truth in what I have spoken ;
and yet—ah, Quinctus ! there is a tear that Philosophy cannot
dry, and a pang that will rise as we approach the gods.

Two [40] things tend beyond all others, after philosophy, to inhibit
and check our ruder passions as they grow and swell in us, and to
keep our gentler in their proper play : and these two things are
seasonable sorrow and inoffensive pleasure, each moderately indulged. Nay, there is also a pleasure—humble, it is true, but
graceful and insinuating—which follows close upon our very
sorrows, reconciles us to them gradually, and sometimes renders
us at last undesirous altogether of abandoning them. If ever you
have remembered the anniversary of some day whereon a dear
friend was lost to you, tell me whether that anniversary was not
purer and even calmer than the day before. The sorrow, if there
should be any left, is soon absorbed, and full satisfaction takes
place of it, while you perform a pious office to Friendship, required
and appointed by the ordinances of Nature. When my Tulliola

[40 From " Two " to " departed " (25 lines) added in 2nd ed.]

was torn away from me, a thousand plans were in readiness for immortalizing her memory, and raising a monument up to the magnitude of my grief. The grief itself has done it: the tears I then shed over her assuaged it in me, and did every thing that could be done for her, or hoped, or wished. I called upon Tulliola : Rome and the whole world heard me ; her glory was a part of mine, and mine of hers ; and when Eternity had received her at my hands, I wept no longer. The tenderness wherewith I mentioned and now mention her, though it suspends my voice, brings what consoles and comforts me : it is the milk and honey left at the sepulchre, and equally sweet (I hope) to the departed.

The gods who have given us our affections permit us surely the uses and the signs of them. Immoderate grief, like every thing else immoderate, is useless and pernicious ; but if we did not tolerate and endure it, if we did not prepare for it, meet it, commune with it, if we did not even cherish it in its season,—much of what is best in our faculties, much of our tenderness, much of our generosity, much of our patriotism, much also of our genius, would be stifled and extinguished.

When I hear any one call upon another to be manly and to restrain his tears, if they flow from the social and kind affections, I doubt the humanity and distrust the wisdom of the counsellor. Were he humane, he would be more inclined to pity and to sympathize than to lecture and reprove ; and were he wise, he would consider that tears are given us by Nature as a remedy to affliction, although, like other remedies, they should come to our relief in private. Philosophy, we may be told, would prevent the tears by turning away the sources of them, and by raising up a rampart against pain and sorrow. I am of opinion that philosophy, quite pure and totally abstracted from our appetites and passions, instead of serving us the better, would do us little or no good at all. We may receive so much light as not to see, and so much philosophy as to be worse than foolish. I [1] have never had leisure to write all I could have written on the subjects I began to meditate and discuss too late. And where, O Quinctus ! where are those men gone, whose approbation would have stimulated and cheered me in the course of them ? Little is entirely my own in

[[1] From " I " to " state " (25 lines) added in 3rd ed.]

the *Tusculan Disputations* ; for I went rather in search of what is useful than of what is specious, and sat down oftener to consult the wise than to argue with the ingenious. In order to determine what is fairly due to me, you will see, which you may easily, how large is the proportion of the impracticable, the visionary, the baseless, in the philosophers who have gone before me ; and how much of application and judgment, to say nothing of temper and patience, was requisite in making the selection. Aristoteles is the only one of the philosophers I am intimate with (except you extort from me to concede you Epicurus) who never is a dreamer or a trifler, and almost the only one whose language, varying with its theme, is yet always grave and concise, authoritative and stately, neither running into wild dithyrambics, nor stagnating in vapid luxuriance. I have not hesitated, on many occasions, to borrow largely from one who, in so many provinces, hath so much to lend. The whole of what I collected, and the whole of what I laid out from my own, is applicable to the purposes of our political, civil, and domestic state. And my eloquence, whatever (with Pollio's leave) it may be, would at least have sufficed me to elucidate and explore those ulterior tracts, which the Greeks have coasted negligently and left unsettled. Although I think I have done somewhat more than they, I am often dissatisfied with the scantiness of my store and the limit of my excursion. Every question has given me the subject of a new one, which has always been better treated than the preceding ; and, like Archimedes, whose tomb appears now before me as when I first discovered it at Syracuse, I could almost ask of my enemy time to solve my problem.

Quinctus ! Quinctus ! let us exult with joy : there is no enemy to be appeased or avoided. We are moving forward and without exertion, thither where we shall know all we wish to know ; and how greatly more than, whether in Tusculum or in Formiæ, in Rome or in Athens, we could ever hope to learn !

[The following note is not printed at full length, but the omissions are chiefly of Latin passages quoted in support of the opinions expressed in it. It is here reprinted from the Imaginary Conversations of Greeks and Romans. There is also a long passage containing an attack on Plato's theoretical preference for a despotism expressed in Laws, iv., 709. See also vol. i., p. 106.]

REFLECTIONS ON THE CONVERSATIONS ON THE CICEROS.

Some of the opinions here attributed to Cicero, and particularly those on the agrarian law, are at variance with what he has expressed, not only in his *Orations*, but also in his three books, *De Officiis*, which he appears to have written under a vehement fear, that either this or something similar would deprive him of his possessions. Hence he speaks of the Gracchi with an asperity which no historian has countenanced, and of Agis without a word of commendation or of pity. When, however, he perceived that in the midst of dangers his property was untouched, it must have occurred to so sagacious a reasoner that if an agrarian law had been enacted, the first triumvirate could never have existed, and that he himself had remained, as he ought to have been, the leader of the commonwealth. It is to be lamented that he should have mentioned Crassus as a man he did not hate. Dion Cassius, in his twenty-ninth book, says he wrote some tremendous things against him and a good many of them: giving the manuscript, sealed up, into the hands of his son, and ordering that it should be published after his death. Such a politician ought to have foreseen that the injunction was unlikely to be carried into effect. As there was no danger impending over the life of Cicero while Crassus held a place in the triumvirate, it may be suspected that the sealed paper related to another of its members; for it would be impossible to add anything worse to what he already had published against Crassus. . . . The conduct of the Gracchi was approved by the wisest and most honest of their contemporaries. Lælius, the friend of Scipio, desisted from his support of Tiberius, only when, as Plutarch says, he was compelled by the apprehension of *greater evil*. But surely a man so prudent as Lælius must have foreseen all the consequences, and have known the good or the evil of them, and would not have desisted when, the matter having been agitated, and the measure agreed on, every danger was over from taking it, and the only one that could arise was from its rejection, after that the hopes and expectations of the people had been stimulated and excited. Hence we may be induced to believe that Scipio, in compliance with the wishes of the Senate, persuaded his friend to desist from the undertaking. . . . Mutianus Crassus, the brother of Publius, and Appius Claudius, were also his supporters. It is beyond all doubt that Tiberius Gracchus was both politic and equitable in his plan of dividing among the poorer citizens, whose debts had been incurred by services rendered to their country, the lands retained by the rich, in violation of the Licinian law. He was called unjust towards the inhabitants of Latium and the allies, in proposing to deprive them of that which the Romans had given them, but instead of which, to indemnify themselves for the grant, they had imposed a tribute. Gracchus wished to allay the irritation of the people, and to render them inoffensive to the state, by giving them useful occupations in the cares and concerns of property. The Latin allies would have been indemnified: for the tax imposed on them would have been removed, and the freedom of the city granted to them. The Senate would perhaps have been somewhat less hostile to Tiberius Gracchus if he had not also proposed that the money left by Attalus to the Roman people should go to its destination. They were stimulated, if not by interest, by power, to invoke the assistance of Scipio against the popular party ; and he was conducted home by them the day before his death ; which appears rather to have been hastened by the fears and jealousy of the Senate than by the revenge of the opposition, none of whom at that time could have had access to him, his house being filled and surrounded by their adversaries. The Senate had reasons for suspicion of Scipio. They dreaded the dictatorial power to be conferred on him, in order that he might settle the commonwealth; they were dissatisfied at the doubts he entertained of guilt in Gracchus, of whom he declared his opinion that he was justly slain if he had attempted to possess the supreme power, which expression proves that he doubted, or, rather, that he disbelieved it, and is equivalent to the declaration that he did not deserve death for any other of his actions or intentions. They also clearly saw that a man of his equity and firmness would not leave unpunished those who had instigated Popilius Lænus, Opinius, and Metellus to their cruelties against the partisans of Gracchus. Opinius alone had put to death, by a judicial process, no fewer than three thousand Roman citizens, whose only crime was that of demanding what had been left them by Attalus and promised them by the rulers of the state. . . . It has been the fashion, and not only of late years, but for ages, to represent the Roman form of government, when unperverted, as aristocratical. This is erroneous. Cicero himself says—" nihil sacro sanctum esse potest, nisi quod plebs populusve jusserit." The people chose all the great functionaries, excepting the interrex : he appointed the dictator, who is falsely thought to have possessed absolute power, even during the short period for which he was created. Polybius, an author to be depended on in whatever he relates as fact, mentioning the appointment of Fabius Maximus to the dictatorship, goes out of his road to pay homage to the fasces of the Tribunes. "*Whereas* the counsel," says he, "*is preceded by twelve axes,* the dictator *is preceded by sixteen : the counsels must refer many things to the Senate : but the dictator is independent of every other power, excepting the tribunes.*" B.6. Now, dependency is not headship. Polybius, who wrote thus, lived intimately with Scipio ; and Scipio is represented as hostile to the constitution of his country, and a stickler for royalty ! He certainly was no zealous advocate of the tribunitial power, yet his friend had no hesitation in speaking thus of it ; for uch was its acknowledged rank and dignity. When Fabius Maximus would have punished Minutius, the tribunes interposed their authority. The senatorial formula, *Videant Consules ne quid detrimenti capiat Res Publica,* has misled many, and, indeed, misled Cicero himself, who offended against the forms of law when he saved the commonwealth from Catalina. The supreme power was never legally in the consuls, but constantly in the tribunes of the people. . . . Nothing is more common than the interference of the tribunes against the consuls. T. Livius (l. xliv.) relates that the effects of Tiberius Gracchus the elder, who had been consul and censor, were *consecrated* (which, in arbitrary governments, is called *confiscated*) because he had disobeyed an order of the tribune S. Flavius ; a tribune committed to prison the consul Metellus ; the censor Appius was punished in the same manner by the tribunitian authority. Carbo, who had been thrice consul, was condemned to death by Pompey from the tribunitian chair. Drusus, as tribune, sent the consul Phillipus to prison with a halter round his neck, *obtrita gula* (Florus, clv.) One Vectius was slain for not rising up before a tribune. Arrogantly and unjustly as the power in this instance was applied, it was constitutionally. Plutarch relates part of a speech by Tiberius Gracchus, in which the authority is mentioned as a thing settled. "It is hard," he says, "if a consul may be thrown into prison by a tribune, and a tribune cannot be removed from office by the people."

With all these facts in his memory, Cicero still would consider the legitimate government of Rome as an aristocracy; for otherwise how could he himself be aristocratical, which he avows he was? He wrote his treatise, De Republica, ten years before his death, when the greater and more costly part of his experience was wanting. In our dialogue he is represented as on the verge of a political world, of which he has been the mover and protector, while the elements of it announce to him that it is bursting under his feet. Hardly is that man to be called inconsistent, who, guided by recent facts, turns at last to wiser sentiments, opposite as they may be to those he entertained the greater part of his life. If any one shall assert that here is attributed to Cicero an inconsistency unwarranted by his writings, the answer is, that there is manifestly a much greater between the facts he states in these quotations and the conclusions he appears by his line of policy to have drawn from them; and that, taking his own statement, no injustice is done to his discernment and ratiocination in bringing home to him a new inference. Whatever be the defects of this memorable writer, we should disclose them hesitatingly and reluctantly; for in comparison with the meanest of his productions, how inelegant is the most elaborate composition of our times. Few have grasp enough to comprehend at once all the greatness of a great writer; somewhat is generally near at hand to distract their attention; some salient point to allure them; they fly towards it just as birds towards a sudden flash in the night, narrow as may be its space and brief its duration. There are critics who take their station on glittering vanes or fretted pinnacles, and seem to have an appetite for wind. Usually they alight on something strange, and call it original; on something perverse, and call it strong; on something clamorous, and call it eloquent. Cicero is not the author for them; to them he is yet in exile. Attentive study, scrupulous examination, strict comparison, are insufficient; yet even these are wanting to many gentlemen who take the chair and talk fluently about his writings.

Now, let us pass from the philosopher and pleader to the man. Morally he was among the best public men of his age; perhaps the very best, being quite exempt from its besetting sin, peculation. He had no vices, few faults; weaknesses he had, as all men have: his vanity was exorbitant, insatiable; and, more effeminately than any Roman, he was prostrated by calamity. Many deplored his death, many still commiserate it: unreasonably. It was without long suffering, without time for vain regrets, and equally vain expectations. Worse days than the past

were coming: had come. Preferable was it to die by the sudden stroke
of a murderer than by a slowly corroded heart. From M. Antonius—
against whom he had inveighed without remission, and whom he would
have driven out of his country, and have persecuted unto death—from M.
Antonius, who forgot no adherent and forgave no enemy, well might he
foresee what befel him. His enfeebled health and broken spirit could ill
have raised him up against the contemptuous neglect of the colder and
crueler and more ungrateful Pompeius. Happily for him and for Italy
the sands of Egypt had drunk the blood of the blood-thirsty; and a
generous enemy (if enemy he must be called) paid to Cicero those
honours, which, from his first reception at Pharsalia, he never had received.
Cæsar knew perfectly what the other never could be taught, the glory of
preserving one grand pillar, although not erect, amid the demolitions
and cinders of the commonwealth.

VI. TIBULLUS AND MESSALA.[1]

Tibullus. Messala? this is indeed a delight to me. A visit in
Rome would have been little better than an honor.

Messala. My dear Tibullus! didst thou not promise me a
great reward if I would come to thy villa in the autumn? Confident that no urbanity can escape thy memory or thy performance,
here I am.

Tibullus. Little, too little, is whatever I could have promised.

Messala. Little? didst thou not promise me in presence of all
the Muses, that Delia should cull the ripest apples for me?—and
thou well knowest how fond I always was of them.

[1 Messala, the patron of Tibullus, was one of the finest characters of his
time. After the death of Cæsar he joined the party of Brutus, though he
had taken no part in his conspiracy. Upon the defeat of his party at
Philippi he surrendered himself to Antony, until the infatuation of that
general for Cleopatra caused him to unite himself to Augustus. To the
military talents of Messala was due in great measure the victory of
Actium, and he also rendered important service in suppressing a
dangerous insurrection in Aquitaine. The family estate of Tibullus had
been confiscated during the civil war, but was in part restored to him at
Messala's request. The poet's gratitude for this service made him the
affectionate friend of his patron, whom he accompanied to Aquitaine
(Tibull. i. vii.). Landor gives in this Conversation a pretty picture of
the country life of Tibullus with his lady-love, Delia, to whom he wrote
many of his best poems. The first elegy was clearly in Landor's mind as
he wrote. There are described "The great apples that fall easily into the
hand," and there come the well known lines quoted below, Te spectem,
&c. (Imag. Convers., Gks. and Rom., 1853. Works, ii., 1876.)]

Tibullus. **On** the Garumna and on the Liger, **after a tedious** march, we often found them refreshing.

Messala. What then must they be, gathered by the hand **of** Delia, the beloved of my brave Tibullus?

Tibullus. She shall gather them instantly.

Come, Delia! come from behind that curtain. Here is Messala. Do not let **his** eloquence win thy heart away from me, **and** forget for a moment all thou hast ever **heard** about his military actions and his high nobility.

Delia. Albius! Albius! for shame! how dare you take such a liberty with so great a man, as to put my hand into his?

Tibullus. Because he **is** what thou callest him: I **take no** liberty with any **other.**

Messala. Albius Tibullus! **I never** thought **thee such a** flatterer **before.** Were I **in** power, **or in favor** with the powerful, thou **wouldst** be more discreet and silent. Neither the **heir** of Julius, **nor** his bosom friend the patron **of poets,** has ever **won** a verse or **a** visit from thee.

Tibullus. And never shall, though **each** of them I believe hath his merit. Was **it to** either I owe the preservation of half my patrimony?—of **this** villa?—of the apple that is growing on the tree for thee? **Friends** who watch over us are to be thanked; **not** robbers **who leave us bruised on the road,** throwing back into **our** faces a few particles **of the booty.**

Messala. Come along, come **along!** let us gather the apple.

Tibullus (to Delia). He will **not** hear me; thanks pain him, much **as he** loves the grateful. Go on, **my** Delia.

Delia. Say more about him before **we reach** the orchard.

Tibullus. His intervention, **his** authority, his name, saved for us all **we** have. **But come, we must** overtake him; he walks swiftly on.

Messala! you **were** always first **in the** field of battle: I will be **up** with you in **this.**

Messala. **Oh** the active girl! she **has** caught thee by the tunic in ten paces.

Delia. Sir! sir! **what** are you doing?

Messala. My pretty one, I am lifting thee **up to** gather me two or three of those red and yellow apples: **they are** better than **such as are nearer** the bottom of the tree.

Well done! What! another, and another, and **another?**
Throw the next down into the bosom of Albius, who is making a
sack of his vest for its reception : and now put one, only one, into
thy own.

Behold! thou art now safe down again. Give me the apple
out of its hiding-place.

How she blushes! Ha! she runs away.

Albius! that little girl is the delight of thy youthful years, and
will be, I augur, the solace of thy decline.

Tibullus. She stands listening behind the statue, pretending
to admire it, or to see somewhat in its features she never saw
before.

Didst thou hear him, my Delia? Light of my life! art thou
sorrowful?

Delia. I did hear; I own it. Sorrowful? No, no!

But how can I hope, sir, to be always a delight to him? What
on earth, as my mother used to say, is always? I was fifteen
years old, and two more are nearly gone, since—

Messala. Since Albius was made happy and Delia was made
immortal. Is it so?

Delia. I must grow old at last!

Tibullus. And so must I.

Delia. Oh! no, no, no! that can never be.

Messala. Lady, it is well to think so : Aurora thought it of
Tithonus. Your ages united are somewhat under mine. Never
take such notice of my scanty and gray hairs; frightful as they
are, they are truthful.

Delia. If they seem gray, it is only because you are in the
sunlight.

Messala. Ah, Delia! I am much nearer the starlight than
the sunlight. Day is fast closing with me. But my life has not
been unserviceable to my friends or to my country. Yet what,
after all, am I ?

Ye glories of the world! how rapidly, how irrevocably, ye
depart! Men who have shaken the Forum and the Senate-house
with their eloquence are soon deserted, soon forgotten. The
stoutest are in need of support; and their props are often of the
most carious materials. Brief is the glimmer of the sword. The
timber of the chariot, which hath borne up the conqueror to the

Capitol, outlasts him ; and the cicada, who lives her three days, lives all her three more merrily than he his proudest.

Tibullus. Light are our ashes ; our wishes, our hopes, our lives, are lighter. Who then upon earth is great and powerful ?

Messala. The poet. The poet is the assessor of the gods : he receives from them, and imparts to whomsoever he chooses, the gift of immortality. It is several years, fair Delia, since Albius wrote a panegyric on me, and you were beginning to try what you could do toward the framework of another.

Tibullus. I do not repent that I wrote it, O Messala, though I never wrote anything so badly since. I was almost a boy, and the weight of the matter bore me down.

Messala. Certainly it is less excellent, and it ought to be, than what Delia hath since inspired. Tell me Delia, now we are in confidence and at home all three, do not you think our Albius a fine, handsome creature ? Come, I will allow you to blush a little, it is so becoming, but not allow you to be silent any longer.

Delia. Make him answer first, whether he really thinks me so ; for he would never tell a story to you.

Messala. Shame upon him ! it appears that he has already told you one so incredible.

Delia. Morning, noon, and—

Messala. Go on, go on.

Delia. I have spoken.

Messala. And you believed him ?

Delia. Rather more at first than now ; but never quite. O sir ! make him tell the real truth ; pray do.

Messala. I will answer for Albius that he always proves his word, sooner or later.

Delia. I do not desire it just at present ; I can wait.

Fie, Albius ! Albius ! do men ever snatch up our hands and kiss them in presence of the great ?

Messala. Let me intercede and answer for him. In the presence of the happy they do, whether of mortals or gods.

Delia. You too are a little in fault, if I may dare to say it. I have not forgotten the apple-tree, sir !

Messala. What a memory ! Are you certain there may not be something of the fabulous in so remote an occurrence ?

Tibullus. To-morrow we will retrace our steps, and learn over again this dubious and half-obliterated page of history; what say you, Delia?

Delia. Ask what says our noble guest. But it will be your turn to-morrow, my Albius, to throw down the apples. It made me tremble all over. There is no reason why we should not go into the orchard at some early hour of the morning, were it only to see whether any thieves have broken in; for they do not heed the dogs, although loose.

Audacious! audacious! and you smile, do you? Ah! you may well look down. Certain men have methods of making dogs[2] lie quiet, when they resolve on committing a robbery in the dark. I have half a mind to tell Messala of somebody I know, very sly and treacherous, who, within my recollection, made even Molossians lie quiet and forget their duty. You blush; that is proper. Well, perhaps I may let you off this once, and say nothing about it now you are penitent. Beside, it was a good while ago, and not here. Mother thought it was witchcraft, and she lustrated the house with eggs and sulphur.

Messala. If any task is to be imposed on him, order him to write another elegy, complaining of your severity and atoning for his offence. Apollo will punish him for extolling me above my merits by making him inadequate to yours.

Tibullus! it occurs to me that he, whom I have heard you mention as the best poet[3] of the present day, wrote two poems in his youth such as I wonder he should acknowledge and republish, —the *Culex* and the *Ceiris.*

Tibullus. He compensated for them soon after, by verses more harmonious than ever had been heard before in our tongue. How beautiful are those at the commencement of the first eclogue, and those of the goatherd at the close of it; and those to Lycoris traversing the Alps, in the last!

Messala. You have cited the few verses worth remembrance. He says somewhere that Apollo pulled his ear and admonished him. The god should have pulled it again, and harder, for

[2 "Upon the threshold sits the guarding dog. Yet if you bring an ample gift, the watchfulness abates; the bars unlock themselves, the dog himself is mute." ii., iv., 32.]

[3 Virgil.]

neglecting his admonition when he composed his *Pollio*. He did indeed take away from him on that one occasion the gift of harmony.

Tibullus. Restored soon. How admirable are some passages in that poem on husbandry, which he has given us lately !

Messala. Admirable in parts, but disproportionate. In the exordium, he has amplified Varro's Portico, which already was too spacious for the edifice.

Tibullus. Indeed, there was exordium quite sufficient at

Teque sibi generum Tethys emat omnibus undis;

which would be followed appropriately by the distant line—

Da facilem cursum.

Messala. What think you of the Scorpion drawing his arms in, that Octavius may have room enough?—or the despair of Tartarus at missing such a treasure?—or the backwardness of Proserpine to follow her mother? Here are together eight such verses as I would give eighty bushels of wheat to eradicate from the poetry of a friend. The Greeks by the facility of their versification are often verbose and languid, but they never exhaust so much breath before they start. A husbandman does his work badly with a buskin fastened round the ankle, and an ampulla swinging at the girdle.

Our Mantuan's *Winter* is unworthy of even a secondary poet : no selection of topics, no arrangement, no continuity; instead of which, there is a dreary conglomeration, where little things and great are confounded. Was ever bathos so profound as in—

Æraque dissiliunt vulgo vestesque rigescunt,—

unless two lines lower, where—

Solidam in glaciem vertêre lacunæ.
Stiriaque impexis induruit horrida barbis.

Tibullus. Let us climb over the ice and snow, leap across the *lacunæ*, and wipe away the *stiria*. His summer storm is such as Jupiter might have sent down to show his power, and Apollo might have hymned to his Father's glory.

Messala. Very soon you will take Proteus under your

patronage. There are some, I am told, who really find in the story of Eurydice [4] a noble effort of poetry.

Tibullus. It grieved me to see that excrescence.

Messala. Proteus had no pity for Cyrene whom he must have known from his infancy, but abundance of it for a dead man's head which he never could have heard of while it was on the shoulders; which head moreover was carried down a river a thousand miles distant from his haunts, and sang all the way. Frigid was indeed the tongue that sang there, and almost as frigid the tongue that sang about it. Such puerility is scarcely for the schoolroom, but rather for the nursery, and comes very nigh the cradle. We have talked about this before, by ourselves, and without any intention of gratifying the malignity of minor song-men.

Tibullus. Propertius tells me that he has lately seen the commencement of an epic by him, and that, if the remainder is equal to the two first books, it will rival the Iliad.

Messala. May we live to read it! At all events may he to complete it!

Tibullus. Pleasant will it be to me to feel the slight shudder of Delia on my bosom, when I read to her the battles.

Messala. Where is she? she has slipped out.

Tibullus. Perhaps she is gone to crown the Penates, for she is pious and grateful.

Messala. Two qualities not always found together. Frequently have I remarked, in the most devout, the most arrogant, quarrelsome, and unjust.

Have you room in your chapel for Caius Julius, our latest god?

Tibullus. Highly as I esteem him, I have not procured his

[4 See Georgic, iv., 317, seq. Aristæus, the shepherd son of Cyrene, was consumed with grief at the loss of his bees. At his prayers his mother went with him to enquire the cause of his loss from Proteus, "the old man of the sea." He, after the usual ceremonies, was compelled to explain that the nymphs had inflicted this loss upon Aristæus, because it was in running away from him that Eurydice had trodden on the snake. Virgil calls it "a huge Hydra," from whose bite she died. This brings in the whole story of Orpheus' journey into Hades, and his death, and how his head floated down the Hebrus to the sea, while "the chilly lips, with chilly voice, still cried aloud the name of Eurydice."]

statue. Gods are great by necessity, mortals by exertion: and what exertions were ever so animated or so unremitted as his?

Messala. All of them tended to the glory of his country, out of which parent soil his own shot up exuberantly, and at last (it seems) reached the heavens.

Tibullus. In my humble opinion, and I hope I am falling into no impiety when I say it, we have gods enow already. Those of Egypt we have in our kitchens,[5] and those of Gaul are not worth conveyance from their woods. We require no importations.

Messala. Formerly, gods made men; at present, men make gods. Where will this fashion have an end? Perhaps you may live to enlarge your sacristy.

Tibullus. I find an object of worship in every field. Wherever there is a stake or a stone crowned with flowers,* I bend before it, and thank the gods for inspiring the hearts of men with gratitude. I feel confident they are well-pleased at these oblations, however poor their worshipper, and however he mispronounce their names.

Messala. While the gods came from the potter, men were virtuous and happy; when they came from the goldsmith, they retained the heat of the furnace, and dazzled and deluded. Priests assumed their similitude, and encrusted one another with the same metal.

Tibullus. Barbarous nations have beheld these prodigies; may Rome never see within her walls a worse Pontifex than Caius Julius.

Messala. Nevertheless, by his oration in the Senate, as Crispus Sallustius hath recorded it, he seems to have verged on atheism. I do not mean hereby to question his aptitude for the office, which others at Rome, after him, have equally well discharged with no firmer belief in the deity, and less resemblance.

Tibullus. If you enter our little sanctuary, you will see the Lares not crowned as usual with rosemary and myrtle, but with myrtle only. The reason is: Delia had gathered both from under the villa-wall, to decorate the little deities, inobservant that a bee

---

    * Nam veneror seu stipes habet desertus in agris,
       Seu vetus in trivio florida serta lapis.
    [5 Cats.]

was inside the blossom of a rosemary; and, beginning to press
it round one of the images, she was stung. The sting was forgotten in the omen.

Messala. What omen is there in so ordinary an occurrence?

Tibullus. "O Albius!" cried she, "something sad will
happen; my piety is rejected, and my love, my love"—Sobs
interrupted her; and she would never tell me afterward what she
was then about to say.

Messala. Simpleton! But at present there are no signs
either of sting or omen. Propertius, whom you just now mentioned, is an imitator of yours, at a distance. His elegies are
apparently tasks undertaken by order of a schoolmaster. He is
uneasy at the loss of a little farm under Perusia, which the triumvirate allotted to the legions. Civil wars bring down these curses;
and not always the most heavily on those who took a prominent
part in them. Probably he is more poet than philosopher; and
he may never have reflected that many things occur, in the course
of every man's life, which he deems unfortunate, and which his
friends deem so too, and upon which they not only condole with
him at the time, but commemorate and discourse upon long after.
Little are they aware that, unless these very things had happened,
the pleasure they are enjoying at that moment, in social intercourse with him, might not exist. Fortune, who appears to
have frowned on him with her worst malignity, in debarring
him from that which he groaned for, and was within a step of
attaining, may there have been his very best friend. If the farm
of Propertius had been larger, it might have cost him his life.
Such prices, we know, have been paid occasionally. When, in
the heat of midsummer, I went to visit a neglected property of
mine among the hills near Sulmo, I was visited by his friend,
Ovidius Naso,* with whose *Epistles of Heroes and Heroines*, on
their appearance last winter, you were, I remember, much delighted. He, like the generality of young poets, meditates a grand

* Tibullus and Propertius, with few more, enjoy the good fortune to
escape from mutilation in the extremities of the name. Following the
French, but neither the Italians nor Germans, we treat Ovid and Virgil
and Horace less ceremoniously; and appear to be more familiar with them
than their contemporaries were. It would be affectation in common
discourse to say *Virgilius,* or *Ovidius,* or *Horatius:* it would be worse
than affectation to represent a Roman saying *Horace,* or *Virgil,* or *Ovid.*

work : and, unlike the generality, is capable of executing it. Practice itself can hardly add to his facility ; and love itself is hardly more ingenious and inventive. He excels in sentences, never dogmatical, never prolix, never inopportune. In every department of eloquence, and particularly in poetry, we look for depth and clearness ; a clearness that shows the depth : here we find it.

Before I left Ovidius when I returned his visit, he read to me the commencement of some amatory pieces, at which, if I smiled, it was in courtesy, not in approbation. From the mysteries of religion the veil is seldom to be drawn, from the mysteries of love never. For this offence, the gods take away from us our freshness of heart and our susceptibility of pure delight. The well loses the spring that fed it, and what is exposed in the shallow basin soon evaporates. I wish well to Ovidius, for he speaks well of everybody. Poets are enrolled in the Cadmean legion : each one cuts down his comrade ; but Ovidius stands apart, gentle and generous, uniting the moral to the sensual voluptuary. He is kinder to Propertius than Horatius Flaccus is, who turns him into ridicule under the name of Callimachus. Our pleasant lyrist is disposed to praise nobody at a distance from the Palatine.

Tibullus. Judicious in his choice, he praises Virgilius and Valgius and Varius and Tucca. In his Satires he is equally discreet, equally refined. Satire ought to strike at the face, as Cæsar ordered the soldier to do on the field of Pharsalia ; far from mortal, the stroke should never be outrageous or repeated. Coarseness and harshness are no proof of strength, as some would fain inculcate. On the contrary, there is no true satire which departs from graceful pleasantry, and which either runs into philosophical sententiousness or acrimonious declamation. Satire draws neither blood nor tears : laughter and blushes are the boundaries of her dominion.

Messala. Perfectly just remarks ; and Horatius is no violator of them. Many of his Odes are so light, so playful, so graceful, that nothing is comparable to them in the literature of Greece. Seldom is he energetic or impressive ; seldomer, even when he attempts it, pathetic. He who tickles the bosom is the least likely to touch the heart. I could pardon him a few of his deficiencies, if he were less parsimonious of praise toward men like you, and if his nymphs poured less of cold water into the cup containing it.

Tibullus. Conscious of his own merits, as every man who possesses any must be, however he may dissemble it, Horatius can ill endure that Catullus and Calvus [6] should be preferred to him, as they are by many.

Messala. I think I have allowed him all his due.

Tibullus. Not quite: add also his great variety. Recent or ancient, surely none is comparable to him in this.

Messala. In the stock of his Gynæcæum, none. Seriously, it is a pity that he who, on his Tiburtine and Sabine farm, is master of so many true and solid, should in worse wantonness have devised so many fabulous, mistresses. It takes away from us all illusion, all sympathy: we laugh at an Ixion raising a cloud to embrace it. But is there any man, Albius, who can read without tenderness your *Te spectem?* [7] Believe me, you are the only elegiac poet, Greek or Roman, whom posterity will cherish. Imperishable are those things only which have been created in the heart.

Tibullus. Forget not then your favorite Catullus, the creator there.

Messala. Earnest and impressive, no poet rests so perfectly on the memory. He is the only one whose verses I could remember after the first reading: I mean his Hendecasyllables and Scazons.

Tibullus. Painful, very painful is it, that the lover of Lesbia should revile her so coarsely as he did before he left her; if indeed he ever left her at all, or ever possessed her. For it appears to me quite impossible that a tender heart, however rancorous it may have become under infidelities and indignities, should ever lose its fineness of fibre, should ever sink into deep corruption. Willingly then would I believe that many of his poems, as you suppose of Horatius's, are merely exercises of ingenuity.

[6 The passage referred to is Satires, i., 10. 16; where Horace speaks of " Hermogenes and his monkey friend who can sing nothing but Calvus and Catullus."]

[7 Elegy, i., 1. 59. "On thy face may eyes gaze in my dying hour; thine be the hand I then hold in my failing grasp."]

Messala. In the elegiac measure, excepting the verses on his brother's funeral, he was less successful. Ovidius hath utterly ruined it. Of all metres, the pentameter is the least harmonious, and the least adapted to the expression of sorrow; to which Mimnermous and Tyrtæus and Solon never applied it. Frisky as it is, it is not frisky enough for Ovidius. With better judgment, you correct the gambols of the first hemistich by the gravity of the spondee : he, wherever he can, renders it dactylic. Often have I defended him against the charge of affectation, but there is no defence for it in terminating every pentameter with a dissyllable. This is a trick unworthy of a school-boy. Catullus and you have scorned it ; Propertius hath followed your example; the Genius of our language cries out against the entanglement, and snaps the chain.

Tibullus. That bust in the corner of the room is the bust of Lucretius; and I know not whether there is any other of him: I bought it at the decease of his widow.

Messala. How different from the opposite! poor Cicero's. He always carried anxiety and hurry in his countenance : that little head of his appears as if it never could lie down to rest.

Tibullus. I saw him but once, and it was shortly before his departure. Lucretius I never saw at all.

Messala. I wish he had abstained from his *induperator* and *endogredi.* Language is as much corrupted by throwing decayed words into it as by the rank and vapid succulence of yesterday's sudden growth. If part is ancient, let all be ancient. When Lucretius complains of our poverty in language, he means only in terms of art and science. Let us stand up for its dignity, and appeal to Plautus for its responsibility. Cicero and Cæsar have brought it to perfection ; there are already signs of its decline. Many of those who were educated at Athens have introduced lately a variety of Hellenisms ; the young poets are too fond of them : among your merits is abstinence from this (not very unpardonable) intoxication.

Plautus and Terentius, who drew largely from Greek originals, are less Greek in their phraseology than many who write now. Lucretius I see is lying on the table. Ovidius, who admires even his contemporaries, is a warm admirer of him, and declares that his work on Nature will perish only with Nature herself.

Nothing is so animated and so august as his invocation. His friend Memmius outlived him; but not long enough to see the termination of those discords which he prayed Mars, at the intercession of Venus, to abate. Little did he imagine that a youth who claims descent from her should be enabled to compose them. Octavius was then a boy, thirteen or fourteen years old, just sent by the munificence of his uncle, Caius Julius, to study at Athens. Happily he found there a protector, in a wealthy and clever though dissolute friend a few years older—Cilnius Mecænas—to whose counsels he owes probably his life, certainly his station and security.

Tibullus. It is the glory of Mecænas to have derived no part of his riches from the proscriptions.

Messala. He had large estates in the most fertile districts of Etruria: but that is no diminution of his merit; others as affluent were rapacious and insatiable. His weakness, one among many, lies in his affectation of family. Were he really a descendant of a Lucumon, the pedigree would have been drawn out and exhibited: indeed, it is a wonder that a fictitious one never was substituted. Flaccus says that his ancestors, both maternal and paternal, had formerly commanded "great legions." There is no record of these great legions having performed great actions. If they ever had, he would have pointed to them and have named the battle-field. He has not omitted to tell us who slew Asdrubal, nor the name of the river on whose banks he fell. He brings forward his patron's royal origin on every occasion, and truly with small dexterity. It seldom or never has any thing to do with the subject. Take for instance the first ode; the worst in the book, excepting the second. And there are other places quite as remarkable for a similar want of connection.

Tibullus. With various little weaknesses he is really an estimable man, although it never may have occurred to him that no one has a right to claim antiquity of family unless he can distinctly show an ancestor who hath rendered a signal service to the Commonwealth.

Messala. To Cilnius however it is mainly owing that our manners are softened, our dissensions pacified, our laws amended, and the remainder of our properties secured.

Tibullus. And Commonwealth? The old nut has only a

maggot and dust within it; and the squirrel at the top of the tree, having laid up or eaten all the sounder, thinks it ill worth while to come down and crack it.

We are safe at present; and that is somewhat: but who on earth can insure us that Thracian or Dacian, or Gaul or German, shall not, within a century or two, advance on Rome?

Messala.   Blindness is the effect of straining the eye too far. Empires have fallen, and will fall: the harder crush the softer, and soften too. Destruction and renovation are eternal laws. A decayed nation, like a decayed animal, fattens the field for enterprise and industry. Egyptians, Babylonians, Medes, the mountaineers of Macedon and Epirus, have vanquished in succession, and now are lying like idle and outcast beggars at the gates of Rome. Albius! be certain of this: if we ever lose our preponderance, we shall deserve to lose it. A weak nation, when it is reduced to subjection, may be pitied; but a nation once powerful by its institutions, military and civil, when it falls, although short of subjugation, is despised. The genius of Julius Cæsar, a man without an equal in the history of the world, would have restored our State. Generals whose sole ability lay in the arts of corruption were opposed to him; and, fortunately for the Senate who appointed them, they failed. In Spain and Africa there still breathed a military spirit; but in his presence it breathed its last. Antonius and Cassius were the only great leaders who survived him: Cassius outlived his cause; Antonius his glory. Agrippa, when he had driven him into Pelusium and upon his sword, turned his heel on the luxuries of Egypt, stood aloof from those of Rome, and was venerated at his death greatly more than those who have recently been deified.

Repose is necessary now to our exhaustion. We must look carefully to our agriculture; we must conciliate our provinces. In no case, however, is military discipline to be neglected, or the soldier to be kept long inactive. We will enjoy the Saturnian age when Saturn comes back again; meanwhile, let us never be forgetful that Mars is the progenitor of our race.

VII. TIBERIUS AND VIPSANIA.[1] *

Tiberius.　Vipsania, my **Vipsania,** whither art thou walking?
Vipsania.　Whom do I see?—my Tiberius?
Tiberius.　Ah! no, no, no! but thou seest the father of thy

[1 Tiberius "married Agrippina, the daughter of Marcus Agrippa, the granddaughter of Cæcilius Atticus, the Roman knight, and correspondent of Cicero; but he was compelled to put her away after one son had been born to him by her, and when she was again pregnant; and in her stead to marry suddenly Julia, the daughter of Augustus, whereat he suffered much anguish of mind. . . . And even after the divorce he regretted Agrippina, and when once, and only once, he saw her, he fled from the meeting with such eager and swelling eyes that care was taken that he should never meet her again." Suetonius Tiberius, vii. In all probability the divorce of Tiberius and his marriage to Julia were part of the schemes contrived by Livia to ensure his accession to the empire. (Imag. Convers., iii., 1828. Works, i., 1846. Imag. Convers., Gks. and Rom., 1853. Works, ii., 1876.)]

* Vipsania, the daughter of Agrippa, was divorced from Tiberius by Augustus and Livia, in order that he might marry Julia, and hold the empire by inheritance. He retained such an affection for her, and showed it so intensely when he once met her afterward, that every precaution was taken lest they should meet again.

There [2] can be no doubt that the Claudii were deranged in intellect. Those of them who succeeded to the empire were by nature no worse than several of their race in the times of the republic. Appius Claudius, Appius Cæcus, Publius, Appa, and after these the enemy of Cicero, exhibited as ungovernable a temper as the imperial ones; some breaking forth into tyranny and lust, others into contempt of, and imprecations against, their country. Tiberius was meditative, morose, suspicious. In the pupil of Seneca were dispositions the opposite to these, with many talents, and some good qualities. They could not disappear on a sudden, without one of those shocks under which had been engulfed almost every member of the family.

[2 Note in 1st ed. reads: "I have mentioned in a former volume my persuasion that the Claudii were deranged in intellect. There are few who, after the perusal of the three (i.e., volumes) will suspect me of apologising for the vices of princes: but those who endure them are to be condemned still more severely. The Claudii who succeeded to the empire were by nature no worse men, and in some respects much better, than several of their race in the times of the republic, altho' power ripened

little Drusus. Press him to thy heart the more closely for this meeting, and give him——

Vipsania. Tiberius! the altars, the gods, the destinies, are between us,—I will take it from this hand;[3] thus, thus shall he receive it.

Tiberius. Raise up thy face, my beloved! I must not shed tears. Augustus! Livia! ye shall not extort them from me. Vipsania! I may kiss thy head—for I have saved it. Thou sayest nothing. I have wronged thee; ay?

Vipsania. Ambition does not see the earth she treads on; the rock and the herbage are of one substance to her. Let me excuse you to my heart, O Tiberius. It has many wants; this is the first and greatest.

Tiberius. My ambition, I swear by the immortal gods, placed not the bar of severance between us. A stronger hand, the hand that composes Rome and sways the world—

Vipsania. —Overawed Tiberius. I know it; Augustus willed and commanded it.

Tiberius. And overawed Tiberius! Power bent, Death terrified, a Nero! What is our race, that any should look down on us and spurn us? Augustus, my benefactor, I have wronged thee! Livia, my mother, this one cruel deed was thine! To reign, forsooth, is a lovely thing. O womanly appetite! Who would have been before me, though the palace of Cæsar cracked and split with emperors, while I, sitting in idleness on a cliff of Rhodes, eyed the sun as he swung his golden censer athwart the heavens, or his

at last their malady into ranker growth and deadlier poison. Appius Claudius, . . . country. Tiberius was a man of greater genius than any of the rest; sorrowful, meditative, morose, suspicious. In the last Nero were dispositions . . . engulphed, in successive generations, almost every member of the Claudian family. Cruelty, if we consider it a crime, is the greatest of all, but I think we should more justly consider it, in men of education, as a madness; for it quite destroys our sympathies, and, doing so, must supersede and master our intellect. It removes from us those that can help us, and brings against us those that can injure us; whence it opposes the great principle of our nature, self-love, and endangers not only our well-being but our being. Reason is then the most perfect when it enables us the most to benefit society: reason is then the most deranged when there is *that* over it which disables a man from benefiting his fellow men—and cruelty is *that*.]

[3 First ed. reads: "hand of thine, and thus shall," &c.]

image as it overstrode the sea?* I have it before me; and, though it seems falling on me, I can smile at it,—just as I did from my little favorite skiff, painted round with the marriage of Thetis, when the sailors drew their long shaggy hair across their eyes many a stadium away from it, to mitigate its effulgence.[4]

These too were happy days: days of happiness like these I could recall and look back upon with unaching brow.

O land of Greece! Tiberius blesses thee, bidding thee rejoice and flourish.

Why cannot one hour, Vipsania, beauteous and light as we have led, return?

Vipsania. Tiberius! is it to me that you were speaking? I would not interrupt you; but I thought I heard my name as you walked away and looked up toward the East. So silent!

Tiberius. Who dared to call thee? Thou wert mine before the gods—do they deny it? Was it my fault—

Vipsania. Since we are separated, and for ever, O Tiberius, let us think no more on the cause of it. Let neither of us believe that the other was to blame: so shall separation be less painful.

Tiberius. O mother! and did I not tell thee what she was? —patient in injury, proud in innocence, serene in grief!

Vipsania. Did you say that too? But I think it was so: I had felt little. One vast wave[5] has washed away the impression of smaller from my memory. Could Livia, could your mother, could she who was so kind to me—

Tiberius. The wife of Cæsar did it. But hear me now; hear me: be calm as I am. No weaknesses are such as those of a mother who loves her only son immoderately; and none are so

---

* The Colossus was thrown down by an earthquake during the war between Antiochus and Ptolemy, who sent the Rhodians three thousand talents for the restoration of it. Again in the time of Vespasian, "Coæ Veneris, item *Colossi* refectorem congiario magnâque mercede donavit." *Suetonius in Vesp.* The first residence of Tiberius in Rhodes was when he returned from his Armenian expedition; the last was after his divorce from Vipsania and his marriage with Julia.

[4 First ed. reads: "effulgence from the brightest effigy of the brightest god. These," &c. Note on Colossus added in 2nd ed.]

[5 First ed. reads: "One wave has washed away a thousand impressions of smaller from my memory."]

easily worked upon from without. Who knows what impulses she received? She is very, very kind ; but she regards me only, and that which at her bidding is to encompass and adorn me. All the weak look after Power, protectress of weakness. Thou art a woman, O Vipsania! is there nothing in thee to excuse my mother? So good she ever was to me! so loving.

Vipsania. I quite forgive her : be tranquil, O Tiberius!

Tiberius. Never can I know peace—never can I pardon— any one. Threaten me with thy exile, thy separation, thy seclusion! Remind me that another climate might endanger thy health!—There death met me and turned me round. Threaten me to take our son from us,—our one boy, our helpless little one, —him whom we made cry because we kissed him both together! Rememberest thou? Or dost thou not hear? turning thus away from me!

Vipsania. I hear; I hear! Oh cease, my sweet Tiberius! Stamp not upon that stone : my heart lies under it.

Tiberius. Ay, there again death, and more than death, stood before me. Oh she maddened me, my mother did, she maddened me—she threw me to where I am at one breath. The gods cannot replace me where I was, nor atone to me, nor console me, nor restore my senses. To whom can I fly; to whom can I open my heart ; to whom speak plainly?* There was upon the earth a man I could converse with and fear nothing ; there was a woman too I could love, and fear nothing. What a soldier, what a Roman, was thy father, O my young bride! How could those who never saw him have discoursed so rightly upon virtue!

Vipsania. These words cool my breast like pressing his urn against it. He was brave : shall Tiberius want courage?

Tiberius. My enemies scorn me. I am a garland dropped from a triumphal car, and taken up and looked on for the place I occupied ; and tossed away and laughed at. Senators! laugh, laugh! Your merits may be yet rewarded—be of good cheer!

---

* The [6] regret of Tiberius at the death of Agrippa may be imagined to arise from a cause of which at this moment he was unconscious. If Agrippa had lived, Julia, who was his wife, could not have been Tiberius's, nor would he and Vipsania have been separated.

[[6] Note added in 2nd ed.]

Counsel me, in your wisdom, what services I can render you,
conscript fathers!

Vipsania. This seems mockery: Tiberius did not smile so,
once.

Tiberius. They had not then congratulated me.

Vipsania. On what?

Tiberius. And it was not because she was beautiful, as they
thought her, and virtuous, as I know she is; but because the
flowers on the altar were to be tied together by my heartstring.
On this they congratulated me. Their day will come. Their
sons and daughters are what I would wish them to be: worthy to
succeed them.[7]

Vipsania. Where is that quietude, that resignation, that sanctity,
that heart of true tenderness?

Tiberius. Where is my love?—my love?

Vipsania. Cry not thus aloud, Tiberius! there is an echo in
the place. Soldiers and slaves may burst in upon us.

Tiberius. And see my tears? There is no echo, Vipsania;
why alarm and shake me so? We are too high here for the
echoes: the city is below us. Methinks it trembles and totters:
would it did! from the marble quays of the Tiber to this rock.
There is a strange buzz and murmur in my brain; but I should
listen so intensely, I should hear the rattle of its roofs, and shout
with joy.

Vipsania. Calm, O my life! calm this horrible transport.

Tiberius. Spake I so loud? Did I indeed then send my voice
after a lost sound, to bring it back; and thou fanciedest it an
echo? Wilt not thou laugh with me, as thou wert wont to do,
at such an error? What was I saying to thee, my tender love,
when I commanded—I know not whom—to stand back, on
pain of death? Why starest thou on me in such agony? Have
I hurt thy fingers, child? I loose them; now let me look!
Thou turnest thine eyes away from me. Oh! oh! I hear my
crime! Immortal gods! I cursed them audibly, and before the
sun, my mother!

[7 First ed. reads: "them, and ready too." I would not make them
love me, as they must do, for it: but this will pass away.]

VIII. EPICTETUS AND SENECA.[1]

Seneca.   Epictetus, I desired your master, Epaphroditus, to
send you hither, having been much pleased with his report
of your conduct, and much surprised at the ingenuity of your
writings.

Epictetus.   Then I am afraid, my friend—

Seneca.   *My friend!* are these the expressions—Well, let
it pass.   Philosophers must bear bravely.   The people expect it.

Epictetus.   Are philosophers, then, only philosophers for the
people ; and, instead of instructing them, must they play tricks
before them? Give me rather the gravity of dancing dogs. Their
motions are for the rabble ; their reverential eyes and pendant paws
are under the pressure of awe at a master ; but they are dogs, and
not below their destinies.

[1 In this Conversation Landor has treated in a dramatic form the
subject which in the Conversation between Plato and Diogenes is treated
by him critically—the contrast between the true or practical philosophy
of life and the false or theoretical. Epictetus is well fitted to represent
the first, and Seneca not undeserving of being made to play the part of
the second. The effect of the teaching of Epictetus on his time was
great ; Aulus Gellius frequently quotes from the book in which Arrian,
his disciple, expounded his master's opinions. In one passage (Aul. Gell.,
ii., 9. 1) he says—"Concerning that noble philosopher Epictetus, it is too
fresh a tale, that he was a slave, to need repeating. There are two verses
written by him of his own lot, wherein he obscurely hints that it is not
only those hated by the gods who in this life have to struggle with many
kinds of trouble, but that there are secret causes of such disaster past the
discovery of most men. "I," he says, "was born a slave, and lame, a
beggar in poverty, and dear to the gods." He was a slave and then a
freedman of Epaphroditus, who was one of the brutal gang of freedmen
surrounding Nero. Tigellinus, who is mentioned in this Conversation,
was also one. Seneca was a philosopher of another kind. He was wealthy,
perhaps by inheritance from his father, but possibly from more discredit-
able sources. He had flattered Claudius and instructed Nero, doing his
best to restrain his pupil by gratifying his least intolerable desires. It is
doubtful whether Seneca and Epictetus ever could have met. If they did so,
it must have been just before Nero compelled his master to kill himself.
(Imag. Convers., iii., 1828. Works, ii., 1846. Imag. Convers., Gks. and
Rom., 1853. Works, ii., 1876.)]

Seneca. Epictetus! I will give you three talents to let me take that sentiment for my own.

Epictetus. I would give thee twenty, if I had them, to make it thine.

Seneca. You mean, by lending to it the graces of my language?

Epictetus. I mean, by lending it to thy conduct. And now let me console and comfort thee, under the calamity I brought on thee by calling thee *my friend.* If thou art not my friend, why send for me? Enemy I can have none : being a slave, Fortune has now done with me.

Seneca. Continue, then, your former observations. What were you saying?

Epictetus. That which thou interruptedst.

Seneca. What was it?

Epictetus. I should have remarked that, if thou foundest ingenuity in my writings, thou must have discovered in them some deviation from the plain, homely truths of Zeno and Cleanthes.

Seneca. We all swerve a little from them.

Epictetus. In practice too?

Seneca. Yes, even in practice, I am afraid.

Epictetus. Often?

Seneca. Too often.

Epictetus. Strange! I have been attentive, and yet have remarked but one difference among you great personages at Rome.

Seneca. What difference fell under your observation?

Epictetus. Crates and Zeno and Cleanthes taught us that our desires were to be subdued by philosophy alone. In this city, their acute and inventive scholars take us aside, and show us that there is not only one way, but two.

Seneca. Two ways?

Epictetus. They whisper in our ear, " These two ways are philosophy and enjoyment : the wiser man will take the readier, or, not finding it, the alternative." Thou reddenest.

Seneca. Monstrous degeneracy.

Epictetus. What magnificent rings! I did not notice them until thou liftest up thy hands to heaven, in detestation of such effeminacy and impudence.

Seneca. The rings are not amiss ; my rank rivets them upon my fingers : I am forced to wear them. Our emperor gave me one, Epaphroditus another, Tigellinus the third. I cannot lay them aside a single day, for fear of offending the gods, and those whom they love the most worthily.

Epictetus. Although they make thee stretch out thy fingers, like the arms and legs of one of us slaves upon a cross.

Seneca. Oh horrible ! Find some other resemblance.

Epictetus. The extremities of a fig-leaf.

Seneca. Ignoble !

Epictetus. The claws of a toad, trodden on or stoned.

Seneca. You have great need, Epictetus, of an instructor in eloquence and rhetoric : you want topics and tropes and figures.

Epictetus. I have no room for them. They make such a buzz in the house, a man's own wife cannot understand what he says to her.

Seneca. Let us reason a little upon style. I would set you right, and remove from before you the prejudices of a somewhat rustic education. We may adorn the simplicity of the wisest.

Epictetus. Thou canst not adorn simplicity. What is naked or defective is susceptible of decoration : what is decorated is simplicity no longer. Thou mayest give another thing in exchange for it ; but if thou wert master of it, thou wouldst preserve it inviolate. It is no wonder that we mortals, little able as we are to see truth, should be less able to express it.

Seneca. You have formed at present no idea of style.

Epictetus. I never think about it. First, I consider whether what I am about to say is true ; then whether I can say it with brevity, in such a manner as that others shall see it as clearly as I do in the light of truth ; for, if they survey it as an ingenuity, my desire is ungratified, my duty unfulfilled. I go not with those who dance round the image of Truth, less out of honor to her than to display their agility and address.

Seneca. We must attract the attention of readers by novelty and force and grandeur of expression.

Epictetus. We must. Nothing is so grand as truth, nothing so forcible, nothing so novel.

Seneca. Sonorous sentences are wanted to awaken the lethargy of indolence.

Epictetus. Awaken it to what? Here lies the question; and a weighty one it is. If thou awakenest men when they can see nothing and do no work, it is better to let them rest: but will not they, thinkest thou, look up at a rainbow, unless they are called to it by a clap of thunder?

Seneca. Your early youth, Epictetus, has been, I will not say neglected, but cultivated with rude instruments and unskilful hands.

Epictetus. I thank God for it. Those rude instruments have left the turf lying yet toward the sun; and those unskilful hands have plucked out the docks.

Seneca. We hope and believe that we have attained a vein of eloquence, brighter and more varied than has been hitherto laid open to the world.

Epictetus. Than any in the Greek?

Seneca. We trust so.

Epictetus. Than your Cicero's?

Seneca. If the declaration may be made without an offence to modesty. Surely, you cannot estimate or value the eloquence of that noble pleader?

Epictetus. Imperfectly, not being born in Italy; and the noble pleader is a much less man with me than the noble philosopher. I regret that, having farms and villas, he would not keep his distance from the pumping up of foul words against thieves, cut-throats, and other rogues; and that he lied, sweated, and thumped his head and thighs, in behalf of those who were no better.

Seneca. Senators must have clients, and must protect them.

Epictetus. Innocent or guilty?

Seneca. Doubtless.

Epictetus. If it becomes a philosopher to regret at all, and if I regret what is and might not be, I may regret more what both is and must be. However, it is an amiable thing, and no small merit in the wealthy, even to trifle and play at their leisure hours with philosophy. It cannot be expected that such a personage should espouse her, or should recommend her as an inseparable mate to his heir.

Seneca. I would.

Epictetus. Yes, Seneca, but thou hast no son to make the match for; and thy recommendation, I suspect, would be given him before he could consummate the marriage. Every man wishes his sons to be philosophers while they are young; but takes especial care, as they grow older, to teach them its insufficiency and unfitness for their intercourse with mankind. The paternal voice says, "You must not be particular; you are about to have a profession to live by: follow those who have thriven the best in it." Now, among these, whatever be the profession, canst thou point out to me one single philosopher?

Seneca. Not just now. Nor upon reflection, do I think it feasible.

Epictetus. Thou indeed mayest live much to thy ease and satisfaction with philosophy, having (they say) two thousand talents.

Seneca. And a trifle to spare—pressed upon me by that god-like youth, my pupil Nero.

Epictetus. Seneca! where God hath placed a mine he hath placed the materials of an earthquake.

Seneca. A true philosopher is beyond the reach of Fortune.

Epictetus. The false one thinks himself so. Fortune cares little about philosophers; but she remembers where she hath set a rich man, and she laughs to see the Destinies at his door.

IX. VIRGILIUS AND HORATIUS.[1]

ON THE ROAD TO BRUNDUSIUM, WITH AUGUSTUS AND MECÆNAS.

Virgilius. Horatius! raise yourself up from the litter and look before you. From this last spur of the Apennines, I discover the Adriatic beyond Brundusium.

Horatius. Let me wipe my eyes first, for the keen air of the mountain and the eastern breeze have made them water, and they

[1 This Conversation refers to the journey described by Horace in Satires, i., 5. Cf. especially the lines where he describes how " at Sinessa, Varius and Virgil met us; brighter spirits the world does not hold, nor dearer friends of mine. How we embraced! how glad we were to meet." The Conversation is full of Horatian allusions. (*Athenæum*, March 9th, 1861. Works, ii., 1876.)]

are not so clear-sighted at the best as yours are. I would fain have turned myself round a few hours later. I am no Persian; seldom do I salute the sun, and never at his ascension. There is, methinks, blue in the distance, whether sea or cloud. Heartily glad shall I be when we reach Brundusium. The ribs of yon lean cattle bear a journey best. We liquefy like the waxwork of a witch.

Virgilius. Yonder we shall have leisure to reflect on the cities, municipalities, and scenery left behind us, and to meditate on what has occurred within our own memory at the seaport to which we are going, and on the fate of those commanders who sailed thence with their armies and adherents.

Horatius. Miserable fate indeed for most of them : but, without that miserable fate of theirs, you would never have recovered your little field of buttercups on the marsh of Mantua, nor on me would have been bestowed the snug white cottage overlooking the crags of Tusculum.

Virgilius. Have you never sighed about your paternal heritage, Venusian or Appulian? I think you have expressed a doubt by which of these names you ought to call it.[2]

Horatius. By Bacchus! a sigh would have blown away all that property. My sighs I reserve for my poetry, as most poets do. I lived in the town; and a dirty town it is. My shoe never shall stick in its mud again. The best of fathers sent me early in life to Athens. There I was wild for freedom, as the most generous and intelligent boys are apt to be ; for neither generosity nor intelligence are necessarily prudent, though intelligence may look grave and appear so. Marcus Brutus was my hero. I followed him to battle. Having money in my pouch, I was made a captain. You know the sequence. Looking at me now, you might hardly think I could run away ; but remember, Apollo has wings to his shoulders, and Mercury[3] to his feet. Each of them lent me aid.

[2 There was no doubt about its being Venusian. Horace's doubt was whether it was Lucanian or Appulian. Sat., ii., 1. 34. The township lay across the border.]

[3 Odes, ii., 7. After Philippi, Horace says, " Swift Mercury bore me through the enemy, and I trembled speeding through the unyielding air."]

Virgilius. You do not appear to be so tired by our journey as I am.

Horatius. Yet I have more weight to carry. However, let me confess to you that I shall be rejoiced at reaching the city. There, when we have rested, we may talk about the vicissitudes of the world, of cities devastated and reduced to mounds of earth, of Thebes and Mycenæ, of Sybaris and Croton, of nations once opulent, now the haunt of boars and wolves.

Virgilius. Rome itself, for many centuries, lay in the same condition. The Etrurians abandoned it from the increasing insalubrity of the air. A band of robbers took possession of the hills and dilapidated walls and roofless houses. They made incursions on the Latins and Sabines, and seized their cattle and their wives. About a hundred freebooters were strong enough to resist a thousand or more of husbandmen unaccustomed to war. Presently they were joined by lawless men from all quarters, to whom they alone could give laws.

Horatius. If the Senate were now in full feather and with claws unclipped, it would peck out your eyes for thus tracing its origin. History has in vain attempted to cover and conceal it. Cato has traced the Etrurians far beyond it; but he shut his eyes on the origin of Rome. He was too patriotic to speak fairly. He was a strict observer of religion, as were his progenitors. They made use of all the gods they found in the cities they had taken. Many yokes of oxen were insufficient to transport them into Rome from Veii. You want only Ceres and Pales to overlook your husbandry, with Jupiter to assist them occasionally with a shower.

Virgilius. We two may indulge in pleasantry, but be careful to abstain from touching the popular belief in any deity. If those among them who are beneficent become discarded, the people may return to Saturn, to whom no altar is now dedicated, and to Diana, such as she was supplicated at Aulis on the sacrifice of Iphigenia. Let them be contented with the gods who are pacified with a few bunches of flowers and a few plates of fruit, with a slice of bread to make it wholesome.

Horatius. My mouth begins to water at the thought of them. I hope breakfast will be ready soon. The country hereabout is fertile in fruit-trees. Blessings on Lucullus! the wisest and most provident of conquerors. He brought from Armenia the apricot and cherry, and the peach from the confines of Persia.

Virgilius. Some of these we shall probably find on the table in another hour.

Horatius. Or I shall raise an outcry. In your Georgics you discourse largely on the better sorts of apples and pears, which indeed are more excellent in Italy than elsewhere, but not a word about those richer fruits, worthy to crown the table of Xerxes and Darius. In regard to them, the Greeks were barbarians. When I see them before me, I do not repeat:

> " Persicos odi, puer, apparatus." [4]

Virgilius. That is a sweet little ode of yours. Valerius Catullus was the first who introduced among us the Sapphic metre, and he uses it only twice or thrice, copying her best. You excel her infinitely, both in the variety and in the quality of yours. But, my dear Horatius, what induced you to be for once ungracious, and to throw a pebble at your neighbor of Verona?

Horatius. Where have I done it?

Virgilius. Remember your verse:—

> " Nil præter Calvum et doctus cantare Catullum."

Horatius. It is unpleasant to be shoved away when we are walking up toward others who are before us.

Virgilius. Acknowledge that we may sing an old song without reproach or reproof. No poet, Roman or Greek, is nearly so graceful as these two. The scazons of Catullus are perfect. Some prefer his phaleucics; I do not, beautiful as they are. You have composed more grandly. Be contented with having written better odes than rattled by the chariot-wheels of Pindar, and do not fear that you are—

> " vitreo daturus nomina ponto."

Horatius. I found in the metre of Alcæus enormous difficulties

[4 Mr Austin Dobson's brief version demands quotation.
> " Davus, I detest
> Persian decoration ;
> Roses and the rest,
> Davus, I detest.
> Simple myrtle best
> Suits our modest station ;
> Davus, I detest
> Persian decoration."]

to overcome, and in these I exerted all my strength. The dithyrambic is unsuitable to the genius of our poetry. It admits and requires compound words, over which Ennius alone had the mastery. You have taken from him, in the few pages of that grand poem which you permitted me to read, *omnipotens* and *armipotens.*

Virgilius. We must be parsimonious of wealth long hoarded, and open the treasury but seldom, nor for other than solemn occasions. There are two young poets who abstain from it, although one of them is somewhat rash here and there.

Horatius. Who are they?

Virgilius. Ovidius Naso and Albius Tibullus.

Horatius. I know Albius a little, shy as he is of company. He was the companion and friend of Messala during the late wars in Gaul; but his placid temper leads him to the retirement of a country life and the enjoyment of his Delia. He excels both Catullus and Ovid in the elegiac. His preference of the spondee as one foot in the first hemistich of the pentameter is judicious. Ovidius is too frequently dactylic in it. Solon and Tyrtæus have left us the earliest specimens. The polysyllabic close renders the verse more animated. In Ovidius it gambols; in Tibullus it murmurs like the ring-dove.

Virgilius. Ovidius, a short time ago, recited to me several passages of a poem on the transformation of men and women into flowers and other things. I was surprised at his ingenuity and facility of versification; and greatly more at a contest of Ulysses and Ajax for the armor of Achilles, quite Homeric.

Horatius. When you have completed your grand epic, now so successfully begun, we shall see Homer's rival. Your commencement of the Æneid is equal to his of the Iliad; which, indeed, is the continuation of another song, and probably of another singer, but Homer's composition. Who was the goddess he invoked? All the goddesses might contend for it, as three did not long before in the same region. In the first sentence, he says that the bodies of the Greeks were left a prey to dogs and *all* birds. Now there are many birds which would have kept aloof, having no taste for flesh, and a salutary fear of dogs and vultures. Some other word than πασι would have been more appropriate; perhaps it was a verb. The dogs themselves, I suspect, would rather have tucked up their legs under their bodies at home than have crossed the Grecian camp.

Virgilius. Here I accede to your proposition ; but I differ widely from you when you say, *aliquando bonus dormitat Homerus.* Attentive as I have always been to him, I have never caught him asleep, or other than wide awake. You may discover a dozen or twenty epithets which the verse rather than the sense required, some of them inappropriate.

Horatius. You have done wonders with a language so inflexible as ours, in which almost every heroic verse is either a dissyllable or trisyllable.

Virgilius. The rich may indulge in superfluities. The Ionian muse is somewhat too fond of playing voluntaries.

Horatius. Your first and second books are prodigies of genius. Continue, and you will have recorded the most memorable events of the most memorable nations, and have turned the eyes of future ages back toward them. Apollo and Neptune by their united power raised the walls of Troy ; Virgilius, single-handed, will have raised an imperishable Rome.

X. ASINIUS POLLIO AND LICINIUS CALVUS.[1]

Calvus. Welcome, thrice welcome, to our beautiful lake again, O Pollio. Benacus smiles at Sirmio, and Sirmio at Benacus, on this happy day.

[1 Asinius Pollio and Calvus are two of those famous writers of antiquity whose fame only has come down to our times. The former was not only a writer but a statesman, and a general as well. Up to the death of Cæsar he had been one of the dictator's lieutenants, and on his death he for a time served under Antony. But he soon gave up a military life and devoted himself to literature. He was a poet and the friend of poets. His influence saved for Virgil his paternal estate, and both Virgil and Horace sang his praises. Calvus had also played some part in the world. He was celebrated for his oratory, as well as for his poems. There is a well-known story that when he prosecuted Vatinius, the defendant was so much stirred by the prosecutor's eloquence, that he leapt up, exclaiming, " Am I to be condemned because this is a clever fellow ? " Calvus was a friend of Catullus, and in this and the following Conversation there are many allusions to the latter's poems. (*Fraser's Magazine*, Nov. 1855. Works, ii., 1876.)]

Pollio. Certainly, my friend Calvus, the water is calm, the sky serene, and the little promontory seems to revel in their enjoyment.

Calvus. We have been expecting you all the month, and we began to doubt whether you had not joined the party in the journey to Brundusium.

Pollio. Augustus and Mecænas, and their poets, could do very well without me. When I travel, I am uncomfortable in much company : I require facility of movement and roominess of accommodation.

Calvus. I know not whether Virgilius Maro has written to you any thing. If he has, I hope it is better than the incoherent verses with which he celebrated your son's nativity.

Pollio. It is seldom that we have seen each other of late. He prefers the Tiber to the Mincius, and laurels to rushes.

Calvus. He deserves the greenest of the one and the softest of the other, with as many doves and swans as haunt them. I doubt whether he ever visited our neighbor here, Valerius Catullus. They tell me he has written even nobler verses.

Pollio. It is reported that he is engaged on an epic. Certain it is that in his *Georgics* there are passages more harmonious, larger in sweep and swell, than the noblest of our friend's, in whose best hexameters the ear is at times disappointed, awaiting the fulness of harmony. In the iambic, in the scazon, in the phaleucic, no poet of Italy or Greece is comparable to him, whether in beauty of expression, in tenderness, or in terseness. Indeed the Greeks, owing to the wonderful flexibility of their language, run occasionally to waste in poetry; there is too much of slenderness in their grace. The many thousands of short pieces, which they call *epigrams* or *skolions* collected in our libraries are not worth, if put together, a dozen [2] of Catullus. He has, however, a rival in the travelling equipage of Cæsar and Cilnius. Their amiable friend, Horatius Flaccus, who, with Virgilius and other songsters of the same aviary, was carried in one cage with them to Brundusium, has given us in verse a description of the voyage. On reading it, I exclaimed in my piety, *Thanks, O ye gods and goddesses, I was not of the party !*

Calvus. The description is often delightful where what is described is greatly the reverse.

[2 First ed. reads : " twelve or thirteen."]

Pollio. Flaccus has an abundance of wit, yet it seems to have been all shaken out of him and scattered and lost upon the road. Never was any thing duller than this little journal.

Calvus. And yet what charming odes he has written!

Pollio. No poet so many of such various merit. Those which he has composed in the metre of Alcæus far excel the best of his master in choice of subject; that is, in celebration of heroism. Judiciously has he chosen this measure, the most sonorous of all the lyrical, for great men and great exploits: a rule which Alcæus has not rigidly observed. With the same sense of propriety and fitness, he usually employs the skittish Sapphic on what is light and pleasurable.

Calvus. And yet poor Sappho herself did not.

Pollio. She was pleased with a pattern of her own device, and worked it admirably.

Calvus. It was first introduced into this country by our old friend Valerius,[3] who condescended to translate her best mode.

Pollio. Let me enjoy a look at his villa. Ah! there it stands! Several others appear to have been recently built in its vicinity. Villas should never have any near. Baiæ and Tybur are less pleasing to me than they would be otherwise, for want of privacy.

You know a great deal more about the Benacus and the Sirmio than I do. Cæcilius, the earliest friend of Valerius now living, unless you yourself are, brought me several years ago to visit the lake before us. He was desirous of visiting once more the terrace where the two young poets had contended which of them could run the faster on the feet of verse: they chose the lightest both of construction and of material. On the next day Valerius sent him, from the bedchamber, a few lines which are to be found collected in his volume.

Calvus. Cæcilius, who never was jealous about his poetry, was very jealous about his lake. "Compare Benacus with Larius! O Calvus! Calvus!"

Pollio. In truth he was right. However, I begin to think the scenery here as beautiful as ever. We know the munificence of Caius Julius to those who served him faithfully: and it mattered not to him whether they were Gauls or Romans. It was by this

[3 Valerius Catullus.]

equity and impartiality that he conciliated all who served under him. Every brave and intelligent man was recognized by him, and placed where he would be the most efficient. His discernment was unclouded, his justice was unwarped. O Calvus! what do you believe is the reason why the Roman power has been, and continues to be, paramount? It is mainly by this system. Look toward other States, the kingly and the aristocratic, and then consider what it is which has reduced them to a subordinate station under us. It is, the unworthy raised above the worthy; it is, science and energy superseded by birth and rank. The family of Julius, although he had the policy, or perhaps the vanity, of tracing it up even to the gods, was less ancient than fifty others. He was not invidious of those fifty others; he made use of them as a master, he encouraged them whenever they did good service; but he never rewarded them more highly for it than he would a tribune or a centurion. In the Senate he was a Sulla, in the camp he was a Marius.

Calvus. But would not Sulla have preserved the constitution of his country? Why do you smile, Asinius?

Pollio. My dear Asinius! there are still poetical visions floating round about your head. Constitution! has the dead man any? Proconsulates and commands were given to the mercenary and rapacious. Military spirit existed yet; and it wafted at last by its strong aspiration a vigorous and a wise man to the Capitol, and the shouts of the soldiery shook down the rotten fabric that encumbered it. States, like men, have their growth, their manhood, their decrepitude, their decay. Caius Julius, even had he been willing, could not have propped up so worm-eaten a fabric. He called stout workmen in, and pulled it down. It was time that something better should be substituted. No death ever was so deplorable to his country as Cæsar's. I am far from being an admirer of Cicero's policy, much as I admire his eloquence. He excited the murderers of the greatest man the world had ever seen, of the man who would have protected his life and preserved his dignity. He fell by ungrateful hands, as Julius had fallen; yes, poor Cicero fell by hands equally ungrateful and more ignoble.

Calvus. Neither so vindictive as Sulla nor so sanguinary as Marius, yet Caius Julius cared little for human blood, whether it ran upon the earth or stagnated and corrupted under: and in these sentiments he found congeniality among the Gauls, than whom no people is more indifferent to the duration of life, or less indifferent to its enjoyments. Never had leader more faithful followers, or followers a more indulgent leader. Rise up a moment. Now look at these architectural villas on either side of us. The ground and the materials were given by the bounty of Cæsar; and one of the proprietors showed me the plan of his, drawn by the very hand of the Dictator. To-morrow, if you please, we will sail under the habitations of these recent occupants. Probably we shall be invited by one or other of them, if they recognise my bark, for they are as urbane as their illustrious commander; and their sons, now grown up to man's estate, are no less intelligent than graceful.

Pollio. Many thanks, my dear Licinius, but we must delay the excursion; for I had a few days of fever on the marshes of the Po, and am scarcely yet so strong as I was when I set out.

Calvus. Indeed! Believe me, I grieve to hear it. Can we procure you no remedies or restoratives?

Pollio. My friend! my friend! talk not to me of remedies: I will take no more of them. In the beginning of my malady I was impatient both of restraint and of delay, and sent for a physician. When he had felt my pulse and had made me put out my tongue for examination, he ordered that I should eat nothing but a small morsel of bread; and he carried to me, late in the evening, what he called a composing draught. It did indeed compose me wonderfully; but it brought me such a series of dreams, in about twelve or thirteen hours, as I doubt whether I could relate in as many days.

Calvus. Pray indulge me with as many of them as you can recollect. Let me hope that I myself was among them, with my friend Catullus, and his skiff, and his father's illustrious guest, of whom we have been speaking.

Pollio. Not you, nor Catullus, nor the skiff; but certainly I did see in my dream the Dictator, the Pontifex Maximus. I fancied I saw him go out of the door of Jupiter's temple, and heard whispers from the ministers who swept it, and soon after from some in rags and tatters, and ultimately from others in richer vestments. They laid their heads together and, after some consultation, they agreed that they, one and all, had as good a right to the office of Pontifex as the Dictator. In the next moment, the statue of Jupiter was beardless; in the next, some dirty and nauseating habiliments were thrown over his shoulders. And then came forward a barber who clipped his eyebrows close, and oiled and soaped one side of his head, leaving the other side intact. This barber, who succeeded so well in comedy, changed the sock for the buskin, and performed on Jupiter what Jupiter had performed on Saturn. There was a whisper, and then a vote, that the number of the Vestal Virgins should be increased and unlimited. After many sidelong glances, the vote was gravely carried. Before long, I seemed to see a couple of Cupids bearing a house across the sea, and setting it down on the borders of the Adriatic. No sooner was this over, than a modest young girl, with a child in her arms, was brought into it. She seemed bewildered, and begged and entreated them to let her go quietly home again. Several priests then stripped her of her clean and modest attire, and, caring little for her repugnance, crowned her hair with costly jewels, painted her face, and covered all parts below with a robe of gossamer and gold. At this, the infant cried aloud and woke me.

Calvus. Curious dream, indeed !

Pollio. This is only what appeared before my eyes. What was spoken I do not remember so well ; and it is lucky for you. It is only in a dream, and hardly there, that so many incongruities and contradictions ever came together. In the midst of these, by way of interlude, there were wrestlings and fightings and stabbings ; and above there, where the sceptre and eagle of Jupiter had stood, was a banner dropping with blood, surmounted by three letters—PAX.

Calvus. This is indeed, O Pollio, such a dream as a man weary and feverish from a long journey might well fall into. But perhaps there may previously have been some little agitation of the nerves ; for you are aware that every part of Italy is infested by thieves of one description or other, and that wherever there are rich way-*farers* there also are sly and alert way-*layers*. The road on which Julius Cæsar passed and repassed has now its own legions under darker colors : the vulture has taken place of the eagle. Enough of this matter for to-day. You, who travel usually with many attendants, have doubtless brought with you the usefullest of them all.

Pollio.   Cooks?

Calvus.   Perhaps I was wrong in my estimate.   Really I did not mean cooks, but books.

Pollio.   Yes, indeed, I have brought both.   Without the cooks there is no good digestion, and without good digestion no enjoyment of that which is falsely thought to be most remote from the dinner-table.   From ill-concocted food rise ill-concocted ideas; and Imagination is much indebted to what she most despises.

Calvus.   Oratory is mute since the establishment of the last Triumvirate, now above twenty years ago; but poetry seems to be still as flourishing as when Lucretius and Catullus were living. Have you brought any thing new along with you?

Pollio.   Not much; only some satires (and would you believe it?) written by Horatius.

Calvus.   I am confident that, whatever he does, he does well.

Pollio.   You shall have them in the morning at breakfast, and judge for yourself.

Calvus.   I am little fond of satire; but I will read whatever he writes.   I know imperfectly the character of the Apulians; but certainly the Romans are far from a well-tempered people: there is somewhat of the wolf in them yet.   Lucilius was a mere butcher.

Pollio.   Horatius is no butcher; he is an anatomist.   Both draw blood: but under the one we writhe; under the slender beak of the other the blood is sucked out gradually, imperceptibly, blandly: we smile in our slumber, and are first aware of our wound and our debility when we wake.

Calvus.   If Horatius is truly of such a stamp, I shall prefer him, not indeed as a poet, yet as a satirist, to my old friend of the Sirmio.   It was hardly worth his while to dirty his hands by besmearing his neighbor's house.   Horatius may never have written so fine a satire as that of Catullus on Egnatius, but on the other hand we may be certain that he runs no risk of committing an attack on Cæsar.   Justly did Marcus Tullius say that the verses of Catullus left an indelible mark on the conqueror of the

Gauls, and justly did he praise that conqueror's equanimity.   It was not patriotism which excited the spleen of my Valerius, for his lines were written long before the passing of the Rubicon. That he once admired Cæsar I well know; that he always despised and hated Pompeius I know equally.   We agreed, and I believe that you are of the same opinion, that never was man less amiable, less capable of friendship, less accessible to the claims of justice and humanity.   He threatened, as Cicero tells us, fire and sword to the whole of Italy, and was indignant that Sulla should have possessed the power of doing it, and he, Pompeius Magnus, should not.   He never performed one signally grand or truly generous action.

Pollio.   Curious! that two madmen, the one raving-mad, the other melancholy-mad, should be the only two men denominated *The Great.*

Calvus.   By whom?—by a madder world.

Pollio.   Neither of them had to contend with the strength and stature, the impetuous onslaught, the indomitable courage, the vigour that springs afresh from every fall, of that nation which most despises death, and most venerates Julius Cæsar.

Calvus.   Ah, Pollio! Pollio! do past days never turn their faces back upon you?   Do they never remind you that he became our lord and master?

Pollio.   Indeed they do: curses on those who imposed on us the sad necessity!   We enjoy, at least in the decline of life, a season of tranquillity.

Calvus.   It may perhaps end with him who closed last the Temple of Janus: can any man tell?

Pollio.   Between to-day and to-morrow there is night: can any man see across?   It is wise to make the most and the best of what is at hand.   In some measure we may frame the future,— in none foretell it.

Calvus.   I remember the time when your temper was less calm, and your endurance of a usurper less patient.

Pollio.   Usurpers are not always the worst of evils.   They are obliged, for their own security, to bring forward in others the most energetic and most inventive minds.   Corrupt and rotten States are the hotbeds of usurpation.   Men of powerful intellect are propelled toward their similars: the grovelling mind is quiescent;

and, if it grumbles, it grumbles like a swine in search of the chestnuts other swine before him have eaten.

Calvus.   It is a blessing, O Asinius, to find you in such high spirits, and particularly after such exhaustion.   They who fancied you jealous of the glory which Cicero and Cæsar had acquired in eloquence have been much mistaken.

Pollio.   Not much, my Calvus!   I was, and I continue to be, jealous of both.   Cicero, far below Demosthenes in vigor and compression, and farther still below him in purity and consistency of patriotism, stands high above the highest of Greek or Roman in the wisdom of his ethics.   His style is equalled only by Cæsar's.

Calvus.   Grammarians have fancied that Cæsar borrowed the style of Xenophon.

Pollio.   Never have I perused a more interesting volume than the *Anabasis.*   Generally, but not there, his style is maidenly, mincing, prudish, and (if one may be vernacular in your company) *pursed up.*   While I am reading him I fancy I hear a lisp. Jealousy peers out through his mock-modesty.   He never once mentions in his *History* the name of Epaminondas, the worthiest man and most scientific general of all the Greeks.   This jealousy is worse than mock-modesty, and very different; it is sheer impudence.   Epaminondas had won such a battle as never was won before, and never since until the battle of Pharsalia.   In each of these fights the conqueror had to contend with forces not only more numerous, but of equal discipline and equal experience ; and within sight of their own fields, their own houses, their own wives and children, in the Spartan.

Calvus.   Certainly here you have done justice to Cicero and Cæsar, with no injustice to Xenophon.   No man ever can praise too highly such writers as Herodotus and Thucydides, but surely the Greek philosophers have been over-rated.

Pollio.   I am inclined to believe that many more have praised them than have read them.   Praise is a species of traditionary wealth : long possession is its security ; we gain nothing by finding flaws in the title-deeds.

Calvus.   Generously spoken!   Let us be contented with filching and detracting a little from our contemporaries, especially if we are neighbors and friends.   Seriously, I am glad to find you more genial than I expected. You never had any asperity, but often some reserve: I now see none.

Pollio. It is with men as with fruits: some grow hard and corrugated, some insipid, while others are the sweeter, and not the less sound, the longer they hang upon the tree. What are those girls about, just under the window?

Calvus. Trimming bay and myrtle.

Pollio. Yes, my Calvus! these grow, I see, upon other parts of the shore beside the peninsula so celebrated by your Catullus. Take them, take them! neither bay nor myrtle befits the brow of Pollio.

SECOND CONVERSATION.[1]

Pollio. Our excursion on the water has refreshed and invigorated me greatly.

Calvus. And what opinion have you formed to yourself of our Gallic hosts?

Pollio. Indeed a high one. Never were soldiers more frank and hearty, more considerate and urbane.

Calvus. Unquestionably they had been informed of your arrival at my villa.

Pollio. Who, I wonder, could have given them the information?

Calvus. Truly I am ignorant of this.

Pollio. Then why suggest the fact? Insidious rogue!

Calvus. Did you not observe on the table a volume with your name superscribed?

Pollio. I saw one with yours; and under it, in large letters, Caius Valerius Catullus.

Calvus. This was very graceful and delicate in the new occupant of his house. Catullus, after the death of his brother in

[1] **Landor** supposes that the Gauls, settled in the neighbourhood of the Italian lakes, were descendants of the Teutons and Cimbrians defeated by Marius. It is worth notice that in this Conversation Landor's tone is more favourable to the Gauls than in his earlier writings. (*Fraser's Magazine*, Nov. 1855. Works, ii., 1876.)]

the Troad, left no near relative ; and when ultimately he went to reside at Rome, his villa soon fell into decay.

Pollio. It seems now again to be in good repair ; and the library is well stored.

Calvus. Even more so than ever. The number of books has been largely increased by the proprietor.

Pollio. Holy Jupiter ! and perhaps this very man's grandfather was a Teuton or Cimber, shaggy as a goat and fierce as a tiger, who fought against Caius Marius.

Calvus. I believe he is a Teuton by descent : the Cimbers are less reclaimable ; they continue to be ferocious and treacherous.

Pollio. He cautiously abstained from mentioning Marius, when he boasted of the prowess his countrymen had displayed against their adversaries. He only bowed to the compliment I paid him on the gallant resistance they made in the most formidable battle that ever nation fought against nation. It was no affair of the manly with the effeminate ; it was no game of play for a diadem of purple : it was for the mastery and dominion of the world. Had we lost, the city of Rome (had any such city been left standing) might have forfeited even its old name, and another have been given to it, which you and I, if we existed to hear it, might have found difficult to pronounce.

Calvus. Our hospitable friend was grateful toward Cæsar, and loud and even obstreperous in praising him. The Gauls have sufficient reason to extol the one and to abominate the other. In my opinion, differ as you may from it, he was on the whole an evil to us, although, had he lived, he would have adorned our city and amended our constitution.

Pollio. But without Marius we should have had no city to be adorned. You and I should have been hewing wood and drawing water, or perhaps have been suspended here in wicker baskets,[2] to be a burned offering to their gods.

Calvus. We might, indeed ; we might even have been educated to bow the head and bend the knee, and howl our prayers and praises before those hideous demons.

Pollio. Anything rather than the wicker basket. In the house we visited, I remarked the statues of Mercury and Apollo and Bacchus. Here is, methinks, an improvement.

[2 **Cæsar.** De Bello Gallico, vi., 16.]

Calvus. Some of the elderly men look grimly inauspicious on these images, which they fancy to be smiling at them. But in their absence the younger dance round about them, which they do well; and sing, which they do execrably. Some of them write verses not unworthy of the house we have left behind us.

Pollio. There is more there of the amatory than of the hymn. I remember, though, a hymn or two in Catullus. Diana must have found it difficult to keep her countenance at hearing him, devoted so little to chastity, celebrate her praises; and Hymen must have tucked up his saffron robe when he came forward, in a somewhat loose attire, at the marriage of Manlius and Julia. It is pleasant to find that the gloomy old gods are left behind in their gloomy old woods. They did Cæsar no harm, and Cæsar did them none. Our ancestors brought out of every conquered city every god they found within, and treated them respectfully and reverentially. Julius was no such god-collector: there was barely room in his tent even for a tessellated pavement.

Calvus. He was very moderate in the objects of his worship, and the few did as much for him as he could have hoped from the many. Taranis,[3] and the rest of the foresters, will never come to their full sturdy growth in the relaxing climate of our Italian regions. Religions, like the sun, take their course from east to west: traversing the globe, they are not all equally temperate, equally salubrious; they dry up some lands, and inundate others. Ours is not likely to be much altered or much enlarged. We have given Latin names to Grecian gods.

Pollio. In my opinion, that religion is the best in which there is the least of fraud and violence, the most of forbearance and sincerity.

Calvus. Wise and good-natured gods will never quarrel about the names they are called by. Do parents whip their children for imperfect pronunciation?

Pollio. I would not be surety for morose and ferocious men, intoxicated by the wine-cup of their priests, keeping the peace toward you, if you declined their mysteries and orgies. They call you blind, and knock out your eyes for being so. The Gauls are tolerant, gay, and genial. I do not imagine that they sang so

[3 Lucan. Pharsalia, i., 446, gives Taranis as the Gallic name of their chief god.]

cheerfully and blithely in their woods as at the dinner-table we left, somewhat late.

Calvus. There are few nations, none perhaps, without their songs; but Italy seems to excel in the vocal.

Pollio. In Egypt there are no songsters, even among the birds; and no dancers but among the snakes, which are very agile and graceful in their movements, and seem to be endowed with a fine ear both for time and tune. . I never have heard them, in the exercise of their profession, hiss at one another, as your poets do: and yet the hiss is the natural voice of both.

Calvus. We have certainly this facility both by nature and practice. Luckily my Catullus hath spared me, though we were intimate: indeed, I do not remember a poet of note (and I have lived familiarly with several) who has thought me worth the cast of a pebble or burr. A few whose causes and characters I defended have, I am told, spoken ill or slightingly of me. Certain proof that I wanted, if not abilities, at least judgment and discretion.

Pollio. Handfuls of dirt, thrown by hands that can hold but little, fall and are scattered ere they reach what they are aimed at; parent Earth receives them into her bosom, and smiles with serenity at their idle sport. Calvus, when you have performed a good office, think yourself well repaid for it by impunity. We may learn somewhat from the foolish, more from the wicked. We are not obliged to sit on the same bench with either, nor to con the same lesson: but they are always worth watching, and sometimes of studying as curiosities.

Calvus. Assuredly not the rarest.

Pollio. I think it improbable that the versifiers of the colony should decry, rather than celebrate, your manifest superiority.

Calvus. Never have I had any proof or signification of it. Our own countrymen have the character, in general, of more mutual evil-speaking than any other: our neighbours are exempt from a malady by which the sight is distorted and the heart corroded. Whether by proximity or disposition, I partake the character of those about me, and feel no slight pleasure in applauding their attempts at poetry. Many of the rising generation have written such verses as are worthy of being recited on the terrace of Catullus, under which his little skiff, which he

dedicated to Castor and Pollux, is still lying with its oars in it.
The possessor has caulked it afresh, and preserves the old sails
religiously. The youths are much given to scenic representations;
some of them have even attempted tragedy: but there they fail;
in comedy they are admirable. No peculiarity of character escapes
their observation, and they hit it with a precision and a delicacy
truly Attic. Terentius is more in favor with them than Plautus
is; and you would sometimes fancy that they are acquainted with
Aristophanes.

Pollio. They may partly owe the purity of their taste to Cæsar,[4]
who, as you well remember, praises it in Terentius, while he
regrets in him the deficiency of comic humor.

Calvus. Yes, I remember his opinion conveyed in verse, and
principally for its too strong expression, "unum hoc *maceror* : "
doleo is weak after this, and *doleo* is itself almost an exaggeration.

Pollio.[5] We all are hypocrites, my friend, in court and out of
court. Among the epistles you receive, whatever the occasion,
try to recollect how very few there are without, "*I am deeply
grieved,*" or, "*I am heartily glad:*" yet the writer's grief,
probably, was no deeper than the extremity of a well-pared nail,
and the gladness did not penetrate the thin fluid round the skin of
the heart. There is an ampulla in the plainest speech. In one
way or other (if not to you, to themselves) most men delight in
lying; all in being lied to, provided the lie be soft and gentle, and
imperceptible in its approaches.

I do, however, think that Cæsar would have been better pleased
had there been somewhat more of hilarity in Terentius.

Calvus. Surely, if hilarity was gratifying, he heard enough
of it in his triumph on the conquest of the Gauls. Perhaps he
wrote the verse in question before that other was sung by his
soldiers with such sprightliness,—

" Gallias Cæsar subegit," &c.

Now again to Metres: this verse suggests the thought. Is it
not remarkable that the trochaic, so lugubrious in cadence, where

[4 The allusion is to the epigram of Cæsar on Terence, quoted by
Suetonius in his Life of Terence.]
[5 From " *Pollio* " to " preceptors " (30 lines) added in 2nd ed.]

the syllable that follows the first falls weaker under it, should be chosen to express jocularity and exultation?

Pollio. It always hath been so, both in Italy and Greece. Indeed, I think there is a sound of animation in it well adapted to the march of soldiers, although the tragic poets in their choruses have applied it differently. The anapest, preceded by the iambic, was the favorite of Aristophanes. He appears to me to be the greatest master of harmony in all the dramatists.

Calvus. We Romans do not always act in obedience to our Greek preceptors. Boys are taught, in the level lawn of poetry where they now are exercised, that a dactylic word should never occupy the second seat in the hexameter. The sentence here, however, is quite as metrical as it need be. The two great masters of harmony, in which they are coequals, Homer and Theocritus, frequently place a dactylic word in the second place; and Cæsar, I think, did it designedly; for " maceror hoc unum " comes as readily in the collocation.

Pollio. Very true. Cæsar appears to have preferred Terentius to Plautus; Cicero the contrary. Comedy owes but a moderate debt to either; yet they are the two most authoritative masters of Latinity. Plautus is richer in words than any other Latin writer, but coined fewer than Aristophanes. Those of Plautus are still current throughout the empire; those of Aristophanes were laid aside with the machinery of the day. Cicero was intimately versed in Plautus, and acquired from him a fondness for diminutives. It may appear incredible, but such is the fact, that the orator and philosopher has more of them in his writings than Plautus and Terentius and Catullus put together.

Calvus. Diminutives are more adapted to light poetry and amatory epistles. The Gauls are become the most festive people in the world, having been throughout many ages, and until recently, the most ferocious and sanguinary. If evil times should return to us, I know not where we shall be safer than among them.

Pollio. Beyond the boundaries of Italy I would never willingly reside.

Calvus. Neither beyond nor within those boundaries is any place more beautiful than our Sirmio; no, not even Sorrentum.

Pollio. Enthusiastic patriot! Take and be contented with what I freely concede to you. Yes, indeed, Sirmio is a beautiful peninsula; **but there** is another yet more beautiful: it **is that** which diverts the **waters of the** Larius into the **Addua.** Cæcilius is residing there; **and it is** there he composed **the** poem which **you** and Valerius so much admire.

Calvus. I do not wonder that such a pleasant companion and such exalted a genius should detain you in the vicinity of Comum; **but, in** warmth and constancy of friendship for Pollio, Calvus will never yield even to Cæcilius.

Pollio. Only give up **the** Lake.

Calvus. Look yonder. Do you not see Castor and Pollux **over** the little skiff? They shall fight for me, and **I will** never yield.

Pollio. Remember, they are now with the Gauls, who give the beautiful **Lake** fresh animation with their lively songs and dances. Do they ever **converse with you** on literature?

Calvus. Frequently.

Pollio. They are so quick in perception that **I am sure their** observations are **usually** just.

Calvus. The young critics are singing from morning **till** night **the verses of** Catullus; and they like him the better on discovering in the most elegant **of poets** a few **words** which they claim as belonging to them.

Pollio. What words **are** those?

Calvus. *Ploxemum,* for instance, and *basium.* *Ploxemum* is the hurdle-framed cart of this country: *basium* is certainly a more expressive word than *osculum,* and is used instead of it wherever **the** colonies of Gaul have extended. *Osculum* is confined to a narrow **region** of Italy, and indeed is peculiarly Latin. *Suavium* is Plautine: our delicate poets of late repudiate it; **but in** the **Latian field** it may be heard occasionally.

Pollio. In that field there **are still some** remnants of the **Saturnian** age. Do you remember a certain exclamation of a rustic in the Forum? Or have you forgotten the honest fellow in the ring, who, applauding your eloquent speech against Vatinius, exclaimed, **and** threw both arms above his head, "*Dii magni! salipusium disertum!*" [6]

[6 The quotation is from Catullus, **xxv.** It may perhaps be rendered "Gods! what a splendid little spark of wit." Vatinius himself was so much moved by the attack that he is said to have exclaimed—"Ought I to be condemned, because my accuser happens to be eloquent?"]

Calvus. I remember it well; and no part of the applause,
from my hearers of every rank and condition, was received by me
with greater glee.   I doubt whether my critic in the crowd, or
you, or Varro, or Cæsar himself, could have told me, on first
hearing it, the origin of the word, plain as was its signification.
It seems to be a compound of *sal* and *pusus*.   The heir of *Pusus*
is *Pusillus :* the termination *ium* is indicative of fondling; as for
example in *Glycerium,* &c.   It is worth something to be of small
stature, when it raises up a man's elbows above his shoulders, and
makes him appeal to the gods to confirm the justice of his
admiration.

Pollio. If I could have spoken as well, and if so tall a man
as I am could have excited any such wonder in him, he might
perhaps have cried out, "Look at that heron! who could believe
that such a long neck and heavy wings should ever raise him
above the marsh?"   The expression of your encomiast might
have puzzled the great writer on *Analogy*.

Calvus. What an admirable work!

Pollio. And consequently how many impertinent things have
the ignorant and inconsiderate written against it.   The aim and
intention of the author was to bring our language under rule and
order; they were in all things his function and his delight.   He
succeeded in the army, in the city, in the provinces; and he
would also have introduced the same propriety in the language.
Partly by the indifference of authors, partly by the ignorance of
transcribers and the negligence of dealers who employ them, our
spelling has lost its fixity.   Marcus Tullius ridiculed the writer
who wrote *cives* for *civeis ;* yet latterly the courtiers have favoured
and their master has countenanced the novelty.   It is not easily
that you find a copy of Plautus or Terentius, in which the
spelling is theirs throughout.   Even Crispus Sallustius, now
living, has been unable to preserve his orthography[7] in all the
copies.   He has indeed thus been accused of archaisms; and
wherefore?   Because, feeling the certainty that some elder
writers have spelled better than the generality of the later, he has
bowed to their authority in preference.

[7 Landor is here speaking of himself in the person of Sallust. In all
the early editions of his writings his spelling is full of archaisms which
he here defends.]

Calvus. His manners ill corresponded with the austerity and sanctitude of his style. In his Preface to the *Catilinarian Conspiracy*, he describes one source of luxury, in which the Romans are immersed, by a very coarse expression, such as would have better befitted the censor Cato in his shortest tunic. Notwithstanding, I greatly admire his historical works, and especially the speeches he introduces. Here I am not led toward, but actually pass into, the wider and more varied grounds of another noble historian, Titus Livius of Patavium. It has been reported in this part of the country that you have censured him for what you designate by the name *patavinity*,[8] and pray tell me how it is, for I can discern in him nothing that is not rigorously Roman.

Pollio. I am no censurer of him, but on the contrary an admirer. No writer, Greek or Latin, is more grave and stately, I had almost said august.

Calvus. There is much of eloquence and much of poetry in him. Inconsiderate men will perhaps tell us that historian sought to keep clear of poetry. If they mean *fiction*, they are partly, and but partly, in the right; for fiction is inseparable from the remoter and higher regions of history. History is essentially dramatic, and the most interesting portions of it are in dialogue. Give us action, and we will reflect upon it. When we are agitated by the movement of events we are impatient of being jogged, and of being told in weighty words what we ought to think about them. We are among the dead and the living; in one quarter is the legionary trumpet, in another the funeral horn. Suffer us in this field to be excited, in the next we will repose.

Pollio. Not only the dramatic, not only the imaginative, but even the fabulous may enter history, provided it be announced for what it is. The fabulous is often not only the most pleasant, but also the most instructive in her pages. Caution and dexterity are required to introduce it.

Calvus. The historian, to be worthy of the name, must occasionally exercise the poet's office. It is impossible that any man could have heard what passed between Tarquinus and Lucretia in her bed-chamber; yet Titus Livius brings out the very words which we must believe he spoke. No verse in Latin or Greek could have uttered them with equal significance.

[8 See Quintilian, viii., 1. 3.]

Note the order of words.   *Sextus Tarquinius sum : ferrum in manu est : moriere si emiseris vocem.*   I have remarked to many this admirable collocation.   He would win her to compliance by his name, which bore along with it his royal rank, his martial courage, his lofty stature, and that prowess of limb which in woman's eyes is manly beauty.   The verb follows the noun, not a syllable precedes it.   He then intimidates her : the sword is there ; the verb again stands behind.   She must see at once the whole extent of her danger : death is announced,—unconditional ? inevitable ? no : but, *si emiseris vocem.*   We know in what manner our friend Cicero would have fabricated the sentence : we are quite certain his ear (pardon the expression) would have overlapped his understanding, and the sentence would have been this : *Ego sum Sextus Tarquinius ; in manu autem ferrum est ; si vocem emiseris moriere.*   In the middle of this oration the girl would have jumped out of bed, and have run downstairs before it ended.

Pollio.   You have hit upon it, Calvus.   Such would have been Cicero's arrangement.   Both of us in the Forum have been obliged to study the position of our words, knowing that the passions have sensitive ears : and the Senate too must be won over by the delicacy of the repast we set before it.   Even the lowest of the populace is contented no longer with street music.

Calvus.   In my enthusiasm for Livius, it is probable I have made over and over again the same observations, to you and others ; but if they have dropped out of your memory, if they are just, and above all if they are brief, the repetition is not unpardonable.

Pollio.   They who are afraid they are repeating what they have said before may sometimes think they have spoken or written what they never have ; and thus an animated being (such is a thought) is lost to the Creation.

Calvus.   I am confident you will forgive me thus praising my contemporaries.   I know there is a penalty for the offence, and I know there are some of the praised who themselves would inform against me,—crying, *I, lictor, colliga manus.*

Pollio.   Never mind them.   ' I have known men, and have known them too well, who would abstain from doing you a wrong were it not for the sake of defending it, and thus experienc-

ing the pleasure of laying out their talents.   An apostate friend is
triumphant when he can make you complain of him : never give
him this advantage over you.   Praise as loudly as you will the
citizen of Patavium, who hath restored the Commonwealth of
Rome, who hath raised up again before us the rushy cottage of
Romulus, and surrounded it with walls expansive as the heavens!
Up they rose, bolder and bolder in the face of danger : Hannibal,
who scaled the Alps, despaired at the sight of them.

Calvus.   Titus Livius hath manned those walls.   Titus Livius
hath ornamented the temples within them, placing god after god
in mansions worthy of them, and filling them with adorers almost
as venerable as the adored.

Pollio.   I have animadverted on the peculiarities of his style
without acrimony or invidiousness : others more accustomed to
decoration, and more fond of it, call them defects.   A future
age, recurring to antiquity, may admire him more highly than the
present, and more justly.   Copiousness is now, and has been long,
the fashion : and fashions not only run into extremes but into
contrarieties.   Marcus Brutus called the style of Cicero Asiatic.
We may be Ionian and avoid the rigidity of the Egyptian.   It is
better to attract than to drag and bind.   Our next generation
may run counter to the present.   Strong youth often affects
austere manliness ; but the beard of Camillus looks ill upon young
faces.   Livius, in the unruliness of adolescence, broke loose from
Roman authority and resolved to assume a style as different as
possible from Cicero's, and preferred the Patavine.

Calvus.   Gently, gently ! Pollio !   Could Cicero, if his
whole lifetime had been devoted to it, have composed such a
history as that of Livius ?   His language, so admirable in every
thing else, was unfit for it : his back would have been bent,
bowed down, and broken, under the weight of armor and
viaticals which Titus carried with him easily and far.

You have not yet quite satisfied me in the use of your expression : I mean *Patavinity.*

Pollio.   My censure was slight.   My meaning is that he
employs the diction of his countrymen in small matters.

Calvus.   I never have remarked it.   Can you recollect such ?

Pollio.   They are hardly worth noticing.   He uses *ab* for *a,*
and *ex* for *e.*

Calvus. If you and I avoided this usage, Terentius and Cæsar have countenanced it. Livius, no friend to his party and principles, comes nearer to him in style than any other has come ; unless it be M. Brutus. Nothing can be more perfect in composition than the *Commentaries.*

Pollio. I am quite of your opinion ; and it has often struck me as a curious coincidence, that Brutus, to the extent of his abilities, imitated him. Cicero has made more of Brutus, as a writer and a philosopher, than he found in him.

Calvus. No common case. Gold coin is oftener clipped than brass, and more easily abraded. These are not the days when a Brutus is overvalued. It was the more generous in Cicero to praise him, since he was invidious both of his authority and celebrity. Asiatic never was Cicero, although he sometimes wore at the bottom of his rhetorician robe a flounce too many.

Pollio. Every thing in its season. Neither our language nor the tone of our voice is the same in public as in private, with a stranger as with a friend. You indulge, and well you may, in the fanciful and facetious with me ; you never would have done so with Pompeius, nor with the people in the Forum to any extent. You might with Cicero and Cæsar ; they were genial and congenial : and both of them would have listened to your remarks with almost as much pleasure as I have been doing.

Calvus. Well ! we will leave them, and Brutus too, where they are, and again to Livius.

Pollio. He, like Brutus, is indifferent to the close of his sentences. Now surely, by blunting the point, the edge of the sword is none the more efficient ?

Calvus. I would rather be deaf than hear, or expect to hear, a verb at the termination of almost every period.

Pollio. Cicero may have been too fond of it in the earlier of his *Orations,* but where is there a greater variety than in the structure of his sentences ? His ear was as internally polished as you poets may imagine the conch of Nereus. He sometimes is exuberant. Conciseness may be better : but where there is much wealth we may excuse a little waste, especially when it falls not unworthily. I confess to you I love a nobility and amplitude of style, provided it never sweeps beyond the subject. There are people who cut short the tails of their dogs ; and such dogs are proper for such masters: but the generous breeds, coursers of the lordly stag, and such as accompanied the steps of Hippolytus and Adonis, were unmutilated.

I admire in Cicero much beside his forensic eloquence.

Calvus. It grew weaker in the presence of a greater man. No such faint whimpering voice Demosthenes raised to heaven when his country fell exhausted and prostrate, and when, throwing his strong arms around her, he failed to raise her up again. Cicero fell as low as his country, and each simultaneously, at the feet of Cæsar. Ambitious men (and never was man more ambitious than Marcus Tullius) are like children who are beginning to swim: their only thought is how to keep the head above-water; and by this anxiety and effort they sink.

Pollio. Cicero swam upon cork and bladder when he was strong and expert enough to strike on without, and to breast the current. He wanted the vigor of character, and perhaps too the vigor of language, we find united in Demosthenes, whose furnace poured forth incessantly its torrent of purified iron; no part of his fabric was constructed for the fusion and elaboration of softer ornamental metals. Cicero's whole house was decorated with rich filigree, with vases that vibrated and rang at a stroke of the knuckle, and with innumerable graceful little images.

Calvus. But how beautiful, plain, and simple are not only his *Dialogues*, but also his two brief Treatises on *Friendship* and *Old Age.* He was perfectly aware that authors ought not to dress themselves in purple and fine linen every day.

Pollio. Assuredly he was. We would allow them a daily change of the fine linen, but would advise them to reserve the purple for solemn and rare occasions. Now Cicero did this. What is become of his poetry I know not. At this moment it occurs to me that no orator but yourself ever wrote passably in poetry, Greek or Latin.

Calvus. True enough—excepting the exception. Do not quarrel with Titus for invading my boundary; but rather let us turn back again toward Tusculum, where the questions are less litigious. With greatly more propriety may it be said of Cicero than of Socrates, that he made Philosophy a good domestic house-wife. She had wandered in the fields over the world, like another Ceres, distracted by her search; she also had plenty of poppies and other flaunting flowers about her bewildered head, but there was scarcely an ear of corn on her brow or on her bosom, scarcely a grain that would bear the winnowing. Cicero took Philosophy by the hand. She found herself at last in a cool and quiet room ; and she came out from it in a modest robe, reaching down to her feet, but not sweeping and scattering the dust about her.

Pollio. In Cicero and his society we find no sophisms or quibbles, but fair discussion and diligent investigation of important truths. The familiar and facetious are not forbidden to enter, or to bear a due part in the conversation. There is no indecorous mirth, no loud banter ; but everything chaste, comely, quiet, with gracefully subdued festivity.

Calvus. Poor Cicero! How often, my Pollio, have we attempted in our earlier days to imitate his tone and gesture ; until our voices changed, deeper but less melodious, and our thews grew sharper, hardier, more prominent, determined to have their own way.

Whoever would enter public life, or more wisely prefer the private, let him, regardless of the rustics he will meet, take his morning walk on the road to Tusculum.

NOTE ON LANDOR'S METHOD OF WRITING GREEK.

The Greek quotations in this and preceding editions of the Imaginary Conversations are printed in a manner which to some eyes will appear uncouth. In some passages the accentuation is approximately accurate, in others there is no accentuation, or next to none, and the breathings are wrongly placed and often incorrect. An examination of the passages, in which Greek is used, shows that this double method is the result of the fashion in which Landor's books were printed. In the editions published between 1824 and 1829 the accentuation is approximately correct. There can be no doubt that this is due to the scholarly care of the friend who relieved Landor of the task of superintending the printing of the volumes so published. It is not likely that Landor ever corrected his own proofs; it is possible that he never even saw them. But Julius Hare was too much of a scholar to allow the book to go forth disfigured by ungainly Greek. The 1846 edition had not the benefit of such care. Landor's Greek was printed exactly in the fashion in which it was written. Like many of his contemporaries, Landor probably never, or almost never, wrote a Greek accent. The Greek quotations that occur in the works of Peacock and Shelley show that a man in those days did not consider himself disqualified from using a Greek quotation because he did not know how to accentuate it. It is, therefore, not surprising that Landor should have written his Greek in this fashion, and seen it so printed without any sense of horror. In the present day we are more critical. Unaccentuated Greek is to a scholar's eye what a dropped H is to his ear. It is with some anxiety that the present editor has followed Mr Forster's example in allowing these unadorned specimens of Greek orthography to remain. But he has preferred in the Classical Conversations to venture upon this course. In the few Greek quotations, however, which occur in the remaining volumes, he has thought it well to force the eccentricity of Landor's genius to conform to modern usage.

DIALOGUES OF SOVEREIGNS AND STATESMEN.

DIALOGUES OF SOVEREIGNS
AND STATESMEN.

———— ✳ ————

I. RICHARD I. AND THE ABBOT OF BOXLEY.[1]

THE Abbot of Boxley was on his road to Haguenau in search of Richard, and[2] the appearance of the church-tower in the horizon had begun to accelerate his pace, when he perceived a tall pilgrim at a distance, waving his staff towards some soldiers who would have advanced before him : they drew back.

"He may know something of the Lion-heart," said the abbot, spurred his horse onward, and in an instant threw himself at the pilgrim's feet, who raised and embraced him affectionately.

[1 "Accordingly when they heard of the captivity of the king, Walter the Archbishop of Rouen, and the other justiciars of the lord king, sent the Abbot of Boxley and the Abbot of Robertsbridge into Germany to look for the King of England. And when they had gone through the whole of Germany and had not found the king, they entered into Bavaria and met the king at the town called 'Oxefer,' through which he was being taken to the Emperor, to confer with him on Palm Sunday. And hearing that these abbots were come from England, the king behaved to them cheerfully and affably, asking of the state of his kingdom, and the faithfulness of his vassals. . . . And they made answer as they had heard and seen. So, talking with them, the king complained of the treachery of his brother John . . . who had joined himself with the King of France against his brother . . . But when the king was in the most grief at this, suddenly he broke out into speech thus, comforting himself. 'My brother John is not the man to conquer dominions for himself, if there were any to oppose him, even were it with a slender force.'" Hoveden, iii., 198 (Chronicles and Memorials); Imag. Convers., i., 1824. i., 1826. Works, i., 1846. Works, iii., 1876.)]

[2 From "and" to "pace" (2 lines) added in 2nd ed.]

Abbot. O my **King**, my King! the champion of our faith at the mercy of a prince unworthy to hold his stirrup! The conqueror of Palestine led **forth** on foot, a captive!—a captive of those he commanded and protected! Could Saladin see it—

Richard. The only prince in the universe who would draw his sword for me against the ruffian of Austria. He alone is worthy to rescue me, who hath proved himself worthy to fight me. I might have foreseen this **insult.**[3] What sentiment of magnanimity, of **honor**, of humanity, ever warmed an Austrian bosom?

Tell me, declare to me, Abbot, speak it out at once,—is this the worst of my misfortunes? Groans burst from me; they cleave my heart: my own English, I hear, have forsaken me: my brother John is preferred to me,—I am lost indeed. What nation hath ever witnessed such a succession of brave kings, two hundred years together, as have reigned uninterruptedly in England? Example formed them, danger nurtured them, difficulty instructed them, peace and war in an equal degree were the supporters of their throne. If John succeed to me, which he never can by virtue, never shall by force, and I pray to God never may by fortune, what will remain to our country but the bitter recollection of her extinguished glory? I would not be regretted at so high a price: I would be better than the gone, presumptuous as is the hope; but may the coming be better than I! Abbot, I have given away thrones, but never shall they be torn from me: rather than this, a king of England shall bend before an emperor of Germany,[4]* but only to rise up again in all his majesty and strength.

[3 For "insult" 1st ed. reads "result," and adds "glory" and "gratitude" to the list of un-Austrian sentiments.]

[4 1st ed. reads: "Germany, but shall bend as an oak before the passing wind, only," &c.]

* Opinions have changed on most things, and greatly on titles and dignities. A consul is appointed to reside in a seaport: a Roman senator was often, in political weight and in landed property, beneath the level of an English gentleman; yet not only a Roman senator, but a Roman citizen, held himself superior to kings. It might well be permitted our Richard to assume a rank above any potentate of his age. If almanacs and German court-calendars are to decide on dignities, the emperors of Morocco and Austria shall precede the kings of England: learned men have thought otherwise. On this subject hear Leonardo Aretino:—

Abbot. God grant it! Abandoning a king like Richard, we abandon our fathers and children, our inheritance and name : far from us be forever such ignominy! May the day when we become the second people upon earth, Almighty God, be the day of our utter extirpation !

Richard. I[5] yet am king,—yea, king am I more than ever, who even in this condition rule over hearts like thine.

Genii and angels move and repose on clouds ; the same do monarchs, but on less compact ones, and scarcely firm enough for a dream to pillow on.   Visions of reluctant homage from crowned heads, and of enthusiastic love from those who keep

"Quid enim mea refert quemadmodum barbari loquantur, quos neque corrigere possum si velim, neque magnopere velim si possim?   De rege tamen et imperatore idem sentio quod tu, et jampridem ridens barbariem istam, hoc ipsum notavi atque redargui.   Tres enim gradus majorum dignitatum apud Romanos, de quorum principe loquimur, fuere ; rex, dictator, imperator.   Ex his suprema omnium potestas rex est ; post regem verò secundum tenuit dignitatis locum dictatura ; post dictaturam imperium *tertio gradu* consequitur.   Hujusce rei probati est, quod Octaviano imperatori optime se gerenti Senatus Populusque Romanus dignitatem augere, pro imperatore dictatorem facere decrevit, quod ille non recepit, sed flexo genu recusavit, quasi majoris status majorisque invidiæ dignitatem existimans, Imperatoris nomen modicum ac populare, si ad Dictatoris fastigium comparetur.   Majorem vero esse regiam potestatem quam dictaturam ex eo potest intelligi, quia Julius Cæsar, Dictator cum esset, affectavit Regem fieri."

The dignity of a sovereign does not depend on the title he possesses, which he may with equal arrogance and indiscretion assume, but on the valor, the power, the wealth, the civilization, of those he governs. This view of the subject the Aretine has not taken.

Rank pretends to fix the value of every one, and is the most arbitrary of all things.   Roman knights, corresponding for the most part in condition with our wealthier yeomanry and inferior esquires, would have disdained to be considered as no better or more respectable than the kings they hired.   In our days, an adventurer to whom a petty prince or his valet has given a pennyworth of ribbon looks proudly and disdainfully on any one who has nothing else in his button-hole than the button.

Few authors are sounder than Plutarch ; and no remark of his more judicious than the following on Juba,—at which, however, there is not a deputy-commissary or under-secretary who would not laugh :—

"His son, named also Juba, was carried in triumph while yet a child : and truly most happy was his imprisonment, by which, barbarian as he was, he came to be numbered among the most learned writers."

[5 First ed. reads: "I cease not to be king who rule," &c.   One line below, from "Genii" to "all" (7 lines) added in 2nd ed.]

them so, have passed away from me, and leave no vacancy. One thought commemorative of my country, and characteristic of my countrymen, is worth them all.

Abbot. Here are barely, I reckon, more than threescore men; and, considering the character both of their prince and of their race, I cannot but believe that the scrip across my saddle-bow contains a full receipt for the discharge of my sovereign. Certain I am that little is left unto him of the prize he made in the caravan of Egypt.

Richard. The gold and silver were distributed among my soldiers; for the only prizes worthy of me were Saladin and Jerusalem. I have no hesitation in esteeming Saladin not only above all the potentates now living, which of a truth is little, but, from what hath been related to me, above all who have ever reigned,—such is his wisdom, his courage, his courtesy, his fidelity; and I acknowledge that, if I had remained to conquer him, I would have restored to him the whole of his dominions, excepting Palestine. And the crown of Palestine which of the crusaders should wear? which among them could have worn it one twelvemonth? I would do nothing in vain; no, not even for glory. The Christian princes judged of me from their own worthlessness; Saladin judged of me from himself: to them he sent pearls and precious stones, to me figs and dates; and I resolved from that moment to contend with him and to love him. Look now toward the Holy Alliance. Philip swore upon the Evangelists to abstain from aggression in my absence.[6] Collecting an army on the borders of Normandy, he protests that his measures are pacific, invokes Heaven against usurpers, and invades the province. He would persuade me, no doubt, that a squadron of horse on the low grounds is a preventive of agues, and a body of archers on the hills a specific for a fever. Ay, Abbot, and his bishops lead him forth and light him on; his nobility follows him with alacrity and applause. In the whole extent of France there is neither sword nor crozier unsullied by perjury. Where upon earth was there ever a people so ready to swear and to forswear, to fight and to fly? Equally enthusiastic in opposite causes, and embracing them without breathing betwixt, their

[6 First ed. reads: "absence. He invades Normandy and sanctions usurpation. Saladin," &c., omitting 27 lines.]

enthusiasm is always in proportion to their number. A Frenchman, like a herring, loses his course when he loses his company,
and his very instinct (in truth he has little else) forsakes him.
The bravest kings with him are those who cast down conscience the most readily, and those whose appetites are the most
grovelling are the best.   As in the black-puddings of our
country-folk, if blood is wanting, it must be made out by fat.*

Abbot.   Times ought to be very quiet, and nations very
prosperous, when rulers are valued like bears and porpoises for
their fur and grease.   The perfidy of a rival may justly have
excited the disdain but ought never to have turned aside the
arms, of Richard.   The cause of truth and righteousness is thine,
O King! and when hast thou deserted what thou hast once
upholden ?

Richard.   Saladin was defeated, and Jerusalem would have
fallen ; but God will forgive me if, leaving his bones and
sepulchre to his own care and protection, I chastise a disloyal
rather than a loyal enemy.

Abbot.   I wish my liege could have taken him prisoner, that
he might have saved such a soul by infusing into it the true faith
under baptism.

Richard.   Ay, that indeed were well.   Tunny-fish[7] under
oil, men under baptism,—those alone of both creatures are
worth a November melon.   So said the Bishop of Hermopolis
one day after dinner ; and I wish he could have kept awake
and sober, to edify us more at large thereupon.

A word in your ear, my Abbot.   Saladin lives in a country
where prophet comes after prophet, and each treads out the last
vestige from the sand.   I am afraid it would not hold.

Abbot.   Better as it is then.

---

* The ancient fare of our kings differed from that of the commonalty
in plenteousness only.   If Richard did not dress his own dinner, like
Achilles, he knew at least the composition of the few plain dishes then
in use.   Indeed, the *black-pudding* was of such moment that it shook the
whole Christian world.   Michael Cellularius, patriarch of Constantinople,
condemned the Bishop of Rome, Leo IX., for eating unleavened bread in
the eucharist, and *black-pudding* at home.

[7 From "Tunny-fish" to "thereupon" (5 lines) added in 2nd ed.
From "A" to "Abbot" added in 3rd ed.   The footnote below on
" happiness" appears in a slightly different form in the 1st ed.]

Richard. There are many in foreign parts who cannot be brought to comprehend **how** a sprinkle of water should prepare **a** man's eternal happiness,* or the curtailment **of** a cuticle his eternal misery.

Abbot. Alas, my liege, society **is froth above and** dregs below, and we have hard work to keep **the** middle of it sweet and sound, **to** communicate right reason and to preserve right feelings. In voyages you may see too much and learn too little. The winds and waves throw about you their mutability and their turbulence. When **we** lose sight of home, **we lose** something else than that which **school-boys** weep for.

Richard. By[8] the **keenness** of your eye, compassionate as it **is, I** discover, my good Abbot, that you have watched and traced **me from the** beginning **of** my wanderings. Let me **now** tell my story,—to confession another time. I sailed along **the** realms of my family ; **on the right was** England, on the left was France : little **else could I discover** than sterile eminences **and extensive** shoals. They fled behind me : **so** pass away generations ; **so** shift **and sink and** die away affections. In the wide ocean I was little **of a monarch ;** old men guided **me,** boys instructed **me ;**

---

* If **Richard had** lived a few **centuries** later, he would **surely have been** less **a freethinker** than we **hear** he was. Fra Sabastiano **di Geisu** related **to Pietro della** Valle, that a Persian *male-witch* (stregone), **taken** in the fact of witchcraft, was asked whether he **could** eat the heart of **a** Portuguese captain, **in the** same manner as he had **just** eaten **the** heart of a cucumber; that is, merely by looking at it. He replied **in** the negative ; **for** that **the** Franks had **in** the breast something like a corslet, of such hardness that **no** witchery could penetrate it ; which, beyond doubt, **says Petro, can be** nothing else than the virtue of baptism, the armor **of faith, and the** privilege of being **sons of** the Church. This honest traveller falls, **in** almost every letter, **on some** unlucky comparison be- **tween the idolatry of his native country** and of those he visits. " It **appears," says he,** " that a great part **of the** worship paid **to** their idols consists **in nothing but** music and **singing,** &c., **to** pass the **time** gaily and luxuriously." He speaks of the **right reverend** their fly-flappers as " making **a** wind and driving off the flies **from the** idols in the palanquin, *offering that obsequiousness which we use toward **the** Pope, with fans made from the tails of white peacocks.* And there were not wanting about the idols many of them *religious,* and many many torches, with the splendor where- of the night was lighted **up."** Who would not imagine this description to have rather **been made by a** Hindoo in **Rome,** than by a Roman in Hindostan ?

[8 From "**By**" to "is" (2 lines) added in 2nd ed.]

these taught me the names of my towns and harbors, those showed me the extent of my dominions : one cloud, that dissolved in one hour, covered them.

I debark in Sicily, place my hand upon the throne of Tancred, and fix it.   Again we sail, and within a day or two, behold ! as the sun is setting, the solitary majesty of Crete, mother of a religion, it is said, that lived two thousand years.   Onward, and many bright specks bubble up along the blue Ægean ; islands, every one of which, if the songs and stories of the pilots are true, is the monument of a greater man than I am.   We leave them afar off—and for whom ?   For creatures of less import than the sea-mews on their cliffs ; men praying to be heard and fearing to be understood, ambitious of another's power in the midst of penitence, avaricious of another's wealth under vows of poverty, and jealous of another's glory in the service of their God.   Is this Christianity ?—and is Saladin to be damned if he despises it ?

Before[9] I joined my worthy brotherhood of the faith, I was tossed about among the isles and islets, which in some places are so thickly set, you may almost call them sea-stars.

A sailor's story is worth little without a tempest : I had enough of one to save my credit at the fireside and in the bower.

The despot or emperor of Cyprus* (I forget his title) threw into prison the crew of an English vessel wrecked on his coast ; and, not contented with this inhumanity, forbade the Princess of Navarre, my spouse, and the Queen of Sicily who attended her, to take refuge from the storm in any of his ports.   I conquered his dominions, with the loss, on my part, of a dinner, two men, and a bridle.   He was brought before me.   My emperor had an aversion to iron in every form ; therefore I adorned his imperial feet with a silver chain, and invited him to the festivities of my nuptials with Berengere, followed by her coronation as Queen of Cyprus.   We placed his daughter under the protection of Jane,† knowing her sweet temper and courtesy, and reminding her that a lady of rank rises one step higher by misfortune. She hath exchanged the cares of a crown for the gayety of a

[9 From "before" to "bower" (6 lines) added in 2nd ed.]
* Isaac, the usurper of Cyprus, styled himself emperor. [For an account of Richard in Cyprus, see T. A. Archer's Crusade of Richard I., p. 60.]
† Queen of Sicily

court, and I hope that what she lost as princess she will gain as woman. I intend to place her suitably in marriage, and her dowry shall be what my treasury is at the time.

Abbot. We have only to consider now what lies before us. Could not my liege have treated with the Duke of Austria?

Richard. Yes, had he been more nearly my equal. I punished his neglect of discipline: it became in his power to satiate his revenge. Henry is mercenary in the same degree, but perhaps less perfidious, certainly less irritated and hostile. No potentate can forgive the superiority of England: none can forget that I treated him as a trooper and dependant, and that the features of my contempt were too broad for any mask in all the rich wardrobe of dissimulation. Henry alone is capable of ensuring my return. I remember the fate of Robert; and if I am not presently in London, I may be in Cardiff.[10]

Those who have abandoned me must ransom me; I myself will dictate the conditions, and they shall be such as no Emperor of Germany can refuse.[*]

Ride on with me.

[[10] Cardiff, where Robert, Duke of Normandy, was imprisoned by his brothers, William Rufus and Henry, until his death. First ed. reads: "Cardiff. He spoke wisely who said—'There is no confidence in princes;' and he will speak not unwisely who shall say—'There is none for them.' Those, &c." The footnote at the end occurs first in 2nd ed.]

[*] *Emperor* is the title usually given to the heads of the Germanic league; but in fact there never was an *Emperor of Germany*. Adrien Valois, in a letter to Albert Portner, writes thus: "Legi Conringii librum *de finibus Imperii Germanici*, cujus libri titulum jure quis arguat; nullum enim imperium Germanicum fuit unquam, nullum est hodieque; nec imperator etiamsi in Germaniâ sedem habeat, Germanorum imperator est, sed, ut ipse se more majorum appellat, rex Germaniæ et Romanorum imperator." Here we see the *rex* is before the *imperator;* if in the patents of Charles V. it is otherwise, the reason is that the title of king is applied to the dominion of several States which his ancestors had acquired more recently. Valois proceeds: "Si tamen Romanorum imperator vocari debet qui urbi Romæ, non imperat, et ab episcopo ecclesiæ Romanæ, Romæ, ac senatus populique Romani sententiâ, dudum desiit consecrari." This letter is not printed among the works of Valois or his brother, but is of unquestionable authenticity, and may be found entire in the *Amænitates Literariæ* of Schelhorn, Tom. V. p. 542. Valois was a good scholar, but he errs in his Latinity when he objects to the expression *imperium Germanicum ;* for that expression would be correct whether Germany were governed by a king, an emperor, an aristocracy, or a democracy. The Roman State was just as much *imperium Romanum* under the consuls and

II. KING HENRY IV. AND SIR ARNOLD SAVAGE.[1]

Savage. I obey the commands of my liege.

Henry. 'Tis well: thou appearest more civil and courteous, Sir Arnold Savage, than this morning in another place, when thou declaredst unto me, as Speaker of the Commons, that no subsidy should be granted me until every cause of public grievance were removed.*

Savage. I am now in the house of the greatest man upon earth; I was then in the house of the greatest nation.

Henry. Marry! thou speakest rightly upon both points; but the latter, I swear unto thee, pleaseth me most. And now, Savage, I do tell thee with like frankness, I had well-nigh sent a score of halberts among your worshipful knights and sleek woolstaplers, for I was sore chafed; and, if another had dealt with me in such wise, I should have straightway followed my inclination. Thou knowest I am grievously let and hindered in my projected war, by such obstinacy and undutifulness in my people. I raised up the House of Commons four years ago, and placed it in opposition to my barons, with trust and confidence that, by the blessing of Christ and His saints, I might be less hampered in my complete conquest of France. This is monstrous: Parliament

tribunes as under Tiberius or Caligula. The justice of the remark made by Valois is proved by the patents of **Charles V.**, which always began "Carolus V., divinâ favente clementiâ, Romanorum Imperator Augustus, *ac rex Germaniæ*, Hispaniarum, utriusque Siciliæ, Hierusalem, Hungariæ, &c." The late Emperor of Austria formally laid down a title which never belonged to him: he and all his ministers were ignorant of this, and it may be doubted whether there was a statesman in Europe who knew it.

[1 Landor always believed himself to be descended from Sir Arnold Savage, and delighted in the opposition which that worthy offered to Henry the Fourth. Writers of Constitutional History have opined Sir Arnold Savage to have been of a pedantic turn of mind, and might find other matters to cavil at in this Conversation. (Imag. Convers., i., 1824 i., 1826. Works, i., 1846. Works. iii., 1876.)]

* The words reported by Hakewell: *De modo tenendi Parliamentum.*

speaks too plainly and steps too stoutly for a creature of four years' growth.

Savage. God forbid that any King of England should achieve the conquest of all France! Patience, my liege and lord! Our Norman ancestors, the most warlike people on whose banners the morning sun ever lighted, have wrested the sceptre from her swaddling kings, and, pushing them back on their cushions and cupboards, have been contented with the seizure of their best and largest province. The possession of more serfs would have tempted them to sit down in idleness, and no piece of unbroken turf would have been left for the playground of their children in arms. William the Conqueror, the most puissant of knights and the wisest of statesmen, thought fit to set open a new career, lest the pride of his chivalry should be troublesome to him at home. He led them forth against the brave and good Harold, whose armies had bled profusely in their war against the Scot. Pity that such blood as the Saxon should ever have been spilled! * but hence are the title-deeds to our lands and tenements, the perpetuity of our power and dominion.

Henry. To preserve them from jeopardy, I must have silver in store; I must have horses and armor, wherewith to satisfy the cravings of the soldier, always sharp, and sharpest of all after fighting.

Savage. My liege must also have other things, which escaped his recollection.

Henry. Store of hides, and of the creatures that were within them; store of bacon; store of oats and barley, of rye and good wheaten corn; hemp, shipping, masts, anchors; pine-tree and its pitch from the Norwegian, yew-tree from Corse and Dalmat. Divers other commodities must be procured from the ruler of the Adriatic, from him who never was infant nor stripling, whom God took by the right hand and taught to walk by himself the first hour. Moreover, I must have instruments of mine own device, weighty and exceeding costly; such as machinery for beating down walls. Nothing of these have escaped my knowlege or memory; but the recital of some befits a butler or sutler or armorer better than a king.

* The Danes under Harold were not numerous, and there were few vestiges of the Britons out of Wales and Cornwall.

Savage. And yet, methinks, sir, there are others which you might have mentioned and have not, the recital of which would befit a king, rather than sutler, butler, or armorer: they are, indeed, the best and most necessary things in the world to batter down your enemy's walls with.

Henry. What may they be? You must find them.

Savage. Sir, you have found them, and must keep them: they are the hearts of your subjects. Your horse will not gallop far without them, though you empty into his manger all the garners of Surrey. Wars are requisite to diminish the power of your barons, by keeping them long and widely separate from the main body of retainers, and under the ken of a stern and steady prince, watching their movements, curbing their discourses, and inuring them to regular and sharp discipline. In general, they are the worthless exalted by the weak, and dangerous from wealth ill-acquired and worse expended. The whole people is a good king's household: quiet and orderly when well treated, and ever in readiness to defend him against the malice of the disappointed, the perfidy of the ungrateful, and the usurpation of the familiar. Act in such guise, most glorious Henry, that the king may say *my* people, and the people may say *our* king: I then will promise you more, passing any computation, than I refused you this morning; the enjoyment of a blessing to which the conquest of France is in comparison as a broken flag-staff,—self-approbation[2] in government and security in power. A Norman by descent, and an Englishman by birth and inheritance, the humiliation of France is requisite to my sense even of quiet enjoyment. Nevertheless, I cannot delude my understanding, on which is impressed this truth; namely, that the condition of a people which hath made many conquests doth ultimately become worse than that of the conquered. For, the conquered have no longer to endure the sufferings of weakness or the struggles of strength; and some advantages are usually holden forth to keep them peaceable and contented: but under a conquering prince the people are shadows, which lessen and lessen as he mounts in glory, until at last they become, if I may reasonably say it and unreprovedly, a thing of nothing, a shapeless form.

[2 From "self-approbation" to "power" added in 2nd ed.]

It[3] is my office and my duty to provide that this evil, in the present day, do not befall us; and that our late descendants, with the same incitements to bravery, the same materials and means of greatness, may deserve as well of your family, my liege, as we have deserved of you.

Henry.   Faith! I could find it in my heart, Sir Arnold, to clip thine eagle's claws, and perch thee somewhere in the peerage.

Savage.   Measureless is the distance between my liege and me; but I occupy the second rank among men now living, forasmuch as, under the guidance of Almighty God, the most discreet and courageous have appointed me, unworthy as I am, to be the great comprehensive symbol of the English people.

Writers differ on the first appointment of Speaker in the House of Commons, for want rather of reflection than of inquiry. The Saxons had frequently such chiefs; not always, nor regularly. In the reign of William Rufus there was a great council of parliament at Rockingham, as may be seen in the history of Eadmerus: his words are, *totius regni adunatio.* He reports that a certain *knight* came forth and stood before the *people,* and spoke in the name and in the behalf of all. Peter de Montford, in the reign of Henry III., spoke *vice totius communitatis, and consented* to the banishment of Ademar de Valence, Bishop of Winchester. A Sir John Bushey was the first presented by the Commons to the King in full parliament. Elsynge calls him " a special minion " to Richard II. It appears that he, like all his predecessors, was chosen for one particular speech, purpose, or sitting.

Sir Arnold Savage, according to Elsynge, " was the first who appears *upon any record* " to have been appointed to the dignity as now constituted. He[4] was elected a second time four years afterward, a rare honor in earlier days; and during this precedency he headed the Commons, and delivered their Resolutions in the plain words recorded by Hakewell.

The business on which the dialogue is founded may be described by an extract from Rapin, who speaks of *remonstrance* only :—

" Le roi, ayant représenté à ce parlement le besoin qu'il avait d'un secours extraordinaire, les Communes allerent en corps lui présenter une Adresse dans laquelle elles lui remontraient que, sans fouler son peuple, il pouvoit subvenir à ses besoins. Elles exposaient que le clergé possédait la troisième partie des biens du royaume, et que, ne rendant au roi aucun service personnel, il était juste qu'il contribuât de ses richesses

---

[3 From " It " to " you " (5 lines) added in 2nd ed.]
[4 From " He " to " Hakewell " (6 lines) added in 2nd ed.   At end of note " In " to " characteristic " (3 lines) added in 3rd ed.]

aux besoins pressans de l'Etat. L'archevêque de Canterbury disait que leur demande n'avait pour fondement que l'irréligion et l'avarice."

The reformers, we see, **were** atheists in those days, **as in ours : to strip** off what is superfluous was **to expose** the body politic to decay.

In decorating the people's **House of** Parliament, it **is** resolved to admit no memorial of **the man without whom neither** house nor parliament **would exist.   Poetry and fable are thought more** characteristic.

III. OLIVER CROMWELL AND WALTER NOBLE.*

Cromwell. **What** brings thee **back from** Staffordshire, **friend** Walter ?

Noble. I hope, General Cromwell, to persuade **you that the** death **of Charles will be** considered by all Europe as **a most** atrocious action.

Cromwell. Thou **hast already persuaded me : what then ?**

Noble. Surely, then **you will prevent it,** for your authority is **great. Even those who** upon **their** consciences found him **guilty would remit** the penalty of blood, some from policy, some **from mercy. I have** conversed with Hutchinson, with Ludlow,† **your friend and mine,** with Henry Nevile, and Walter **Long :**

*¹He represented **the city of** Lichfield : he lived familiarly with the best patriots of the age, remonstrated with Cromwell, and retired from public life on the punishment of Charles. The memorial of my ancestor's virtues I hold in trust for the benefit **of** our descendants.

[". . . Oliver Cromwell and that Michael (misnamed by him Walter) Noble, . . . **some** of whose blood ran **in** Landor's own veins ; his grandfather, **Robert** Landor of Rugeley, having (in 1732) married the **sole** daughter **and** heiress of Noble's grandson Walter, of Chorley Hall, Longdon, through **whom** Landor's father inherited a good estate."— Forster's Life, **243.** (Imag. Convers. i., 1824. i., 1826. Works, ii., 1846. Works, iii., 1876.)]

†Ludlow, a most **humane and** temperate man, signed the death-warrant of Charles, for violating **the** constitution he had sworn to defend, for depriving **the** subject of property, liberty, limbs, and life unlawfully. In equity he could do no otherwise ; and to equity was the only appeal, since **the** laws of the **land** had been **erased by** the king himself.

[¹ Footnotes **added** in 3rd ed.]

you will **oblige these** worthy friends, and unite in your favor the suffrages **of the truest and** trustiest men living. There are **many** others, **with whom I am** in no habits of intercourse, who are known **to** entertain **the** same sentiments ; and these also **are** among the country gentlemen, to whom our parliament owes **the** better **part** of its reputation.

Cromwell. You **country** gentleman bring **with you into the** People's House a freshness and sweet savor, **which** our citizens lack mightily. I would **fain** merit your esteem, heedless of those pursy fellows from **hulks** and warehouses, with one ear lappeted by the pen behind it, **and the other** an heirloom, as Charles would **have** had it, **in Laud's** star-chamber. Oh ! they are proud and bloody men. **My** heart melts ; **but,** alas ! my authority is null : **I am** the servant of the Commonwealth. I will not, dare not, **betray it.** If Charles Stuart had threatened my death only, **in the** letter **we** ripped **out** of the saddle, **I would** have reproved **him** manfully and turned him adrift : but **others are concerned ;** lives more precious than mine, **worn** as it is with fastings, prayers, long services, and preyed upon by a pouncing disease. The Lord hath led him **into the** toils laid for the innocent. Foolish **man ! he** never **could eschew** evil **counsel.**

Noble. In comparison **with you, he is** but as a pinnacle to **a** buttress. I acknowledge his weaknesses, and cannot wink upon his crimes : but **that** which you visit as the heaviest of them **per-**haps was not so, **although** the most disastrous to both parties,——the bearing of arms against his people. He fought for what he considered his hereditary property ; we do the same : should we be hanged for losing a lawsuit ?

Cromwell. No, unless it **is the second. Thou** talkest finely **and foolishly,** Wat, **for a man of thy calm discernment.** If a rogue holds a pistol to my **breast, do I** ask him who he is ? Do I care whether **his** doublet **be** of catskin or of dogskin ? Fie upon such **wicked** sophisms ! Marvellous, how the devil works **upon good men's** minds ! Friend ! [2] friend ! hast thou lost thy **recollection ? On** the third of June, 1628, an usher stood at the door **of our** Commons-house, to hinder any member leaving it, **under pain** of being sent to the Tower. On the fifth of the same

[2 From "Friend ! " to "exempted" (37 lines) added in 3rd ed. For "He" 1st ed. reads "Charles."]

month, the Speaker said he had received the King's order to interrupt any who should utter a word against his ministers. In the following year, we might have justly hanged him for the crime of forgery, seeing that on the twenty-first of January he commanded his printer, Norton, to falsify the text of his own *Declaration*, in which he had acknowledged our rights, and had been paid handsomely for the acknowledgment. I sorely fear the month of January is marked in the Calendar by the finger of the Almighty, for the heavy chastisement of this misdeed. We must take heed unto our ways, and never again be led into the wicked temptation of trusting the false and the reprobate. Equity might demand from the traitor more than his worthless and pernicious life. Equity might retaliate on him what Eliot and other most innocent and most virtuous men have suffered : pestilential imprisonment, lingering, painful, incurable disease, fetters and thumbscrews, racks, and mutilations. Should the guiltless have suffered these things rather than the guilty ?—the defender of his home and property rather than the robber who broke into them ? If the extinction of a spark prevents worse things than the conflagration of twenty cities, if it prevents the expansion of principles endemically noxious through incalculable ages, such as slavish endurance and all unmanly propensities, I would never take by the collar him who resolutely setteth his foot thereon. Whether a grain of dust be blown away in the morning, in the noon, or in the evening, what matter ? But it imports very seriously whether it be blown in the eyes and darken the sight of a nation. This is the difference between him who dies in the solitude of his chamber, and him whom halberds, by God's ordinance, may surround upon the scaffold.

Noble. From so cruel an infliction let me hope our unfortunate king may be exempted. He was always more to be dreaded by his friends than by his enemies, and now by neither.

Cromwell. God forbid that Englishmen should be feared by Englishmen ! but to be daunted by the weakest, to bend before the worst—I tell thee, Walter Noble, if Moses and the Prophets commanded me to this villainy, I would draw back and mount my horse.

Noble. I wish that our history, already too dark with blood, should contain, as far as we are concerned in it, some unpolluted pages.

Cromwell. 'Twere better, much better. Never shall I be called, I promise thee, an unnecessary shedder of blood. Remember, my good prudent friend, of what materials our sectaries are composed : what hostility against all eminence, what rancor against all glory.[3] Not only kingly power offends them, but every other ; and they talk of *putting to the sword*, as if it were the quietest, gentlest, and most ordinary thing in the world. The knaves even dictate from their stools and benches to men in armor, bruised and bleeding for them ; and with schooldames' scourges in their fists do they give counsel to those who protect them from the cart and halter. In the name of the Lord, I must spit outright (or worse) upon these crackling, bouncing firebrands, before I can make them tractable.

Noble. I lament their blindness ; but follies wear out the faster by being hard run upon. This fermenting sourness will presently turn vapid, and people will cast it out. I am not surprised that you are discontented and angry at what thwarts your better nature. But come, Cromwell, overlook them, despise them, and erect to yourself a glorious name by sparing a mortal enemy.

Cromwell. A glorious name, by God's blessing, I will erect ; and all our fellow-labourers shall rejoice at it : but I see better than they do the blow descending on them, and my arm better than theirs can ward it off. Noble, thy heart overflows with kindness for Charles Stuart : if he were at liberty tomorrow by thy intercession, he would sign thy death-warrant the day after, for serving the Commonwealth. A generation of vipers! there is nothing upright or grateful in them : never was there a drop of even Scotch blood in their veins. Indeed, we have a clew to their bedchamber still hanging on the door, and I suspect that an Italian fiddler or French valet has more than once crossed the current.

Noble. That may be : nor indeed is it credible that any royal or courtly family has gone on for three generations without

[3 First ed. reads : "glory. How the knaves . . . . . for them ! with what fatherly scourges," &c.]

a spur from interloper.   **Look** at France! some stout Parisian saint performed the last miracle there.*

Cromwell.   Now thou **talkest** gravely and **sensibly** : I could hear thee **discourse** thus for hours together.

Noble.   Hear me, Cromwell, with equal patience on matters more important.   We all **have our** sufferings : why increase one another's wantonly?   Be the blood Scotch or English, French or Italian, a drummer's or a buffoon's, it carries a soul upon its stream ; and every soul has many places to touch at, and much business to perform, before it reaches its ultimate destination.   Abolish the power of Charles ; extinguish not his virtues.[4]   Whatever is worthy to be loved for any thing is worthy to be preserved.   A wise and dispassionate legislator, if any such should arise among men, will not condemn to death him who has done, or is likely to do, more service than injury to society.   Blocks and gibbets are the nearest objects to ours, and their business is never with virtues or with hopes.   Justice [5] upon earth has forgotten half her lesson, and repeats the other half badly.   God commanded her to reward and to punish. She would tell you that punishment is the reward of the wicked, and that the rewards of the good belong to him whose delight is their distribution in another place.   She is neither blind, as some have represented her, nor clear-sighted : she is one-eyed, and looks fixedly and fondly with her one eye upon edge-tools and halters.   The best actions are never recompensed, and the worst are seldom chastised.   The virtuous man passes by without a *good morrow* from us, and the malefactor may walk at large where he will, provided he walk far enough from encroachment on our passions and their playthings.   Let us,

---

* [6] The birth of Louis XIV. is somewhat like a miracle to true believers, while among sceptics the principal **doubt is** not whether the child was supposititious, but whether he was so after his birth or before.

[[4] First ed. reads: "virtues ; he may be a good father who was a bad king.   Whatever," &c.]

[[5] From "Justice" to "law" (31 lines) added in 2nd ed.   From "We" to "impediments" (7 lines) added in 3rd ed.   From "Reverting" to "him" (19 lines) added in 2nd ed.   From "*Cromwell*" to "clemency" (19 lines) added in 3rd ed.]

[[6] Footnote not in 1st ed.]

Cromwell, in God's name, turn the laws to their right intention : let us render it the interest of all to love them and keep them holy. They are at present, both in form and essence, the greatest curse that society labours under ; the scorn of the wicked, the consternation of the good, the refuge of those who violate, and the ruin of those who appeal to them.

Cromwell. You have paid, I see, chancery fees, Walter.

Noble. I should then have paid not only what is exorbitant, but what is altogether undue. Paying a lawyer, in any court, we pay over again what we have paid before. If government has neglected to provide that our duties be taught us, and our lives, properties, and station in society be secured, what right has it to one farthing from us? For what else have our forefathers and ourselves been taxed? — for what else are magistrates of any kind appointed? There is an awfulness in symmetry which chastens even the wildest, and there is a terror in distortion at which they strike and fly. It is thus in regard to law. We should be slow in the censure of princes, and slower in the chastisement. Kingship is a profession which has produced few among the most illustrious, many among the most despicable, of the human race. As in our days they are educated and treated, he is deserving of no slight commendation who rises in moral worth to the level of his lowest subject ; so manifold and so great are the impediments.

Reverting to the peculiar case of Charles, in my opinion you are ill justified by morality or policy in punishing him capitally. The representatives of the people ought to super-intend the education of their princes ; where they have omitted it, the mischief and the responsibility rest with them. As kings are the administrators of the Commonwealth, they must submit their whole household to the national inspection ; on which principle, the preceptors of their children should be appointed by parliament ; and the pupils, until they have attained their majority, should be examined twice annually on the extent and on the direction of their studies, in the presence of seven men at least, chosen out of the Commons-house by ballot. Nothing of the kind having been done, and the principles of this unfortunate king having been distorted by a wrong education, and retained in their obliquity by evil counsellors, I would now, on the

reclamation both of generosity and of justice, try clemency.   If
it fails, his adherents will be confounded at his perfidy, and, expecting a like return for their services, will abandon him.

Cromwell.   Whatever his education was, thinkest thou he was
not wise enough to know his wickedness, his usurpation and
tyranny, when he resolved to rule without a parliament; to levy
taxes, to force consciences, to imprison, to slay, at his own arbi-
trament and pleasure?   Some time before the most violent of his
outrages, had he not received a grant of money from us on conditions which he violated?   He then seized forcibly what belonged to the public; and, because we remonstrated against this
fraud and theft, did he not prosecute us as rebels?   Whereas,
when a king acts against the laws or without them, there can be
but one rebel in the kingdom.   Accomplices there may be; and
such we may treat with mildness, if they do not wring and wrest
it away from us and turn it against us, pushing down those who
raised them.   When the leading stag of such a herd is intractably
wild, and obstinately vicious to his keepers, he ought to be ham-
strung and thrown across the paling, wherever he is overtaken.
What! pat his hide forsooth! hug his neck, garland his horns,
pipe to him, try gentleness, try clemency!   Walter, Walter! we
laugh at speculators.

Noble.   Many indeed are ready enough to laugh at speculators,
because many profit, or expect to profit, by established and widen-
ing abuses.   Speculations toward evil lose their name by adoption;
speculations toward good are for ever speculations, and he who
hath proposed them is a chimerical and silly creature.   Among [7]
the matters under this denomination I never find a cruel project,
I never find an oppressive or unjust one: how happens it?

Cromwell.   Proportions should exist in all things.   Sovereigns are paid higher than others for their office; they should
therefore be punished more severely for abusing it, even if the
consequences of this abuse were in nothing more grievous or extensive.   We cannot clap them in the stocks conveniently, nor
whip them at the market-place.   Where there is a crown there
must be an axe: I would keep it there only.

Noble.   Lop off the rotten, press out the poisonous, preserve

[7 From "among" to "it" (3 lines) added in 2nd ed.]

the rest ; let it suffice to have given this memorable example of national power and justice.

Cromwell. Justice is perfect; an attribute of God: we must not trifle with it.

Noble. Should we be less merciful to our fellow-creatures than to our domestic animals? Before we deliver them to be killed, we weigh their services against their inconveniences. On the foundation of policy, when we have no better, let us erect the trophies of humanity: let us consider that, educated in the same manner and situated in the same position, we ourselves might have acted as reprovably. Abolish that for ever which must else for ever generate abuses ; and attribute the faults of the man to the office, not the faults of the office to the man.

Cromwell. I [8] have no bowels for hypocrisy, and I abominate and detest kingship.

Noble. I abominate and detest hangmanship ; but in certain stages of society both are necessary. Let them go together ; we want neither now.

Cromwell. Men, [9] like nails, lose their usefulness when they lose their direction and begin to bend : such nails are then thrown into the dust or into the furnace. I must do my duty ; I must accomplish what is commanded me ; I must not be turned aside. I am loth to be cast into the furnace or the dust ; but God's will be done! Prythee, Wat, since thou readest, as I see, the books of philosophers, didst thou ever hear of Digby's remedies by sympathy?

Noble. Yes, formerly.

Cromwell. Well, now, I protest, I do believe there is something in them. To cure my headache, I must breathe a vein in the neck of Charles.

Noble. Oliver, Oliver! others are wittiest over wine, thou over blood : cold-hearted, cruel man.*

[8 From "I" to "hypocrisy" added in 3rd ed.]

[9 From "Men" to "done!" (6 lines) added in 3rd ed. **Footnote added** in 3rd ed.]

* Cromwell was not cruel. Had he been less sparing of the worst blood in the three kingdoms, the best would never have been spilled upon the scaffold ; and England would have been exempt from the ignominy of Sidney's death, Milton's proscription, the sale of the nation to the second Charles, and the transfer of both to Louis.

Cromwell. Why, dost thou verily think me so, Walter?
Perhaps thou art right in the main : but He alone who fashioned
me in my mother's womb, and who sees things deeper than we do,
knows that.

IV. KING JAMES I. AND ISAAC CASAUBON.[1] *

James. Good M. Casaubon, I am vexed and perturbed in
spirit, to find that my moderation and my zeal, which never
has departed from it, should be opposed and thwarted by the
pontificals.

Casaubon. Touch [2] gently, sire, the hinder quarters of a
vicious horse, and he will lay down his ears and kick ; smite him

[1] For Isaac Casaubon's life see Mark Pattison's biography of that
scholar. After the death of Henry IV., under whose patronage he had
been made librarian of the Royal library in Paris, Casaubon found that the
difficulties he had experienced from his Roman Catholic opponents were
likely to be even greater than they had been during the king's life. He
accordingly accepted James' invitation to come to England, where he was
received with the distinction his learning demanded. Nearly every Sunday James and he had long conversations, chiefly on Theology, of which
this may be supposed to be one. (Imag. Convers., i., 1824;
i., 1826. Works, i., 1846. Works, ii., 1876.)]

* Casaubon wrote a treatise *De Libertate Ecclesiastica*, of which 264 pp.
were printed, when Henry IV., on the agreement of the Venetians with
the pope, forbade the continuation, and attempted to suppress the commencement. Some copies escaped ; and Goldast inserted the 264 pp. in
the first volume of his *Monarchia Imperii*.

Pompous as James was, he was less unbending than many constitutional
kings have been. The royal practice of unnatural stiffness did not prevail in Europe until the minor potentates thought it becoming to
imitate Louis XIV., and took that part of his character which was the
easiest to copy. Unbendingness, in the moral as in the vegetable world, is
an indication as frequently of unsoundness as of strength. Indeed, wise
men, kings as well as others, have been free from it. Stiff necks are
diseased ones.

[2] From "Touch" to "even" (51 lines) added in 3rd ed. This Conversation is much altered in the 2nd ed. and again in the 3rd. It has
been found impossible, without over-weighting the Conversation with
notes, to comment on all verbal alterations. But all important alterations
have been noticed.]

resolutely and stoutly, and, behold! he draws his legs in, and sidles toward you.

James. As I am a king and a Christian, I have a mind to act vigorously and with my whole courage. Methinks it would not be misplaced. What are these doughty bishops of Rome, forsooth, that they should lay hands thus rudely upon God's anointed? I shudder at their violence, though I see it athwart times gone by. Raymond the Sixth, Count of Toulouse—God forfend that any thing mischievous should lie upon the number, I being, as you know, the sixth monarch of my name in Scotland—what think you, Casaubon?

Casaubon. I see no reason why your Majesty should apprehend any.

James. Raymond then, a descendant of Charlemagne, was dragged to the Church of Saint Ægidius, naked to the waist and with a halter round his neck, to be flogged by a monk while the pope's legate was at dinner. His son, although a Catholic, yet being the begotten of a reputed heretic, was stripped, not of his shirt, like the father, but of all his domains and hereditaments. He fought, however, so valiantly (which I would likewise do were I not unaccountably afraid of a naked sword) that the pope could extort from him only the county of Venaissin, the richest of his lands indeed, with seventy-three castles, on the other side of the Rhone, and 13,800 marks in silver.

Casaubon. Crimes, of which the heresy of princes is the richest, fertilize Saint Peter's patrimony. The celebrated Queen Giovanna, of Naples, a descendant from the brother of Saint Louis, accused of privity to the murder of her husband—

James. I do not believe a word of it; a fabrication, a forgery! Proceed forthwith to the pope's part in the business; there lies the guilt: say on.

Casaubon. The beautiful young queen had need of his protection. Although the people of Provence had obliged her to swear upon the Gospels that she would alienate none of her dominions, his Holiness, a few months afterward, compelled her to sell him Avignon.

James. Ay, and never paid her. I know not which is the more execrable; that a vicar of Christ should be guilty of simony, and of exacting the commission of a perjury, or that a people should require an oath from a prince.

Casaubon. The people, sire, have sometimes been suspicious; and overwatchfulness hath made them feverish: but pontiffs in all ages have mounted and ridden hard both restive rulers and well-broken ones.

James. Afore God! my back shall never bend under them. If they run restive with me, they shall bleed in both flanks ere the last leg quit the stirrup.

Casaubon. Not only counts, lords paramount, as your Majesty hath recited, but even kings[3] have been stripped bare, and emperors unbreeched, by the popes, who followed them up into their very dreams, threatening them as disobedient children, rod in hand. The Emperor Maximilian swore to defend the freedom of religion as declared in the Confession of Augsburg. Terrified by the pope's denunciations, he rescinded the diploma; and he protested, in excuse of such conduct, that he saw Pius shaking a scourge over his shoulder in his sleep. Pius the Fifth, too, commanded Charles the Ninth, of France, to revoke the Edict of Orleans on religious toleration. The holy father was introduced into the farce by the *Most Apostolic* and *Most Christian* Majesties. They prevailed on his Holiness that he should oblige them to loosen and lay aside their sacred obligations. On timorous and treacherous men like these depended, and still depend, the prosperity and improvement of the human race. Charles and Maximilian, the reverse of Achilles, abhorred the gates of hell far more than falsehood.

James. No promises, oaths, or treaties, are sacred any longer than these holinesses and beatitudes will permit. Even Cæsars are super-Cæsared by their tenants of the vatican. Nothing is too high or too low for the vultures of the Seven Hills. Not only churches and kingdoms are their quarry, but they swoop into colleges and kitchens, and order what our manciples shall bring into the buttery. One would think they might at least be as complacent as owls are to owlets, and cats to kittens. No such thing; nor do they keep under their own hedges, but prowl far a-field. They pull a tag from the fur of a lawyer if it looks a little too rough, or doth not sit to their liking. Thus, in 1220, unless I mistake the year, Honorius, by his *Interdict*, took away

[3 " Kings " to " hand " (4 lines) added in 2nd ed. From " The " to " at " (42 lines) added in 3rd ed.]

from the University of Paris the power of conferring degrees in civil law. So we see not only the consolations of religion are snatched at once from the innocent as well as from the guilty, whenever a pope cries for a penny and cannot get it; but even the rights of the injured are left without defence. The worst is, that anointed kings are treated so unceremoniously. Gregory the Seventh excommunicated the Emperor Henry the Fourth, and refused him absolution until he had sitten at his gate three days, and barefoot. Soon afterward he repents of this clemency, deposes him, and raises a duke of Suabia to the throne. His successor would put anybody upon mine, excepting the rightful master. But I advise him never to grapple with such a wrestler as I am, until he hath well oiled himself, or I may peradventure make him blow his fingers and caper. I came forward with the olive branch in my hand, little thinking it a plant for a toad in his rage to spit at.

Casaubon. Your Majesty could entertain but feeble hopes of accommodation where avarice and pride are the directors of every council. The advantage, however, which I pointed out to your Majesty is obtained, inasmuch as you have hung your proofs upon the highest peg in the chambers of the vatican : and these manifest to the world below the sincerity of your heart, and the solidity of your arguments.

James. And[4] yet they call me *sectary!*

Casaubon. Those who dissent from the domineering party have always been thus stigmatised. When the pope called Luther, and afterward your Majesty, by such an appellation, a small particle of learning might have shown him that the title better suited himself. According to Cato, in his "Treatise on Husbandry," "*Sectarius* porcus est qui gregem præcedens ducit."

James. I am truly and completely a Catholic. How can ever the name be refused me without a manifest and gross injustice?—acknowledging as I do the Three Creeds, the Œcumenical Councils, and every doctrine taught as necessary to salvation in the four first centuries of Christianity. And being so in all sincerity, I could have wished that whatever leads to fellowship and concord were tolerated and encouraged. It is not the interest of kings to carry the forest-laws into churches. On

[4 From " And " to " sincerity " (13 lines) added in 3rd ed.]

this principle and persuasion, I admitted many papists to offices about my person, not expecting that they would prepare for me such a blazing fire so early in the season ; yet, such is my spirit of peace and conciliation, though I would rather keep them out of my cellar and my kitchen, I should not however be loth to go with them, if their priests would allow me, to the communion-table.

The Gospel says, *This is my body ;* it does not say *how.* I am far from angry with the mass-maker for knowing more about it than I do, or than my Master chose to tell my betters, His apostles and disciples ; or for insisting on transubstantiation, the name of which was not in existence for some hundred years after He left the earth. Let every Christian take the sacrament; let families, friends, dependants, neighbours, take it together; let each apply to it his own idea of its import and its essence. At a commemoration dinner, one would wish something which he does not see upon the table ; another is desirous that the dish which stands before him were away : yet surely both may find that wherein their tastes agree ; and nothing, of what is present or of what is absent, can alter their sentiments as to the harmony of the meeting or the object of the entertainment. Such feelings—let me ascend from the little to the great, from the ordinary to the solemn—will the Christian's be at the sacrament of the eucharist. The memory of that day when it first was celebrated makes me anxious to open my arms toward all, and to treat the enemies of my throne with the charity of the Gospel.

We gratify our humors in sovereignty, in Christianity our affections ; in this always our best, in that often our worst. You know not, M. Casaubon, how pleasant a thing it is to converse naturally, because you have always done so ; but we kings feel it sensibly, those at least among us to whom God hath vouch-safed a plain understanding. It is like unto a removal from the curtained and closed chamber of sickness, where every footfall is suspended and measured, every voice constrained and lowered, into our native air again, amid the songs and piping of our shepherds, and the wilder and more exuberant harmony of our woodlands. To you, the whole intellectual world lies open : we must speak in epigrams or in oracles. The book, however, which I hold in my hand teaches me that the practice should be laid aside, and that we ought not to be ashamed of acknowledging a sort of relation, at home, with those whom in the house of God we call our brethren. If I fall rather short of this, I do not pretend to tell a man how he should sing, or how he should pronounce his language, or upon which side he should lie in bed ; * much less would I admonish him in what manner he should think on subjects which concern not me. Everybody[5] knows that I am a great deal more liberal and merciful than the lady who occupied the throne before me ; yet surely my Cousin Elizabeth ought to have been more tolerant of those who believed too much : she who believed that gallants could be in love with her at seventy. I would exclude none from the benefit of law, none from the enjoyment of dignity : I would establish the Catholic peers in that House from which their friends Garnet and Catesby would, to serve their own purposes, have exploded them. What think you ?

Casaubon. I see not how your Majesty can receive as your counsellors, or indeed as any part of those who are to govern, judge, or administrate, men who profess that another has by right a greater power in this realm, not only than your Majesty, but than all the three estates conjointly. They are bound to assist in · placing the instruction of your people out of your hands ; they are bound to murder you if you resist the authority of the pope, or even if they are informed by him that such an action is of advantage to the Church : indeed any one may murder you, let him only be persuaded by two or three factious but learned men that it is conducive to the interests of his *Holiness.*

James. It[7] is impossible that the common sense of mankind shall permit such a pest as popery to exist much longer ; but there will be smoke and stench for some time after the explosion. So long as this nuisance is reeking on the earth, religion will be

---

*[6] Yet never did king interfere so minutely in the private concerns of his subjects. Here, as men are apt to do, he claims exemption from the very failing to which he was most liable.

[5 From "Everybody" to "seventy" (6 lines) added in 3rd ed.]

[7 "It" to "virtues" (87 lines) added in 3rd ed. Portions of this long addition and of the two following speeches of Casaubon and James appear, in an altered form, as a footnote in both the 1st and 2nd editions.]

[6 Note added in 3rd ed.]

a prostitute, civilization a starveling, and freedom a dishonest outcast and maimed beggar. This grieveth me : for it is only in
king's palaces that freedom can be properly educated and worthily
entertained.

Casaubon. But, sire ! what security for the palace when the
parliament-house is blown up ? Garnet, being asked whether he
held it lawful to extinguish the innocent with the guilty, answered
in the affirmative, if as much advantage were derivable from it as
would compensate for the loss of the unoffending. Murder, then,
may be committed, and even without advantage. The Jesuit,
the Catholic in perfection, requires only a balance of good, and
reckons the murder itself as an indifferent and inoffensive method
of obtaining it.

James. The same doctor, in another place, delivered it as his
opinion that the exploit was not only lawful, but would even be
a most glorious one indeed, if it eventually turned out well for
Mother-church. She hath been sharpening her teeth for us until
some of the grinders begin to ache, and the rest are loosening.
This puts her into worse and worse humor, and makes her look
uglier than usual.

What think you now ? am I not liberal enough in all conscience, when I declare my readiness to admit her children about
me, if they will only come without cutlery and crackers ?

Casaubon. If their conscience is not at their own disposal,
can we reasonably hope that their consent will be ? The
question, which your Majesty hath cited, was not an idle nor
a speculative one : it brushed the way to the murder of two
monarchs of France,—Henry the Third and Fourth. The
name itself of the former was inserted in a thesis for *illustration ;*
whether it were lawful to slay, for instance, Henry the Third,
after he had begun to be called a tyrant by a few seditious but
learned men. Such are the expressions.

James. Lamentable ! that the governments of Europe should
have permitted such questions to be agitated by the clergy,
to whom they least appertain. Exterminate the appointed and
anointed of the Lord ! It becomes us to seize, to imprison, and
to punish capitally any religionist, pope or other, who disseminates
or countenances such bloody rebellion at once against king and
God.

Casaubon. The first attempt to murder the Prince of Orange was committed by one who carried in the same pocket with his pistol a string of prayers to the Virgin Mary and the angel Gabriel, and a catechism of the Jesuits.

James. The death of the Prince of Orange was commanded by a lawful king; and, although he might employ worthier instruments, he being anointed, and thereby judge supreme in his own cause, had an unquestionable right to inflict the penalty. He had disobedient subjects to deal with, instigated by the devil of democracy; and the Prince of Orange was a ringleader of republicans, rank and riotous in his love of power; which love I hold unlawful and ungodly in any under the throne.

Casaubon. Sire! What I ventured to commemorate was mainly in demonstration that not only Jesuits and Dominicans were assassins, but, under the influence of the same religion, even kings themselves.

James. Nay, nay, nay, M. Isaac! A king may peradventure slay unadvisedly, rashly, wrathfully; but a king can never be an assassin, even though he should smite unto the death with his own right hand; forasmuch as the Lord hath given him the sceptre in Israel. King Philip, of whom you made reference, did encompass and bring about the decease of his son Charles, and likewise of his brother (not uterine but spurious), John of Austria, as many sound scholars and rational thinkers do surmise; yet reverential awe hath alway stood between him and that untoward appellation of assassin. Therefore, were it only for the sake of rhetoric and euphony, I do think I would cast about for some palatabler word. It beseems and behooves the learned, most of all, to hold their caps before their faces where any foulness is, and not to see it; but, if they have seen it, to put the same before their mouths, and never to let such expressions break out full syllabled. As for the pope, indeed, I do not acknowledge in him either prince or priest; wherefore you may take him and Jacques Clément by the throat again, and deal with them condignly.

Casaubon. Clément, being interrogated on the reasons why he undertook the perpetration of his atrocious crime, said plainly that he did it because the king was preparing to aid and succor the Protestants in Germany; and that, intending thereby a thing offensive to God, he was worthy of death: he added, *The pope is God, and God is pope.*

James.   Christ forgive me! but I am almost fain to cry out, Happy the people whose gods were leeks!   Religion never taught them that perfidy and murder are virtues.   I apprehend that my intentions must be deferred.   O Lord! preserve my life for Thy glory! preserve it for the union of Christians! Casaubon, it is verily, though we enter thereby into bliss, an ugly thing to die.   The malignity of popery may soften: I should be sorry to inflict new pains and penalties.

Casaubon.   I would not inflict any.   I would authorise no inabilities or privations for a difference in mere articles of faith: for instance, it would be tyranny or madness to declare a man incapable of beating the enemy because he believes in transubstantiation: but I would exclude from all power, all trust, all office whoever should assert that any man has legitimate power of any kind within this realm, unless it repose in, or originate from, the king or parliament, or both united.[8]   According to confessors no treason of a priest against a king is criminal.   Emmanuel Sa, in his guide to them, says, "The rebellion of a priest against a king is not treason, because 'non est principi subjectus;'" and again: "Tyrannice gubernans justum acquisitum dominium non potest spoliari sine publico judicio; latâ vero sententiâ potest quisque fieri executor."

James.   Horrible! Christ says, *My kingdom is not of this world*: the pope says, *My kingdom is.*   Pius V. excited to rebellion the subjects of Elizabeth; Clement VIII. (it is ludicrous to hear the titles of these ruffians) ordered all the Roman Catholics, "quantum in ipsis esset, ut post Elizabethæ obitum rex eligeretur, omni sanguinis propinquitate spretâ."   For this purpose it was requisite that the consciences of men should be modified;

[8 First ed. reads: "united.   The Council of Trent has defined and settled the questions at issue in the Roman Catholic creed so that the popes can pretend to teach nothing new for the future; matters of discipline are likewise fixed.   The appointment of ecclesiastical dignities of every degree may be safely entrusted to the native hierarchy in each kingdom.   Your Majesty has then a right to demand from your Roman Catholic subjects that no Papal bull, no order, brief, decree, or mandate of any kind be received in your dominions.   It is singular," &c. (42 lines below.)]

and hence arose *mental reservation*, to which all the abominations of other religions, even of popery itself, are trifles. Christ says, " Let your discourse be yea, yea ; nay, nay ; " the Jesuit says, supported by the pope, " The speech by equivocation being saved from a lie, the same speech may be without perjury confirmed by oath, or by any other way, though it were by receiving the sacrament, if just necessity so require." Cannot a lie be circuitous ? Whatever is said in order to make a man believe an untruth is a lie ; yet a Jesuit has no hesitation to swear it upon the eucharist ; and princes have no hesitation to let Jesuits be the instructors of youth ! Falsely have they been called the supporters of thrones : they never support them but when they can govern from them, by means of deluded or affrighted princes. The papacy is the guardian of governments as a bawd is the guardian of girls,—for profit. Antonius Capellus, a Franciscan friar, says that kings are unworthy of presiding over the church of their dominions, in any way whatever ; and that God in the books of Moses declares his dislike of them. Blasphemy ! Eudæmono Johannes, a monk of Crete, a true Jesuit, extols the son of the Emperor Henry IV. for insulting the dead body of his father, who had been disobedient to the See of Rome. The opinions of these men are not private ; they are sanctioned *facultate superiorum*, by the doctors of theology, and by the chancery of the papal court. The spirit of their church has always been and always will be the same, whenever it can exercise its authority,—arrogant, intolerant, persecuting, unforgiving. Its poison has been sublimated, and its froth and fumes have been condensed, by the Jesuits.

Casaubon. It is singular and anomalous in the political world, that subjects should claim a right of appeal to foreign princes ; and it is absurd to argue that the appeal is made not to the prince but to the priest, when the person is invested with both characters, and acts in both. It [9] was determined in the *Council of the Lateran*, by seventy bishops, in presence of the ambassadors of all the Christian princes, that the Holy See held a jurisdiction *in every place ;* that its authority extended over all ; that it was empowered to decide the causes of princes, to deprive them of their government, and to confer it on others at their own option.

[9 From " It " to " perjury" (9 lines) added in 3rd ed. This appears in part as a footnote in 2nd ed.]

On this principle, in the exercise of this authority, Pope Zacharias gave the crown of France to Charles Martel, ejecting Chilperic, and commanding a whole nation to commit a perjury.

James.[10]　What should I think, if the fellows of Trinity College in Cambridge, or of Christchurch in Oxford, rose from table, and shut themselves in their common-room for the day, and sent me word the next morning that they had appointed a head of the church, enclosing his circular, wherein he ordereth my obedience? Verily, from pure good-will, I should diet and scourge the knaves into their sounder senses, clapping up their headpiece, with his tiara on, in my fool's hospital, and giving him the precedency in it he had claimed outside. And yet, M. Casaubon, the fellows of either college are better scholars and honester men, I trow, than your pediculous friars and parti-colored bald-coot priests, into whose frowsy bodies, incrusted with libidinousness and blood, enters that legion-spirit which overshadows and shakes the world. I have exorcised my three kingdoms; and, by the Lord! if such spirit encroacheth, I will set those at him who shall leave him no easier a horn than Achelöusis, and no more tail than I have.

Casaubon.　It were an easy matter to prove that deacons, called subsequently cardinal-deacons, have no right to elect a pope; that they themselves were not a corporate body many centuries ago, much less an elective one, but rather so many gourds sprung up in one dark night, with nobody then to heed, and nobody now to pluck them.

James.　Nay, but they have though.

Casaubon.　Bishops, priests, and deacons were instituted by the apostles; and what proves that after their time we had no earthly and visible head of the church is this: on the decease of the twelve, the próvincial priests elected them, not without the suffrages of the people.

James.　We may hold back this latter part, M. Casaubon! Never [11] let people know it. All religions have their secrets and conveniences. Saint Cyprian in several places, and particularly in his epistle to Felix the presbyter, doth indeed tes-

---

[10 From "*James*" to "M. Casaubon" (29 lines) added in 2nd ed.]
[11 From "Never" to "conveniences" (2 lines) added in 3rd ed. From "Saint Cyprian" to "Antherus" (20 lines) added in 2nd ed., but slightly altered in 3rd ed.]

tify to the custom you have cited. A bishop thus elected was initiated into his ministry by the other bishops in the nearer dioceses; and it was decreed in the council of Nicæa that no fewer than three of them should attend on this occasion. Bonifacius the Third left the election to the priests and people, but usurped to himself the right of confirming it. Afterward the emperor's will and pleasure were consulted; Louis, the son of Charlemagne, was the first who waived the ceremony. Cardinals were instituted by Pope Marcellus, to bury and baptize. That there was no regular nor certain method of electing popes themselves is manifest by the Council holden at Rome in 610, which established one; but the establishment hath been sapped and subverted.

Casaubon. The violation mentioned by your Majesty of this ordinance, and of that order made in the council of Nicæa, are not the only ones. It was there determined that a bishop removed from a diocese could never be placed in another; which determination was unfixed by Pope Antherus.

James.[12] Well, well: let them overturn and overturn to their hearts' content, so that what they overturn do not fall against our shins. My bishops see no harm in removals, which they designate by the auspicious name of *trans-lation*. It were more prudent on my part, and more to the purpose, to touch upon the popes again.

Casaubon. Your Majesty needs not be reminded that, according to papal infallibility, every potentate in Europe is baseborn.

James. How? Do you mean spurious, or merely that he can be traced by genealogists to a low origin?

Casaubon. I mean a bastard, or the descendant of one; which, as affecting his right to the crown, is the same thing. Innocent III. prohibited marriages within the seventh degree of affinity: by which prohibition there not only is no crowned head, but no nobleman, in Europe, who is not a bastard or the descendant of one. What an immense field, what a forest, what a new world for absolution! What a mine of gold throughout the whole extent, all lying on the surface!

James. Yet those divines who prohibited marriages within the seventh degree put a niece into bed with her uncle, or an

[12 From "*James*" to "expert" (52 lines) added in 3rd ed.]

aunt into a nephew's, and tucked them up and wished them pleasant dreams. Show me the same fraudulence in any other religion, the same venality and impudence in the priesthood, and you shall have my crown for your pains, Master Isaac, and the head that is under it to boot.

Casaubon. Sire, it is easier to find flaws in the ring of Infallibility. At the Council of Chalcedon it was resolved that the Sees of Constantinople and Rome should possess equal authority. One century later a Council was convoked by the Emperor Justinian at Constantinople, where the patriarch presided, and no bishop of the Latin church attended ; none of them understanding Greek any more than they do now. In 680, another Council was assembled there under Constantine the Bearded, who himself presided at it, placing on his right the patriarchs of Constantinople and Antioch, on his left the deputies of Jerusalem and Rome. It was there that Pope Honorius was condemned. In 879, Pope John the Eighth declared that all are Judases who assert the Holy Ghost to proceed from the Father and the Son.

James. Another short vacation for Infallibility !

Casaubon. In 1215, a General Council was holden in Saint John Lateran, by Pope Innocent the Third, forbidding the establishment of religious orders.

James. The greater part of them, methinks, have been founded since.

Casaubon. It was not until this Council that the doctrine of Transubstantiation was established.

James. The only intelligible sense of it is what Christ's vicar gave, when he took away the substance of the Count of Toulouse and transferred it to himself. Lo! here is a practical kind of transubstantiation, in which his successors have had perpetual practice and are admirably expert. These[13] gentles care neither for bishops their equals, nor for synods their superiors. A pope, like the Glaucus of antiquity, has taken his leap, and from a fisherman is become a god. He may advise and enlighten ; he may also command and fulminate : a favorite

---

[13] From "These" to "god" (4 lines) added in 2nd ed. In the 2nd ed. from "These gentles" to "for the dead" (25 lines) is assigned to James.]

designation of one among the supernatural powers which he arrogates to himself from the Divinity.

Casaubon. By a less exertion, he might transfuse in a perennial stream his wisdom and his holiness into a succession of bishops : hence appeals to Rome would be unnecessary. Power is always the more immoderate and the more jealous when it rises out of usurpation ; but those who contend for liberty of any kind should in no instance be its abettors. If the popes had been conscientious or decently honest men, if they could have abstained from laughing in their sleeves when they called themselves the successors of Saint Peter, if they could have been contented with his quiet mediocrity of fortune, his dignified and righteous exercise of authority, their influence upon sound consciences would have been greater and more permanent : and neither would rape and incest and the abominations of Lampsacus and Crete have been committed in their closets, under the images of the saints and under the lamp of the Virgin ; nor would forbearance from evil and activity in good be postponed to frogs and flounders, to horse-hair, hemp and ashes, or prayers to the dead for the dead. Pope[14] John XXII. established a Tariff for sins ; and if Leo X. published in like manner a Brief containing one, it did not as many imagine bring about the Reformation, which, in the midst of general depravity, it was likelier to prevent.

James. But it was a stinkpot in the hands alike of the pious and of the ambitious, swung about in opposition to the thurible, and a piece of furniture from the same chamber.

Casaubon. Enormity was not taken into the account. Impurities and incests, the least likely to be committed, paid least.* That which desolated the house of Œdipus, and filled Greece with horror and dismay, was compounded for at the rate of six shillings ; while that incontinence, which peradventure might be committed by two persons who happened to have the same sponsor at baptism, cost them sixteen. For this is incest too, according to the *Decretals ;* according to the authority of men whose interest is threefold : first, to increase the number of sins ;

[14 " Pope " to " *Casaubon* " (31 lines) added in 3rd ed.]
* The list entitled *Taxæ Pænitentiariæ*, the genuineness or which publication has been denied, was edited at Paris by Toussain Denis, 1520, and at Venice in the *Oceanus Juris*.

secondly, to split them artificially, and to plant them like the cuttings of vines in long and well-labored and well-manured trenches ; and thirdly, to facilitate the means of atonement.

James. I would not say openly, for evil might come there-from, that popes 'might as rationally deduce their origin from Julius Cæsar as from Simon Peter ; yet I will declare and protest that the religion they attempt to impose on us resembles more Julius's than Peter's ; and that the means they employ to get into office are the same as his ; which, after he had ruined his estate by debauchery, would, if he had failed to bribe his electors, have left him without a penny in his pouch. Let me rather mind my own matters : I have nothing to do with crimes out of my kingdom. But *mine* these audacious robbers will not let me call it, if they can hinder me ; these infesters of the king's high-road, through England, through Europe, and beyond.

Casaubon. Infallibility[15] was never claimed by the Bishops of Rome, nor ever thought of, until they were sufficiently powerful for the assertion of any falsehood and any usurpation. Pope Honorius, in later times, gave his sanction to the Ecthesis of Sergius, which was accepted by a synod convoked under him : it was declared heretical by his successors. Where was then Infallibility ?

A[16] question far more important to kings and nations lies before us. The Cardinal Bellarmin, unable to confute the slightest of your remonstrances, came forward in his master's name, threw down the key of Peter and took up the sword, cutting short the question between you, and asserting that the King of England is also in temporals the pope's feudatory and subject. After this, according to the constitution, your Majesty may declare rebels all adherents of the pope in any way whatever, all who hold direct or indirect communication with him, all who receive or give intelli-gence for the furtherance of his machinations and designs.

James.[17] The Pope has many true and just causes for hostility against us ; the truest and justest is this : the Reformation has shown that bishops are appointed by the secular power, though

[15 " Infallibility " to " Infallibility " (7 lines) added in 2nd ed., where this speech is assigned to James.]
[16 " A " to " us " (2 lines) added in 3rd ed.]
[17 From " *James* " to " exploded " (43 lines) added in 2nd ed.]

selected by the spiritual, at least in form. Now, he may be frightened at the apparition of some mighty prince in armor, who although surrounded by the clouds and fogs of his native superstition, calls upon his own bishops to nominate one, and gives his sanction to their nomination. On this principle, Rome may receive her bishop at his hands.

One thing is plain and demonstrable from the Scripture, and admits no doubt nor equivocation, nor can it be interpreted with more or less force ; which is, that the guides of Christians must abstain altogether from political concerns.

Casaubon. May not that, sire, affect the bishops as lords in parliament?

James. They sit there only to give their counsel on such discipline as may be propounded for the clergy. Hence they are called lords spiritual ; two very good words, although rather strange together.

If any one of mine in his pruriency should cast his wild eye askance, and ruffle his mane, and neigh and snort to overleap this boundary, I would thrust the Bible into his mouth forthwith, and thereby curb his extravagance. For, M. Isaac, we do possess this advantage : our bishops acknowledge in spirituals the sole authority of that sacred book ; whereas your papist, when you push him, slinks off from it as he lists, now to one doctor, now to another, now to saint, now to father, now to confessor ; and, as these retire from him and will have nothing to say to him or for him, he has recourse to tradition, which is anywhere or nowhere. If you follow him up into this whispering gallery, and press him closer, he flies at your throat, and swears (by God's help) he will throttle you.

Casaubon. The English have reflected at all times more intensely on religion than any other people in the universe, and began the earliest to examine its innovations and abuses. The *Trialogue* of Wicklif* is the first important work published in this country, and few more important have been published since.

James. I do not like Wicklif ; he would make men equal : let me hear no more of him. Bishop Reginald Peacock went exactly far enough. He resisted the authority of the pope, and

---

* This book was first printed without date, and written about the year 1360. Peacock flourished a century later.

refuted the doctrine of transubstantiation, with several other papalities, and particularly those paganisms which Vigilantius, in ancient times, buffeted and exploded.

Casaubon.[18]   The council of Trent hath defined and settled all the questions at issue in the Roman Catholic creed ; so that popes can pretend to inculcate nothing new for the future. Matters of discipline are likewise fixed.   The appointment to ecclesiastical dignities, of every degree, may be safely intrusted to the native hierarchy in each kingdom.   Your Majesty has a right to demand from your Roman Catholic subjects that no papal bull, no order, brief, decree, or mandate of any kind hereafter be received in your dominions.

Throughout the Christian world, the popes have stipulated with usurpers for almost every accession of authority and power. Bonifacius III. obtained from the emperor Phocas, who had assassinated his master and benefactor Mauritius, an imperial Rescript, ordering that he should be styled *Œcumenicus,* which the papists interpret Universal Bishop.   Mauritius had resolved to confer the title on the Patriarch of Constantinople ; but Gregory, at that time Bishop of Rome, opposed it, " using Christian freedom," says Eusebius, " and declaring that he could not assent to it ; for that no bishop ought to arrogate to himself the style and dignity of Universal Bishop." *   In the East, the Church received with scorn and anger the intelligence of this usurpation ; and the spirit of discord, which never breathed so violently and uninterruptedly in any other religion, and which never has intermitted a moment in the sixteen centuries since peace and good-will were first proclaimed to mankind, induced an Arab to collect a few of his countrymen, disbanded and defrauded by Heraclius, and to preach among them plainer doctrines.   Provinces, kingdoms, empires, gazed, trembled, and bowed before him ; religions, old and young, seceded and slunk away ; not a camel crossed the desert with a grain of incense. While Arians and Catholics were fighting for Christ against the

---

[18 From " *Casaubon* " to " *Casaubon* " (60 lines) added in 3rd ed.   From a footnote to Washington and Franklin in 1st and 2nd ed.   But see also note 8.]

* Orta est contentio, &c. Carrionis Chron: L. 4. p. 272.   Venetiis, 1540.

command of Christ, the most populous and civilized part of the world revolted from both standards.

James. To establish things as now constituted, it was necessary to reverse the prophecy of Isaiah, and, instead of making the rough smooth, to make the smooth rough.

Casaubon. Hence we find perpetually the terms, pernicious errors, impious doctrines, execrable heresies ; and rarely a word about the perniciousness, impiety, and execrableness of cruelty, malice, fraudulence, lust, avarice, and ambition. Hence the people are not permitted to read in their houses the precepts of our Saviour, but are ordered to believe the legend of Saint Handkerchief or Saint Eleventhousand ; to embrace the faith of a hot-headed enthusiast who tells us he believes a thing because it is impossible, and to place confidence in a lying old dotard who asserts that he filed his teeth in order to speak Hebrew.

James. It must be confessed his followers have sharpened theirs for worse purposes. Mahomet, of whom you were speaking, borrowed the best of his doctrines from the Christians, and the Christians the worst of theirs from him. Pope John VIII. declared that they who died fighting against the infidels should obtain the entire pardon of their sins. So, whoever wished to commit a rape or murder had only to make haste, and to run from one holy city to the other. As the predecessors of Pope John clipped something from the older religions, so Pope John crooked his finger and filched these spicy and intoxicating comforts from the goatskin of the Arab.

Casaubon. Among the various religions that have been established in the world, the papal is the only one which, as though it wished to ridicule and parody the Athanasian creed, insists that a kingdom shall have two *chief* magistrates ; * that

---

* Casaubon must be supposed to mean two magistrates, each of whom pretended to power independently of the other. For in Sparta were two kings ; and in Japan was a kind of pope, reported to possess an equal authority with the emperor. Where any such magistrate exists, a short time is requisite for his growth into inordinate power : where there is a hierarchy there will be usurpation. The Japanese pope, or dairo, is reduced to order, and his chief privileges are the keeping of twelve wives, with as many concubines as are necessary for the prosperity of the State and the interests of religion. The number of these, no doubt, would be diminished, if no serious danger were to be apprehended from the example of innovation.

nevertheless one of these shall be *superior* to the other, and
that he of right is so who has never seen the country, never will
see it, never had parentage or progeny or land or tenement in it ;
that a kingdom neither conquered nor hereditary, neither bequeathed nor surrendered by itself, must admit an alien arbitrator
whenever it pleases him to raise a question, and that this alien
arbitrator shall always give an irreversible verdict in his own
favor ; lastly, that a kingdom, to the detriment of its defence, of
its agriculture, of its commerce, of its population, of its independence, shall raise a body of men for the service of this intruder,
unlimited in number, enormous in expenditure, which he alone
shall discipline, he alone shall organize, he alone shall direct and
control.   Mahomet left a family, and was far from deficient in
impudence, but he wanted the assurance to claim for his own
successors what the pretended ones of Saint Peter claim for
theirs : here, however, we have somewhat worse than common
absurdity, or than common arrogance, to contend with.

James.[19] A harlot was not contented with debauching your
servants, with getting drunk at your expense, and with picking
your pocket of some loose money every time you approached
her ; she became impatient for your strong-box and title-deeds,
and invoked the Blessed Virgin to witness that, unless she had
them, you should never, as she hoped for salvation, leave the
room alive. She now is angry that you have turned her off ;
is [20] ready to bring attestations by the thousands that she is fairer
and cleaner and safer than any other ; reminds you, as peculiar
to herself, that you may enjoy her as well asleep as awake, as
well by proxy as in person ; complains of your levity and violence, boasts of her sweet temper, affection, and fidelity ; pouts,
pants, and swells, and swears that neither you nor yours shall
enter her house again.[21] I see not therefore what we can do
better than to cut her laces and put her decently to bed, slipping
out of the door with as little noise as possible.

[19 " *James* " added in 3rd ed.]
[20 From " is " to " person " (4 lines) added in 2nd ed.]
[21 First ed. reads : " again. Nicodemus," (7 lines below), &c. Second
ed. reads : " again. *James.* I see not . . . . . possible. *Casaubon.* Rather
act so in . . . . . . unreasonable. Nicodemus," &c. Three lines below
1st ed. reads : " question on any subject of doubt to a theophagous pope
from some," &c.]

Casaubon. Rather should we act so in every case, than exchange a pledge with the perfidious, or reason with the unreasonable.

James. Nicodemus asked our Saviour, *How can these things be ?* and his divine instructor heard and answered him with complacency : put the same question to his vicar, issuing from some mountain monastery or some súburban lane, and the fellow will illuminate you with a cart-load of faggots.

The [22] French displayed long before the English a resolution to defend the prerogatives of royalty against the usurpations of the popedom. Vigilantius, afore cited, a Frenchman by birth, although a bishop in Spain, condemned the celibacy of priests, the adoration of relics, and the lighting of lamps and candles by day in churches. Pierre Bruis, neither less intelligent nor less holy, took up and maintained his doctrines, which had languished six centuries, and taught them for twenty years at Toulouse. He was burned alive : for the Roman shepherds have not only their shears but their tar-pot. Henri le Moine followed his doctrine, and preached the words of his master with such good effect, that half the nation came back again from Rome to Christ. At the same season flourished Valdo, as you remember, and translated the Bible into French. His followers, called by his name and by that of Albigenses, carried this precious treasure through more than the third and fourth generation, and yielded it up only with their lives to the God who gave it. Indulgences were in vain held forth to this poor and lonely remnant of the apostolic church. Nicolas Oremus, plucking up courage by example, wrote to prove that the papacy is Antichrist, and translated anew the Holy Scriptures into French, by order of King Charles V. Under the next of that name the secretary, Maitre Alain, wrote his *Somnium Vividarium ;* for which I hope, rather than for any other work, my kinswoman Margaret, wife of the Dauphin, gave him a kiss upon the mouth while (it is said) he lay asleep.

The greatest blow of all was received in 1395, when the Sorbonne decreed that the two contending popes might box it out by themselves, and that the people of France should have nothing to do with either. In pursuance of which resolution the kingdom

[22 " The " to " popedom " (3 lines) added in 2nd ed. " Vigilantius " to " plumage " (33 lines) added in 3rd ed.]

was exempt from papal jurisdiction three whole years.   In soberer
times, when the popes were **neither** in the **cockpit nor** upon the
perch, we have proofs before us that the French **knew how to clip
their combs,** shorten their **tails, and** cleanse their plumage.   To [23]
pretermit the **vigor** and firmness **of** Philippe le Bel, who burned
the Bull of Bonifacius VIII. in the streets of Paris by the hands
of the hangman, and, having **seized** *His Holiness* at Anagni,
would have treated him with as **little** ceremony had he not **been**
rescued, Giovanni Buonacorsi **of Lucca** published, under the
reign of Louis XII., a proposition that **the pope was above the
king in temporals.** The Parliament of **Paris condemned him** to
be stripped of his canonical dress, **to put on one of green** and
yellow, **to** carry a candle of the same **colour, to confess before the**
image of the Virgin Mary that **this proposition was contrary to
the** Roman Catholic religion, and **to ask pardon of the king, of**
justice, and of the people : of the people, **because he had put their**
souls in danger ; else the **Parliament of Paris** was **always most**
discreet in its consignment of liberty, **not leaving any in places
where it might do harm,** and placing it **abundantly in the king's**
treasury, **to be** distributed at his royal **will and pleasure.** The
doctors **of** that country, and none but **doctors and princes**
are **fit to** handle the subject, are unanimous that **law and
liberty,** like offices and honors, **can emanate** only from the throne.
I **throw out this** in friendship and generosity, M. Casaubon, feeling **that you, born** and educated as you were at Geneva, might
think erroneously upon a point which **the nicest** hand cannot
separate from religion, and loving **you with all my** heart, and most
anxious for your welfare and salvation.

 Casaubon.   Sire, I will think **thereupon.**

 James.   Friend Casaubon, do **you speak in** the royal sense of
the word, or in the popular ?   **W**e kings, when we say to Parliament or other folk that we **will think** upon any thing, mean
always **that we will** dismiss it from our thoughts.

 Casaubon.   **That** would not be easy to do **with the words of**
your Majesty.

 James.   We **have** already **seen and** examined the anarchal
doctrines of the popish priesthood, **and** can never be surprised at
any atrocity committed by a sect, **the** only one since the creation of

[[23] From "**To**" to "them" (47 lines) added in 2nd ed.]

the world by which fratricide has been protected. Juan Diaz, in the memory of some now living,[*] was murdered in Nuremburg at the instigation of his brother, Alfonso, for having adopted the doctrine of the apostles in preference to the glosses of the popes. His murderers were imprisoned in the jail of Innspruck ; the Emperor Charles V. stopped the proceedings, under the pretext that he himself would take cognizance of them at the approaching diet. I know not whether the facts have been divulgated.

Casaubon. The whole history of the assassination has been published in Latin, under the name of Claudius Senarclæus. I possess one of the few copies that have escaped the searches made in order to suppress them. Medals[24] were coined by order of Gregory XIII. to commemorate Saint Bartholomew's day : on one side is the pope, on the other is the slaughter. He commanded it also to be painted in the Vatican, where the painting still exists. In popes no atrocity is marvellous or remarkable ; but how painful is it to find a scholar like Muretus exulting in a massacre ! Horatius Tursellinus, another eminent scholar, is another proof among thousands that literature, the tamer and subduer of barbarism, cannot penetrate a heart immersed in this searing superstition.

James. Tursellinus is not so rapturous as Muretus, but he counts the number of the victims with a sedate and calm pleasure.

Casaubon. Spondanus, in his *Auctarium ad Annales Baronii,* represents a similar scene on a smaller scale, exhibited two centuries ago in the Valtellina, under the auspices of the Duke of Feria, governor of the Milanese for the Spanish king. "Catholici, mense Julio, omnes Calvinistas, tam incolas quam exteros, occidunt."

James. Is it not wonderful that[25] an ignorant, vicious, and ferocious priest, covered with filth and vermin, being hailed as another god by some dozens of the same caste, instantly treats kings as his inferiors and subjects, and is obeyed in a country like

---

[*] 1545.

[[24] From "Medals" to "occidunt" (18 lines) added in 3rd ed.]

[[25] First ed. reads : "that odious and contemptible as the Italians are to all the other nations of Europe, when hardly the first amongst them, unless it be the son of some Venetian Senator, can find access to the family of any gentleman in England, yet an ignorant, vicious," &c.]

this, high-minded, free, and enlightened? **Is there** any **thing** more **irrational** or more humiliating in the **worship** of the Delai-Lama? **Far** otherwise: he is innocent, gentle, and **beneficent** ; no **murderer**, no instigator **to** assassinations, no **approver** of **massacres,*** no **plunderer**, no **extortioner**, no **vender** of **pardons,** no dealer in dispensations, no forestaller and **regrater** of **manna** from **heaven** or of palms from **paradise**, no **ringdropper** of sacraments, **no** scourer of incests, no forger, no betrayer.†

* **The** following words are part **of an** oration addressed **by him to** Gregory, in the name of Charles IX., **on the** celebration of this **festival:**

" O noctem illam memorabilem, et in fastis eximiæ alicujus **notæ adjectione** signandam, quæ *paucorum seditiosorum* interitu regem **a** præsenti **cædis** periculo, regnum a perpetuâ civilium bellorum formidine, **liberavit!** Quâ quidem nocte stellas equidem ipsas luxisse solito nitidiùs arbitror, et flumen Sequanam majores undas volvisse, **quo** citiùs illa impurorum hominum cadavera evolveret **et exoneraret in** mare! O felicissimam mulierum Catharinam regis **matrem! &c."**

Such **are** the expressions of Muretus, as **the most agreeable he** could deliver **to** the successor **of** him who proclaimed **on earth peace,** goodwill toward **men.** This language of Charity **had been corrected** by Infallibility, **and** altered to *pax hominibus.* . . . *bonæ voluntatis:* terms on which **a massacre is a commentary.**

His **words on the same** occasion are these: " Gregorius **XIII. deinde** pontifex summus **patrum studiis** electus ; *cujus pontificatûs* **initia lætiora** *lætus de Parisiensi Hugenotorum cæde nuncius fecit.* Per occasionem nuptiarum regis Navarri, Calviniani proceres jussu Franci regis oppressi ad LX. millia Parisiis **cæsa** traduntur." Treachery in the mask of Festivity, Murder in that of Religion, **are thus** congratuled and applauded.

† Almost **the only** good, **or rather** almost the only cessation of evil, **permitted by catholic** princes **is the** abolition of the Jesuits, which must **however be** considered as merely **the dismissal of** old servants grown insolent. Princes still maintained **and** supported **the** Inquisition. During the period of these two institutions, more **mischief** has been done to mankind **by** their religion, than by all the other religions that have existed **in the** world. The Jesuits taught youth, but only to a certain and very circumscribed extent, and their principal dogma was the legitimacy of falsehood : **hence** knowledge and virtue have suffered worse from them **than** from **the most** profligate and ignorant of the other confraternities.

Catholicism is the cause, we are informed, why sculpture and painting **were** revived: it is **more** certainly the cause why they have made no progress, and why they **have** been employed on ignoble objects ; on scourgers and hangmen, on beggarly enthusiasts and base impostors. Look at the two masterpieces of the pencil ; **the** Transfiguration of Raphael and the St Jerome of Correggio : can any thing **be more** incongruous, any thing more contrary to truth and history? **We** may be persuaded that the little town of Sicyon produced a greater number of masterpieces than all

O Casaubon! I blush to reflect that dissimulation is necessary to the maintenance of peace. A rotten rag covers worse rottenness: remove it, and half the world is tainted with infidelity. In England, in Holland, in any country where laws are equitable and morals pure, how often would these *Eminences* and *Holinesses* have clasped the whipping-post, and with how much more fervency than they clasp the cross! Bellarmin must have been convinced; he must have struggled against his conscience: heated with that conflict, he advances the more outrageously against me.

Casaubon. Bellarmin throws all your arguments into the fire, and assumes a fiercer attitude; not from any resentment at being convinced, for convinced he was long before, but on the principle that, when we are tired of parrying, we thrust. Your Majesty has now a declared competitor for the throne: but parliament will provide, if the statute of Queen Elizabeth is insufficient, the means necessary to maintain your possession. On the compliance of your Roman Catholic subjects with such conservatory statutes, nothing can be so unjust or so needless, as to exclude from the rights of citizenship or from the dignities of State a body of men who believe not differently from your Majesty, but more.

Popery [26] is an amalgam of every religion and every institution by which mankind in all countries under heaven had been subjugated. Not only the Egyptian and Syrian, the Brahmin and Persian, the Phrygian and Greek, but even the Druidical was found useful in its structure; and thereupon were erected the fulminating batteries of Excommunication. This, which satisfied and satiated the ferocity of the most ferocious race among men, satisfied not the papal priesthood. They conducted their inquisition far beyond it, extinguishing, as they went, all other lights than such as served for illusion. In Spain they succeeded perfectly; nearly so in Italy: in France the machine stuck and

the modern world. The sculptors of Sicyon are celebrated, the painters not: but sculpture was never brought to perfection anywhere until drawing was; and we are instructed by the defect in our own school how much rarer and more difficult is this part. In landscape only, where superstition has no influence, are the moderns to be thought on a level with the ancients. Claude and Titian, Cuyp and Hobbima, were probably not excelled.

[[26] From "Popery" to "suppleness" (25 lines) added in 2nd ed.]

miscarried. The vivacity and courage of the French, and their felicity in ridicule and mimicry, kept them up from suffocation and submersion. The strong moral principle of the English, their serious temper, their habit of long reflection, their unreserved confidence one in another, their dauntless practice of delivering their opinions, their liberality in accepting and exchanging them, and, upon these, the attempering countenance of your Majesty, will deprive the papal poison of its circulation and activity. Threats are yet murmured; but, if your Majesty will cease to notice them, they will die away. There is no echo but from repercussion; no repercussion but from some place higher than the voice. The scourge of reason and humanity, left upon the ground awhile, will break in the hand of the first who strikes hard · therewith: it has already lost much of its weight and suppleness.

Casaubon here finished his discourse, and James made no farther observation. Such was his simplicity, he really had imagined that reason and truth, urged so forcibly by him, would alter the system and conciliate the goodwill of the papal court, and that it would resign a wide dominion for a weighty argument. He stroked his beard, licked softly the extremities of his whiskers, ejaculated, sighed, and sat down quietly. He was, notwithstanding, in a frame of mind capable of receiving with satisfaction whatever could derogate from the dignity of the Roman Catholic rites, when Archibald Pringle, one of his pages, entered the apartment.

"Archy," said his Majesty, who was fond of such abbreviations, "I remember to have chidden you for a wicked little story you told me last winter, touching a Japanese at Rouen. Come now, if you can divest it of irreverence, I would fain hear it repeated. I think it a subject for the disquisition of my bishops, whether the pagan sinned or not; or whether, if he sinned, his faith was of a nature to atone for it."

Such were really, if not the first thoughts, those however which now arose in the king's mind. The page thus began his narration:—

"A young Japanese was brought over to Rouen on the day of Pentecost. He had expressed in the voyage a deep regret at the death of the chaplain, who might have instructed him in the mysteries, and who, the only time he conversed with him, recommended to him zealously the worship of the living God.   He was constant in his desire to be edified, and immediately on his debarkation was conducted to the cathedral.   He observed the elevation of the Host with imperturbable devotion, and an utter indifference to the flattering whispers of the fairest among the faithful ; such as, ' Oh the sweet jonquil-coloured skin !   Oh the pretty piercing black eyes !   Oh the charming long-twisted tail ! And how finely those flowers and birds and butterflies are painted upon his trousers !   And look at that leopard in the centre ! it seems alive.'

" When the service was over, and the archbishop was mounting his carriage-step, he ran after him, and, with eyes half-closed, bit him gently by the calf of the leg.   Vociferations were raised by the attendants, the soldiers, and the congregation, ill accordant with sanctity, and wronging the moral character and pious disposition of the Japanese.   These, however, the good prelate quieted, by waving his hand and smiling with affability.   The neophyte was asked what induced him to bite the archbishop by the leg ; he answered that he wished to pay the living god the same reverence and adoration as the living god had paid the dead one."

" See now," cried James, "the result of proclaiming that the pope is god upon earth.   It led this poor heathen, who amid such splendour and prostrations might well mistake an archbishop for a pope, to the verge of an abyss, dark, precipitous, and profound as any that superstition hath opened in his own deplorable country."

V. PETER LEOPOLD AND PRESIDENT DU PATY.[1]

Among the Frenchmen who within the last fifty years have reflected honor on their country, a distinguished rank is holden by the President Du Paty.   His letters on Italy contain acute

[1 In Mercier Dupaty's Letters from Italy (1735) is contained much information on the legal institutions of the different states he visited in

observations, and his interview with Leopold forms no small portion of their interest. Pleased with the justness of his remarks and the pointedness of his expressions, and perhaps hoping to derive some advantage to the new Code from his deep study and long practice of jurisprudence, Leopold, when he had conversed with him, invited him to return the next day.

At the hour appointed, the grand duke was leaning with his elbow on the chimney-piece, that he might neither rise at the entrance of the President, nor receive him in the manner of a sovereign. The commencement of conversation is trifling, even among the greatest men: this expression, whenever I use it, means men of the greatest genius and worth. The usual courtesies then having been exchanged, Leopold thus addressed his visitant :—

Leopold. I know, M. Du Paty, that your compliments cannot stifle nor supersede your sincerity; and that, if I seriously ask your opinion on the defects of my Code, you will answer me as seriously.

The President bowed, and, observing that Leopold had paused, replied.

President. Sir, I cannot bear in mind all the articles of your Code; and, unless I could, my observations, if not erroneous,

Italy. In his remarks on the Duchy of Tuscany occur the following passages:—"Leopold loves his people: he has suppressed taxes as unnecessary, and dismissed all his troops, only keeping enough to serve as a model. He has pulled down the walls of Pisa, which were very costly to keep up. . . . Finding that a court hid the condition of his people from him, he abolished his court. He has established manufactures and built roads everywhere at his own expense. . . . The prayers offered to God for harvests are no longer the cause of dearth in the fields; the prince has made the year longer by adding to it days which he has converted from superstitious holidays into days of labour. He is occupied in a complete reform of the laws, . . . has simplified the civil code and made the criminal code milder. For ten years no blood has been shed on a Tuscan scaffold." The Conversation between Leopold and Dupaty is given in letter xxvi. Dupaty himself was an eager advocate of reasonable penal legislation; a pamphlet by him in favour of three men condemned to be broken on the wheel, was burnt by order of the Parliament of Paris. He praises in his letters from Italy the English criminal law, which was savage enough, saying, "In England the laws fear to condemn, in France they fear to acquit."—(Imag. Convers. i., 1824; i., 1826. Works, i., 1846. Works, iii., 1876.)]

must be imperfect. On these subjects we may not talk vaguely and fancifully, as on subjects of literature. Where man is to decide on man, where the happiness or wretchedness of one hangs on the lips of another, where a breath may extinguish a family or blight a generation, every thing should be tried particle by particle. To have abolished capital punishments is a proof, in certain circumstances, no less of wisdom than of humanity; but I would suggest to your consideration, whether you have provided sufficiently for the protection of property and of honor. Your prisons are empty; but are you sure that the number of criminals is less? Or are you of opinion that it is better to see them at large than in custody?

Leopold. Here are few assassinations, and no highway robberies.

President. I will explain the reason. In other countries the prostitutes are a distinct class; in Tuscany not: * and where there are no jealousies there will be few assassinations. Supposing a case of tyranny, the Tuscans will wriggle under it rather than writhe; and if even they should writhe, yet they will never stand erect. They commit no murders for the purpose of robbing; and robbery on the highway they rarely hazard, having such facilities for committing safer and more compendious. Every man may plunder the vineyard of another at small risk of prosecution; nor is there a single one in Tuscany that is not plundered every autumn, unless the owner pass his nights in it during the maturity of the grapes. If he prosecutes, he suffers a heavier punishment than the prosecuted. He loses several days of labour, and receives no indemnity; nor, indeed, is there any security against a similar injury the succeeding year. Many

---

* Pomponius Mela says, after Theophrastus, "apud Tyrrhenos conjugia communia." Among the curiosities of this nation, reported by Athenæus in his twelfth book, are these from Theopompus. "Παρὰ δὲ Τυρρηνοῖς ἐκτόπως τρυφήσασιν ἱστορεῖ Τίμαιος. Θεόπομπος δὲ, καὶ νόμον εἶναί φησι παρὰ τοῖς Τυρρηνοῖς κοινὰς ὑπάρχειν τὰς γυναῖκας, ταύτας δὲ ἐπιμελεῖσθαι σφόδρα τῶν σωμάτων, καὶ γυμνάζεσθαι πολλάκις καὶ μετ' ἀνδρῶν, ἐνίοτε δὲ καὶ πρὸς ἑαυτάς, οὐ γὰρ αἰσχρὸν εἶναι αὐταῖς φαίνεσθαι γυμναῖς. δειπνεῖν δὲ αὐτὰς οὐ παρὰ τοῖς ἀνδράσι τοῖς ἑαυτῶν, ἀλλὰ παρ' οἷς ἂν τύχωσι τῶν παρόντων, καὶ προπίνουσιν οἷς ἂν βουληθῶσιν, εἶναι γὰρ καὶ πίνειν δειναί. Τρέφειν δὲ τοὺς Τυρρηνοὺς πάντα τὰ γινόμενα παιδία, οὐκ εἰδότας ὅτου ἐστὶν ἕκαστον."

robberies require impossible proofs; and there are others the crime of which is extenuated by what ought to be an aggravation; namely, because they are also breaches of trust.   Again,[2] what progress can philosophy, or indeed plain common-sense, be said to have made in these countries where, according to law, no criminal is punished with the higher penalty for the worst offences, unless he confess his guilt?

Leopold.   I have retained this statute much against my will, in compliance with those about me.

President.   Sir, good lawyers are often bad legislators; many know perfectly what has been established, and very imperfectly what ought to be.   Those about an arbitrary prince, whose (what scarcely ever happens) benevolence induces him to give laws to his dominions, should be only two,—Equity and Decision. This appearance of gentleness is most illusory.   It originated from the clergy, who slackened crimes and heightened punishments at their pleasure.   You make the criminal his own judge, deciding for himself in what manner he shall be chastised.

Leopold.   Mine is an experiment.

President.   Never let experiments be made on life or law. Let Experience sit on one side of the lawgiver, Justice on the other, with Humanity for assessor.

I know that your Highness has enacted clement laws in order to humanize the people, and that violence might never be added to rapine.   But laws should be formed according to the character of the nation that is to receive them.   The Italians were always more addicted to robbery and revenge than other European people; crimes equally proceeding from idleness and effeminacy.

Leopold.   On[3] the accusation of revenge I have nothing to say; but on what authority do you found your assertion, M. Du Paty, that the Italians were always so addicted to theft?

President.   I will not urge as a proof of it the increasing severity of the ancient laws, which would only demonstrate their imperfection; but I will insist on the documents of the Latin writers *de re rustica,* who give particular directions on the breed of house-dogs for the safe-guard of the farms, however far removed be the subject from cattle and cultivation.   Nothing

[2 From "Again" to "assessor" (10 lines) added in 3rd ed.]
[3 From "On" to "but" (two lines) added in 3rd ed.]

similar has entered into the scheme of any modern author on agriculture. Added to which, there is hardly a Latin writer whether in prose or in poetry, whatever be his subject, who does not say something about thieves ; so familiar was the idea. The word itself extended, in more than one direction, beyond the character it first designated : Plautus calls a soldier *latro ;* Horace, a servant *fur.* The Romans, who far excelled us in the greater part of their institutions, were much behind in what by way of excellence we call the *police.* Hence in early times an opening to theft, among a people less influenced than any other by continence and honor. In many whole provinces of England, France, and Holland, and throughout the kingdoms of Denmark, Sweden, and Norway, the countryman may sleep in perfect security with his doors wide-open ; but, among the Italians, not in a single village, not in a single house, from Como to Reggio. The windows in every dwelling in Florence, even of your own palace, are barricaded by grates of iron ; in other words, every dwelling, your own among the rest, holds forth in the censor's face a libel against the government. The fault is partly in the laws and partly in the magistrature ; for there is no nation so easily coerced by fear as this. I recommend no cruelty : but those laws are cruel which are illusory, dilatory, or costly to such as appeal to their protection ; not those which award a stated and known severity of punishment for proven offences. The latter are no more so than a precipice or a penknife. I may leap down the one ; I may cut my throat with the other : I may do neither.[4]

Sisto Quinto is the only sovereign who appears to have acted uniformly according to the national character.

Leopold. I see in him, however, that cruel laws do not necessarily make a people cruel. The Romans (I would rather call them the inhabitants of Rome) were less so under Sisto Quinto than before or since ; and the English are, and always

[4 **First ed.** reads : "neither. I pay taxes for the security of my person, my property, and my **character** : every farthing I pay beyond for law, if I can demonstrate the equity of my cause, is an injustice. Sestus Quintus is . . . . character. Happy would it have been for his country, had he united to omniscience another attribute of the Godhead, immortality. *Leopold.* In that case, M. Du **Paty,** I should not have had the pleasure of your conversation here. I see," &c.]

have been, the most humane of nations, under penal laws the most iniquitous and atrocious.

President.   I[5] am desirous of learning why the English appear to have been always so.

Leopold.   Look at Spain, at France, at Italy, from 1500 to 1600,—a century in which the human race, both in those countries and in England, seems to have been greatly worse than it ever was before or since,—and you will rarely find an empoisonment, rarely an assassination of any kind, committed in England for policy or revenge ; while every month produces them in rank abundance through Italy, Spain, and France.   I attribute it chiefly to the conscious valor of the English, so long displayed over all their enemies.   The Spaniards, then esteemed the bravest and best soldiers on the continent, fled before them from one region of America to another, and over all the seas, while opulent cities were sacked by a boat's crew of buccaneers.

President.   The glory of self-possession and of abstinence from bloodshed is shared by Sweden in the same age.   And indeed, although it might be called, by a less intelligent and a less impartial judge, invidiousness and detraction, I cannot but remark that some of the best Englishmen of that period were no better than robbers.

Leopold.   Robbers they were ; but they also were better than robbers.   Courage, which ought to be generous, was rapacious ; and Genius, which ought to be tutelary, was destructive.   Few rise to eminence in a calm ; and, of those who attain it in a stormier season, the names the most part are perishable.   Not so Raleigh's.

President.   France has produced many quite as illustrious in the union of wisdom, eloquence, and enterprise as he was ; and, finding such characters are by no means extraordinary, has forgotten them.

Leopold.   I see clearly she has forgotten them, whether I read your historians or your older writers.

President.   In regard to integrity and candor, no wickedness in that or any other age is comparable to Bacon's, another great

[5 From " I " to " themselves " (55 lines) added in 3rd ed.]

Englishman, who solicited and flattered the Earl of Essex, owed his fortune and dignity to him, and dragged him to the scaffold.

I do not wonder at the villanies of men who have nothing but power and pedigree to support them, and whose names are as perishable as those of their spaniels; but I do wonder at one, who is conscious that his must be immortal, fixing a stigma with his own hand upon it, which only the flames that will consume the world can obliterate. The counsellors of Elizabeth were wary and politic; they left magnificent mansions and large estates behind them, and the letters which compose their titles are legible enough: but what were the men intrinsically? Sharpers in Paris are often necessitated to exercise as much ability in doing less mischief. But Bacon—Bacon, to whom the earth had never seen (and was only then about to see) an equal—Bacon to whom Milton and Shakspeare might have risen and looked up reverentially—was lured away by Avarice in the specious form of Ambition; and Ingratitude, the only fiend as odious, cast him down among worse than dead men from the pinnacle of glory.

I now return from the most memorable of the chancellors to the laws themselves. The laws of England have been the subject of eulogy to many learned and sagacious men. I have read them repeatedly and pondered them attentively, and I discover them often dilatory, often uncertain, often contradictory, often cruel, often ruinous. Whenever they find a man down they keep him so, and the more pertinaciously the more earnestly he appeals to them. Like tilers, in mending one hole they make another. There is no country in which they move with such velocity where life is at stake, or, where property is to be defended, so slowly. I have hardly the courage to state these facts, and want it totally to hazard a reflection on them. Can we wonder that, on a Bench under so rotten an effigy of Justice, sat a Scrogges, a Jefferies, a Finch, a Page? The[6] hand of Law strikes the poor; its shadow strikes the wealthy.

[6 From "The" to "wealthy" (2 lines) added in 3rd ed.; from "The" to "President" (91 lines) added in 2nd ed. "The notorious" Scrogges was Lord Chief Justice at the time of the Popish Plot, 1678. Finch, made Lord Chief Justice in 1634, and Lord Keeper in 1640, is perhaps best known for his judgment given against Hampden in the famous case of ship money. Jeffereys was made Lord Chief Justice in 1683.]

The Roman institutions were incomparably better, when the most respectable and the most elevated characters of the republic walked up and down the forum, ready to receive the complaints and to redress the grievances of their fellow-citizens. Such was the practice not only in the time of the republic, but before it under the kings, and after it under the emperors. Law is become in England not only the most expensive, but the most rapacious and the most dishonest of trades; and the most licentious of strolling comedians are those, who, under the title of barristers, accompany the English judges in their circuits. In cross-questioning, as they term it, or examination of deponents against their client, they bear no respect whatever to honor or genius or any kind of worth; and the accuser who has been robbed, defrauded, or otherwise injured has a graver and more intolerable wrong impending over him, not only than what he has already suffered, but even than what the criminal himself, in most instances, has to fear: so shameless is the effrontery, so unrestricted the invective, of barristers. What is peculiar in our times to the English, is, that these alone are the qualities for which the leaders of their Opposition are chosen; and from the Opposition (when the dunghill is well heated) ministers and secretaries, heads and tails, dart across the road before you.

Leopold. I have observed that these worthies begin their course by rowing with their backs against the stream, leaving it to be inferred what feats they can perform when a fare is offered them to go with it. With them we have nothing to do: let us descend again to the lower courts, in which the slowness of reparation is the thing most complained of. Justice in England is perhaps the slower in her movements from a higher sense of the decorous.

President. One would imagine that, in this long minuet of hers, she might take better care not to sweep against and upset the refreshments. Who could suppose that laws instituted to humanize and civilize mankind, and on the operation of which the eyes of the most acute and virtuous are constantly intent, should retain a degree of ferocity greater than on any occasion they are called upon to correct?—and should retain it where the nation has less of it than any other, and where hardly any trace of it is to be discovered out of its tribunals? Yet England, and within these twenty years, saw the worst of tortures inflicted on a criminal, not for his crime, but for his constancy; not for the violation of his country's laws, but for his strict observance of Nature's; not for yielding to the solicitations of poverty, or to the seductions of vice, but for disregarding pain, torture, death itself, that he might not injure his family. Until the year 1772, a man convicted of felony, or petty treason, incurred what is barbarously and foolishly called "corruption of blood," followed by confiscation of goods, if, after or before his sentence, he acknowledged himself guilty; but if, hoping to save from ruin a family he had already brought to shame, he refused to answer the questions of the court, and neither denied nor confessed his guilt, then he was led back to his dungeon, a little bread and water was given to him, he was cast on his back, and he perished by the slow operation of an iron weight upon his breast. Blackstone, in his encomium on the English laws, which he entitles a Commentary on the Constitution, is unable to deny or to dissemble this fact. Nevertheless, the procedures and administration of justice are better in England than in France: in England, it would be an infamy for a person to solicit or even to visit a judge on any case, criminal or civil; in France, it would be thought a folly and an affront not to do it, and the omission of it would be the loss of the suit. We Frenchmen are the most delicate people in the world on points of honor, and the least delicate on points of justice.

Leopold. In other words, the most on imaginary things; the least on real. A man's vanity tells him what is honor, a man's conscience what is justice: the one is busy and importunate in all times and places; the other but touches the sleeve when men are alone, and, if they do not mind it, leaves them. Point of honor you may well call it; for such precisely is the space it occupies.

Nothing is so surprising, and proves to me so manifestly the moral excellence of the English above all other nations, as their juries. That twelve men should be unanimous in order to punish an offender, and that neither fear nor corruption should have influenced an individual in the many hundred thousands who have been jurymen, is a miracle in morals and jurisprudence. No other nation could prudently or safely adopt this institution; no

Italian legislator could modify it in any way; nor indeed does it appear to me advisable, in the most perfect state to which human nature can be brought, that more than nine in twelve should decide on guilt or innocence. For take the better-informed half of the world, put the names into an urn, draw them out at hazard and by twelves, and you will surely find at least three in that number weak, obstinate, or dishonest.

President. Some of the English laws are wonderfully strange, and equally strange are the expressions. I may be punished for " bringing a man into contempt : " as if any one could be brought into it without stirring a step on his own legs toward it. Aristides may have been laughed at, Phocion may have been reviled ; but the judge who should have said that either had been brought into contempt would have been covered with it himself by every citizen of Athens. The English are somewhat less quick in the apprehension of absurdity ; and this expression is not merely an absurdity, but a most pernicious one. The doctrine was inculcated by M. Murray, a Scotchman by birth, but an English judge ; and the opinion of judges in that country, when once acted upon, passes into law. The national character, if I am not greatly mistaken, will within half a century feel the sad effect of this decision. Nothing in the world is such a safeguard of liberty and virtue as the maxim, *Ne quid falsi dicere audeat, ne quid veri non audeat*, or such a loss and misfortune as its abolition. I would punish every thing false against character, and permit every thing true, as being the fairest chastisement of faults and follies, the mildest and surest and most expeditious. On the contrary, an English judge would punish in a fellow-citizen what he applauds in a Roman historian.

Leopold.[7] No tyrant in modern ages or ancient, however barbarous, hath enacted such unjust and cruel laws as the Parliament of England. Where will you point out to me one equal in atrocity to that which authorizes the renegade son of a Catholic to dispossess his father of his estate ? " Honor thy father and mother " is erased from the commandments of the *Reformed* Church by act of parliament. The renegade may be elected to sit in this parliament, and his qualification is founded on the very

[7 From " *Leopold* " to " coast " (17 lines) added in 2nd ed. See Lecky's " Irish Statesmen."]

property from which he has ejected his own father. Translate the English statutes into the language of Madagascar or Mozambic ; read them to the prince of their country,—and what must be the impression ?

President. He would ask with what instrument the English sharpen their teeth ; whether they color them black, red, purple, or yellow ; and would order his subjects to besmear their bodies with some acrid juice or gum, whenever a British vessel is observed upon the coast.

It may, indeed, be doubted whether the laws of England have not been gradually deteriorating for above seven hundred years ; that is, whether they have not been accumulating more anomalies, more uncertainties, more delays, more costs, more contradictions, more cruelties.*   •

Leopold.   In England, a peasant is slaughtered for the slaughter of another's sheep against his consent ; a servant for stealing his master's spoon or wig ; a little vagabond, starving at Christmas, snatches a rag from a hedge, and is recommended to the hangman for correction.   Are these laws better than mine ?

President. No, sir ; they are worse in themselves ; yet your Highness would do well to make the exchange, throwing back to the English, the boy, rag, spoon, and wig. They would suit your people better, and might fairly be laid aside when it had outgrown them : but I suspect they would be serviceable many years.   Punish all crimes, and you will punish few ; remit a single one, and you create a thousand.

Leopold.[8]   In England, great crimes escape through the intensity of law ; in Italy, small ones through its relaxation. Which is the worse ?

President. I dare to answer that the latter is ; because great crimes do not run into smaller, but smaller into greater ; and because, if there were not this reason, multitude turns the scale against magnitude.

I must here observe to you that the privilege of pardon in a prince is the most flagrant of usurpations.   It belongs for the

---

* Shute Barrington, in the year 1776, published *Observations on the Statutes, with a Proposition for new-modelling them.* Bacon, while chancellor, did the same, and ineffectually.

[[8]From " *Leopold* " to " magnitude " (7 lines) added in 2nd ed.]

greater part to the person injured; but not entirely.   The magistrate, who takes cognizance of the particulars, should also give his assent in the name of the community; not, however, in consequence of a private petition or a subsequent representation.

I perceive with pleasure in your Code that fines occur but seldom.

Leopold.   Pray, M. Du Paty, give me your reasons.   If they are the same as mine they strengthen them; if they are different, they are more.

President.   Fines and halters, the minions of English jurists, are the most summary and the least summary of chastisements, and by far the worst.   A great fine does no harm whatever to a man of great fortune: it is a bribe to the laws, and ought as much to be prohibited as a bribe to the judge.   It ruins, not the poorer man, but the poorer man's children; it derives him of what he perhaps may do without, but what they cannot without an injury to society.   If his education was defective, which the offence goes a great way toward proving, theirs must be more defective still, because the means of educating them are taken away or lessened.   In some countries, heavier fines are imposed for injuries or affronts committed against the superior of the offender, slighter for those against the inferior: this, if indeed they are ever equitable in such cases, ought to be reversed; for the inferior is the weaker in calumny and injustice, as in other things.   We cannot strike so hard from below as from above.   The rich and powerful man does not lose even so much as a salute by it, while the artisan or tradesman loses in one instance a customer, in another ten or twenty, in another his livelihood.

Leopold.   In reply to the former of your remarks, I know not what else to say than that all punishments must in some degree touch the innocent; and that the family of every criminal is a loser in estimation, and consequently in property and prosperity, by his punishment, however just.

President.   According[9] to your laws, two witnesses of bad character are worth more than one of good.   But your Highness will excuse me from entering farther on the Code itself, or from touching any single provision in it, since no conversation could do it rightly and satisfactorily; and indeed, I am persuaded

[9 From " According " to " position " (7 lines) added in 2nd ed.]

that your **Highness** would rather hear what I think of the spirit
and its effects, than of any particular point or position.

The first duty of a legislator is to apportion penalties ; **the**
second is to insulate them as much as possible,"and to embank
the waters of bitterness.   I would, therefore, both for the sake of
compensation to the unoffending and to guard against offences,
place the children of criminals in schools or workhouses appointed
for that purpose, and forbid them to keep the paternal name,
which, for more than one reason, should be the first thing forfeited.   A workhouse ought to contain a school, not of writing
or reading, but of industry.   If you wish to make the bulk of
men wiser, do not put books into their hands, which they will
either throw away from indifference or must drop from necessity,
but give them employment suitable to their abilities, and let them
be occupied in what will repay them the most certainly and the
best.   Their thoughts will thus be directed to one main point,
and you will produce good artizans and good citizens.   This is
the wisdom for every day in the week ; and what is higher than
this will never be impeded by it, and will often rise out of it.

Leopold.   I will consider your advice.[10]   Here I may venture
to assert, that, suitable to my character, my laws are circumspect.

President.   I am afraid that, in the practice of jurisprudence,
circumspection more than rarely means dilatoriness.   Delay of
justice is injustice.   When offences are defined and punishments
are apportioned, no circumspection is necessary.   According to
the practice in Tuscany, if I complain of a robbery, a young commissary of police examines me, and writes my deposition, without
reading it over to me, whereby I may acknowledge or challenge
its correctness.   After several weeks, another young commissary
examines me again ; at the same interval a third ; and if my
relation varies a tittle from what is found written by either, no
chance remains of recovering the loss or of punishing the offender.
These young men are paid no better than postilions ; but it seldom
happens that one of the three is not corrupted by the offender.
Travellers cannot delay their journey : their valets know it ;
hence hardly one stranger in twenty but finds himself robbed in
this city.   Witnesses are required where witnesses cannot be ex-

[10 First ed. reads : " advice : I say it as legislator not as prince : for in
our language you know, when we promise to consider we purpose to
neglect. Here," &c.]

pected ; for which reason treachery is the constant companion of violence, and manliness of character is excluded.[11]

I brought with me a letter of introduction to a gentleman here whom I found unwell, and his medical friend by the side of him in choler.   As the invalid laughed, I took the liberty of asking the cause of his good spirits.   "The doctor will tell you his story," said he.   "It was in the beginning of January, and my coachman had been robbed of his great-coat ; he found it again, detected the thief, brought him before the magistrate, and his deposition was written down carefully.   According to custom, I and the coachman shall be called a second time in about forty days, a third in about forty more ; that, if there is any discrepancy in our evidence, which discrepancy often arises from collusion, and oftener from forgetfulness in some minute circumstances, the rogue may enjoy the benefit of the law, and be acquitted.   In the mean time, I must purchase my coachman another great-coat, for justice here keeps nobody warm but the lawyers ; and the stolen one will be eaten by the moths, as is inevitable in cloth at the close of February, if not carefully aired and beaten."

A young foreigner who had refused a favor was waylaid in the street at dusk, and a blow was aimed at his head from behind with a club,—which, if he had not at the moment heard the feet of his assassin, must have killed him, as it required from its massiveness the use of both hands, and the assassin was a remarkably strong man.   The foreigner turned and avoided it, immediately aiming a blow at his adversary.   The facts were proved ; and this blow, necessary for self-preservation, was alleged as the reason why the crime was punished by one

[11 First ed. reads: "excluded.   It is remarkable that in a single week two cases have occurred in point.   A young man in the theatre applauded an actress.   One sitting near him called him a blockhead for his admiration. He replied.   The severer critic, to prove his superior judgment, made a different use of hands, applying them to the face and frill of the applauder, who stood motionless as the prompter himself, and on the following day applied to the police.   It being proved that he returned no blow, the Aristarchus was condemned to a month's imprisonment. A few days before or afterwards (I forget which) a young foreigner, a painter by profession, who had refused a favour to another, was waylaid by him in the street," &c. (20 lines below.)   In 2nd ed. the story of the great-coat is introduced.]

day's confinement.   Yet the offender, it cannot be doubted, had premeditated an assassination, and had carried it as far into effect as he could.   For his attempt he was almost unpunished ; and if he had succeeded in it he would never have been punished at all ; for the witnesses were brought together only by the contest. Had there been no contest there would have been no witnesses : it being a point of delicacy here in Tuscany not to interfere in another man's affairs without strong solicitation ; and the dead can neither ask favors, nor, what is equally necessary, requite them. Cowardice then is a merit, courage a bar to justice.   What can be expected from a people, the least confident in personal strength and honor, when such dispositions are countenanced by such institutions ?

Leopold.   I need not remark, M. Du Paty, that institutions are with difficulty laid aside.

President.   Yet your Highness has abolished a very ancient one, that of monachism, I forbear to say totally, but almost, and without detriment or danger.   Now the forest is thinned, we discover its boundaries and can make our way through.

Leopold.   The business is done then to your satisfaction ?

President.   Not altogether.   In my journey from Pisa to Florence, I inquired what was allotted to each ejected monk, and was informed that it amounted to somewhat less than what each galley-slave could earn in prison : facilities and materials of · which earning are supplied to him by government, but are supplied in no measure to the ejected monk.

Leopold.   The fellows are idlers and rogues : none of them understand, and few of them believe, what they teach.   I am not more imperious and arbitrary with the monks, than the monks have been with princes.   I have removed their cells ; they have removed our palaces.   The Church of Saint Isidore in Seville was opposite the royal palace ; Sanchia, the king's daughter, was praying at a window which faced the shrine of the saint, when he appeared to the family and commanded that the situation of the palace should be changed, as it was unsafe to have a woman so near his ashes.*

Saint[12] Andreas and Saint Podius, two Florentide archbishops,

---

* Luca Tudensis Hist. Mirac. Sti. Isidori, c. xxxv. Bollandus.

[12 From " Saint " to " satisfaction " (7 lines) added in 2nd ed. ; from " In " to " monks " (2 lines) added in 3rd ed.

whose images stand opposite in the cathedral, would serve a sculptor or painter as models for the proudest and bitterest of the fallen angels.   I have never seen such countenances among the living ; for in the galleys we see roguery out of power, and hopeless of authority and respect : those of the Florentines in general express good-nature and self-satisfaction.

In this digression, I am seeking no escape or subterfuge from our monks.   The body is injurious and pernicious from a shuffling show of enthusiasm, of all pests upon earth the most contagious. They who believe nothing make others believe most ; as the best actors in our theatres are those who retain the most perfect command over their feelings, voice, and countenance.   Our spiritual mamelukery is as ambitious of power and riches as if it had children to inherit them, and the money that falls into their hands lies dead, the land indifferently cultivated.   I shall fumigate my old hives, one after another, not minding the buzz from within.[13]

There is now another cry against me,—that I am about to curtail the number of holidays.

President.   The worship of Saint Nicholas, I imagine, would be more easy to abolish than that of any other saint.

Leopold.   Why ?

President.   Because he, making the sign of the cross, brought to life a brace of roasted partridges ; as I saw yesterday, painted and written in the cloister of Santo Spirito.   Surely, he can have few favorers in the Church, who thus abuses the holy weapon : if he had lifted it up and brought down a brace out of a covey, instead of subducting them from the platter, when it had pleased God to put them upon it, he might have expected more fervency of adoration.

Leopold.   A good reason for your belief : and I hope to give as good a one for my design.   It is, because every saint in the calendar has made ten thousand beggars and ten thousand thieves, not counting monks.

President.[14]   In my humble opinion, your Imperial Highness

[13 First ed. reads : " within. I shall next abolish the greater part of their festivals for every saint," &c. (15 lines below).   From " There " to " design " (15 lines) added in 2nd ed.]

[14 From " *President* " to " Capri " (20 lines) added in 2nd ed.]

would have begun better with the abolition of fasts, as they are improperly called.   If your people were mariners, if you possessed a fishery, then indeed there would be a politic and adequate reason for maintaining the institution ; but as the Italians make less use of their coast than any people in the world, as among them only the Venetians have a fishery, there is no sufficient cause or plea for it.   That God is better pleased with a sharp bone than a blunt one, I never can concede.   This I know ; fasts enervate men, and render them unfit not only for the duties of war, but for the occupations of peace.   If salt fish, the only kind within the reach of the common people, be called a fast, the most important effect it produces is that it makes them drink more wine than they would otherwise do, and deteriorates their blood.

The Athenians did not keep fasts ; but their policy led them to eat salted the grillo and the locust, which diminished the number of these insects, and which at all events it was better to eat than to be eaten by.

Leopold.   A flight of locusts in Attica was like a flight of quails to the Bishop of Capri.

Frequently, when I have been vehement against abuses, but silent on my intentions, the clergy have told me that abuses form no part of their religion : they now tremble at what they call innovation, not knowing or dissembling that, in pure religion, there can be no other innovations than abuses.   They talk to me about the religion of our forefathers, conveyed to us in all its purity from the earliest ages.   I am afraid, M. Du Paty, the pear was thumbed at the stalk when it was just ripe, and it rotted almost the next day.

President.   The Priesthood in all religions sings the same anthem.   First, the abuses are stoutly defended ; but when the ground is no longer tenable, then these abuses are to be distinguished and separated from the holy faith.   Since, however, they are always found in its company, you may as well say that the cat's skin is not the cat: the creature will make horrible cries should you attempt to strip it off, and perhaps will die of the operation. If[15] you see a man the greater part of his life in bad company, and growing worse at an age when he ought to act more wisely

[15 From " If " to " not " (4 lines) added in 2nd ed. ; 3 lines below, from " Neither " to " unsafe " (3 lines) added in 3rd ed.]

and more decently, you avoid him, whether his father and mother were honest people or not.

You have done much toward the destruction of a system, where fraud has been incessantly building upon fraud for fifteen hundred years. Neither wit nor wisdom can operate on the vulgar. To speak to them obscurely would be insensate, and to speak to them plainly would be unsafe. The most dexterous attack ever made against the worship of the Virgin—the principal worship among Catholics, which opens so many side-chapels to pilfering and imposture—is that of Cervantes. When [16] we once go beyond the unity of God, who can say where we shall stop? The human mind is then propelled into infinite space, and catches at any thing, from a want of rest.

Leopold. Cervantes wrote some sacred poetry.

President. Perhaps as a cover to his other book.

Leopold. I do not remember in what part of his writings he alludes to the worship of the Virgin irreverently or jocosely.

President. Throughout *Don Quixote*. Dulcinea was the peerless, the immaculate ; and death was denounced against all who hesitated to admit the assertion of her perfections. Surely, your Highness never could have imagined that Cervantes was such a knight-errant as to attack knight-errantry,—a folly which had ceased almost a century, if indeed it was any folly at all ; and the idea that he ridiculed the poems and romances founded on it is not less improbable ; for they contained all the literature of the nation, excepting the garniture of chapter-houses—theology—and pervaded as with a thread of gold the beautiful histories of this illustrious people. He delighted the idlers of romance by the jokes he scattered among them on the false taste of his predecessors and of his rivals ; and he delighted his own heart by his solitary archery, well knowing what amusement those who came another day would find in picking up his arrows, and discovering the bull's-eye hits. Is [17] it possible to misapprehend such a passage as this : " When my lord duke promised you the government of the island, nobody ever thought of such things as

[16 From " When " to " rest " (3 lines) added in 2nd ed. From " *Leopold* " to " book " (2 lines) added in 3rd ed. One line below from " of " to " jocosely " (3 lines) added in 3rd ed.]

[17 From " Is " to " blood-letting " (8 lines) added in 3rd ed.]

scourgings"? **Or that** preceding: "Despatch, and consent to this discipline. I assure you it will redound to the advantage **both** of your soul and body: of your soul, from the charity it **occasions**; and of your body, as you are of a florid complexion, **and will be** all **the** better for a little blood-letting"? Charles **V.** was the knight of La Mancha, devoting **his** labours and vigils, **his** wars and treaties, to the chimerical idea **of making minds,** like watches, turn **their** indexes, **by a** simultaneous movement, **to one point.** Sancho Panza **was the** symbol of the people, possessing sound sense in other **matters, but** ready to follow the most extravagant visionary in **this, and** combining implicit belief in it with **the** grossest sensuality. **For** religion, when it is hot enough **to** produce a rank enthusiasm, burns up and kills **every** wholesome seed entrusted **to** its bosom. A [18] man somewhat more suspicious **than I am** might be afraid **that Cervantes was** casting a sly glance toward the Trinity, when he wrote, **instead of** Tirante el Blanco, **Triante.** It could not be a mistake of his, **the** name of Tirante **being among the** most celebrated in romance; **and** critics and **editors are so sure of** correctness in the **first** editions, **that we find Triante in that of** Madrid. Allusions are made to the Catholic **Church by more than one** personage; but the author had **the good taste, not** to say **the prudence, to** avoid the continuity of **allegory in so long a** work, **and to make it** yield to character. **In the same** manner, Petronius alludes **to** Nero, sometimes in a philo-**sopher,** sometimes **in a** poet, and often in himself; so that the **emperor** stood in a room panelled with mirrors, and turned no-where without seeing his own features.

Leopold. Your **exposition** of the subject **is** quite novel to me, and your observation **on it just.** I **care** nothing **about** the worship **of** maple-trees and marble, **or** the inscriptions under them, or the coronets above; but I am resolved [19] to remove **many gross** impediments to industry, to forbid the observance of **certain old** saints, and to discountenance the canonization of any **new ones in** Tuscany. Noble families have been ruined by **counting a saint** among them; almost as many as **have** been

[18] From "**A**" to "Madrid" (7 lines) added in 3rd ed.; from "Allusions" to "**features**" (8 lines) added in 2nd ed.]

[19] First ed. reads: "resolved if not to forbid at least to discountenance the canonization of more saints in **Tuscany.** Many noble," &c.]

enriched by counting a **pope** : for the process **costs** fifty thousand crowns.   When it happens that a poorer man **or** woman is **made** the **object** of adoration, **then** indeed it is attended with somewhat **lighter expense,** because **the** confraternity **that** solicits it never **does so unless it** has some **powerful** patron at **Rome,** nor unless **the speculation is** sure enough **to be** lucrative.

President. **It** appears **to me, sir,** that even **in a** religion **resting on** peculation and fattening **on** vice, with **violence on** the **right hand and** falsehood **on** the left, giving every **thing to** the **slothful and** taking every thing **from the** industrious, **no evil** is worse than the necessity of periodical **confessions** to priests,—an evil which, **I am** afraid, **your** power **cannot remove, nor your wisdom** remedy.   It does more than **impoverish noble families ;** it **divests** them of **their** respectability.   **What young woman who** has once overcome her sense of shame, **so as to expose before a** stranger **of** another **sex** the first secrets **of the heart and the** disclosing germs of **the** passions, can **retain all** her **delicacy of** character ?   Modesty, **by** lifting up **the veil, is changed in all** her features ; **and,** when she **turns her** first **step aside, is** gone for ever. **Nothing** [20] **could** be invented **so** efficacious **as confession to increase and** perpetuate **the** dominion of the **priesthood, and** nothing **so** efficacious **to** accumulate and secure its **wealth as the** doctrine of purgatory.   **Confession is** good, **if it be made to the person** injured ; ingenuousness, manliness, **a resolution to give satisfaction for a wrong, and a** pledge **to abstain from it in future, are then, and then only,** its seasonable **fruits.**   Confession is not only not good, but positively and greatly bad, if it be made **to** a priest, **as it** always **is in the** Catholic **Church ; because it** transfers the authority of pardoning from **Him who can to him who cannot.**   He whose hay-stack **is burned may pardon the burner of it ;** but he **who only** hears **of its being burned is in no such** situation.   **A** father **may forgive the corrupter of his** daughter ; can a priest ?

Leopold.   **He says he can.**

President.   **He lies, then.**   **God** has given him no such **authority ;** nor can he show that **God has** enabled him to pardon

[[20] **From** " nothing " **to** " nearly all " (74 lines) added in 2nd ed.   At **line 29, 2nd ed. reads:** " pardoning from him who can."   The editor is **inclined to** think this the correct reading.]

any sin whatever on confession made to *him :* but he knows that neither confession to God, nor (what is better) to the injured party, will give him power and domination, by placing the hearts of men, and, with their hearts their stomachs and purses (two other vital parts), within his reach and under his key.

Leopold. The priest inherits, he tells you, his prerogative from the apostles.

President. He may as well pretend to the gift of tongues. Peculiar powers and attributes were conferred on the apostles which never were intended for perpetuity ; and the Catholic Church selects from these whatever can aggrandize it, by whatever means and application.

Leopold. Come, now for purgatory : after this last sentence you want it.

President. Whether there be or be not such a place or thing as purgatory, I think it useless to inquire, since no inquiry will lead me to proof and certainty. Truths, untruths, ambiguities, serve Mother Church most filially. Purgatory has one gateway upon earth ; under which gateway is a till to receive the small coin and great coin of all comers.

" Will you leave your father and mother in the flames for ages, when masses can release them ? O sinner ! you may expect the same hardness of heart in your own children ; and your offences will be the heavier by the addition of this inhumanity practised by you toward your unhappy parents, taught by you to your unhappier progeny." The penitent in the confusion of terror begs and implores the tender priest to say them : and what priest will do it unpaid ? Catholics cure sins as old women cure styes in the eye, —by rubbing them with gold.

Leopold. M. Du Paty, you do not believe then our religion to be of divine origin ?

President. Every good action, every good thought, every thing good, is of divine origin ; but I see nothing of the divine in manifest fraud, swarming with its insects and reeking in its exposure. I see nothing of it in the political invention of priestly institutions, nor in that base metal which solders the Church to the State. As Christians, we can take only the word of Christ for our rule. Neither the dreams of the convent nor the revels of the Vatican are adapted to the present day. We know more things and better than priests and monks have taught us; nor do we esteem those people the more in a tiara than in a cowl, in scarlet and embroidery than in black and white.   When violence and ignorance had usurped the Roman empire and the Greek, reasonably did the few wise men unite against the many unwise, until an equal and a safer share of power was granted them.   Religion opened her august asylum: Peace, Virtue, and Learning took refuge there, and sat quietly at the side of Bigotry and Imposture.   Diversity of opinion did at last spring up; but the great body of the thinking, at least in this country, found the comfort of holding together. Thus by degrees the Church grew on a level with the State, and (what remote posterity will hardly credit) overtopped it.   Times have changed wonderfully since: kings equal monks, and nations equal kings.   Whether it ought to be thus, I dare not ask: certainly it appeared a monstrous thing so lately as two centuries ago.   The first attempts were made by Venice and Holland: one defeated the most powerful king in Europe, and the other broke the league of nearly all.   Let [21] us lower our eyes from States to look at individuals; let us compare the women of Saxony and England with those of Italy and, I say it reluctantly, of France: what a difference!   In Florence, indeed, you see English-women arrogant, presumptuous, suspicious, credulous, and speaking one of another more maliciously than untruly; but Englishwomen in their character as in their clothes contract a great deal of dirt by travelling.   Of this there are many causes: the filthiness of our continental inns, so shocking to decency, and to nothing of which kind are they accustomed in their own country; the immodest language they hear from all classes, and nearly from all individuals, a thing utterly unknown among them at home; conversations on topics to which not even the most vulgar wretch in England ever alludes in presence of a female; and intercourse with others of their countrywomen who, from a long residence abroad, have been deeply imbued in foreign manners.   This [22] impudicity, this utter insensibility to decency in conversation, seems to have

[[21] From "Let" to "us" (2 lines) added in 2nd ed.   First ed. reads: "you rarely see an Englishwoman of character: they are chiefly those who are little respected at home; arrogant," &c.]

[[22] From "This" to "Seine" (18 lines) added in 3rd ed.   Instead of this passage occurs one which Landor was wise to omit.]

always been a characteristic of the Italian race. Many things are daily said at the tables of the first society, which ought only to be heard in schools of anatomy or medicine. At a time when corruption was thought, truly or falsely, to be less profound and less general than at present, we find the novelist Bandello—a person of education, a courtier, and at last a bishop—addressing to a lady of rank, whom he esteemed for her understanding and her virtue, a story of Messalina, in which such expressions are used by him as the sailors of Caieta, her paramours, would have hesitated to employ. Boccaccio, too, who flourished much earlier,—the purest and soundest heart, the companion of the highest, the bosom-friend of the wisest and the best,—represents to us seven unmarried ladies of the first families, of the noblest principles, of the most elegant and courteous manners, listening to the recital of such stories as would drive away five out of any seven washerwomen on the Seine.

Leopold. What the English ladies may be in their interior I do not pretend to know ; but when I compare their manners and address with those of my Florentines, or indeed with those of any other nation, it is far beyond my prerogative to grant them the precedency. Ours are accused of levity at church : they go thither, it is objected, to make love. Be it so. I never saw a Florentine girl or woman who did not come out in better humor than she entered, nor an English who did not come out in worse. The heart may surely be as impure from gall as from love ; and, if we must err on either side, let it rather be toward the kind affections than toward the unkind. The Florentine opens her heart, gives it, and resumes it, as easily as her fan ; the Englishwoman abroad keeps hers locked up, as a storeroom for the reputations she has torn, or intends to tear, in pieces. She may be indeed a good mother ; but if she takes alarm or umbrage at every foot that approaches her, I would rather have such a good mother in cub or kennel than in my closet or at my table.

President. The Englishwoman in England is domestic ; she of highest rank superintends the village-school, hears the children their lesson, examines their cleanliness, observes their dress, inquires into their health, remarks their conduct, presages their propensities, is amused at their games, and is interested in their adventures. She visits the sick, she converses with the aged, she comforts the afflicted, and she carries her sons and daughters with her, to acquire the practice of their duties. Those in England are all diffidence; those in Italy all defiance. Awkward beyond all other women upon earth, they happily are the most so when they are copying what is bad.

If we desire to know with certainty what religion is best, let us examine in what country are the best fathers, mothers, sons, daughters, wives: we shall there also find the best citizens, and of course the best Christians.

Leopold.[23] The Catholic has one advantage over others, in the fixedness of its dogmas.

President. These have been interpreted according to the convenience of the hierarchy. One pope, on more than one occasion, has flatly contradicted another; and not only has this been done where the contradicted pope has been declared an anti-pope (exquisite solution!), but where anti-papacy was never dreamed of. Benedict XIV., in the formulary called the "act of faith" prefixed to the elementary works of education, and even to the alphabet, makes the children say "they believe that the Son of God will bestow on the good the eternal glory of paradise, and on the wicked the eternal pains of hells." Children, who have not a penny in their pockets, may believe it; but old men and women, who carry a warm purse in fob or sack, entertain another belief. They are assured that the wicked are not liable to eternal pains, if they leave enough behind them for masses. In vain will any one tell me that masses will relieve from purgatory only, and not from hell. Where is the instance of a wealthy man told on his deathbed that the Church cannot save his soul by masses, or that he has not been confirmed in his credulity that it can? Pay handsomely for masses, and hell is out of the question. When you are there, indeed, you are too late; make haste!

Leopold. Popery, with her worst abuses, hath had her converts; and even from among the reformed, and men neither vicious nor ignorant; explain me this.

President. Reasons and reason are different things. In all religions, there have been believers who reflected with equal intensity. Those you mention, serious and melancholy triflers, attach much importance to things of little. After attempting to

[23] From "*Leopold*" to "haste" (22 lines) added in 2nd ed.]

penetrate and pass the crowd of fathers (as they are called) and
saints and martyrs, and knowing that before them lies a vast extent of perplexity and confusion, they stop, exhausted and spirit-
less, cast back a look of anguish over the ground they have plodded
through, hesitate, close their eyes, and sink upon the bosom of
Infallibility. As if the Almighty had ever invested with his
attributes a senseless and vicious priest, studious of nothing but
the usurpation of power and the aggrandisement of family; a
creature stained, as the greater part hath been, with murder and
incest and other enormities, at which Nature is confounded, and
Piety in consternation!

If[24] the popes are the servants of God, it must be confessed
that God has been very unlucky in the choice of his household.
So many, and so atrocious, thieves, liars, and murderers are not
to be found in any other trade; much less would you look for
them at the head of it.

Leopold. Take care they do not catch you, and treat you as
Julius II. was about to treat Ariosto.

President. I will not touch his Galatea under his eye; for
little am I disposed to be the hero of an eclogue, and less than
any of a piscatory one.

There are offences which popes will not pardon; those
namely, that affect their power: otherwise the[25] best among
them permit for money what they and their statutes condemn.
Prohibitions are merely a preparation for indulgences; sins are
wealth, masses save souls, virtues are insufficient.

Leopold. I have under my windows here in Florence no
fewer than three uncles married to their nieces, by express
permission from the "Holiness of our Lord,"—the title always
given to him in our gazettes. A little more wealth, with hardly
any more impudence, and we (unless I check it) may see brother
and sister, father and child, united by the sacrament of matri-
mony.

[24 From "If" to "one" (10 lines) added in 2nd ed. From "There"
to "otherwise" (2 lines) added in 3rd ed.]

[25 First ed. reads: "*Leopold.* The best . . . insufficient. Would you not
relieve your father from the agonies of hell, when a petticoat tied by
you round a priest's mistress can accomplish it? Do you hesitate?
Would not you, unnatural wretch! desire that your children should perform
the same service for you. I have under," &c.]

President. Let me return to my monks, who, whatever may be the abuses of their institutions, have nothing to do with such abominations.

Leopold. While they are monks, no; but scatter the dragon's teeth upon a warmer mould, and up springs a body of the same troopers.

Those of Rome were desirous, not many years ago, of beatifying one of your countrymen. "Such a rarity," said Benedetto Sant-Anna, its partisan and its promoter, "was the brilliant device of Father Nepomuceno, and should have gloriously greased our platters."

Benedetto Sant-Anna Torbellini is the natural son of a prince whom I esteem. Neglecting his studies, he was placed in a monastery at Rome, where he was remarkable for his musical powers, and his influence on the minds of his fair auditors. An intrigue with the adopted niece of a cardinal was his ruin. "It is not enough, then, Benedetto," cried his Eminence, "that you treat me with this ingratitude; me, who from your earliest youth have treated you with paternal kindness! We have known each other's foibles; but such an affront in my own library, under my own eyes, is unpardonable."

In vain he protested that, guilty as he was, this aggravation of his guilt was unintentional; that for the universe he would not have wounded the feelings of his early friend and benefactor, who certainly had been toward him a great deal more than ever father was; that his Eminence at no other time could have been irritated by any levity in him; that he thought the library a sanctuary unentered by human foot; and that he and Costanza had almost blinded themselves, by dusting the cushion where—

"Begone from my sight, villain! leave Rome instantly," cried the cardinal.

He obeyed, bringing me a letter; on which, knowing his state of probation, I did not hesitate to place him at the head of my young fifers, and he will shortly be leader of my band. His account of the sanctification is this :—

A poor devil had been observed every day, for twenty years, saying his prayers and beating his breast upon the bridge of Sant-Angiolo; and it sounded like a drum from inanition, voluntary

or involuntary.   During the performance of these religious duties,
a boy who had gone over to the buttress, on such an occasion as
is usual here in such places, fell from it, and was taken up by a
barge a little way off.   We have receipts for doing every thing,
miracles not excepted.   On the death of the Frenchman, one
Labre, who was attended in his last moments by Father Nepomuceno, it was resolved to make a saint of him, as having saved by
his intercession the boy who tumbled from the buttress.   Deposi-
tions were made upon oath that he was seen praying at the time,
and that he neither called out for assistance, nor exerted any other
human aid.   Such unequivocal proofs of piety and faith interested
all the holy city in his behalf.   His clothes, after being well
shaken on the bridge and sprinkled with holy water, were removed
to the convent.   Benedetto Sant-Anna had the charge of giving
them the odor of sanctity, by sprinkling them daily with the
powder of a Tonga bean, a substance then unknown at the
capital of the Christian world.   They were kissed inside and
outside, and some of the more pious in this operation licked them
furtively.

You must have observed at Rome, M. President, a vast
number of lame beggars.   No single war, in ancient or modern
times, could have lamed so many as now become lame every
year ; nearly all are cheats.   A consultation was holden by the
elder monks ; and it was resolved to collect these rogues and
vagabonds, and to restore the use of their limbs in the church of
the monastery.   Two younger members of the confraternity
were commissioned to joke with some, and to pay a paolo to
others.   At the morning appointed for the solemnity, the cloisters
were filled with these creatures upon crutches and the church,
arrayed in silks of yellow and red, was admirably well attended.
Every one was in full dress : the ladies with naked bosoms, the
gentlemen with swords, out[26] out of pure respect to Mother
Church.   Suddenly the cloister-door flew open, and a tremendous
sound was heard from the pavement to the roof.   Tatters rustled
round, crutches and knees, and bosoms covered with parchment
and bladders, made a noise greater than that of an attack with
bayonets.   Waves of mendicants, one bending over another, poured
in.   It was an edifying sight.

[26 From " out " to " Church " added in 3rd ed.]

An old beggar, really lame, and not in the secret, heard by chance of the ceremony, and hopped in after the rest. Many prayers were offered up to the beggar-saint; the censer was waved frequently before his picture; motions of the hands in various figures were made over the supplicants.[27] Some walked like boys; others walked indeed, but felt pain. Again crosses were made, again breasts were beaten, groans and thanksgivings were mingled, till at last pain and stiffness were unfelt by all; old sinews were knitted anew, lost bones recovered, and even the maimed and mangled left their late supports in the nave of the church as incumbrances, and perhaps as offerings, and walked firm and erect to finish their thanks in the refectory. One only remained. Father Nepomuceno, who led the rear, approached him marvelling, and said majestically and somewhat angrily, " Arise ! " The beggar, strengthened in faith, made an effort.

" Do not you find yourself better ? " said Father Nepomuceno.

" Rather better," replied the mendicant.

" Rise then, instantly ! "

He raised himself vehemently, and his crutches and knees and knuckles rattled in unison upon the floor.

" Thou man of little faith ! away ! " exclaimed Father Nepomuceno. He led him into his cell, and cried furiously, " What means this ? "

" God knows," replied the poor, good, patient creature ; " it is God's will."

" Have you prayed ? " asked the father, hastily.

" Thrice a-day regularly since I could speak."

" In church ? and always to the Virgin ? "

" Yes," replied the penitent.

" Have you confessed ? "

" Yes."

" Have you scourged yourself for your manifold sins ? "

" Alas ! how can I scourge myself ? " cried the beggar, with tears in his eyes from so painful an inability. " I can only beat myself when I lie down ; and beside, I can commit no offence to any one, which God forbid I should ever wish to do."

" No offence to any one ! Is that no offence ? How ! no

[27 First ed. reads : " Supplicants, and all received signal benefit."]

offence do you think it, to talk thus presumptuously? We are
all sinners : unless we did works of charity and penitence, what,
in the name of heaven, would become of us? Vile wretch! I
must open your eyes. You have secret crimes unexpiated ; you
have brought dishonor upon him who would have been your
patron, and whose manifold mercies you have just witnessed
toward the more deserving."

Upon this he took down a scourge, and bade the beggar kiss
it : the contrite man complied. The father unconsciously drew
it through his left hand, and found that it was one adapted to
his own shoulders. He threw it down indignantly, and seized
from across the back of an arm-chair a[28] broad embroidered
garter, stiff with brazen threads double-gilt, and embossed with
the letters EUFROSINA—LAURA-BEATRICE—RADICOFANI,—with
which, and without any further ceremonials, he scourged the
lame beggar heartily, exhorted him to faith, humility, and
penitence, and dismissed him weeping and praising God that his
eyes were opened.*

President. I am not the advocate of these Orders ; but each
contains, I know, many virtuous individuals ; many have resigned

[[28] First ed. reads: "an old cord, with which," &c.]
* It will hardly be credited that the following is an extract from a
Gazette in our times: "Firenze, giovedi 19 Decembre, 1822. La re-
ligione de' *Servi di Maria* che ha avuto origine in questa capitale, ci ha
dato in quest' anno il contento di vedere due de' suoi figli, nostri Toscani,
sollevati all' onore degli altari, cioè il B. Ubaldo Adimari, nobile Fiorentino
di cui ne furono già fatte le festi nella basilica della SS. Annunziata di
questa città, ne' tre giorni della scorsa pasqua, cioè 7, 8 e 9 Aprile, e nella
chiesa di monte Senario il di 16 nello scorso maggio, in cui ricorreva la
solennita dell' Ascenzion del Signore, e il B. Bonaventura Bonaccorsi,
nobile Pistojese, del quale oltre le solennissime feste celebrate in Orvieto,
dove passò alla gloria e si conserva il di lui sacro corpo, ne' giorno 11, 12, e 13
dello scorso Ottobre, il di 14 del corrente, giorno della sua *preziosa morte*,
ne fù con decente sacra pompa solennizata la memoria nella predetta
basilica della SS. Annunziata. *Rendiamo pertanto graziall' Altissimo, per
averci concesso in questi due Beati Comprensori due potenti avvocati al suo divin
trono !* "

According to this, God is ready enough to receive thanks and per-
fumery from whoever offers, without the introduction of squire or chamberlain, but is somewhat slow to grant pardon without such powerful
advocates as Signor Bonaventura Bonaccorsi or Signor Ubaldo Adimari,
in their saintly embroidered shoes and pink-satin robes of glory.

all pretensions to patrimony in behalf of brothers and sisters, relying on a secure possession of their hoods and cells.   I may not be greatly benefited by their processions or their prayers, but surely as much by them as by the cutlass and pistol of the highwayman.

Leopold.   The[20] greatest of abuses is the bequest of gold and jewels to the Virgin and Saints.   Since, however, it would shock the piety of the people to forbid it, the only plan I can think of is to decree that such gifts be confided to the municipality in trust and guardianship, and kept under lock and key ; and, if the Virgin or Saint do not come and take them within the year, that it be considered as a proof no such things are wanted by them, and that they freely give them to the sick and poor.   No roguery of priestcraft, no stupidity of idolatry, is so gross as in this practice, which I imagine my scheme will tend speedily to correct.   I do not know whether I am of a profession so good at telling stories as at raising them ; however, since I hear most of the occurrences that happen in my little territory, I will relate to you another anecdote.

Marchese Riccardi had the finest reliquary in Italy.   When he was on his death-bed, the Dominicans came about him, and his confessor was firmly of opinion that his road to Paradise would be smoother, if the relics were given to their church.   He was persuaded of the fact : he left the Dominicans his relics.   I inquired of his son the other day, whether it was not with some regret that he presented to the Dominicans so great a treasure.

" Not at all," said he.

" I understand the reliquary to have been valued at eight thousand crowns," answered I.

" The reliquary, yes," replied he ; " but I never heard the value of the relics."

" What then, Marchese, did you only give *them?* "

" My father," said he, " would have felt a torment the more, if the reliquary had gone out of the family.   We may hope for other relics to fill it again ; and just at this time there are some real ones that will be sold reasonably."

[20 From "The " to "correct" (10 lines) added in 2nd ed.   From "I " to " anecdote" (5 lines) added in 3rd ed.   From " Marchese " to " assented " (116 lines) added in 2nd ed.]

I asked him what he meant. He told me that a worthy friar had been despatched from Rome, on a mission to Ravenna, with a present of relics to the cathedral. He was so sober a man that, whenever he drank an extraordinary glass of wine, it confused his intellect. On his arrival at Forli, he could not contain his joy nor moderate his pride on the treasure he was conveying. The box was of cypress, curiously carved, and extremely old ; a brass lock was fastened upon it with pins of the same metal. The brotherhood of the convent where he lodged looked upon it with a variety of eyes, on hearing that it contained a treasure ; for he uttered not a word upon the nature of it. Some believed it was of diamonds ; others of emeralds ; others of rubies : all however were convinced from the lightness that the jewels were unset. There is hardly a town in Italy where the people are idler than at Forli. The lay-brothers of the convent whispered the report in every street ; and among the curious who assembled at the convent-gate was an officer, a native of Ravenna, named Filiberto Quinci. He indeed was curious to see the treasure, and, not without hope that he might be ordered to convoy it, came to say that there was an old munition waggon fit for this service ; little thinking that treasures could be light things, nor having heard any expression but, " Have you seen the treasure ? " What was his surprise on beholding a box nine inches long and seven broad, with a crucifix on the top to guard it ; and what was his delight at finding a friend of his early youth in the trusty friar !

" Paolo Naccheri ! is it you ? " cried he.

" Filiberto ! Filiberto ! " cried the monk. They embraced : necks and shoulders, beards and tears, met. They went away, and would sup together. The friar drew forth his handkerchief, and produced a thick slice of Bologna mortadella, some cheese, seven or eight livers, with lard enough to fry them in, and some bay-leaves and rosemary. There was also a piece of new goat-milk cheese, indented like Dover cliffs by his hunger on the road : this he threw back into his cowl. The lieutenant, when he saw all the provisions, blushed a little, and was resolved not to be outdone. He had observed a goose in the morning at the shop of a poulterer, the only poulterer in Forli, and who refused to sell any smaller portion than a whole leg, with which it was stipulated that half the head and half the neck and the

whole foot should be weighed.   A noble of the city sent his
cook several times to negotiate about it ; but the poulterer
was inflexible, and the noble retreated.   The lieutenant did what
was never done there since the days of Lombard King Aistulphus :
he stewed three-parts of a goose together, and inserted the cheese,
the liver, the mortadella, the bay-leaves, the rosemary, and the
lard.   The monk declared that the dish was fit for the marriage
of Cana in Galilee.   The lieutenant said that such was his
friend's courtesy ; but that in his anxiety to serve him he had
forgotten the figs and the aniseed, and begged him not to spare
the lemon and sugar that were beside him : if it wanted oil, the
oil in the lucerna was as fresh as any.   The pleasure of meeting
gave activity to their digestive powers, and to the antecedent
ones ; exhortations, jokes, recollections, wine, religion, women,
passed in turn : and now struck the *ventiquattro*.*   The monk
hurried toward the convent, embracing his friend at the door, and
promising to return.   He did indeed, and shortly,—pale, speechless, agonizing.

"What is the matter, my dear Naccheri?" exclaimed the
lieutenant.

"I am undone!   I am lost for ever!   The casket is broken
open ; the relics gone ! "

"Have you no suspicion of the thief?"

"None whatever."

"Some person in the convent?"

"Sacrilege! Impossible! "

"Leave the matter to me : I have detected and taken up
many rogues."

"Oh for Christ's sake!   It would be a scandal! "

"Leave it, I say, to me : I will accuse no friar, I promise
you.   Bring me the box by daylight."

Disturbed and disorderly were the slumbers of the monk : he
attributed his loss to the levity of his conversation, which he
confessed to the Virgin, begging her however to remember that
he had mixed it with religion.   Among other thoughts in his
imperfect sleep, he fancied that the relics were again in the

* 24 o'clock, one hour after sunset, when the monks should be in the
convent.   Almost the only question asked openly by the Italians is, *Sono
sonate le* 24?— so teeming with big events is that hour.

casket. He started up ; walked toward it ; closed the lid, turning his eyes away from it, as unworthy to behold it ; and, repeating in a tremulous voice, *Fiat voluntas tua !* again placed it under the guardianship of the crucifix. Before the dawn of day, he rose and dressed himself, if such an expression is applicable to friars ; and having said a litany, together with a proper psalm,— *By the waters of Babylon we sat down and wept,*—he wiped his eyes, covered the precious casket, and carried it to his friend, to whom he related his sufferings and his dream.

"May I look at it, unworthy as I am?" said Filiberto.

"Take it, take it ! Behold it !" answered the friar, sobbing piteously.

The lock was unforced, but the brass nails were standing out from it : they had been removed and replaced.

"Are you quite sure they have taken the relics?"

"Sure, sure ; even the wrapper."

"I must confer with another upon these nails," said the lieutenant ; "they may lead to the discovery of truth." He had drawn one out slily.

"No, no, no !" cried the friar.

"One is wanting," said his friend : "you yourself will be suspected of curiosity and unbelief, if this should be missed. Another must be made quickly !"

Fra Paolo shuddered and assented, but[30] remarked that it was impossible for any human hand to imitate the embossed and ancient nail.

"Leave it to me," said Filiberto : "you must not appear in the business ; the nut is out, I may be trusted with the shell."

He took it into his bedroom, and having selected the larger bones of the goose from their two plates, and washed them in a lixiviate, and rubbed them with ashes, he enwrapped them in a cartouche-paper, deposited them in the casket, fastening the nails, particularly the one he had removed. He then ran to the outer room, and, "Father ! father !" cried he, "I will have nothing more to do with it : I am unworthy ! I can aver and swear that a nail was wanting, and I believe in my conscience that several were loose."

[30] From "but" to "nail" (3 lines) added in 3rd ed. From "Leave" to "perukes" (47 lines) added in 2nd ed.]

The father answered not; he took the casket in his hand, looked at it, raised his eyes to heaven, and swooned. The lieutenant rubbed his temples with vinegar and gunpowder, scratched his gums with a flint, and poured some brandy down his throat, muttering in a low, gruff voice, what he never would have done but for a friend, *Ave Maria! presto!* The friar's senses returned, but it was long before he could find a channel for the effusion of his piety. At last he repeated three times, as the most proper on the occasion, the words in which the Lord was praised for having glorified his hand-maiden. "Sinner as I am," exclaimed he, "I dare neither doubt nor believe that the miracle is complete in all its parts." He closed his eyes; the flesh crept upon his bones; he lifted up the casket in his two hands above his head, and chanted in a tremulous voice, *Fiat voluntas tua!*

The lieutenant said that he doubted, from the lightness of the box, whether a single bone was restored. "Bones are not heavy, it is true," added he; "but a young girl's bones have a good deal of marrow in them."

"None whatever," answered the holy man; "they were as dry as a palm branch* on the anniversary, and very small; for she was the youngest of the eleven thousand."

"One miracle is as good as another," said the lieutenant; "two trusses of hay from the same stack smell and weigh pretty much alike. Let us hope, however, that the pretty saint has protected her bones and vindicated her virginity."

Again Fra Paolo chanted, *Fiat voluntas tua!* Indignant at the robbery, he returned no more to the convent, and resolved to say nothing of his charge again until he reached Ravenna. There it was received with the ringing of bells, and the display of tapestry and bed-coverlets from the windows, and the array of all the pillars of all the churches in the richest silks, and of all the saints in spangled shoes and powdered perukes: their[31] faces were reddened, their eyebrows blackened, and their nails gilt afresh. The clergy, the military, the various fraternities marched

---

* These palms are really olive-twigs, placed over the crucifix by the bedside, and renewed on Palm-Sunday.

[31 From "their" to "afresh" (2 lines) added in 3rd ed.; from "The clergy" to "Riccardi" (48 lines) added in 2nd ed.; "You" to "orders" added in 3rd ed. The addition to the 1st ed. is 239 lines in all.]

before and after it into the cathedral. Four **knights** supported **it,**
eight marquises assisting them; and his excellency the governor,
adorned with all his orders, holding over it the umbrella. Cannon
was fired as it entered the portal, and again as it ascended the steps
of the high altar. Nothing of jubilee is celebrated here, nor, I
believe, in the rest of Europe, without the instruments of violence
and slaughter. Many a belly felt the butt-end of a musket, for
yearning too affectionately after the youngest of the eleven
thousand, in the nave of the duomo. The crowd was immense.
Happy the youth who was next to his beloved on that day, for
he was near indeed, and she wanted protection upon all sides. If
she reproved him for **any** thing, the Ambrosian hymn, echoing
through **the** vault, intercepted it.

The **bones had been verified upon the oath of** surgeons and
physicians, denominated **on** such occasions the "expert," in
presence of the archbishop, the canonics, and **the** prothonotary.
It was ascertained that the *os pubis* had been fractured, by the
same violence as was offered by the executioner to the daughter
of Sejanus,—a farther proof of martyrdom; it being remembered
by one of the canonics that, according **to** the Roman laws, virgins
must undergo this indignity **before** the last punishment. The
condition of the bones was admirable. She must have **been very**
young, poor child! If such another *os pubis* **could be found**
among her sisterhood, it would be decorous **and reverential to**
compose a pair of spectacles with them for the **"Holiness of** our
Lord." Several old priests declared that they saw much the
better, on merely looking through the mysterious curvature in its
present state; and a wart of long standing was removed from the
nose of one by it, after forty days, as was evident to all Ravenna.
The inauguration of the relics took place on the twenty-ninth of
July; on the thirtieth of September the lieutenant Filiberto
Quinci was mortally wounded from behind the wall **of** a vineyard, **by an** assassin whose brother **he** had disarmed and **was**
leading **with** his hands tied behind him toward the city prison of
Forli. He confessed to a Jesuit the fraud he had committed,
who absolved him the more readily **as it** was committed in its first
stage against a **dominican.** The **pain** of the wound **made** him
exert his **voice;** and perhaps he **cared** little for secrecy, in the
greater hope **of** expiating his offence; so that many of his friends

and attendants heard the recital, and divulged it. Nevertheless, it was agreed and certified that a miracle had really been performed; and that, although some of the bones had been stolen, several were yet remaining, and endued with such efficacy as to convert the baser into the more precious,—the goose's into the virgin's. It is reported that the greater part of the original are brought into Tuscany, and will be sold here: this report is the comfort of Riccardi.

You may smile at the credulity of even the higher orders: I trust however, M. Du Paty, that the laws and establishments are better in Tuscany, and information more advanced, than in the other States of Italy. Closing[32] the cells of idleness and imposture, I have opened schools and manufactories for the children of the poor.

President. Unless the ladies and gentlemen can be induced to visit and superintend them, I doubt their efficiency.

A House of Industry was established at Como. Virtuous mothers have been led frequently out of it, heavy with child, and have died from inanition in the streets; their allowance of food being only one scanty meal in the twenty-four hours; while prostitutes, thieves, assassins, poisoners, have enjoyed purer air and more comfortable accommodation in prison, and have been supplied twice in the day with more wholesome food, and each time more abundantly. In both instances, a discouragement is holden forth to honesty, a reward to crime.

Sovereigns know more correctly the state of other countries than of their own. We may be too near great objects to discern them justly; and the greatest of all objects to a prince is the internal state of his people.

Leopold. Your observation is just. The persons we employ have more interest in deceiving us than others have. I can trust one,—Gianni.[33] I send none abroad; so that I am rather less liable to deception than my brethren are. As the gentlemen of Tuscany seldom travel farther than to Siena or to Pisa, the expense of a coffee-house-keeper, under the title of plenipotentiary, is saved me everywhere.

[32 From "Closing" to "established" (6 lines) added in 3rd ed.; 1st ed. reads: "*President.* I observed nearly the same inequality at Como."]

[33 See cancelled passages printed at the end of the Conversation.]

President. **Your Highness is as desirous of** abolishing idle offices as **others** are **of** creating them.

Leopold. I am not afraid of losing my place from a want of party friends, and have **no** very poor relations to support. Since[33] I send no envoys, there are certain States which seem resolved to punish **me** by sending worse than **none.**

It often happens, that those who are very wealthy are far from forward in displaying **what** they possess ; thus happens it **that, in** countries which abound **in** talents and genius, the governors **are** careless how little of them is exhibited in **their** appointments to foreign courts. I should **be** happy to see as ministers at mine, M. President, men like you, with whom I could converse familiarly and frankly on matters of high importance ; and **no** greater compliment could be paid me by the princes, my friends and allies. To delegate as their representatives young persons **of** no knowledge, no conduct, **no** respectability, proves to **me a** neglect **of** their duty and an indifference **to** their honor, **and no less** evidently shows the opinion they entertain of me to **be un-** worthy and injurious. Trifling men in such situations may **suit** indeed small courts, but not where **the** sovereign **has** any credit for the rectitude of his views and the **arduousness of** his under-takings.

This reflection leads me back again **to an** inquiry into the last **of** your positions, that **my** Code provides but faintly and ineffect-ually for the protection of character. **The** States of Italy are the parts of shame in **the** body politic of Europe. I would not hold out an ægis to protect a snail : the gardener **does** not shelter his plants while they are underground. I declare **to** you, M. Du Paty, that, whenever and wherever **I find a** character to protect, I will protect it.

President. I am **averse to** the perpetual maintenance of great armies ; but without somewhat of **a** military spirit there can be little spirit for anything,—as we **see** in China and India. That the Florentines should have conquered **the** Pisans quite astonishes **me** when I look upon them : at present they could not conquer a **hen-coop** guarded by **a cur.** Boccaccio,[34] in his eclogue entitled

---

[33 See cancelled passages printed at the end of the Conversation.]
[34 From " Boccaccio " to " Baldelli " (4 lines) added in 3rd ed.]

Lipis, calls the Florentine by the name of Batracus (frog), as being the most loquacious and timid of animals.   Such at least is the explanation given by his countryman and commentator, Baldelli.

Leopold.   The Italians, when they were bravest, were like tame rabbits; very pugnacious among themselves, but crouching, screaming, and submitting to be torn piecemeal by the smallest creatures of another race.   In the consulate of Marcus Valerius (brother of Publicola) and Postumius, the Sabines were conquered; thirteen thousand prisoners were taken in two battles: in the second no Roman was slain.

I want no armies.   If ever I should want them, I can procure a much better commodity at the same price; the rations of a Bohemian and of a Tuscan are the same: I would not change a good farmer for a bad soldier.   I want honest men and no other glory than that of making them.

President.[35]   If you abolish the convents of monks, you act consistently in abolishing your armies: for the natives of Florence are the smallest and weakest men in Europe; and, whenever we meet one stronger than the generality, we may be sure he derives his origin from the convent.   The monks are generally stout, and their offspring is healthy; but this continues for only one generation.   The children of your soldiers are mostly weak, like those of your citizens; and from the same cause, indiscriminate venery. The monks have their choice, from the facilities afforded to them by the sacredness of their order, and by the beneficence of confession; advantages in which the soldiery does not participate. In Protestant countries, the people are always both cleanlier and healthier than in Catholic; but I have observed that the religious in the former are mostly the weakest men in the community,—in the latter, universally the strongest.

Leopold.   As my soldiers are useless to me in the field, I shall call them out more frequently in the churches, when I have reduced the number of ecclesiastics.   On great festivals we have decently smart files of them in the nave.   I shall indulge the people with a larger number, and oftener.

President.   In Tuscany there are persons of integrity; few

[35 From " *President* " to " oftener " (20 lines) added in 2nd ed.]

indeed, and therefore the more estimable.[36]   Wherever there is a substitute for morality; where ceremonies stand in the place of duties; where the confession of a fault before a priest is more meritorious than never to have committed it; where virtues and duties are vicarious; where crimes can be expiated after death for money; where by breaking a wafer you open the gates of heaven,—probity and honor, if they exist at all, exist in the temperament of the individual.   Hence 'a general indifference to virtue in others; hence the best men in Italy do not avoid the worst; hence the diverging rays of opinion can be brought to no focus; nothing can be consumed by it, nothing warmed.

The language proves the character of the people.   Of all pursuits and occupations, for I am unwilling to call it knowledge, the most trifling is denominated *virtù*.   An[37] alteration in a picture is *pentimento*.

The Romans, detained from war and activity by a calm, termed it *malacia*; the Italians, whom it keeps out of danger, call it *bonaccia*.   I[38] am ashamed to confess that we Frenchmen have borrowed this expression, without a suspicion of its import. We are, it is true, the most courageous people in the world; but we have always been the most subject to panics by land, and to despair by sea.

Leopold.[39]   On *malacia* and *bonaccia* let me remark, that, although the latter supplanted the former, as *Beneventum* did *Maleventum*, yet *malacia* descends not in a direct line from *malus* (a thing evidently unknown to those who substituted in its place *bonaccia*), but from μαλακός.   *Malus* itself has the same origin. Effeminacy and wickedness were correlative terms both in Greek and Latin; as were courage and virtue.   Among the English, I hear, softness and folly, virtue and purity, are synonymous.   Let

---

[[36] First ed. reads: "estimable.   One honest Italian is worth one hundred thousand honest Englishmen, for such, I imagine, to be the proportion. Wherever," &c.]

[[37] From "An" to "*pentimento*" added in 3rd ed.]

[[38] First ed. reads: "*bonnacia*.   Love of their country is so feeble that whatever is excellent they call *pelegrino*."   From "I" to "sea" (5 lines) added in 2nd ed.]

[[39] "*Leopold*" added in 3rd ed.; from "on" to "people" (10 lines) appears as a footnote in 1st ed.]

others determine on which side lies the indication of the more quiet, delicate, and reflecting people.

President.[40] If a footman sends a scullion to a tailor, it is an *ambasciata*. Sbirri are eminently *la famiglia*, quite at home ; but what is admirable is *pellegrino*.

So corrupt are they, that softness with them must partake of disease and impurity : it is *morbidezza*.

Three or four acres of land with a laborer's cottage are called a *podere*. Beggarly magnificence of expression ! Every house with a barn-door, instead of a narrower, is *palazzo*.

I saw open in a bookseller's window a boy's dictionary, " Dictionarium Ciceronianum," in the page where *heros* was, and found its interpretation, *barone, signore*.

Such is their idea of contemplation, and of the subjects on which it should be fixed, that, if a dinner is given to a person of rank, the gazettes announce that it was presented *alla Contemplazione della sua eccellenza*.

A lamb's fry is *cosa stupenda :* a[41] paper kite is *aquilone*.

Their idea of fighting is exemplified in the word *tirare*, which properly means to *drag*.

Strength which frightens, and finery which attracts them, are *honesty :* hence *valentuomo* and *galantuomo*.

A well-dressed man is a man of honor ; *uomo di garbo*.

Spogliare is *to undress ;* the spoils of a modern Italian being his shirt and stockings.

Pride is offended at selling any thing ; the shopkeeper tells you that he *gives* you his yard of shoe-ribbon : *dà,* not *vende*.

A *trinket* is a joy, *gioia ;* and a *present* is a *regala,* though it be a bodkin.

One would imagine that *giustiziato* means requited : it means *hanged :* as if justice did nothing else, or had nothing else to do.

---

[40] From " *President* " to "*pellegrino* " (3 lines) added in 3rd ed. ; 2 lines below from " three " to "*signore*" added in 2nd ed.]

[41] From "a " to "*aquilone* " added in 3rd ed.; from " their " to " drag " (2 lines) added in 2nd ed.; 3 lines below from " *Spogliare* " to " stockings " (2 lines) added in 2nd ed. ; 2 lines below 1st ed. reads : " *vende*. Misfortune is criminal: the captive is a wicked man *cattivo* ; " from " A " to " gioia " added in 2nd ed. ; from " and " to " bodkin " added in 3rd ed. ; from " one " to " do " added in 2nd ed.]

Leopold.[42] I can furnish you with another example in my own profession. *Governare* means to *govern* and to *wash the dishes.* This indeed is not so absurd at bottom ; for there is generally as much dirty work in the one as in the other.

President. *Meschino,* formerly *poor,** is now *mischievous* or *bad.*

Leopold.[43] I am no etymologist, and more than an etymologist is wanted here ; but let me remark to you that the word *meschino* is still in use among us in the same double acceptation, as the word *wretch* is among the English ; and you Frenchmen, too, employ the word *méchant,* which comes from it, in the same manner. The words signify to us that wretchedness and wickedness go together.

President. I see it. Things strike us in another language which we pass over in our own ; and words often lose their original meaning. What is general may become particular, and what is particular may become general. *Amazzare* is *to kill.* The meaning was originally to kill with a *club.* We now say *il gatto ha amazzato un topo,* although we have the best grounds for believing that cats never killed rats with clubs, even in the heroic ages.

An Italian thinks he pays me a compliment by calling me *furbo,* holding it as the summit of felicity and glory to overreach. But on the other hand, if roguery is praiseworthy, misfortune is criminal : the captive is a wicked man, *cattivo.*

A person is not rendered vile by any misconduct ; but if he has the toothache, he is *avvilito.*

With[44] all the admiration and aptitude of the Italians for poetry, any grimace or trick of the countenance is called a *verso.* *Fa tanti versi.* We call *valiant* the man who defends his own or his country's honor by his courage : the Italians call valiant a famous fiddler or well-winded fifer,—*valente suonotare.* In Italy,

---

[42 From "*Leopold*" to "other" (4 lines) added in 2nd ed.]

* Teseo era stato anch' egli un certo protettore e difensore, e benignamente e con amorevolezza haveva ascoltato i preghi degli uomini *meschini,—Vite di Plutarco da M. Ludovico Domenichi, MDLX.*

[43 From "*Leopold*" to "*cattivo*" (19 lines) added in 2nd ed.]

[44 From "With" to "*versi*" (3 lines) added in 2nd ed.; and from "We" to "synonymous" (5 lines) added in 3rd ed.]

the *fabulous* is the common speech : *favalla* and *lingua* are synonymous.

Opera was among the Romans *labor*, as *operæ pretium*, &c. It now signifies the most contemptible of performances, the vilest office of the feet and tongue, whenever it stands alone *by excellence*. *Anima*[45] the *soul*, is also the *mould of a button : animella* (the endearing form), a *sweetbread*.

Ostia, a sacrifice (*hostia*), now serves equally to designate the Almighty and the wafer that seals a billet-doux. This, too, we have in common. Poisoning was formerly so ordinary an operation here, that what other nations call a violent death was called an *assisted* one. " Nacqui l'opinione, dispersa allora, ch' egli mancava di morte *aiutata* piutosto che naturale," says Bentivoglio on Don John of Austria.

Leopold.[46] Beware, M. President, that no learned man in his idleness take you farther to task on the same subject. I would wish to retaliate on you as gently as possible, but I find in one of your expressions that characteristic sportiveness which attends your cruelties, when you commit any. *Amende honorable*, as your jurists call it, is thus defined by them : " Le condamné est à genoux en chemise, la corde au cou, une torche à la main, et conduit par le bourreau." This *honorable* way in which an offender is persuaded to correct his error is, according to time and person, accompanied by flagellations and other ceremonials of honor and devotion, in which the humble minister of justice, the hangman, has the goodness to lend him all the assistance in his power, and indeed to take upon himself this most painful part of the duty ; the person who makes the expiation to honor and the laws only lending the superficies (or a little more) of his body, while the precursory section of his amendment is going through.

There are idoms for which no philologer can account ; such as

---

[45] From " *Anima* " to " *sweetbread* " (2 lines); and two lines below from "This" to " Austria " (6 lines) added in 3rd ed. In the 1st ed. there are in a footnote on *Ostia* two Latin epigrams the first of which is worth quoting.

> " Oblita butyro quanta es mea crustula. Quanta
> Vel sine butyro quum deus esse potes."]

[46] From " *Leopold* " to " through " (16 lines) added in 2nd d. ; and from " There " to " one " (3 lines) added in 3rd ed.]

personne for *nobody*, and *à même* for *ability* to perform. You *lend* an oath,—vous prêtez serment,—do you ever *keep* one ?

I [47] have found in twenty of your authors, at the least, the expression, *faire retentir sa voix au milieu ; entonner* is also in common use, a proof of a noisy people : and perhaps some might be found of a vain one. I must fight for my Tuscans ; they have other phrases which prove their good nature,—not the least of merits in any man or any people, and among the first to be commended by a prince.

Their oaths and exclamations, instead of *peste* and other horrors, are, by the kindest and most lovely of the gods,—*per Bacco ! per Bacco d'India ! Fe di Bacco ! Corpo di Bacco ! per Dingi Bacco !*

President. What can that mean ?

Leopold. *Dingi* is an abbreviation of *Dionigi* (Dionysius). Then, *per Diana !* or [48] by the most beautiful of our indigenous plants, as *Cappari ! Corbezzoli !*

President. I do not understand the latter.

Leopold. *Corbezzoli* are the berries of the arbutus : your French *corbeil* comes from the twigs, which are used in making baskets and panniers; and another word, which you like less, *corvée*,—loads of stone, earth, manure, carried on the backs of men and women in crates of this material. Let us now leave the fields again, for cities and manners.

We may discern, I think, the characters of nations in their different modes of salutation. We Italians reply, *Sto bene ;* the ancient Romans, *valeo ;* the Englishman, I am *well;* the Frenchman, *I carry myself well.* Here, the Italian, the best formed of Europeans, stands with gracefulness and firmness ; in short, *stands well.* The Roman, proudly confident in his strength, said, *I am stout and hearty.* The Englishman feels throughout mind and body this " standing well," this calm, confident vigor, and says, I *am* well. The Frenchman *carries himself* so.

President. It is dangerous to retort on princes.

Leopold. I invite it.

[47 From " I " to " *Corpo de Bacco* " (10 lines) added in 2nd ed. ; and from " *per Dingi* " to " *Diana* " (5 lines) added in 3rd ed.]
[48 From " or " to " material " (8 lines) added in 2nd ed. ; and from " Let " to " that " (15 lines) added in 3rd ed.]

President. By this condescension I am encouraged to remark, that a stranger [49] is much amused by the designation of your Italian tribunals, the *ruota criminale*, &c. ; as if Justice had her wheel, like Fortune, or rather used the same.

Leopold. Such is the idea the thing itself presents to us ; the word is deduced from the *rolling* and *unrolling* of papers, and is analogous to the *volumen* of the Romans, and the *roll* of the English, which likewise gives an appellation to a court of judicature.

President. Your Highness will permit me to add one more example. If injustice is done and redress claimed, it is requisite to perform an execrable act, if the words mean any thing,— *umiliare una supplica.* Baser language was never heard in the palace of Domitian, who commanded that he should be called lord and god. I could select many such expressions. In this perversion of moral feeling, it is not to be expected that the laws can always stand upright. It is dangerous for a foreigner not to visit a commissary of police ; but to omit in an address to him the title of *illustrissimo* is fatal. I conversed the other day with an English gentleman, who had conducted his wife and family to Pistoja, for the benefit of the air. He rented a villa at the recommendation of the proprietor, who assured him that the walls were dry, although built recently. Within a few days it rained, and the bed-chambers were covered with drops. His wife and child suffered in their health : he expostulated ; he offered to pay a month's rent and to quit the premises, insisting on the nullity of an agreement founded on fraud. The proposal was rejected ; a court of judicature declared the contract void. The gentleman, to prove that there was nothing light or ungenerous in his motive, gave to his banker, M. Cassigoli, the amount of the six months' rent, to be distributed among respectable families in distress. The proprietor of the house, enraged at losing not only what he had demanded but also what was offered, circulated a report in the coffee-houses, and wherever he went, that the gentleman might well throw away his money, having acquired immense sums by piracy. He appealed to the local tribunals, with a result far different from the former. The commissary, to whom the business was referred by them, called the offender to him in

[49 From "a stranger" to "same" (3 lines) added in 2nd ed.; from "*Leopold*" to "*President*" (5 lines) added in 3rd ed.]

private, without informing the plaintiff of his intention. Hence no proof was adduced, no witness was present, and the gentleman knew nothing of the result for several weeks after. It was an admonition to be more cautious in future, given to a man who had in succession been servant to two masters, both of whom were found dead without illness ; a man who, without any will in his favor, any success in the lottery, any dowry with his wife, any trade or profession, any employment or occupation, possessed 12,000 crowns. Where justice is refused, neglected, or perverted, the *Presidente del buon Governo* is the magistrate who receives the appeal. The foreigner stated his case fully to the president, from whom he obtained no redress, no [50] answer, no notice.*

[[50] " No answer, no notice " added in 3rd ed. The footnote assumes its present form in the 2nd ed. In the 1st ed. in place of the first 16 lines another anecdote is given, which is not reprinted here.]

* Dr Lotti of Lizzano, on the confines of the Modenese, the reputed son of the Emperor P. Leopold, to whom (if I may judge from the coins) he bore a perfect resemblance, was the most learned and courteous man I have ever conversed with in Tuscany. He was rather fond of wine ; but with decorum. I spent one of the happiest days of my life in his society, and was about to repeat my visit the following summer, when I heard that my quiet, inoffensive, beneficent friend had been stoned to death by a parishioner. No inquiry was instituted by government: he had nothing but erudition and virtue to recommend him, and the tears and blessings of the poor. I asked how so unmerited a calamity could have befallen so warm-hearted a creature, and in the decline of life : the reply was, *Chi sa ? forse uno sbaglio. Who knows ? perhaps it was done by mistake.* What a virtuous and happy people must that be, to which such a loss is imperceptible ! I saw him but three times, and lament it more than I think it right to express, at the distance of nearly two years. Rest thee with God, kind, gentle, generous Lotti !

A courier, who had been in the service of Prince Borghese, went openly by day into the Postmaster's office, stabbed him in the body, fired a pistol through his hand, was confined at Volterra, and released at the intercession of Prince Borghese in six weeks.

Whoever shall publish a periodical work, containing a correct and detailed account of irregularities and iniquities in the various courts of law throughout Europe, will accomplish the greatest of literary undertakings, and will obtain the merit of the stanchest, the truest, and the best of reformers. No subject is so humble that it may not be recommended by a fit simplicity of style ; no story so flat that it may not solicit attention if edged by pointed remarks. The writer will perform one of those operations which are often admired in Nature, by eliciting a steady, broad, and beautiful light from rottenness and corruption.

Leopold. As I covered **my** ears at the commencement, I must at the conclusion. Scandalously as my servants acted, the rank and character **of** the injured gentleman were imperfectly known to the commissary and the president, who also are **ignorant** that many of the best families in England **are** untitled. **Here** counts and marquises **are** more plentiful **than sheep** and **swine ;** and there are orders of knighthood where **there is not credit for a** pound of polenta.[51]

President. **Your** predecessors **have softened what was** already **too soft ;** and **your** Highness must give some consistency **to** your mud, **by** exposing and working it, if you desire to leave **upon it** any durable or just impression. I am afraid it will close **upon your** footstep the moment **you** go away.

Leopold. **I** hope **not.** Tuscany **is a** beautiful landscape with bad figures : **I** must introduce better.

President.[52] To speak without reserve **or** dissimulation, **I** have **remarked this** difference between the gentlemen of Florence and those of other nations. While others **reject disdainfully and** indignantly **from** among **them** any member **who has acted** publicly or privately **with** dishonor, these interest **themselves** warmly **in** his favor, **although** they never **had** visited **or known** him. It must be from **a powerful** sympathy, **and** in the hope, **more or less remote** and **obscure, that** they may benefit **in** the **same manner in the same circumstances.**

Leopold. **I** begin with **what forms the moral** character, however **my conduct** may be viewed **by the Catholic** princes. Few among **them are** better than whipped **children, or** wiser than unwhipped ones. They are **puppets in the hands of** priests : they nod their heads, **open** their mouths, **shut** their eyes, and their blood is liquefied or congealed at the touch of these impostors. I will lessen their **influence by** lessening their **number.** To the intent of **keeping** up a numerous establishment **of** satellites in the church **militant, a priest is** punished more severely for performing twice in **the day the most** holy of his ceremonies than for almost any violation of morality. But the popes, perhaps, have in secret a typical sense **of the** Mass, permitting the priest to celebrate it only

---

[51 First ed. reads: "polenta, and the bravest of whose members would tremble to mount a goat in their worst breeches. *President,*" &c.]

[52 From " *President* " to " Leopold " (10 lines) added in 2nd ed.]

once, in remembrance that Christ was sold once only. When we arrive at mystery, a single step farther and we tumble into the fosse of fraud. The Romish Church is the general hospital of old and incurable superstitions from the Ganges to the Po. It is useful to princes as a pigsty is to farmers; but it shall not infect my palace, and shall do as little mischief as possible to my people.

President. Your Highness, by diminishing the number of priests, will increase the rate of Masses. A few days ago I went into San Lorenzo, and saw a clergyman strip off his gown before the altar with violence and indignation. Inquiring the reason, I was informed that four *pauls* had been offered to him for a Mass, which he accepted, and that on his coming into the church the negotiator said he could afford to pay only three.[53] There are offices in the city where Masses are bargained for publicly. Purgatory is the Peru of Catholicism; the body of Christ in some of our shops is at the price of a stockfish, in others a fat goose will hardly reach it, and in *Via de' Calzaioli* it is worth a sucking-pig.

Leopold. The Roman States are worse in proportion.

President. There are more *religious* in that territory than slave-masters in our American islands, and their gangs are under stronger and severer discipline. The refuse of manhood exercises the tyranny of Xerxes in the cloak and under the statutes of Pythagoras.

Leopold. It[54] is curious and interesting to observe the fabrication of those insects, which from the bottom of the Sea of Galilee have been adding, year after year, particle on particle, and have ultimately filled up almost the whole expanse with their tortuous and branching corallines.

When violence and usurpation were distracting the Roman empire, can we wonder if the possessors of knowledge and the lovers of quiet clung together, and contrived the best and readiest means possible of preserving the little they retained? The sanctuaries of religion, abandoned by the old gods and old wor-

[53 In 1st ed. there is a footnote here which is not reprinted. It contains a scandalous story concerning the avarice of a Florentine nobleman.]

[54 From "It" to "corallines" (5 lines) added in 3rd ed. and then from "When" to "excommunicated" (158 lines) added in 2nd ed.]

shippers served the purpose well. Persecution rendered the new
guests only the more united ; pity at their sufferings, admiration
at their virtues, drew many toward them ; miracles were invented,
encouraged, propagated. There is something of truth in every
thing. Like gold, it is generally found in small quantities ; and,
as is said of gold, it is universal : even falsehood rests upon it.
Contrivances, which at first were requisite and necessary for the
security of a weak and unprotected religion, now began to
multiply for its extension and aggrandizement. The credulous,
the rich, the slothful, stood prepared for the mark that was to be
impressed on them by the coarse, indiscriminating letters of the
age. The literary now chose their emperor, as the military chose
theirs, only giving him another title inaugurated by religion. A
quieter craft, observing the instability of power, devised and
executed at leisure the institutions best adapted to its maintenance ; and by degrees such barriers were erected about the church,
as neither in extent nor in strength had ever surrounded the
pretorium. The pious, who came from a distance to venerate
the simple edifice—the house of a god born in a manger—could
not pass nor even look over the ramparts, and were driven away
or punished as criminals if they inquired for it. Somewhat
earlier, when the name of pope had not yet been invented, instead
of surprise at any worldly advantages the pastors derived from the
tractability of their flocks, it might rather be excited at their
moderation. This, however, soon was over ; and such rapacity
succeeded as no other religion, no other government, no tyranny,
no conquest hath exemplified. In our days, the commander of
the faithful in the West is contented if we pay and clothe his
military, permitting them to be taken off our lands for him, and
allowing him to discipline them, even in our streets and houses.
The more virtuous our subjects are, the less contented is he.
Every execution-day is a rent-day to him : no fellow is hanged
but the halter is his purse-string. The most notorious robber
that ever infested Tuscany was no sooner upon the gibbet than
forty or fifty idler-thieves, in white surplices half-way down the
hams, ran about our streets, soliciting the eleemosynary *paolo* from
citizen and peasant, to liberate the sinful soul earlier out of
purgatory. Can we imagine that crimes will be rigorously
reprehended by those who derive a revenue from the multiplicity
and magnitude of them ?

President. What purgatory may be to any of the dead I cannot tell; but I see it is a paradise to a great portion of the living. How many dormitories and refectories are warmed with it! How many gardens, lined with orange and citron, are brought into blossom by its well directed fires! Not Styx, nor Acheron, nor Phlegethon, but Pactolus is now the river that runs through the infernal regions, leaving its golden sands on the papal shore, the patrimony of Saint Peter.

Leopold. What do you imagine was the reason, M. Du Paty, why celibacy was imposed on the priesthood, not when it was chaste and virtuous, but at a time when neither the heads of the Church nor her other members were any longer pure?

President. There cannot be conceived a better reason for so extraordinary and unnatural an ordinance, than that the concubines and wives of such dissolute men were, as you may suppose, eternally at variance; and ecclesiastical polity was well aware that they would arouse by degrees, and excite to inquiry, a supine and dormant world. The pope therefore put down, and suppressed under the piscatory signet, the more clamorous of the parties. Among the first Christians all things were in common but their wives; among those of the papal reformation, the wives seem the only things that were so.

Leopold. I am apprehensive, M. Du Paty, you will be thought here in Italy to entertain but little reverence even for those higher authorities (if any are higher than the pope) on which the foundations of our faith repose; it being known that men of letters in France, including the dignitaries of the Church, are inclined to philosophy.

President. Sir, I wish they were; for then they would teach and practise Christianity, which is peace and good-will toward men. The partisans of popery have evinced by their conduct that either the book whereon they found their religion in itself is false, or that those dogmas are which they pretend to draw from it; otherwise they would not forbid nor discountenance its circulation and publicity. In copying the worst features of every religion, they should at least have omitted this. The Egyptian, the Hindoo, and other priesthoods, kept their sacred books secluded from the people, and said perhaps that they were thus commanded, whether by dog or by calf, or some such deity; but if the pope

believed in the gospel, or ever read it, he must know that his predecessors (as he calls the apostles) were commanded to disseminate
it among all the nations of the universe.

Leopold.   Catholicism does not appear to be quite so poly-
theistical among you Frenchmen as among us.

President.   An Italian, a Spaniard, or a Portuguese has no
thought whatever of praying to God.   The expression, common
in our language, is unknown in theirs.   Desirous as I always was
of finding out the opinions of men on this subject, I accosted one
who had been praying, at the entrance of a village, to an image
of earthenware in a niche against a cottage.

"You pray then, my good young man! I am .happy to observe
that you think of your Creator in the days of your youth!"

He looked at me with wonder.

"Were not you praying to the Father of mercies?"

"Oh, now · I understand.   I was praying, sir, to his mother
and Saint Zenobio."

"Excellently done!   But do you never offer up a prayer to
God himself?"

His reply I must give in his own language :—

"Mi canzona!   Ad Iddio medesimo! solo, solo! ma davvero
non sono si poco garbato."

Accustomed, as the people of these countries have been for
centuries, to ask favors by means of valets, who speak to the
ladies' maids, and they to their mistresses, whence the petition
goes up to the husband or *cavaliere serviente,* they pursue the
same steps in their prayers to Heaven: first a prayer to Saint
Zenobio; then, with his permission, to the Virgin; who again is
requested to seize a suitable opportunity of mentioning the matter
to her son; or, at her option, to do it herself, and let him know
nothing about the business.   Such are the thoughts of those who
think the most deeply.

Leopold.   What can be the reason why the pious in your
country, and sincere Catholics, speak oftener of God than of
his son or parent?

President.   The reason, I presume, is that our ancestors the
Gauls worshipped one superior Being,—though, from indifference
to the truth in such matters, Cæsar asserts the contrary,—and
that hence we still talk as monotheists; while other nations, who

were formerly polytheists, retain the language of such ; and would, perhaps, although the religion of the country had retained no shadow or resemblance of it.*

Leopold. No prince ought to be indifferent to religion ; but every one ought to the forms and sects of it, so long as they abstain from pretensions of interference with the State. This is an offence which, at the least, should be punished by their suppression. I am supposed to exercise an arbitrary power in this country ; yet my interference in the affairs of religion is less extensive than that of your Louis XIV. In his Declaration of 1682, he says : " Pour l'intérêt de l'Eglise de notre royaume, de laquelle nous sommes premier et universel protecteur." According to the former of these words (premier), he takes precedency of the pope in the Church ; and according to the latter (universel), he quite excludes him.

President. Many of our bishops think otherwise ; although the most acute and clear of reasoners, and the most eloquent of expositors, Bossuet, was in this campaign the champion of the king.

Leopold. Of your bishops there are many who think otherwise ; first because many of them think little, and possess no learning ; and secondly and mainly, because they have a better chance of being cardinals by adherence to the papacy, certain that they cannot lose their bishoprics by it. Surely I have as much power in my monasteries as the popes have in my music-shops.

President. That is clear.

Leopold. Nevertheless they have forbidden, under pain of excommunication, to copy the *miserere* of Allegrini, which is only to be sung in the pope's chapel, and by eunuchs. This is an order more conformable to the taste of Nero than to the office of Christ's vicar.

President. A countryman of mine, Choron, infringed the edict, and may have his throat cut for it ; the offender being excommunicated.

* If Du Paty were now living, what would he say about the report on the project of a law in France against *sacrilege*, in which the reporters use the word *deicide* (god-killing), and are guided by the Jesuits, who would burn you alive for materialism !

Leopold.   Although [55] I would admit but one system of laws and one head of them, I would willingly see several religions in my States, knowing that in England and Holland they are checks one upon another.   The Quaker inverts his eye and rebukes his graceless son, by observing how industrious and tractable is the son of some fierce Presbyterian; the Catholic points to the daughter of a Socinian, and cries shame upon his own, educated as she was in the purity of the faith, in the religion of so many forefathers.   Catholicism loses somewhat of its poisonous strong savor by taking root in a well-pulverised, well-harrowed soil.   As competition levels the price of provisions, so maintains it the just value of sects.   Whatever is vicious in one is kept under by the concourse of others, and each is emulous to prove the superiority of its doctrines by honesty and regularity of life.   If ever the English could be brought to one opinion in politics or religion, they would lose the energy of their character and the remains of their freedom.   In England, the Catholics are unexceptionably good members of society; although the gentlemen of that persuasion, I hear, are generally more ignorant than others, partly by the jealous spirit of their Church, and partly by an ungenerous exclusion from the universities.   They keep a chaplain in their houses, but always a man of worth, and not combining as in Italy a plurality of incongruous offices.   Here, a confessor, in many instances, is tutor to the children, house-steward to the father, and *cavaliere serviente* to the mother.   He thinks it would be a mockery of God to call her to confess, without a decent provision of slight transgressions; and he cures her indigestions by a dram, her qualms of conscience by a sacrament.

President.   Both morality and learning require the sound of feet running fast behind, to keep them from loitering and flagging. When Calvinism had made and was making a rapid progress in France, the Catholic bishops were learned men; indeed so learned, that Joseph Scaliger, himself a Calvinist, acknowledged in the latter part of his life their immense superiority over the rising sect.   At present, there is only one bishop in France capable of reading a chapter in the Greek Testament, which every schoolboy in England, for whatever profession he is intended, must do at eleven years of age.   I would then recom-

[55 From "Although" to "them" (2 lines) added in 3rd ed.]

mend a free commerce both of matter and of mind. I would let men enter their own churches with the same freedom as their own houses ; and I would do it without a homily on graciousness or favor. For tyranny itself is to me a word less odious than toleration.

Leopold. I am placed among certain small difficulties. Tuscany is my farm : the main object of proprietors is their income. I would see my cattle fat and my laborers well clothed ; but I would not permit the cattle to break down my fences, nor the laborer to dilapidate my buildings. I will preserve the Catholic religion in its dogmas, forms, discipline, and ceremonies : it is the pommel of a sovereign's sword, and the richest jewel in his regalia ; no bull, however, shall squeeze out blood under me, no faggot sweat out heresy, no false key unlock my treasury. The propensity will always exist. The system has been called *imperium in imperio,* very unwisely : it was *imperium super imperio,* until it taught kings to profit by its alphabet, its ciphers, and its flagellations. You complain that I have softened my mud : this is the season for treading and kneading it ; and there are no better means of doing so, none cheaper, none more effectual, than by keeping a gang of priests on the platform. America will produce disturbances in Europe by her emancipation from England. The example will operate in part, not principally. Wherever there is a national debt, disproportionately less rapid in its extinction than in its formation, there is a revolutionary tendency : this will spread where there is none ; as maladies first engendered in the air are soon communicated by contact to the sound and healthy. Various causes will be attributed to the effect ; even the books of philosophers. All the philosophers in the world would produce a weaker effect in this business than one blind ballad-singer. Principles are of slower growth than passions ; and the hand of Philosophy, holden out to all, there are few who press cordially. And who are those ? the disappointed, the contemplative, the retired, the timid. Did Cromwell read Plato ? Did the grocers of Boston read Locke ? The true motives in political affairs are often improbable. Men who never heard of philosophy but to sneer at it after dinner will attribute to it those evils which their own venality and corruption have engendered ; and not from a spirit of falsehood, but from incompetency of judgment and reflection.   What is the stablest in itself is not always so in all places: marble is harder and more durable than timber; but the palaces of Venice and Amsterdam would have split and sunk without wooden piles for their foundation.   Single government wants those manifold props which are supplied, well-seasoned, by Catholicism.   A king indeed may lose his throne by indiscretion or inadvertency, but the throne itself will never lose its legs, in any Catholic State.   Never will a republican or a mixed constitution exist seven years where the hierarchy of Rome hath recently exerted its potency.   Venice and Genoa afford no proofs to the contrary: they arose and grew up while the popes were bishops, and ere mankind had witnessed the wonderful spectacle of an inverted apotheosis.   God forbid that any corrupt nation should dream of becoming what America is!   If it possesses one single man of reflection, he will demonstrate the impracticability of citizenship where the stronger body of the State, as the clergy must morally be, receives its impulse and agency from without, and where it claims to itself a jurisdiction over all, excluding all from any authority over its concerns.   This demonstration leads to a sentence which policy is necessitated to pronounce, and humanity is unable to mitigate.

President.   Theories and speculations always subvert religious, never political, establishments.   Uneasiness makes men shift their postures.   National debts produce the same effects as private ones, —immorality and a desire of change; the former universally, the latter almost.   A man may well think he pays profusely, who pays a tenth as an insurance for his property against the perils of the sea.   Does he reason less justly who deems the same sum sufficient for the security of the remainder, in his own lands, in his own house?   No conquered people was ever obliged to surrender such a portion of its wealth, present and reversionary, as in our times hath been expended voluntarily in the purchase of handcuffs and fetters for home consumption.   Free nations, for the sake of doing mischief to others, and to punish the offence of pretending to be like them, have consented that a certain preparation of grain shall be interdicted in their families; that certain herbs shall never be cultivated in their fields and gardens; that they shall never roast certain beans nor extract certain liquors, and that certain rooms in their houses shall admit no light.   Domitian never did against his enemies what these free nations have done against themselves.

The sea-tortoise can live without its brains,—an old discovery! Men can govern without theirs,—an older still !

Leopold.[56] I indeed see no reason why different sects in religion should not converse in the streets, as they are walking to their churches and chapels, with as much good-will and good-humor as schoolboys of different ages and classes going up at the same hour and for the same purpose to their appointed forms and respective teachers. Both parties are going for learning and improvement : the younger is the wiser; how long shall it continue so ?

President. I can calculate the period to a day. It will continue while the clergy is a distinct body ; while a priest is a prince ; while he who says at one moment, " I am a servant, the servant of servants," says at another, " I am a master, the master of masters ! "

So long as society will suffer these impositions, and toil under these tax-gatherers, and starve and contend and bleed for them, animosity and hatred will deface and desecrate the house of prayer and peace. The interest of the class, and above all of the chiefs, requires it ; for, from the moment when men begin to understand and support one another, they will listen to them no longer, nor endure them.

Leopold. I am influenced little by opinions : they vary the most where they are strongest and loudest; here they breathe softly, and not against me, for I excite the hopes of many by extinguishing those of a few. What I have begun I will continue ; but I see clearly where I ought to stop, and know to a certainty, which few reformers do, where I can. Exempt from intemperance of persecution as from taint of bigotry, I am disposed to see Christianity neither in diamonds nor in tatters : I would sell her red and white, to procure her a clean shift and inoffensive stockings.

I must persuade both clergy and laity that God understands Italian. Ricci, Bishop of Pistoja, is convinced of this truth ; but many of his diocesans, not disputing his authority, argue that, although God indeed may understand it, yet the saints, to

[56 From " *Leopold* " to " them " (20 lines) added in 2nd ed.]

whom they offer up incense and in whom they have greater confidence, may not ; and that being, for the most part, old men, it
might incommode them in the regions of bliss to alter pristine
habits.

Warmly and heartily do I thank you, M. Du Paty, for your
observations : you have treated me really as your equal.

President.   I should rather thank your Imperial Highness for
your patience and confidence.   If I have presented one rarity to
the Palazzo Pitti, I have been richly remunerated with another.
There are only two things which authorize a man out of office
to speak his sentiments freely in the courts of princes,—very
small stature and very small probity.   You have abolished this
most ancient institution, in favor of a middle-sized man, who can
reproach himself with no perversion or neglect of justice, in a
magistrature of twenty years.

· [The following footnote on Gianni is reprinted from 1st ed. with a
few omissions.   "At my last arrival on the continent, it retained among
its ruins two great men, Kosciusko and Gianni : the one I had seen in
England, the other I visited in Genoa.   He was in his ninetieth year ;
an age to which no other minister of king or prince or republic has
attained.   But the evil passions never preyed on the heart of Gianni : he
enjoyed good health from good spirits, and those from their only genuine
source, a clear conscience. . . .   Patient, provident, moderate, imperturbable, he knew on all occasions what kind and what intensity of
resistance should be opposed to violence and tumult.   I will adduce two
instances.   Ricci, bishop of Pistoja and Prato, had excited the indignation of his diocesans, by an attempt, as is related in the dialogue, to
introduce the prayers in Italian, and to abolish some idle festivals and processions.   The populace of Prato, headed by a confraternity, broke forth
into acts of rebellion ; the bishop's palace was assaulted, his life threatened.
The church bells summoned all true believers to the banner ; the broken
bones of saints were exposed, and invited others to be broken.   Leopold,
on hearing it, shocked in his system of policy, forgot at the moment
the mildness of his character, and ordered all the military at hand to
march against the insurgents.   Gianni was sent for ; he entered the very
instant this command was issued.   *What disturbs your Highness ?* said he,
mildly.   "You ought to have been informed, Gianni," answered the
Grand-Duke, "that the populace of Prato has resisted my authority and
insulted Ricci.   My troops march in a body against these wretches."
*I have already dispatched a stronger force against them than your highness has done,
which, by your permission, must remain in the city.*   "On free quarters until the
madmen are quiet.   But how could you collect a stronger force so
instantaneously ?"

Instead of two regiments I dispatched two crosses, instead of cannon and ammuni-

tion waggons, a nail-box, a **hammer**, *and a clean napkin. If reinforcements are wanted, we* **can** *find a dice-box* **at** *Riccardi's and a sponge at Rospigliosi's on good security. At this hour, however, I am persuaded that the confraternity is walking in procession and extolling to the skies not your humanity but your devotion."* It was so.

The *maximum* or *assize* had been abolished by Gianni: lands and provisions rose in value; the people was discontented, broke into his house, drank his wine, cut his beds in pieces, and carried off the rest of his furniture. Leopold, who had succeeded to the Empire of Germany, and was residing at Vienna, decreed that the utmost severity should be exercised against all who had borne any part in this sedition. It was difficult to separate the more guilty from the less; particularly as every man, convicted of delinquency, might hope to extenuate his offence by accusing his enemy of one more flagrant. Gianni, who could neither disobey nor defer the mandate of the Emperor, engaged Commendatore Pazzi to invite some hundreds of the people to a banquet in the court-yard of his palace. Now, while the other families of those Florentines who in ages past had served this bustling little city, were neglected for their obscurity, shunned for their profligacy, or despised for their avarice and baseness, that of Riccardi was still in esteem for its splendid hospi-tality, that of Pazzi for its patronage of the people. The invitation was unsuspected; they met, they feasted, they drank, profusely; every man brought forward his merits; what each had done, and what each was ready to do, was openly declared and carefully recorded. On the following morning, before day-break, forty were on the road to the galleys. The people is never in such danger as from its idol.]

[Second ed. reads here: " support. Among the residents in Florence, I speak in confidence, M. President, I remember none of even ordinary talents, or, according to what I could judge or could learn from report, of the slightest political or literary reputation. Not long ago a young person was sent hither in that capacity, who had more dogs than books, and more mistresses than ideas. He rode hard, drank hard, and fiddled hard, and admitted to his society, as such people usually do, the vilest and most abandoned of both sexes. At Milan, his course was arrested by a deficiency of means; he had already drawn on his bankers here for sums, beyond such even as the prodigality of his government had enabled him to deposit in their hands. With this heavy debt upon him, he drew on them again from Milan, at one single time, for four thousand crowns. The draft was dishonoured, with a protestation that their concerns were inadequate to such frequent and vast demands. He replied with a vehemence of language, such as most tribunals would have severely punished in a private character, and such as, if presented in complaint to me, would have obliged me to insist on his recall. When he thus retired to rest himself for about a year, after the labours of his office, he left behind him a pack of hounds, a groom, a chargé d' affaires, a chasseur, and several other domestics. The amusement of these delegated powers was cat-hunting in the spacious gardens belonging to the legation. Every day the diversion was pursued, until the neighbourhood was so

infected with rats, that serious remonstrances, light as the subject may
appear, were presented to me by gardeners, grocers, oilmen, booksellers
and stationers, and other trades; and I condemned to extermination by
poison the more innocent of the offenders.

The Sieur Dorcas, the secretary I mentioned, a necessitous and un-
educated young person, no sooner found himself in possession of a hundred
pounds a year, than he bought a pony, hired the best saddle and bridle
that were to be let out, presented a bunch of flowers (when the season was
somewhat advanced) to the woman of highest rank he met at the *cascine*,
and manifested his resolution to be *cavaliere serviente*, wherever he found
beauty and cookery. He soon introduced himself to Madame Mozzi,
a lady of great personal attractions, good-humoured, witty, well-informed,
and whose house enjoys the reputation of an admirable kitchen. The
next morning he addressed a note to her, declaring that she had pleased
him, and desiring to know at what time she would be ready to receive
the first visit of so distinguished and ardent a lover. She answered him
as frankly, and proposed that the interview should take place on the
ensuing evening. Sieur Dorcas ran to the milliner's, bought a worked
frill; to the perfumers, bought a bottle of eau de Cologne; and borrowed
a clean cambric handkerchief to pour it on. Observing that his gloves
bore the mark of the bridle, he put them into his pocket before he knocked
at the door. This he did once, and softly. It opened, as if by magic.
A servant with a lively countenance ushered him upstairs. He passed
through an antechamber filled with fine pictures; every countenance
seemed to smile on him, every landscape bloomed. He had little taste
or time for them; onward he followed the servant. The doors of the
apartment flew open to him. The whole family was assembled; Sieur
Dorcas was announced; all eyes were fixed upon a personage who had
announced himself as the performer of so topping a part. Madame Mozzi
and her *aja* rose from their seats, and the former, after smiling most
graciously, turned again to the company, and presented Sieur Dorcas,
as the attaché, who would have done so much honour to them all, if he
had not fixed his attentions on the least worthy of the family. They
made their obeisances to Sieur Dorcas: 'And now,' said Madame Mozzi
to her *aja*, 'you will do me the favour, my dear friend, to read the elegant
note of the British Diplomatist.' The *aja* put on her spectacles and read
it through. The husband took Sieur Dorcas by the hand, apologized
for the necessity he was under of leaving him so soon after his introduction, and wished him all possible success in his negotiation. The other
relatives complimented him on the frankness of the English character,
of which they protested they never had seen before so charming a
specimen; and the lady told him, with an air of concern, and tender
reproof, that she found him somewhat more cold than his note had
promised. He bit his lips, lifted up one side of his shirt-collar, bowed
as well as he had learned to bow, and withdrew. He found the servants
ranged upon the stairs; his conductor told him it was usual to give a
mancia on the first good fortune, and hoped he would not forget it. As
it often happens," &c.]

VI. KOSCIUSKO **AND PONIATOWSKI.** [1]

Poniatowski. A short and hasty letter, brought by my courier, will have expressed to you, general, with what pleasure I obtained leave of absence for ten days, that I might present you my affectionate homage here in Switzerland.

Kosciusko. No courier can have arrived, sir ; for we hear the children at play in the street, and they would have been earnest to discover what sort of creature is a courier.

Poniatowski. I myself am no bad specimen of one : I have traversed three kingdoms in five days ; such a power of attraction hath Kosciusko on Poniatowski.

Kosciusko. Poniatowski ! my brave countryman, I embrace you heartily. Sit down, rest yourself,—not upon that chair ; the rushes are cut through in the middle : the boys and girls come in when I am reading in the window or working in the garden, and play their old captain these tricks.

Poniatowski. I must embrace you again, my general ! Always the same kind tender heart, the same simplicity and modesty ! There is little of poetry or of ingenuity in the idea that your nativity was between the Lion and the Virgin.

Kosciusko. [2] O Poniatowski ! my countryman, comrade, and friend ! how long it is since we met ! I require a few moments to recollect your features : the voice, and the heart that gives it utterance, are the same. I am indeed a revolutionist : I invert the order of established things. Usually the countenance is remembered when benefits are forgotten : from defect of sight, which these gashes have injured, your countenance was only such

[[1] The exploits of Kosciusko were performed in the year 1794, when for a time, with far inferior forces, he resisted the combined armies of Russia, Prussia, and Austria. After his defeat and captivity in Russia, he went to live in retirement in Switzerland. In 1807 Napoleon, who was about to invade Poland, entreated him to return to Poland and take command of the Polish troops. The position, which Kosciusko refused was filled by Poniatowski, who, less clear sighted than his old chief, allowed Napoleon to use him as his tool. For Kosciusko Landor had a great admiration. See cancelled note on Gianni in the preceding Conversation, and a letter published in the *Examiner* of Nov. 1, 1851. (Imag. Convers., i., 1824. i., 1826. Works, i., 1846. Works, iii. 1876.]

[[2] From " *Kosciusko* " to " more " (26 lines) added in 2nd ed.]

to my apprehension as to make me wonder whose it could be, while your services were fresh in my memory; services than which, in ages of heroism, no man ever rendered more pure or more illustrious to his country. I do not marvel that you have lost the bloom of youth, knowing your anxieties; but how happens it, that, after such exertions, such privations, such injuries (for all honors but one conferred on you, and that, too, by the voice of your countrymen, are such),—how happens it, Poniatowski, that you appear more robust than ever, and retain to the full your activity and animation?

Poniatowski. Hope is the source of them; the aroma without which our bodies are putridity, the ether without which our souls themselves, so long as they are here on earth, are cold and heavy vapor. If we could but have saved our Poland, O my general! less men can rule her. Of all arts this is the easiest, and exercised by the most imbecile. The laws should rule; for courts we have always in readiness a cushion, a king, and a crier: can any wicked wretch want more?

Kosciusko.[3] Ah, scoffer!

Poniatowski. I will ask the question, then, not scoffingly, but in sober sadness. I ask it in the name of our country; I ask her defender and protector; I ask you, chief of Poland! first of mankind! why are you not with us? Oh, with what enthusiasm would our legions follow you! Return among us and command us.

Kosciusko. Where is Poland!

Poniatowski. She rises from her ashes with new splendor: in every battle she performs the most distinguished part;—do you sigh at hearing it?

Kosciusko. Poniatowski! her blood flows for strangers, and her heroism is but an interlude in the drama of Ambition. She is intoxicated from the cup of Glory, to be dismembered with the less feeling of her loss. When she recovers her senses, in vain will she look around for compassion or for gratitude. Beyond a doubt, I am a feeble and visionary politician: nevertheless, I will venture to express my opinion, that gratitude, although it never has been admitted among the political virtues, is one; that whatever is good in morals is also good in politics; and that, by

[3 From " *Kosciusko* " to " us " (5 lines) added in 3rd ed.]

introducing it opportunely and dexterously, the gravest of old politicians might occasionally be disconcerted. Do not let us be alarmed at the novelty: many have presumed to recommend the observance of justice; and gratitude is nothing more than justice in a fit of generosity, and permitting a Love or a Genius to carry off her scales.

Poniatowski. We live in an age when no experiments of this kind are tried, and when others are exhausted.

Kosciusko. True, we see nothing in battle but brute force, nothing in peace but unblushing perfidy. War, which gave its name to stratagems, would recall them, and cannot: they are shut up within the cabinet and counter, where they never should have entered, and the wisest of them are such as would disgrace the talents of a ring-dropper.

If the person to whom fortune seems to have given the disposal of mankind had known any thing of our national character, he would have augmented the dominions of Poland, instead of diminishing them; if he had known as much of policy as a peasant, he would have united with it Royal Prussia and Hungary, and its southern boundaries would have been the Danube and the Dnieper. Every German province, excepting a few I am about to mention, would have been erected into a kingdom, under the most powerful or the most popular of its princes, its nobles, its civil magistrates; representatives would have been elected, standing armies would have been abolished. Thus the existence of the governors and the prosperity of the governed would have been his work, and that work would have been indestructible. The erection of twenty kings in twenty minutes would have abundantly gratified his vanity,—a consideration not unimportant when we discourse upon crowned heads, and particularly upon heads crowned recently, or indeed upon heads of any kind subject to the vortexes of power. The Scandinavian Peninsula should have been strengthened by the junction of Denmark, Mecklenburgh, and Pomerania, forming a barrier against the maritime force of England, and (united by confederacy with Poland) against the systematic and unsuspected march of Muscovite aggression. No German kingdom should have contained much more than a million of inhabitants; for it was his business to lessen both the kingly authority and the kingly name.

History hath given us no example of a man whose errors are so manifold and so destructive. I confess that I have been mistaken in foretelling his downfall : I calculated from observations on mankind in ages less effete. I could not calculate the forces that resisted him : for I knew only the military and financial, and this but numerically ; I knew not by whom and where and to what specific object it was to be applied. Fortunate (if usurpers ever are) to spring up in a season of rankness and rottenness, when every principle or vitality had been extinguished in the State, either by the pestilence of despotism or by the tempests of democracy ; when they who came against him from without were weaker in judgment than himself; and when the wildest temerity was equally sure of success as the most prudent combinations and best measured conduct! No general versed in war has been consulted by the principal of the belligerents ; but persons the least practised in it have been employed as commanders-in-chief. The good people of England is persuaded that to open a campaign is as easy as to open an oyster, and to finish it is a thing to be done as quickly as to swallow one.

Poniatowski. England will alter her system from one of these two causes: Either (at the end of twenty years perhaps) the families of her aristocracy will be sufficiently enriched, which is the prime motive in her undertakings ; or a serious and earnest effort will be made against increasing danger, and some general of capacity will at last be appointed to satisfy the clamors of the people, and to keep the government, or rather the governors, unshaken. [4] But come, let us cease to speculate on the English, and indeed on everything else than our own beloved Poland. You have reason to shake your head, and to hold your hand over your eyes : you have reason to complain of ingratitude ; but it is rather on the side of fortune than of princes, who, in good truth, owe you little.

Kosciusko. We hear many complaints of princes and of fortune ; but believe me, Poniatowski, there never was a good or generous action that met with much ingratitude.

Poniatowski. Not [5] Sobieski from Austria ?

[4 See end of Conversation for cancelled passage.]
[5 From " Not " to " ungrateful " (8 lines) added in 3rd ed. Sobieski, king of Poland, saved Vienna from the Turks. The Emperor Leopold broke faith with him and thus forced him into a disastrous treaty with Russia.]

Kosciusko. Sobieski had his reward : God, who alone was great enough, bestowed it.

Poniatowski. But then his kingdom? what befell that? and from whom? Condescending, as you have often been, to the meanest peasant for the slightest service, grateful as I have seen you to an undistinguished soldier for moistening your horse's bit after a battle, do you thus speak of the ungrateful? You to whom no statues are erected, no hymns are sung in public processions; you, who have no country! And you smile upon such injuries and such losses!

Kosciusko. My friend! I have lost nothing; I have received no injury; I am in the midst of our country, day and night. Absence is not of matter: the body does not make it; absence quickens our love and elevates our affections; absence is the invisible and incorporeal mother of ideal beauty. Were I in Poland, how many things are there which would disturb and perhaps exasperate me! Here I can think of her as of some departed soul; not yet indeed clothed in light nor exempted from sorrowfulness, but divested of passion, removed from tumult, and inviting to contemplation. She is the dearer to me, because she reminds me that I have performed my duty toward her. Permit me to go on. I said that a good or generous action never met with much ingratitude. I do not deny that ingratitude may be very general; but, even if we experience it from all quarters, there is yet no evidence of its weight or its intensity. We bear upon our heads an immense column of air; but the nature of things has rendered us insensible of it altogether : have we not likewise a strength and a support against what is equally external,—the breath of worthless men? Very far is that from being much or great which a single movement of self-esteem tosses up and scatters. Slaves make out of barbarians a king or emperor; the clumsiest hand can fashion such misshapen images : but the high and discerning spirit spreads out its wings from precipices, raises itself up slowly by great efforts, acquires ease, velocity, and might by elevation, and suns itself in the smiles of its Creator.

[Second ed. reads : "unshaken. I have heard, however, that Pichegru and Dumourier have sometimes been consulted by that cabinet. *Kosciusko.* The name of the latter I remember in old gazettes ; and I will readily believe that he may have given his advice. Pichegru had no influence there ; he received no marks of confidence, few of courtesy. His wisdom, his modesty, his taciturnity, his disdain of puppets in power, beating each other, head against head, and chuckling each other's language when uppermost, a disdain his stern countenance ill concealed, would be my proofs and vouchers, if I had not also his own declaration. He was incomparably the best general in Europe, and could not often have failed in what he thought expedient. He had, however, two great defects, either of which might have brought his loyalty into suspicion : he wore no other powder in his hair than what it collected on a march ; and he put on boots when he should have put on buckles. *Poniatowski.* I have heard young Englishmen of distinction say, that they could hardly suppose him to be a Frenchman, unless from his ugliness : that he spoke slowly, contradicted no one, interrupted no one, delivered no opinion of his own unasked, nor indeed at all when he could adduce another's, never aimed at a witticism, never smiled at a misfortune, an awkwardness, or a sneer, never sang, never danced, never spat upon the carpet, or in the presence of a lady, bowed ungracefully and gravely, and had been seen to blush. *Kosciusko.* They might have added, that he refused to execute the decree of the convention, when no quarter was to be given to them ; that he hazarded his life for his humanity ; and that he invaded and conquered the richest country in the world, and took not away from it one grain of gold. If he had been facetious and eloquent, he would have been almost a Phocion : no other man in Europe can be weighed against his scabbard. *Poniatowski.* The French accuse him of betraying the Republic. *Kosciusko.* He saw one thing clearly and firmly believed another. He saw that the French character could retain no stamp of republicanism, and he believed that the Bourbons would be chastened by adversity. As the Republic must die by a natural death or a violent one, he preferred the former, and he desired that the supreme magistracy should return to that family which had the most orderly and peaceable for its partisans. He knew enough of the Bourbons to be certain that they never would recompense his services, and enough of human nature in its most exalted state, to feel that a man as great as himself could alone be his rewarder. We hear many complaints," &c.]

VII. WOLFGANG AND HENRY OF MELCTAL.*

Wolfgang. Old man, thou knowest, I doubt not, why thou art brought before me.

Henry. For having been the preserver of Arnold.

* Landenberg, who governed the country for Albert of Austria, sent to drive away a yoke of oxen from Henry of Melctal. His son Arnold, complaining of the violence, was told that *peasants might draw the plough*

Wolfgang.   For harbouring and concealing an outlaw.

Henry.   We all are outlaws.

Wolfgang.   What! and confess it?

Henry.   Where there is law for none, what else can we be?

Wolfgang.   In consideration of thy age and heretofore good repute, our emperor in his clemency would remit the sentence passed on thy offence, taking only thy plough and oxen in punishment of disobedience.

Henry.   Ploughs and oxen are not instruments and furtherers of disobedience.   Why were they taken from me before?   Had they never been seized by his apostolic majesty, and had not the great man Gessler told me that I, a hoary traitor, should be yoked in place of them, my valiant son had never cursed him and his master.

Wolfgang.   I turn pale with horror.   Curse the right hand of the Almighty!

Henry.   We were told that man was his image, long before we ever heard that a dry marten-skin on the shoulder, and a score of cut pebbles on the head, made any creature his right hand.   This right hand does little else than, like children, strip the image, or, just as they do, break the head of one against the head of another.

Wolfgang.   What particular hardship couldst thou complain of?

Henry.   Only that, whenever there was a fine day, my oxen were taken for the emperor's use, and that my boy was forced to guide them.

Wolfgang.   You had many days left.

Henry.   Ay, verily; all winter, from the first of November to the first of April.   While the snow was from five to three feet deep, I might plough, sow, and harrow.   A green turf was an imperial rescript; and I never saw one in the morning but I met a soldier at my gate ere noon, and my two poor beasts were unhoused.

themselves if they wanted bread.   Arnold struck him with his staff, broke two fingers, and fled to a friend at Uri.   On this, the father in his extreme old age saw his cattle driven from his farm, his goods confiscated, his house seized,—and nothing else; for his eyes were burnt out.   [(Imag. Convers., iii., 1828.   Works, i., 1846.   Works, iii., 1876.)]

Wolfgang.   Factious man! the mildest governments in the world have always exacted this trifle in payment for their protection.   Where there is little coin, there must be labor or its produce; and how much better it is to give the half, or rather more, to a lawful master, than the whole to robbers? But indeed this half is not given: all in right is Cæsar's. Thy Bible says, "Give unto Cæsar that which is Cæsar's, and unto God that which is God's."   It does not say, " Keep anything," which it would do if anything remained.   Dost whistle, rogue?

Henry.   I cry you mercy, Sir Wolfgang.. About the Scripture I dare argue nothing; but about the thieves,—what thieves have we here?   Who is disposed to take away kid or pullet from us?   Cannot we, who are in our own houses, defend them as well as those who are some hundred miles off?   And, when we cannot, is not our neighbor as ready to help us as they are?   Yet our neighbor would blush to ask a spoonful of salt for doing it.

Wolfgang.   Malcontent! what wouldst thou say if thy master should forbid thee to turn thy barley into malt, or to plant thy garden, or any plot of it, with hops?

Henry.   I dare not imagine this wrong.[1]   To order me how to crop my garden or how to mix my tankard!   To forbid the earth to give its increase in due season is the heaviest and the rarest curse of God.   Never, I trust, will our nation be so heartless as to endure a like interdict from the wrath of man.

Wolfgang.   There is no danger:[2] nevertheless, why not profit by example, and avoid the chances of mischief?   The tortoise, well protected as it is, draws in its head at the touch of a child.

Henry.   I will do the same when I am a tortoise.   But we Switzers have our rights and privileges : we may kill even a hare

---

[1 First ed. reads: "wrong. The doctor may tell me what I shall best eat, and the priest how I shall best cook it ; but neither the emperor nor the great man Gessler has committed such an act of tyranny as to order," &c.]

[2 In 1st ed. a speech of Henry's is here interpolated, which is not reprinted ; it contains a dull story, which stops the whole action of the Conversation.]

if we find him in our corn, provided the land be our freehold.
What nation in Christendom can say the same, beyond these
mountains? We alone are raised to an equality with the beasts
and birds; we alone can leave our country; we alone pine and
perish if we are long absent from it.

Wolfgang. Is that a privilege?

Henry. No, my lord judge: it may be a want, a weakness;
but those who are subject to it are exempt from many others. Of
what are they not capable in defence of their country, to whom
she is so dear! We see our parents and children carried to the
grave; we lose sight of them, and bear it manfully: on losing
sight of our country our hearts melt away.

Wolfgang. Brave men bear it. I left my country to perform my duties in this; and what country is pleasanter than
Austria, or more productive of cattle and game, of river-fish and
capons?

Henry. All men have a birth-place, Sir Wolfgang; but all
men have not a country. Nay, there are some who have it not,
and who possess almost half a province, with tolls and mills and
chases and courts and prisons, and whatever else can make the
great contented.

Wolfgang. I should be censurable if I listened longer
to such idle and wild discourse. The people of Burgundy are
subject to more hardships than thou art; so are those of Swa-
bia and of France. Be obedient and grateful, seeing that others
fare worse.

Henry. If my ear is frost-bitten, your worship's toe may be
frost-bitten off and never cure me.

Wolfgang. Be comforted and satisfied. The outlawry of thy
son Arnold is reversed, on payment of a slender fine for the proclamation of it, and of another for its annulment, not much heavier.
We have fresh accusations against him, which our clemency will
not bring forward unless he trespass in future.

Henry. Of what offence is the boy accused?

Wolfgang. Of the seditious song he was heard to sing last
winter, which he is known to have composed. We have three
witnesses, who will declare upon their consciences that they
believe by *eagle* he means the emperor, our lord; by *hooked-nosed
wolf*, the arch-chancellor; by *dozing bear*, the metropolitan.

I say nothing of the *squirrel,* and the uncurling of her tail : no action might lie ; but court ladies, when they relax a little of their coldness and severity, are still to be treated with deference and respect.

Henry. Upon my faith, Sir Wolfgang, I know nothing of the matter : if ever I heard the verses I have clean forgotten them.

Wolfgang.   Anastatius Griffenhoof! read aloud those seditious rhymes marked Z.

> Storm Morgarten's larch-plumed crest,
> Search the sun-eyed eagle's nest,
> Tear from hook-nosed wolf his prey,
> Drag the dozing bear to day, ·
> O'er the forest shout the deer,—
> Dogs and men have voices here.
> Freedom here shall make his stand,
> Happy, happy, Switzerland!

> You whose pliant legs with ease
> Clasp and win the tallest trees,
> Swarm the flat-head tawny pine,
> Bring a gift to Adeline ;
> Squirrel rolled into a ball,
> Squirrel, young, nest, nuts, and all.
> While her balmy breath she blows
> In the grandam's icy nose,
> See the tail, it quits the chin ;
> Feel the heart, it thaws within.
> Show her what her touch can do,—
> Ask but half as much for you.

> Fishers ! leave the spangled trout,
> And the pike with pitcher snout,
> Whisker'd carp and green-coat tench,—
> Who for these his shoes would drench ?
> For the otter they were meant,
> Or the saints of lanky Lent.
> Stars are swinging in the lake,
> Come, our heartier fare partake.
> Home again ! the chimney's blaze
> Melts our toils and crowns our days.
> Hal of Melctal has in store
> Seventy full kegs and more.
> He who grudges one of these
> Is less liberal than his bees,
> Or his flowers and flowering trees.

Hal could live without **old** wine,
But without old friends would pine.
Where old wine is, there the cellar
Of that safe and sound indweller
May be very good, which **he**
Who confines it cannot **be.**
Give me rather men of proof
(What say you?) than wall and **roof;**
Rather than a talc-paved **floor,**
Pine-dust bin and iron door.
I have always seen that liquor
Runs, like us, in youth the quicker ;
And that rarely older juice
Sparkles forth from hand profuse.
Here for absent friends is plenty :— '
Toast them all ; and then some twenty
Pretty girls,—your Hal, 'tis said :
Father, do not shake thy head.
Though of thirty **I** had heard,
I would never say **a word.**

 Pour the mead for those who **stay,**
Wormwood for who slink away.
What! my friends! ye drink **no** more?
Then the day indeed is o'er!
Whiter than a marriage shift
See the window ! still they drift
By the thousand flake on flake,—
Each **his** road might well mistake,
And the soberest foot must trip,
For the tricks of snow are deep.
Brunn shall pitch upon his skull.
Glendorp scoop his girdle-full,
· **Pliffer, Borgardt,** Sprengel, Grim,
Lose a cap or break a limb,
And the northern maidens smother
In their **feathers** one or other.
Things ye **never** meet by day,
Things **at night ye** wish away,
Some in linen, some in fur,
Some that moan and some **that purr,**
Wander almost everywhere,
But have never **enter'd** here.

They are out upon the snow,
Scattering it with naked toe ;
Ye shall hear them through the wild
Cry like hungry kid or child.

These are **they**, the wiser think,
Who spite **most the** sons of drink,
And who **leave them** on the waste
With their **faces pale** as paste.

    Thessinger, sit still—be bolder—
Squint not over **that left shoulder:**
I could tell of many **fiercer,**
But, I warrant, none **are** here, sir.
Some that neigh, **and** bray, and rattle
Like the horns of fighting cattle,
Or like (over stones) the log
Of the truant shepherd-dog.
Some, but most in summer **these,**
Shaking under shaking **trees**
(*My* heart too is now afraid),
One-half priest, and one-half **maid!** [3]

    Sleep before the hearth **to-night,**
Still the stouter sticks **are bright,**
And **the** stump will burn till **light.**

    Back, **my** hounds—give **us our turn—**
Shake, lads, shake the matted **fern.**
If the curs have left unsweet
(As mayhap) your russet sheet,
Strew a little **tansy** on it,
Or but tuck **in it the** bonnet,
Hanging just **below your** nose—
So, gay dreams **and sound** repose!

Wolfgang. Call **Abraham Konig** and Rehoboam Storck.
Usher. **Behold them, sir!**
Wolfgang. Abraham Konig, you **shall well and truly—you**
know the rest. What is **your** belief on the words, " Hanging
just below the nose," applied to *rue?*
Konig. It appears to me—
Wolfgang In other words you **are firmly persuaded.**
Konig. **Yes,** as your Honor **commanded** me, I am firmly
persuaded that *rue* means bitterness **and** reviling and threat; for
we say, as your Honor said, you **shall** rue such and such a thing :

[3 In the 1st ed. there are 58 **lines of verse between this** and the
following line, which were excluded in the 2nd ed. They are not worth
reprinting.]

and then, as your Honor remarked, *just below the nose* is the mouth, so that this reviling and bitterness and threat must hang about their mouths.

Wolfgang. Rehoboam Storck, are you likewise firmly persuaded of the same?

Storck. I am.

Wolfgang. And what do you believe is meant by the dogs being kicked up from the hearth, as having an ill scent?

Storck. I do firmly believe that the meaning is what your Honor ordered me to consider and deliver; namely, saving your Honor's presence, that the higher magistrates were meant thereby, who have indeed an ill savor in the country, and who were to be traitorously and violently dispossessed of their warm places, and that they were to rue their misdeeds.

Wolfgang. What misdeeds, carrion? Proceed; what dost understand by the bitter herb being tucked just under the nose?

Storck. Hemp, mayhap.

Wolfgang. How, idiot!

Storck. Your Honor has confounded me.

Wolfgang. The devil confound thee!

Storck. Verily, I think he hath done so.

Wolfgang. What is under the nose?

Storck. The neck.

Wolfgang. Thou dolt!

Storck. The teeth, in young folks.

Wolfgang. I could flay thee alive. But one witness who sweareth stoutly to the citation of *well and truly* is enough: I called another for form's sake.

Usher. Sir—in your Honor's ear, if so it please you. If you read the verse again, you will find the word not to be *rue*, but *tansy.*

Wolfgang. Hush, idler! Judges are no botanists—look again.

Usher. Of a truth the written word is *tansy.*

Wolfgang. The erased word, I uphold it, was *rue.* Rehoboam Storck, did not this same libellous and most seditious man, Arnold, son of Henry of Melctal, call thee a felon, not having proven thee such?

Storck. He did.

Wolfgang.   On what plea or count?   Why dost thou not speak?

Storck.   I went out at dusk, may it please your Honor, to cut the roots of sundry young trees, belonging to the said Arnold—as he said.

Wolfgang.   Was it so dark that nobody could see thee?

Storck.   I wish it had been.

Wolfgang.   Simpleton! it would then have been felony. Hearing these loose lines, can any one doubt their aim and intent?   But let them pass.   I am authorized, as I told you before, to reverse thy son's outlawry and to commute thy own sentence; at the same time I am also commanded to denounce unto thee, that, if ever thou seest thy son again, thou be deprived of eye-sight.

Henry.   I am deprived of eye-sight if I do not see him.   Of sun and snows we have seen enough at seventy.   Ho! Arnold! Arnold! help!

Arnold.   Father! who hurts thee?   Who threatens thee?   Off, gentlemen!   Off, strangers!   Off, soldiers!   Slaves, miscreants, Austrians, stand off!

Wolfgang.   Murder in my presence!

Henry.   They bleed all five under thy yew-stick—one is dying —I was faint: I am not so now; fly, in the name of God! Again, I pray thee, Arnold, if thou lovest thy father, go, begone! I command thee.

Arnold.   O God! I heard thy name and was disobedient: my father has commanded and I obey—forgive me, O my God!

Wolfgang.   Seize him, the traitor.   Dastards—but perhaps it may be better to catch him anywhere else.   Who would have thought it! fair as morning, ardent as noon, and terrible as midnight on the shoals.   Thou at least canst not run so fast.

Henry.   I hope I cannot.

Wolfgang.   Anastasius, call the priest, Reginald Grot, to strengthen him with admonition, and Sigismund Lockhart, the greffier, to translate the sentence into the vulgar tongue; and to read it before the people, in the name of his Apostolic Majesty the Emperor and King, Albert, by the grace of God, *et cetera;* and in the public square to provide that the sentence be well and duly executed, forthwith.

Henry. Send also for the great man, Gessler; tell him to come and see a sight: he has not many more such to see. Welcome, good Reginald! welcome too, my worthy master Lockhart! Come, thy band sits well enough, let it rest; begin.

Lockhart. The instrument must be translated,—a good hour's labor yet, to the ablest clerk.

Henry. Reginald, thou pressest my hand, and sayest nothing. Dost thou turn thy back upon me? Is this thy comfort?

Reginald. There is a Comforter who has given thee strength, and taken mine from me; keep it, good old man: do my tears hurt thee?

Henry. They do, indeed; go home, blessed soul! I never knew thy temper until now. Many have turned away from me before, but none to hide their compassion at my sufferings. What a draught of sight have I taken with my lord-judge, Wolfgang! It lasts me yet, and will last me for life. O my young eagle, my own Arnold! I shall never see thee more upon the rocks of Uri; never shall I tremble at thy hardihood, nor press thee to my bosom for reproaching thee too much about it. But I shall hear thy carols in the woods of Underwald. Let them be blithe as usual; let them be blither still, for I shall more want pastime, and shall listen for sweet sounds all day long. Do not ask me again, as in the *Lay of the Leap,* whether thou hast given me the heart-ache. I was always in thy songs before they ended, even where spring and summer, even where youth and fair maidens, were discoursed of. Prythee, do not go on so. Above all, I charge thee, Arnold, never say, "O my poor father! art thou blind for me!" I was fancying my Arnold at my side. Foolish old man, with my eyes yet open, and their two balls unbroken. Is this the place? Blow away, boys! the weather is misty; it will not light: this arrow head is too blunt; have you nothing better? My old eyes are sunken and tough. Ay, that seems sharper: put it just under the piece of mountain-ash; it will soon redden there. Well done, boy, that is right.

VIII. WASHINGTON AND FRANKLIN.[1]

Washington. Well met again, my friend Benjamin! Never did I see you, I think, in better health : Paris does not appear to have added a single day to your age. I hope the two years you have spent there for us were spent as pleasantly to yourself as they have been advantageously to your country.

Franklin. Pleasantly they were spent indeed, but, you may well suppose, not entirely without anxiety. I thank God, however, that all this is over.

Washington. Yes, Benjamin, let us render thanks to the Disposer of events, under whom, by the fortitude, the wisdom, and the endurance of our Congress, the affairs of America are brought at last to a triumphant issue.

Franklin. Do not refuse the share of merit due to yourself, which is perhaps the largest.

Washington. I am not of that opinion ; if I were, I might acknowledge it to you, although not to others. Suppose me to have made a judicious choice in my measures, the Congress then made a judicious choice in me ; so that whatever praise may be allowed me is at best but secondary.

Franklin. I do not believe that the remainder of the world contains so many men who reason rightly as New England. Serious, religious, peaceable, inflexibly just and courageous, their stores of intellect are not squandered in the regions of fancy, nor in the desperate ventures of new found and foggy metaphysics, but ware-housed and kept sound at home, and ready to be brought forth in good and wholesome condition at the first demand. Their ancestors had abandoned their estates, their

[1 The characters in this Conversation are not much more than mouth-pieces for Landor's views concerning the Roman Catholic religion, Ireland, the character of the English government, and other political subjects. There are no allusions to the details of the lives of the two friends. Franklin's embassy to Paris and the daring fashion in which Washington stopped the epidemic of small-pox in his army, in the face of the superior forces of Lord Howe, are the only incidents mentioned. In the first edition the Conversation begins (8 lines below) *Washington.* Yes, Benjamin, &c. (Imag. Convers. ii., 1824; ii., 1826. Works, i., 1846. Works, iii., 1876.)]

families, and their country, for the attainment of peace and freedom; and they themselves were ready to traverse the vast
wildernesses of an unexplored continent, rather than submit to that
moral degradation which alone can satisfy the capriciousness of
despotism.   Their gravity is converted into enthusiasm; even
those among them, who never in childhood itself expressed by
speech or countenance a sign of admiration, express it strongly in
their old age at your exploits.

Washington.   Benjamin, one would imagine that we both had
been educated in courts, and that I were a man who could give,
and you a man who could ask.   Prythee, my friend, be a philosopher in somewhat more than books and bottles; and, as you
have learned to manage the clouds and lightnings, try an experiment on the management of your fancies.   I declare, on my
conscience, I do not know what I have done extraordinary,
unless we are forced to acknowledge, from the examples to which
we have been accustomed, that it is extraordinary to possess
power and remain honest.   I believe it may be; but this was a
matter of reflection with me: by serving my country I gratified
my heart and all its wants.   Perhaps I am not so happy a creature
as he who smokes his pipe on the bench at the tavern-door; yet
I am as happy as my slow blood allows; and I keep my store of
happiness in the same temperature the whole year round, by the
double casement of activity and integrity.

Franklin.   I do not assert that there never was a general who
disposed his army in the day of battle with skill equal to yours,—
which, in many instances, must depend almost as much on his
adversary as on himself; but I assert that no man ever displayed
such intimate knowledge of his whole business, guarded so
frequently and so effectually against the impending ruin of his
forces, and showed himself at once so circumspect and so daring.
To have inoculated one-half of your troops under the eye of the
enemy—

Washington.   Those actions are great, which require great
calculation, and succeed in consequence of its correctness; those
alone, or nearly alone, are called so, which succeed without any.
I knew the supineness of the British general, his utter ignorance
of his profession, his propensity to gaming, to drinking, in short
to all the camp vices.   I took especial care that he should be in-

formed of my intention to attack him, on the very day when my army was, from the nature of its distemper, the most disabled. Instead of anticipating me—which this intelligence, credited as it was, would have induced a more skilful man to do—he kept his troops unremittingly on the alert, and he himself is reported to have been sober three days together. The money which he ought to have employed in obtaining just and necessary information, he lost at cards; and when he heard that I had ventured to inoculate my army, and that the soldiers had recovered, he little imagined that half the number was at that moment under the full influence of the disease.

Attribute no small portion of our success to the only invariable policy of England, which is to sweep forward to the head of her armaments the grubs of rotten boroughs and the droppings of the gaming-table; and Benjamin, be assured that, although men of eminent genius have been guilty of all other vices, none worthy of more than a secondary name has ever been a gamester. Either an excess of avarice, or a deficiency of what in physics is called excitability, is the cause of it; neither of which can exist in the same bosom with genius, with patriotism, or with virtue. Clive, the best English general since Marlborough and Peterborough, was apparently an exception; but he fell not into this degrading vice until he was removed from the sphere of exertion, until his abilities had begun to decay, and his intellect in some measure to be deranged.

Franklin. I quite agree with you in your main proposition, and see no exception to it in Clive, who was more capable of ruining a country than of raising one. Those who record that chess was invented in the Trojan war would have informed us if Ulysses, Agamemnon, or Diomedes ever played at it; which, however, is usually done without a stake, nor can it be called in any way a game of chance. Gustavus Adolphus, and Eugene of Savoy, and Marlborough, and Frederick of Prussia, and Charles XII. of Sweden, and William III. of England had springs and movements within themselves, which did not require to be wound up every night. They deemed it indecorous to be selvages to an ell of green cloth, and scandalous to cast upon a card what would cover a whole country with plenteousness.

Gaming is the vice of those nations which are too effeminate

to be barbarous, and too depraved to be civilized, and which unite
the worst qualities of both conditions; as for example, the rags
and lace of Naples, its lazzaroni and other titulars. The Malays,
I acknowledge, are less effeminate and in all respects less degraded,
and still are gamesters; but gaming with the Malays is a substitute
for betel: the Neapolitan games on a full snuff-box. Monarchs
should encourage the practice, as the Capets have done constantly;
for it brings the idle and rich into their capitals, holds them from
other intrigues and from more active parties, makes many powerful
families dependent, and satisfies young officers who would otherwise want employment. Republics, on the contrary, should
punish the first offence with fine and imprisonment, the second
with a public whipping and a year's hard labor, the third with
deportation.

Washington. As you please in monarchies and republics, but,
prythee, say nothing of them in mixed governments: do not
affront the earliest coadjutors and surest reliances of our Commonwealth. The leaders of party in England are inclined to
play; and what was a cartouche but yesterday will make a rouleau
to-morrow.

Franklin. Fill it then with base money, or you will be over-
reached, little [2] as is the danger to be apprehended from them in
any higher species of calculation. They are persons of some
repute for eloquence; but if I conducted a newspaper in that
country, I should think it a wild speculation to pay the wiser
of them half-a-crown a day for his most elaborate composition.
When either shall venture to publish a history, or even a speech of
his own, his talents will then be appreciated justly. God grant
(for our differences have not yet annihilated the remembrance of
our relationship) that England may never have any more painful
proofs, any more lasting documents, of their incapacity. Since
we Americans can suffer no farther from them, I speak of them
with the same indifference and equanimity as if they were among
the dead.

Washington. But come, come! the war is ended, God be
praised! Objections have been made against our form of government, and assertions have been added that the republican is ill-
adapted to a flourishing or an extensive country. We know from

[2 From "little" to "calculation" (2 lines) added in 3rd ed.]

the experience of Holland that it not only can preserve but can make a country flourishing, when Nature herself has multiplied the impediments, and when the earth and all the elements have conspired against it. Demonstration is indeed yet wanting that a very extensive territory is best governed by its people : reason and sound common-sense are the only vouchers. Many may fancy they have an interest in seizing what is another's ; but surely no man can suppose that he has any in ruining or alienating his own.

Franklin. Confederate States, under one President, will never be all at once, or indeed in great part, deprived of their freedom.

Washington. Adventurers may aspire to the supreme power illegally ; but none can expect that the majority will sacrifice their present interests to his ambition, in confidence or hope of greater. He never will raise a standing army who cannot point out the probable means of paying it, which no one can do here ; nor will a usurper rise up anywhere, unless there are mines to tempt the adventurous and avaricious, or [3] estates to parcel out with laborers to cultivate them, or slaves to seduce and embody, or treasures to confiscate.

Franklin. The objections bear much more weightily against monarchal and mixed governments ; because these, in wide dominions, are always composed of parts at variance in privileges and interests, in manners and opinions, and the inhabitants of which are not unreluctant to be employed one against the other. Hence, while we Americans leave our few soldiers to the States where they were levied, the kings of Europe will cautiously change the quarters of theirs, and send them into provinces as remote as possible. When they have ceased to have a home, they have ceased to have a country ; for all affinities are destroyed by breaking the nearest. Thrones are constructed on the petrifaction of the human heart.

Washington. Lawless ambition has no chance whatever of success where there are neither great standing armies nor great

[3 Second ed. reads: " or large and well cultivated estates to parcel out, and labourers to cultivate them, or many slaves to seduce and embody, or rich treasures to confiscate, or enemies to invade, whose property may be plundered. *Franklin,*" &c.]

national debts.[4]   Where either of those exist, freedom must waste away and perish.   We are as far from the one as from the other.

Franklin.   Dangers grow familiar and unsuspected; slight causes may produce them, even names.   Suppose a man calling another his subject, and having first received from him marks of deference, and relying on his good-temper and passiveness, and exerting by degrees more and more authority over him, and leaving him at last to the care and protection of his son or grandson : we are well acquainted with the designation ; but we are ignorant how deeply it cuts into the metal.   After a time a shrewd jurist will instruct the subject in his duties, and give him arguments and proofs out of the name itself.   What so irrefragable !

The Latin language,—which answers so nearly all our demands upon it from its own resources, or, not having quite wherewithal, borrows for us a trifle from the Greek,—neither can give us nor help us to find, directly or circuitously, a word for *subject*. *Subditus*, the term in use, is not Latin in that sense, whether of the golden, the silver, or the brazen age : it means *substitutes* primarily, and then *subdued* or *subjected*.   Yet people own themselves to be subjects, who would be outrageous if you called them vassals,—an appellation quite as noble.

Poetry,[5] closing her eyes, has sung until people slept over it, that liberty is never more perfect or more safe than under a mild monarch : history teaches us the contrary.   Where princes are absolute, more tyranny is committed under the mild than under the austere ; for the latter are jealous of power, and entrust it to few.   The mild delegate it inconsiderately to many ; and the same easiness of temper which allows them to do so, permits their ministers and those under them to abuse the trust with impunity.   It has been said that in a democracy there are many despots, and that in a kingdom there can be one only.   This is false : in a republic the tyrannical temper creates a check to itself

[4 First ed. reads : "debts; (I am not speaking of usurpation but of encroachment) where," &c. ; 4 lines below from " Dangers " to " noble " (21 lines) added in 2nd ed.]

[5 First ed. reads : " Excellent pens have written, I know not from what motive, that liberty," &c.]

in the very person next it ; but, in a monarchy, all entrusted with
power become tyrannical by a nod from above, whether the nod
be of approbation or of drowsiness. Royalty not only is a
monster of more heads, but also of more claws, and sharper.

It is amusing to find us treated as visionaries. All the gravest
nations have been republics, both in ancient times and in modern.[6]
I shall believe that a king is better than a republic, when I find
that a single tooth in a head is better than a set, and that in its
solitariness there is a warrant for its strength and soundness.

Washington. Many[7] have begun to predict our *future* greatness ; * in fact, no nation is ever greater than at the time when it
recovers its freedom from under one apparently more powerful.
America will never have to make again such a struggle as she
made in 1775, and never can make one so glorious. A wide territory does not constitute a great people, nor does enormous wealth,
nor does excessive population. The Americans are at present
as great a people as we can expect them to be in future. Can we
hope that they will be more virtuous, more unanimous, more
courageous,. more patriotic ? They may become more learned
and more elegant in their manners ; but these advantages are
only to be purchased by paying down others equivalent.

Franklin. All acquisitions, to be advantageous, must have
some mart and vent. Elegance grows familiar with venality.
Learning may perhaps be succeeded by a Church Establishment,
—an institution perversive of those on which the government of
America is constructed. Erudition (as we use the word) begins
with societies, and ends with professions and orders. Priests and
lawyers, the flies and wasps of ripe and ripening communities, may

[6 First ed. reads : " modern. The Dutch, the Venetians, the Spaniards,
will always, unless an insuperable force oppresses them, aspire to the
dignity of manhood ; the Neapolitans and the French will dream of it
and shake it off. I shall," &c.]

[7 From " Many " to " zero " (25 lines) added in 2nd ed. ; the 13 lines
spoken by Washington are there assigned to Franklin.]

* Of the Americans, in late years, Madame de Stael says, *There is a
people which will one day be very great,* placing her fine impressive pen on
the broad rude mark of the vulgar, who measure greatness by the standard of aggression. America was never so great as on the day when she
declared her Independence, and never will be greater ; although she will
constitute *two* great empires, more powerful and more unassailable than
any now existing.

darken and disturb America. A few of these (we will allow)
are necessary ; many are, of all the curses that the world is subject
to, the most pernicious. These guardians have been proved in
every country the poisoners of their wards—Law and Religion.
They never let us exist long together in an equable and genial
temperature : it is either at fever heat or at zero.

Washington.[8] The solid sense of our people, their speculative
habits, their room for enterprise around home, and their distance
from Europe ensure to them, if not a long continuance of peace,
exemption from such wars as can effect in a material degree their
character or their prosperity. We might have continued the
hostilities, until a part or even the whole of Canada had been
ceded to us. The congress has done what, if my opinion had
been asked, I should have urgently recommended. Let Canada
be ours when she is cultivated and enriched ; let not the fruit be
gathered prematurely : indeed, let it never be plucked ; let it fall
when our bosom can hold it. This must happen within the
century to come ; for no nation is, or ever has been, so intoler-
ably vexatious to its colonies, its dependencies, and its conquests
as the British. I have known personally several Governors, many
of them honest and sensible men, many of them of mild and easy
character ; but I never knew one, nor ever heard of any from
older officers, who attempted to conciliate the affections, or
systematically to promote the interests, of the governed. Liberality has been occasionally extended to them,—the liberality of a
master toward a slave, and only after grievous sufferings. Services
have then been exacted, not hard perhaps in themselves, but in a
manner to cancel all recollection and deaden all sense of kindness.
The French and Spaniards act differently : they extract advantage from their undisturbed possessions, appealing to the
generosity of their children, and softening their commands by
kind offices and constant attentions. Wherever a French regi-
ment is quartered, there are balls and comedies ; wherever an
English, there are disturbances in the street, and duels. Give
the Spaniard a bull-fight, and you may burn his father at the
stake, commending him to the God of Mercy in a cassock painted

[8 First ed. reads: " *Washington.* Let us look forward ; let us consider
what our country will be a century after our departure ; for the sound
sense of," &c.]

with the flames of hell. The English (and we their descendants are most deserving of the name) require but justice ; whatever comes as a favor comes as an affront. To what a pitch then must our indignation be excited, when we are not permitted even to pay that which is required of us, unless we present it with the left hand, or upon the nose, or from our knees amid the mire ! The orators of the British parliament, while they are coloring this insolence and injustice, keep the understanding of the people at tongue's length.

Franklin. In good truth, then, the separation is no narrow one. I have been present while some of them have thrown up the most chaffy stuff two hours together, and have never called for a glass of water. This is thought the summit of ability, and he who is capable of performing it is deemed capable of ruling the East and West.* The rich families that govern this assembly have made us independent ; they have given us thirteen provinces, and they will people them all for us in less than fifty years. Religious and grave men, for none are graver or more religious than the beaten, are praising the loving mercies of God in loosening from their necks the millstone of America. What a blessing to throw aside such an extent of coast, which of itself would have required an immense navy for its defence ! No one dreams that England, in confederacy with America, would have been so strong in sailors, in ports, in naval stores, as to have become (I do not say with good management, I say in spite of bad) not invincible only, but invulnerable.

Washington. If she turns her attention to the defects of her administration in all its branches, she may recover not much less than she has lost. Look at the nations of Europe, and point out one, despotic or free, of which so large a portion is so barbarous and wretched as the Irish. The country is more fertile than Britain ; the inhabitants are healthy, strong, courageous, faithful, patriotic, and quick of apprehension. No quality is wanting which constitutes the respectability of a State : yet, from centuries of misrule, they are in a condition more hopeless than any other nation or tribe upon the globe, civilized or savage.

Franklin. There is only one direct way to bring them into

* Pitt may be complimented on his oratory in the words wherewith Anacreon congratulates the tettinx,—ἀπαθής, ἄναιμ', ἄσαρκε.

order, and that appears so rough it never will be trodden. The chief misery arises from the rapacity of the gentry, as they are styled, and the nobility, who, to avoid the trouble of collecting their rents from many poor tenants, and the greater of hearing their complaints, have leased their properties to what are called *middle-men*. These harass their inferiors in the exact ratio of their industry, and drive them into desperation. Hence slovenliness and drunkenness; for the appearance of ease and comfort is an allurement to avarice. To pacify and reclaim the people, leases to middle-men must be annulled; every cultivator must have a lease for life, and (at the option of his successor) valid for as many years afterward as will amount in the whole to twenty-one. The extent of ground should be proportionate to his family and his means. To underlet land should be punished by law as *regrating*.

Washington.[9] Authority would here be strongly exercised, not tyrannically,—which never can be asserted of plans sanctioned by the representatives of a people, for the great and perpetual benefit of the many, to the small and transient inconvenience of the few.

Franklin. Auxiliary to this reform should be one in church-livings. They should all embrace as nearly as possible the same number of communicants. Suppose three thousand souls under each cure: a fourth part would consist of the infirm, and of children not yet prepared for the reception of doctrine. The service, as formerly, should be shorter, and performed thrice each Sunday; so that all might in turn be present, and that great concourse would be avoided, which frequently is the prelude to licentiousness and brutality. Abolishing tithes, selling the property of the crown, of the church, and of corporations, I would establish a fund sufficient to allow each clergyman, in addition to his house, one hundred and forty pounds annually.[10] Each would be remunerated, not for his profession, but for services done toward the

[9 In 1st ed. the following five lines form part of Franklin's speech.]
[10 First ed. reads: "annually. The catholic priest should have the same number of communicants, and should receive a gratuity of fifty pounds annually, and should also possess his parsonage house: offerings and gifts as at present would accrue to him from the piety and gratitude of his parishioners. The church as established by government would be maintained in its supremacy and the papal priest would be remunerated," &c.]

State by his attention to the morals of his communicants. If the people pay forty pounds for taking up a felon, would they not willingly pay four times as much for reclaiming a dozen ?[11]

Washington. I do not know ; for we must never argue that men or their rulers are the likelier to do a thing because it is rational or useful. If ever the poorer clergy are rendered more comfortable, it will be only when the richer are afraid of losing a part of their usurped dominions. English and Irish bishops, who possess ten and twelve thousand a year, will be the last to relieve the necessities of their brethren ; and their selfishness will not alienate from them those who are habituated to long abuses. The fine linen of popery sticks close to the skin ; and there is much of it in the wardrobe of the English Church.

On all subjects I can talk dispassionately, and perhaps the most so on that topic which renders the great body of mankind the most furious and insane. Never would I animadvert on the tenets of the Catholic or any other church, apart from civil polity. But I am suspicious, if not inquisitive, when I see questionable articles day after day smuggled in, and when I am pushed aside if I venture to read the direction or lift up the wrapping. Articles of faith are innocent in themselves ; but upon articles of faith what incontrollable domination, what insupportable prerogatives, what insolent frauds, what incessant tyranny have been asserted and enforced !

Franklin. I am ready to be of that church, if you will tell me

[11 **First ed. reads** here : " dozen. I would grant eight hundred pounds yearly to **each** protestant bishop, obliging him **to constant** residence in his diocese ; **four of** these are sufficient : I **would grant two** thousand to one archbishop. The catholics should have the same number, and their stipends should **be the** same : for although **the** priests are ignorant and **vulgar** men in all catholic countries, **it** is highly requisite for the maintenance of order, **that the** bishops and archbishops here should possess whatever gives **authority.** Knowledge in some measure gives it ; but splendour **in a much greater.** Elagabalus would **attract** more notice and lead after him more **followers** than Lycurgus, **and not merely** from the lower orders **but also from the** higher. *Washington.* True enough : and indeed some **of the wise become as the** unwise in the enchanted chambers of Power, whose lamps **make every face of the** same colour. Gorgeousness welts all mankind into **one inert mass, carrying** off and confounding and consuming all beneath it, like a torrent of lava, **bright amidst** the darkness, and dark again amidst the light. The reductions," &c., (48 lines below). From " *Washington* " to " commodity " (26 lines) **added** in 3rd ed.]

which it is, in which there are the fewest of them. Show me that a single pope in one country tells fewer lies and sits quieter than twenty in another, and he is the pope for my money, when I lay it out on such a commodity. The[12] abuses of the clergy were first exposed by the clergy, the lower assailing the higher. If something more like equality, something more near moderation, had pervaded all, fewer sects would have arisen, and those fewer less acrimonious. Dogmas turn sour upon too full stomachs, and empty ones rattle against them. Envy, which the wolves and bears are without, and the generous dog alone seems by his proximity to have caught from us,—Envy, accompanying Religion, swells amid her genuflexions to the Episcopal canopy, at seeing so much wealth so ill distributed. The low cannot be leaders without a change nor without a party. Some unintelligible syllable is seized ; and the vulgar are taught to believe that salvation rests upon it. Even this were little : they are instructed that salvation may be yet perhaps insecure, unless they drag others to it by the throat, and quicken their paces at the dagger's point. Popery first laid down this doctrine ; the most abominable and monstrous of her tenets, and the only one that all establishments, splitting off from her, are unanimous in retaining.

Washington. The reductions you propose would bring about another ; they would remove the necessity of a standing army in that unfortunate country, and would enable the government to establish three companies for fisheries,—the herring, the cod, and the whale,—and to enrich her remote dominions with the super-abundance of a discontented peasantry. The western part of Ireland in another century may derive as great advantages from her relative position with America, as the eastern from hers with the mercantile and manufacturing towns of Lancashire. The population is already too numerous, and is increasing, which of itself is the worst of curses, unless when high civilization regulates it ; and the superflux must be diverted by colonization, or occupied on the seas by commerce. Manufacturers tend to deteriorate the species, but begin by humanizing it. Happy those countries which have occasion for little more of them than may supply the home consumption ! National debts are evils, not so much because they take away from useful and honest gains, as because

[12 From "The" to "retaining" (18 lines) added in 2nd ed.]

they create superfluous and hishonest ones ; and because, when carried as far as England would carry hers, they occasion half the children of the land to be cooped up in buildings which open into the brothel and the hospital.

In assenting to you, I interrupted your propositions ; pray go on.

Franklin. I would permit no Englishman to hold in Ireland a place of trust or profit, whether in Church or State. I would confer titles and offices on those Irish gentlemen who reside in the country ; and surely they would in time become habituated to a regular and decorous mode of life. The landlord and clergyman might in the beginning lose something of current coin ; but if you consider that their lives, houses, and effects would be safe, that provisions would be plentiful in proportion to the concessions they make, and that in no year would their rents and incomes fail, as they now do at least thirty in each century, you will find that their situation, like the situation of their inferiors, must be improved.

Washington. Many will exclaim against the injustice of taking from one class alone a portion of its property as insurance-money.

Franklin. Not from one alone ; property should be protected at its own cost : this is the right and the object of governments. The insurance is two-fold ; that of the private man and that of the community : the latter is the main consideration. I perceive nothing arbitrary, nothing novel, in its principle.* The [13] King of England and Ireland, as head of the Church, succeeds by consent of Parliament to the disposal of benefices. He surely can do in his own kingdom what the pope can do in another's, where ecclesiastical property (if any can be called so) is concerned. The religion of a State is established for the correction

---

* There is an argument which could not be attributed to Franklin, because it is derived from an authority to which he never appealed, and the words containing it are unlikely to have lain within the range of his reading :—

" Le Pape peut révoquer la loi établie par lui ou par prédécesseur, et oster *mesme sans occasion* les effects procédens d'icelle, et le bénéfice valide à un chacun : car il a entière disposition sur les bénéfices."—*Em. Sa.* p. 528.

[13 From "The" to "exciseman" (16 lines) forms part of the footnote in 1st ed.]

of its morals, and its morals are requisite to the maintenance of
the laws. Religion, then, in the view of a statesman, is only
a thing that aids and assists the laws, removing from before
them much of their painful duties, and lessening (if good and
effectual) the number of their officers and executioners. So that
in political economy there is between them a close and intimate
connection, and both alike are subject to regulations in them
from the same authority. Where there is a State religion, the
salary of a clergyman should be as much subject to the State as
the stipend of a custom-house officer and exciseman. If a
government exerts the power of taxing one trade or profession,
it does the same thing or more. Suppose it should levy a tax of
a hundred pounds on every man who begins the business of an
apothecary or lawyer, is not the grievance even heavier, as
pressing on those whose gains are yet uncertain and to be derived
from others, than it would be if bearing upon those whose emoluments are fixed, and proceed from the government which regulates
and circumscribes them? But they have been accustomed, you
will say, to the enjoyment of more. So much clear gain for
them; and I hope they may have made a liberal and prudent use
of the superfluity. Those who have done so will possess minds
ready to calculate justly their own lasting interests, and the
interests of the community for whose benefit they have been
appointed. If there is any thing the existence of which produces
great and general evil, and the abolition of which will produce
great and general good in perpetuity, the government is not only
authorized by right but bound by duty to remove it. Compensation should be made to the middle-men for all losses; it should
be made even to the worst: these losses may as easily be ascertained, as those occasioned to proprietors and tenants through
whose lands we open a road or a canal.

Washington.[14] Methods, far short of what you indicate, will
be adopted, and will fail. Constitutional lawyers will assent that
Ireland be subject to martial law for thirty years in the century,
and to little or none for the remainder, but will not assent that
every thing unlawful be unnecessary and unprovoked. In consequence of which, within the lifetime of some in existence we
shall have two millions of Irishmen in America, reclaimed from

[14 " *Washington* " added in 3rd ed.]

their ferocity by assuaging their physical and moral wants, and addicted to industry by the undisturbed enjoyment of its reward. Experience seems to have given no sort of instruction to their rulers : they profit by nothing old, they venture on nothing new.

Franklin. We[15] are informed, by the scientific in chemistry, that a diamond and a stick of charcoal on the hearth are essentially of the same materials. In like manner, those among men, who to the vulgar eye are the most dissimilar in externals are nearly the same in mind and intellect ; and their difference is the effect of accident and fortune, of position and combination. Those who, governing the political, influence in a high degree the moral world, can perform at once what Nature is myriads of years in accomplishing : they can convert the stick of charcoal into a diamond, by the aliment and situation they allow to it. Our government will find its interest in doing so : others will pursue their old occupation in reducing the diamond to its dark original, and exercise their divine right of keeping it unextracted.

If I were a member of the British Ministry, I should think I acted wisely, not in attempting to prove that the Constitution is the best in the world, but in demonstrating, if I could, the reverse. For in proportion as they labor to extol it, in the same proportion do they oblige us to suppose them its most impudent and outrageous violators, or, at the least, ignorant of its spirit and incapable of its application. Otherwise, how could this excellent form be the parent of deformity ? How could the population, where the country is so fertile and the race so industrious, contain a larger number of indigent families, and those among the most laborious and the most virtuous, than any other upon earth ? [16]

Washington. If the Constitution were what it is represented, its agents could not abuse it ; and, if its agents could not abuse it, America would not have been at this time separated from England ; nor would Ireland have been condemned to a massacre

[15 From " We " to " unextracted " (13 lines) added in 2nd ed. *Franklin* added in 3rd ed.]

[16 First ed. reads: " earth. Such is the beneficence of the supreme power, unmixed evil, in its exposure to the air and heavens, may contract or produce, by a certain stimulating agency, a somewhat of good, however scantily and slowly, but evil never flows from good unmixed. If the constitution," &c.]

once at furthest in **two** generations ; nor would the British people be more heavily taxed in its comforts and its necessaries than the Algerines and Turks, when its industry is so much greater, and when **its** territory has not been occupied **nor** invaded nor endangered **by** an enemy.

Franklin.[17]   The Persian despots never debased the **souls of the** nations they had conquered, **and do not** appear **to have** coveted **their** purses.   Herodotus calls the taxation of the Ionian States **a** tranquillizing and pacificatory measure.   No portion of **the** globe was **more** advantageously situated **for** commerce than the Greek **republics in** Asia ; no soil richer, no climate healthier, no people **more** industrious.   Æolians, Ionians, and Dorians, together with Pamphylia, Lycia, **the** islands of Rhodes, Cos, **Samos,** Chios, and Sestos,—on the whole exceeding four hundred miles by forty,—were taxed unalterably at four hundred talents (about £105,000) by Darius, according **to a** scale *submitted to their deputies* by his father, Artaxerxes.   **Italy** in the time of **Nero** contained at the lowest computation twenty-six millions of inhabitants, and paid less **in** taxes than **the City of** London with **its** appurtenances.   Appian **states that Pompey** imposed **on** the Tyrians and Cilicians a hundreth **of their income.**   Hadrian **was** accused **of** great severity **toward the Jews** in having somewhat augmented the rate which Vespasian had decreed, and which, according to Zonaras and Xiphilinus, **was** about sixteen pence **on** each.   Strabo remarks that Egypt brought a revenue of about £180,000 to the **father of** Cleopatra, which was doubled **by** Augustus.   When **he** was declared Imperator against **M.** Antonius, the Senate **decreed** a temporary property-tax **of a twentieth.**   Plutarch, **in his** *Life of Pompey,* informs us that **he** levied on Asia £192,000.   M. Antonius had exacted in advance at one time the tribute of ten years.

Washington.   **The** possibility of levying in **a** single year the ordinary taxes **of** ten is a proof how extremely light were the impositions on the **richest** subjects of the Roman empire.   Laboring under the enormous debt of £200,000,000, the English could **not** in any emergency **pay** the rate of three years anticipated.

[17 From *"Franklin"* to " scourge them " (41 lines) added in 3rd ed.   This rather pedantic passage appears in **an** appendix to the Conversation between Pericles and Sophocles in **the** 1st and 2nd editions of that dialogue.]

Franklin. The nations of Asia had recently paid more heavily : for it was objected to them as a reproach, and as a cause for this exaction, that they had raised for Cassius and Brutus in the one preceding year what was now demanded for ten.

Washington. So long as the English tolerate the absorption of their wealth under the patronage of their peerage, wars and taxation will severely scourge them. Wars, the origin of taxation, are systematical in their periods, however little so in their conduct, and must recur about every twenty years as a new generation springs up from the aristocracy, for which all the great civil employments however multiplied are insufficient, and which disdains all other professions than the military and the naval. But [18] when this devourer hath exhausted and concentrated in itself nearly all the land and riches of the nation, then it will begin to discuss the question whether it can gain most by suppressing the Church establishment, or by maintaining it in its rankness.

Franklin. May it not happen that the question be tried before a session of other jurors ; and that the benches of the Lords Spiritual have nothing else upon them than the benches of the Lords Temporal with the legs uppermost ? If State religions were abolished, the world would be quieter and better ; in England the national debt would be liquidated in a century, and in Ireland the public tranquillity would be established in a year. Among our own injuries on the part of England, this never bore upon us ; namely, to pay for hearing what we knew or for what we disbelieved. If there existed no establishment in England, fear would be entertained of Puritanism.

---

[18] From " But " to " uppermost " (9 lines) added in 3rd ed. From " If " to " pillow " (18 lines) added in 2nd ed. In the 2nd ed. the following passage is inserted thus " established. When the catholic sees the protestant freed from the heaviest of taxations, that of paying in the clergy a body he does not appoint, a body bound like a dead weight upon him, he will presently claim a similar advantage. The sect that bears the lighter burden will become the more numerous by being the more flourishing. This alone in my opinion can ever give the protestants in Ireland a true legitimate and durable assembly. Among . . . disbelieved. *Franklin.* If there existed no establishment in England or in Ireland, great fears would be entertained of novel sects and greater still of old ones ; of puritanism for instance and of Popery. *Washington.* Against," &c.]

Washington. Against what could Puritanism act? It over-threw the Established Church in her state of inebriety; it kicked into the streets her crosiers and mitres, and other such ensigns of barbarism and paganism and despotism. When it finds nothing to quarrel with out of doors, it will quarrel at home.

Franklin. It grows strong by being kept in the cool, and bunged up by the ecclesiastical excise.

Washington. Benjamin, I do not like to meddle with relig-ions, nor indeed to speak about them. All of them appear to me inoffensive, excepting the Popish, which not only would have a hand in every man's pocket, but an ear on every man's pillow.

Franklin. [19] I know not whether the Irish are very fervent in their devotion to the Bishops of Rome. Probably they are unaware of some among the benefits they have heretofore received from them. Few, I dare say, have ever heard that their Holy Father, Hadrian the Fourth, solemnly gave his sanction to Henry the Second to invade and subjugate their country. This, I dare likewise say, would be loudly contradicted by the few who know it. Indeed, I must correct my words before I go farther. Hadrian did not give his sanction; he sold it. A tax was to be paid the Holy See on every Irish family. So that the Holy See was as much interested as Henry himself that the conquest should be effectual and complete. The Holy Father chose rather a tax on families than a capitation; for although many thousands of men would be exterminated, few whole families would.

Washington. We may talk together in private of these his-torical facts; but if we mention them to people whose eyes might be opened by them, we shall render them in the same degree our enemies as we are their true friends.

Franklin. I knew a certain man who would take the most nauseous medicine in health, because he had paid money for it at the apothecary's when he was ill; at the same time he would not eat a fresh salad at the next door. Things are valued by the places they come from. If a reasoner were to say what a Saint hath said about the Blessed Trinity, in most countries he would be called an infidel, and even in some of the most tolerant he would be subject to fine and imprisonment.

[19 From " *Franklin* " to " *Washington* " (35 lines) added in 3rd. ed.]

Washington.   How was that?

Franklin.   St Augustine says, "We talk of Three Persons merely for the sake of talking."

Washington.   Oh the knave!

Franklin.   And scholars do say that the Latin expression is an ugly one : "Dictum est Tres *Personæ,* non ut aliquid diceretur, sed ne taceretur."

Washington.   Instead[20] of sending to a rotten old city, the most profligate and the most venal on earth, for spiritual advice and counsel,—which always comes to you in the form of a command, and enclosing an order to pay a pretty round sum to the bearer,—could not every city and every hamlet find some worthy inhabitant capable of giving his opinion upon those matters, if indeed there be any such, which the Disciples of Christ were unable or inattentive or indifferent to elucidate and explain? I see nothing worth a quarrel in them ; and certainly there is nothing which the blessed Author of our religion would recommend us to fight about. If there were no hierarchy in England and Ireland, the people of both countries would be brotherly and contented. They would mind their own business, and not the business of those who fare sumptuously on their credulity, and ride in rich housings on their fiery animosities. The revenues of ecclesiastics would overpay the just demands of a protecting and frugal government. Let the Protestant Church be no longer a hireling ; and the Popish will drop away rag after rag, image after image, to the great emolument of the barber's shop. The poor people of that persuasion would not long be so foolish and besotted as to pay tithes where the heretic pays none. Inequality would shake their creed, extortion would open their eyes, and they would feel on that occasion what they now feel on another,—that they were not, as they ought to be, in the same condition as the Protestant. The parties will never be peaceable until the banners are thrown into the dust between them, and each tramples upon his own. Absurdities in worship would soon cease if nobody gained by them. Within half a century, the whole people would find in their hand and hearts nothing else than the unencumbering and

[20] From " Instead " to " *Franklin* " (112 lines) added in 2nd ed.].

unexhausting page, which, if its spirit were received in its purity, might well be denominated the Book of Life. So mischievous a use, however, has been made of it for above a thousand years, that if you take, as churches would force you, their glosses and interpretations for part of it, then indeed may it be called more properly the book of imposture and extortion, of darkness and destruction.

Franklin. We may become so habituated to tyranny as neither to feel nor see it. The part on which its poison has been perpetually dropping is deadened; else would it be possible that throughout a whole nation, incomparably the most enlightened of any upon earth, young men should be sent from a distance,—quite unknown to the parishioners, and often of a vicious or loose character, and for the greater part of a light one,—to teach the experienced as well as the inexperienced their duties, and to be paid for a lesson which has been already taught by others?

Washington. Supposing an establishment to exist at all, the uttermost that a grave and reflecting people could reasonably be expected to endure is that the bishop or presbyter, chosen by the clergy of the diocese, should nominate at least three natives of it, in order for the parishioners to appoint one of them to the vacant benefice. They should agree with him upon the stipend, which they would do amicably, just as they agree with an apothecary for his attendance on the paupers. He should be removable for any offence against the laws, or for any habits which they and the bishop should declare to be inconsistent with his office.

Franklin. These remarks of yours are reasonable. In regard to the appointment of clergymen, the Roman Church is more observant of propriety than the English. It rarely if ever happens that a parish priest is sent from a distance to his cure: he almost always is chosen from among his townsmen or provincials. This difference would be a subject of wonder to me, if I did not likewise see the representatives of boroughs, not selected as they were formerly from among the most respectable of the burgesses, but invited for the greater part from a distance, and utterly unknown both morally and politically by those who depute them to parliament. Can any thing be more disgraceful to the inhabitants of a city, than to declare by their actions that none of them is worthy of confidence, or capable of transacting their affairs? And either this must be the inference, or we must attribute their conduct to the most scandalous venality.

Washington.[21] I would obviate present evils by present remedies, as in the case of Ireland. Many good things cannot be done, many indifferent ones may be: if, indeed, those are to be called indifferent which are only so at the time, and very far from it in the consequences. Religion, I agree with you, is too pure for corporations: it is best meditated on in our privacy, and best acted on in our ordinary intercourse with mankind. If we believe in Revelation, we must believe that God wishes us to converse with him but little, since the only form of address he has prescribed to us is an extremely short one. He has placed us where our time may be more beneficially employed in mutually kind offices; and he does not desire us to tell him hour after hour how dearly we love him, or how much we want from him: he knows these things exactly.

Franklin. These, however, are the things which occupy the pulpit; and the ceremonies attending them and the modes of doing them, together with disquisitions on His body and parentage, have cost the lives of millions. In money, too, and lands I have calculated what Europe has paid for them; but the sum total, if I could repeat it, would confound the head of any arithmetician; nor was there ever a man in the world could remember the figures, if he had heard them but once or twice read to him. The despots of France never exacted by their detested *corvée* so large a portion as the pastors claim in England,—a tenth forsooth of every man's industry; and this tenth is taken off the ground untaxed, while the other nine parts are liable to new deductions. If truths are plain, they ought not to cost so much; if not plain, still less are they worth it. The tyrants of Sicily demanded a tenth of the corn, but not a tenth of oil or wine or hay or legumes, or fruits of any kind, in which the island was equally abundant. This satisfied them, and sufficed to keep the bodies and minds of their subjects in order and subjection.

Washington. We never had to complain of England for per-

[21 " *Washington* " and the following " *Franklin* " added in 3rd ed.]

secuting us by her fox-hunters in the Church; nor indeed, to speak honestly and freely, so much of any persecution as of idle and unprofitable vexation.

Franklin. The conduct of England toward us resembles that of Ebenezer Bullock toward his eldest son, Jonas.

Washington.[22] I remember old Ebenezer; and I believe it was Jonas who, when another youth after giving him much offence and seeing him unresisting would fain fight him, replied, " Nay, I will not fight thee, friend ; but if thou dost with that fist what thou threatenest, by the Lord's help I will smite thee sore, marking thee for one of an ill and unprofitable flock ; and thou shalt walk home in heaviness, like a wether the first morning he was made one" Whereat he took off his coat, folded it up, and laid it on the ground, saying, " This at least hath done no harm, and deserveth good treatment." The adversary, not admiring such an object of contemplation, went away muttering more reasonable threats, conditional and subjunctive. Ebenezer, I guess, aggravated and wore out his son's patience ; for the old man was rich and testy, and would have his comforts neither encroached upon nor much partaken.

Franklin. My story is this. Jonas had been hunting in the woods, and had contracted a rheumatism in the face which drew it awry, and either from the pain it occasioned or from the medicines he took to cure it, rotted one of his grinders. Old Ebenezer was wealthy, had little to do or to care about, made few observations on his family, sick or sound, and saw nothing particular in his son's countenance. However, one day after dinner when he had eaten heartily, he said " Son Jonas, methinks thy appetite is not over-keen : pick (and welcome) the other half of that hog's foot."

" Father," answered he, " I have had a pain in my tooth the last fortnight ; the northerly wind does it no good to-day. I would rather, if so be that you approve of it, eat a slice of yon fair cheesecake in the closet."   .

" Why, what ails the tooth?" said Ebenezer. "Nothing more," replied Jonas, " than that I cannot chew with it what I used to chew." " Drive a nail in the wall," quoth stoutly and courage-

[22 From " *Washington* to " this " (16 lines) added in 2nd ed.]

ously Ebenezer, "tie a string to one end, and lace the other round thy tooth."

The son performed a part of the injunction, but could not very dexterously twist the string around the grinder, for his teeth were close and the cord not over-fine. Then said the father kindly, "Open thy mouth, lad! give me the twine: back thy head,— back it, I tell thee, over the chair."

"Not that, father! not that; the next;" cried Jonas. "What dost mean?" proudly and impatiently said Ebenezer. "Is not the string about it? Dost hold my hand too, scape-grace? Dost give me this trouble for naught?" "Patience, now, father!" meekly said Jonas with the cord across his tongue; "let me draw my tooth my own way."

"Follow thine own courses, serpent!" indignantly exclaimed Ebenezer. "As God's in Boston, thou art a most wilful and undutiful child." "I hope not, father." "Hope not! rebel! Did not I beget thee and thy teeth, one and all? Have not I lodged thee, clothed thee, and fed thee, these forty years; and now, I warrant ye, all this bustle and backwardness about a rotten tooth! Should I be a groat the richer for it, out or in?"

Washington. Dignity in private men and in governments has been little else than a stately and stiff perseverance in oppression; and spirit, as it is called, little else than the foam of hard-mouthed insolence. Such at last is become the audacity of Power, from a century or more of holidays, and riot, it now complains that you deprive it of its prerogative if you limit the exercise of its malignity. I lament that there are those who can learn no lesson of humanity, unless we write it broadly with the point of the sword.

Franklin. Let us hope, however, that we may see the day when these scholars shall be turned out of school.[23]

Washington. The object of our cares and solicitudes, at present, is the stability of the blessings we have obtained. No attempt against them is dangerous from without, nor immediately from within; but the seeds of corruption are inherent, however latent, in all bodies, physical and political; guards therefore should be stationed, and laws enacted, to deter adventurers from attempts at despotism.

[[23] In 1st ed. the Conversation ends here.]

Franklin. Other offences, even the greatest, are the violation of one law : despotism is the violation of all. The despot then should be punished, not only by loss of life, which the violation of only one law may incur, and which leaves no pain, no repentance, no example, but also with exposure and scourges, as among the Romans. Conspiracies are weak and frivolous : the hand of every man should be directed against him whose hand is directed against every man. Societies, on the contrary, should be instituted to recompense the avenger of humanity : every land should be his country, every free citizen his brother. The greatest men, according to what is taught in schools and colleges, are those who have offered the greatest violence to reason and humanity. Destroyers of freedom are more celebrated than its founders,— Pompey than Pelopidas, Cæsar than Timoleon,—just as we hear more of him who burns a house than of him who builds one.

Washington.[24] In the proper choice of teachers, and in the right course of education, are to be found the best preventive laws against despotism. Wherever there is a political church, of whatever creed, supported by the shoulders of the people, whether against their will or partially with it, there will be much dissatisfaction and much intolerance. Unhappily most of Christ's doctrines are superseded or explained away. There is one indeed which was never in fashion, and which, where all are good, is among the best. *Commune with thine own heart in thy chamber, and be still.* This, if attended to in England and Ireland, would speedily send Episcopal thrones into the lumber-room.

Franklin. When certain men cry loudest, they feel least. Indeed, there is a great deal less of bigotry in the world than is usually supposed, and a great deal more insincerity. Our faith is of little moment or concern to those who declaim against it. They are angry, not at our blindness, but that the blind will trust his own dog and staff rather than theirs ; and, what is worse, that he will carry the scrip. This is wilfulness : they would fain open his eyes to save him from the sin of it ;

[24 " *Washington* " added in 3rd ed.; 3 lines below, from "wherever" to "affections" (25 lines), added in 3rd ed. from the appendix affixed to this Conversation in 1st and 2nd eds.]

and they break one or two bones because he will not take them for his oculists.

Washington. Love of power resides in the breast of every man, and is well regulated and discreet in few. Accompanied by genius, it is likewise too frequently accompanied by pride and arrogance. Although it assumes to itself the highest character, it is really among the weakest of our affections. Christianity, in its unadulterated form, is perfectly adapted to control it: in its adulterated, it has been the main support of aggression and iniquity. If ever we reduce it in America to an *Establishment* (as people call it), its spirit flies, and its body so weighs upon us that we cast it down, or let it slip quietly from our arms. For Christianity is in itself of such simplicity, that whoever would make an Establishment of it must add imposture : and from imposture grows usurpation.

Franklin.[25] Every mother, if left to herself, would teach her child what that child during the whole of its lifetime pays dearly for being taught, and what from such payment makes often an unkindly and unjust impression on him. He is obliged to purchase a commodity he does not require, and one which (sometimes it may happen), he has a larger store of than the patentee and vender. The most pious and moral men upon earth are the inhabitants of New England ; and they are so because their consciences have never been drilled nor swathed ; and because they never have been taught to divide their offering— the prayer and psalm on this side, the bag of wheat and truss of clover on that—between God and the ministers of the Church.

Washington. While such men as the New England men are existing, our independence and liberty are secure. Governments, in which there are Establishments, will, without great prudence, fall into danger from sects : every new one gives a fresh security and an additional stability to ours.

Franklin. A mixture of sects is as advantageous to a political system as a mixture of blood is to the strength and perpetuity of the human race. Every thing wants gentle, insensible, unrestricted renovation,—air, fire, earth, water, the vegetables, the animals, man, States. To you, fellow-citizen and defender, the

[25 In the 2nd ed., Franklin speaks without interruption down to "gradually and occasionally" on page 275.]

most beneficent on record is principally owing. If America had been conquered, the breath of Freedom had been stifled in every region of the world, and we should have lamented the fate even of the people who in their blindness had enslaved us.

Looking to what may happen in future, on the ground you have marked out to me, I recollect an admirable law of Solon, which enacts that in case of usurpation the magistrates should resign their offices : and that he who continued his functions after the extinction of the popular power should, together with the subverter of it, be punished with death by any private citizen. Let jurists decide whether it be not right and expedient to punish, not usurpers only, but (if in compliance with the vulgar use of language we must distinguish them) conquerors, too, in this manner; on the principle that every individual may recover his own property, and slay the spoiler who detains it aggressively. And let moralists judge, whether a few of such chastisements on choice subjects would not cool in a great degree the lusts of spoliation and conquest. We will not be morose and captious with the lovers of peace and order; we will concede to them that it is a dangerous question to agitate whether an arbitrary but salutary imprisonment now and then, with now and then an un-lucky but well-meant torture, should be resisted or endured : for such things (they will tell us) happen occasionally in the most flourishing and best-regulated governments. But when consti-tutions are destroyed and legal magistrates are displaced, every man may pick up the broken laws; and it is a virtue to exercise the most solemn and the most imperative of them gratuitously. That of Solon, moderate as he was, goes farther. A similar law was enacted at Rome on the abolition of the decemvirate.*

Washington. Our constitution is flexible and yielding by reason of its homogeneousness and its purity. Like the surface of our country, it may in some measure be changed by improve-ments and still preserve its character and features. The better part of what we have imported from England is retained for the present, because it is difficult to introduce new regulations in times of trouble, and that the mischievous should not burst in

---

* Ne quis ullum magistratum sine provocatione crearet: qui creasset, eum jus fasque esset occidi, neve ea cædes capitalis noxæ haberetur. *Liv.* iii. 55.

between the old paling and the new. Several of these must be repealed, but gradually and occasionally.

Franklin.[26] In England, more have been made and repealed again within one century than in all the rest of the universe within three ; not reckoning, as would be unfair, what has been effected by revolutions. The worst have lasted the longest.*
Barrenness is perennial ; fertility is the produce of a season.

Washington. The whole system of representation, on which every thing depends of law and liberty, has been changed within our memory.

Franklin. Except the Chancery-court.

Sedet æternumque sedebit.

It has carried more ruin and desolation into innocent families than all the gaming-houses and other haunts of vice in the three kingdoms. Orphans, charities, schools, hospitals, are absorbed by the hundred, and swallowed up in this inland Maëlstrom.

Washington. The English talk of other grievances, and hardly notice this : we may be so near an object as not to see it in its full extent, nor clearly.

Franklin. A sailor condemned to be hanged was thus admonished : " Prepare yourself to appear before your eternal judge." " What does his lordship mean ? " said he to the jailer who was conducting him away. " Sure, I can have nothing to do with

---

[²⁶ Second ed. reads : " *Washington* " for " *Franklin*." And the speech continues unbroken down to " dearly " (17 lines).]

* Nevertheless, it is proved and declared from the Bench that the mass of the people live in comfort, not to say in affluence ; for Mr Justice Best informs us that *most of the industrious part of the community live upon nothing else than bread and water*. That the laws are liberal is proved also and declared from the Bench by the same high authority. He tells us that writers of newspapers ought to report *nothing* of the King but what has been communicated by the Ministry. Mr Justice Best, being raised to the Peerage, said, " *I bullied them into it*." At a public dinner, he proposed the health of George IV., enumerated his manifold virtues, and stated the benefits he had conferred on the nation. Upon which Mr T. Erskine begged to remind him of one omission, and to suggest that the national thanks should be humbly offered to his Majesty for the late abundant harvest. We may hope that ere long allied kings, instead of sending each other stars, snuff-boxes, and crosses, will amicably exchange ministers, jurists, and judges ; all good and useful for all.

my Lord Chancellor! I have neither land nor tenement ; and he would turn up his nose at my jacket and trousers."

There is no country where laws are so disproportionate to offences, so sanguinary, so disputable, so contradictory, so tardy, so expensive. Now these are the six principal defects of laws, and to which it would be difficult to add a seventh of weight : for laxity cannot co-exist with them. More fortunes have been wrecked upon the quicksands of British jurisprudence than ever have been engulfed by any one despotism ; and more crimes are capital in England than were even known by name among the Jews in the time of Moses, or among the Athenians in the time of Draco.

Washington. Sometimes[27] it is not the ignorant who act the most absurdly. Our late enemies are now just as angry with us as if they fancied we were mocking their mutability ; some of them are more alarmed at the form of government we have chosen than at any other consequence of our liberation : I think, without reason. Republicanism is fit only for nations grown up, and is equally ill adapted to those in decay and to those in infancy. Europeans do indeed call ours an infant State.

Franklin. Ay, indeed ! I never heard of an infant who kicked its mother downstairs.

Washington. Be graver, Benjamin, and inform me whether, in your opinion, States do not reasonably date from their instruction and experience, and not from this or from that effect of vicissitude ; and whether any nation in the world was ever better informed than ours in its duties and interests.

Franklin. None on record : and God grant that every novelty in our country may be as just and reasonable as that contained in your observation with regard to dates. We are as old a nation as the English, although we are not so old in America as they in England. Crossing the ocean does not make a man younger ; neither does it a people.

Washington. Other accusations than those of juvenility are brought against us, and in appearance weightier. We are accused of the worst ingratitude, in having turned our strength and prosperity against the authors of it. Prosperity and strength never have excited a colony to rebellion, nor is wealth a whisperer to in-

[27 From "Sometimes" to "absurdly" (2 lines) added in 3rd ed.]

dependence. But when arrogance and **injustice** stride forth **into**
a colony strong and prosperous, it takes the advantage of its strength
and prosperity; and then indeed wealth, which has not **been** the
mover, becomes the supporter, of emancipation. Every colony of
England hath evinced a desire of quitting **her** when it could; not
a single one of ancient Rome. Under the government of Hadrian,
Utica, Italica, and **Gades, enjoying the** privileges of municipal
towns, entreated and obtained the **title** of colonies; though
in the former condition they might exercise **all** the magistracies,
and enjoy all the dignities of the republic. Yet Rome, we
are informed, was the subjugator of mankind, and **England** the
protector. .

Franklin. **G**od protect the wretchedest of his creatures from
such **protection!**

Washington. **W**e have spoken of the danger to which every
State, sooner or **later,** is subject from arbitrary power, and on the
principles which ought to be instilled **into every young citizen,**
first to guard against **it,** and then, if unsuccessful in his precautions,
to exterminate it. Aristocracy, in the eyes of many, is as great
an evil, and **more** imminent. Hence we have a **party in force**
against the institution of a Senate; and **indeed, if I could con-**
sider **it as** any thing like an aristocracy **or oligarchy in its gait or**
tendency, I should disapprove of it openly **and loudly.** **But in**
fact **ours is** the only intermediate **body** which **can do good; and**
I think **it capable** of this to a great **extent.** Hereditary Senates,
under **whatever name, are** eternally tearing and consuming the
vitals of their country. Our Senate brings no such evil with it;
on the contrary, every thing about it is **conservative and** prospec-
tive. Its beneficent effects go beyond **itself, and exceed its** attributions: for, as **none** can be elected into it whose **fortunes do not**
show him to **have** been prudent, and whose demeanor has not been
regular and decorous, many spirits which from their nature, from
youth, from zeal, from ambition, would **be** clamorous **and** unruly
among our representatives, are controlled **and** guided by **the** hope
of rising thence **into** this venerable assembly.

Franklin. Tiberius, the wisest of despots, to increase **his** own
power, increased that of the **Senate,** and transferred to it the
business of the *comitia.* In **more** barbarous times, the king and
aristocracy will **contend for** power, **and** the people will lift up its

head between **them ; in** more civilized, when abundance of wealth
produces abundance of **offices, the** two will unite, and the people
sink imperceptibly under them.   For it is requisite in such a
State to the existence **of** both that **the** mass do not become rich
or instructed ; against which evils **wars** and lucrative **places are**
devised, and elections are so managed as to **occasion a vast ex-**
penditure, and to be **accompanied** by as many vices as **can find**
room.   Where Senates **have not** been the executive power **or the**
appointers **of it, they have** been instruments, **but** never intermedi-
aries.   That of papal **Rome** is in nothing **less** respectable than
that of imperial.   The venerable body—consisting [28] of one man,
a robe, and a periwig—went this year before the " Holiness of
our Lord," requesting his permission to **wear** masks **the last week** *
of the carnival.   Who **can** doubt **the** utility and dignity of such
institutions, or that something of such gravity and decorum ought
always to stand between the prince and the people ?

Washington.   Other nations seem to entertain more fears for
us, in the abundance **of** their benevolence, **than we entertain for**
ourselves.   They acknowledge **you and some few** more among **us**
to be honest and well-meaning **persons, and, pressing them** hardly,
do not deny altogether **that you are moderate,** reasonable, capable
of instruction, nay **indeed wise ; yet the merest** youths, whist-
players, and jockeys, **turn their heads across** their shoulders to
give you a word of **advice.   When the** Popular **part, the Sena-**
torial part, the **Executive part are** summarily discussed, the whole
together is taken up **as lightly and** as easily disposed of.   " Republics cannot stand ! " **is the exclamation** of council-board **and**
sounding-board ; **the echo of Church** and Chamber.

Franklin.   I would reduce the question to as few words as
they would.   A single argument is enough for a single truth :
whatever comes after is in part illustration, in part confusion.

When the advantages of kingship and republicanism are opposed,
the **main** inquiry **is** not about forms or families, **not** about the
government of the fewer or the more ; but whether the good shall
control the bad, **or the bad control the** good.   A whole people
cannot long err in its choice.   **One man** or two may agree with a
groom that an unsound horse is a sound **one ;** but twenty will not,

[[28] From " consisting " to " periwig " (2 lines) added in **3rd ed.**]
* This was likewise done in **1824.**

take the twenty even at hazard. The great advantage is, however, when you can send back the horse after trying him, or
change him on discovering his infirmity.

Washington.[29]   There are certain parts of our constitution
which are capable of improvement.   In my situation it would be
imprudent and indecorous to point them out.   But it is better in
its present condition than if it were more centralized and compact.
It is like those bridges which are overlaid with loose planks, and
of which, when the tide is rising rapidly, the platform would be
heaved up and broken if it were more strained into apparent
solidity.

Franklin.   In government, as in other things, we—and not
only we, but even those wiser and greater men, the ministers of
kings—may profit by reading the first half-page in the *Elements
of Geometry,* in which we find that " the right line is the shortest
way from one point to another," and, I would add, *cæteris paribus,*
the easiest and surest.

We were called, a little while ago, the partisans of anarchy.
At that time we could not argue with our opponents, they being
in a state of frenzy, and running loose ; but now that their arms
are tied behind them, and that they are at home and a-bed, we
may reason calmly with them, and tell them that no number is so
near to nothing as one, and no government so near to anarchy as
monarchy.   There is more than one kind of anarchy, though
there is only one known by name ; as there are plants and metals
under our feet, unclassed and undescribed.   We are in the habit
of calling those bodies of men anarchal which are in a state of
effervescence ; but the most anarchal of all are those which surrender self-rule to the caprice of the worst informed and least
tractable members of society.   Anarchy, like other things, has its
certain state and season of quiescence ; and its features are only
the more flushed and discomposed by the somnolence of repletion
and supineness.

Washington.   A third question, of less intense anxiety, is raised
by those who read our fortunes, not in the palms of our hands,
but in the clouds.   At some future day, they portend to us that
every province will be an independent State.

Franklin.   Horrible prediction !   We shall experience the

[[29] From " *Washington* " to " *Franklin* " (9 lines) added in 3rd ed.]

misfortune, then, to have cultivated our wilds ; to have subdivided
and peopled hill, forest, and savannah ; to have excavated quarries,
mines, canals ; to have erected arsenals, to have constructed navies ;
to be so rich, in short, and so powerful as to fear no enemy and
to need no alliance. The time undoubtedly will come when each
province will produce as much as all do now ; so that as easily
and safely as all now stand together, each will then stand alone.
A long experience of their true interests, a certainty that they
depend upon peace and concord, will render wars impossible
among them ; and if any European power should have the temerity
to attack the weakest, not only will our other States chastise that
power, but its own subjects will abandon or subvert it. Repose
from oppression, refuge from persecution, respect for honesty, and
reward for industry are found here. A laborer gains more in
this country than a "professor of humanity" in some of the most
civilized on the other continent. Resolute to defend these advantages, the children of America are for ever free : those of
Europe, many years yet, must thread the labyrinth and face the
Minotaur.

IX. ANDREW HOFER, COUNT METTERNICH, AND THE EMPEROR FRANCIS. [1]

Metternich. Who are you, man ? I hear you have brought
some intelligence from Tyrol. Be brief ; I have little time for

[1 Andrew Hofer's insurrection in the Tyrol was designed to free that
country from the rule of the Bavarians to whom Napoleon had transferred
it, and to restore it to the Austrian Crown. The insurrection was at
first successful, but the Tyrolese were left without assistance and were finally
crushed by the French troops ; the Austrians at the same time were compelled by the campaign of Wagram to consent to the peace of Vienna.
No attempt was made in that treaty to secure Hofer's safety. He was
captured in his hiding-place. Napoleon wrote to Eugene Beauharnais to
order that within twenty-four hours Hofer should be tried and shot.
This was done while the marriage of Marie Louise and Napoleon was
being celebrated. At a later date the Austrian government ennobled the
family of Hofer. It will be seen that there is no historical foundation
for the present Conversation. Lanfrey (English Translation) iii., p. 531.
(Imag. Convers. ii., 1824. Works ii., 1846. Works, iii., 1876.)]

audiences, and am surprised that you should have required one, although you mountaineers are somewhat used to liberties. What, in few words, have you brought from your country?

Hofer. This.

Metternich. No enigmas: at the court of Vienna we understand no other than plain language.

Hofer. Your Excellency commanded me to be brief: I was. This is the heron's feather which moved merrily over the Alps, when not an eagle's was stirring. If the slaughter of thirty thousand enemies is worth a recompense, I come at the instigation of those who followed me, to ask one.

Metternich. I expected it: never was an audience asked of me, or of any other minister, which did not begin or end so. But, friend, many years of war have exhausted the treasury. England is penurious; and we have innumerable young men, of high rank and great promise, disappointed in their hopes of preferment: beside, who ordered you to take up arms?

Hofer. My oath of allegiance, the voice of my country, my hatred of the French, and my contempt of the Italians, by whom principally our towns and villages were garrisoned.

Metternich. You would fain be another William Tell.

Hofer. As willingly as William Tell, now among the saints in heaven, would, if he were living, be another Andrew Hofer. We are creatures too humble for jealousy; we have neither rank nor beauty, neither silk hosiery nor powdered caul; we write no poems, challenge no club for attention, and solicit no clerk for preferment.

Metternich. I have found your name in the French gazettes, and you have just now mentioned it, I think; but really I quite forget what it may be.

Hofer. Andrew Hofer.

Metternich. Such is the tenderness of the Emperor, my master, for those who have served him faithfully, that although you are no longer his subject, yet, as you are a person of known bravery and of some repute in your country, if you will only change your name and enter into the service as an Austrian, I myself will venture to mention you as worthy of the earliest promotion, and, within three or four years at furthest, I entertain the best-founded hopes that you may be made a corporal.

Hofer. Excellent sir, I do not ask so much.

Metternich. A little money, if I could dispose of it, should not be wanting—but—

Hofer. Pardon me, sir, an interruption to the current of your kindness. I have grain and wine under a certain rock I could mention, with two hundred crowns, and my freehold may be valued at twelve hundred more ; and I have children who are brave and healthy, who love their father and fear God.

Metternich. You want something, and it is neither money nor promotion. I believe I am as acute as most people, yet here I confess my dulness.

Hofer. If I have devoted my little property, which is always dearer to the possessor than a great one, as every shrub and hillock is familiar to him, and the scene of some joviality, some tenderness, or some kindness ; if I have hazarded and exposed my life in all places and seasons, for him whom we both are serving,—grant me only a cell or a dungeon in this city. I have a country to defend, I have a family to educate, I have duties to teach and to perform ; and your Excellency knows that the French police has traced me into the Austrian States, and has demanded that I should be delivered up. Never shall this happen. I could not preserve the dominions of my master, but I will preserve his honor. Little did I ever dream of prisons ; to us Tyrolese they are horrible as hell, and like hell the abodes of crime only ; but he whom I have sworn to obey must do nothing unworthy of his name and station. Rather would I waste away my strength in this dreary asylum ; rather would I live among the unholy and unjust ; rather would I, if such be God's ordinance, lose the blossoming of my brave lads at home, which is worth a thousand times more, not only than all the future, but than all the past of life. There are those about them who will tell them of me, and there are places to take them into, on the cliffs and in the valleys, in many a copse and craggy lane, where my name, summer or winter, will sound in their ears right well.

Metternich. Mr Hofer, I cannot enter into these discussions. It appears by your own acknowledgment that there will be little loss on either side. Your children will be taken care of, you say, whatever may happen ; and a trifle at most can be the damage to your affairs. What then do you miss?

Hofer. The sight of my native hills, my homestead, my garden-plot of sweet herbs, the young apple-trees in my croft, the friends of my youth, the companions of my dangers, and the associates of many a freak and frolic requiring no less enterprise. I lose above all—but alas! what are the children of the great to them! You stared at me, sir Count, when I spoke to you of mine. One would imagine that *family* meant coaches, horses, grooms, liveries, and gravy-spoons: one would imagine there is some indecency in the word *child*. Believe me, sir, they are different things with us from what they are with you. If you happen to cherish them, it is that they may carry a lily, a lion, a bear, a serpent, or a bird, when you have done with it. I love in them—yes, beyond my own soul, God forgive me!—the very worst things about them; their unparriable questions, triumphant screams, and boisterous embraces. It is true, I never so talked of them before; but they are now beyond hail or whistle far enough.

Metternich. I shall be happy to expedite the business of your petition, from which it appears to me, my friend, you have somewhat deviated, forgetting the exact place and circumstances where you are.

Hofer. Excuse me, sir, once more. I acknowledge my error. I have been discoursing as if all the cloth in the world were of one color and one fineness, and as if a man who goes upon two legs were equal to one who goes upon eight or sixteen, with a varnished plank betwixt, and another man's rear at his nostrils.

Metternich. The brute! Others may have the same pretensions as you, and it is difficult to protect all we would favor.

Hofer. I stand alone in this proscription. Pretensions I have none: my country has used me as she would a trumpet. I was in her hands what she wished me to be, and what she made me. Whether her brave hearts followed me or followed this feather, what matters it? I am not better than those of them who are with God: had I been, he would have called me among the first. Those who are yet living wish to reserve me for another day, if another, such as brave men pant for, is decreed us.

Francis (*entering*). Sit still: who is that man, Count, stroking his cock's feather with his forefinger?

Metternich. It is the Andrew—Hofer—I think it is written.

Francis. I wish we were fairly rid of him.

Hofer. Sir, your countenance did not inspire me in the beginning with much confidence. When you entered, I observed that you dared not meet an honest man's eye.

Metternich. Audacious! do you know—

Francis. We may draw something from him : let him go on. Are we safe, Metternich? He is a strong rogue : I don't like his looks.

Hofer. It becomes not me to be angry with any one ; but until I asked a favor from you, it would have been well in you to leave his Excellency to his own kind intentions. The little good that drips from the higher sources is intercepted or corrupted by secretaries, clerks, valets, and other such people as you.

Francis. What does he want?

Metternich. A place in prison.

Francis. Give him it.

Hofer. I thank you, friend. If you are idle, as you seem to be, pray show me the way. Come along : we are losing time.

Francis. Make out the order : send him off.

Hofer. The gentleman is gone, then! He gave his advice very fluently, almost as if he directed. When I would have embraced him for his readiness to serve me, his breath drove me back. Oh for a fresh pipe of tobacco! a bundle of sweet hay! a sprig of thyme! a bean-flower! Other creatures have each his own peculiar ill savor, and that suffices for the whole of him ; but men, and in particular those of cities, have beds and parterres and plots and knots of stinks, varying in quality from the dells and dingles to the mountain-top. There are people who stink heart and soul : their bodies are the best of them. Away with these fellows! I would not be a materialist if I could help it ; I was educated in no such bestiality ; but is it possible that God should ever have intended spirits like these to be immortal?

Metternich. Friend, it is not permitted in any public office to exceed the business to be transacted there. I will venture to pronounce that yours is the first reflection ever made in one ; and it affords no proof of your delicacy or discretion. If you wish protection, never hazard a remark of any kind, unless you intend it for publication : in that case the censor will judge of its propriety, and it may do you no harm. Write freely ; write every thing you please : high souls are privileged at Vienna.

Soldier, take this note to the governor, as directed : you may accompany him, Mr Hofer.

Hofer. **To** the governor ! Do favor me, sir, with a prison.

Metternich. **I** do.

Hofer. **But** without sending me to his Excellency the governor of the city.

Metternich. **My note is addressed to the governor of the** prison.

Hofer. **What !** are jailers called **governors ?**

Metternich. God's blood ! the **fellow** asks questions : he examines ranks **and** dignities. Fare you well, Mr Hofer : **God** preserve you, in reward of your zeal and fidelity.

Francis (returning). Is he gone ?

Metternich. This instant, sire.

Francis. The French minister is **very urgent** in the business : what is to be done ?

Metternich. I am afraid he must be **surrendered.**

Francis. The empress says, that all **Europe would cry out** against it, as an action the most ungenerous **and ungrateful :** such are her words.

Metternich. **With your** Majesty's **permission, I** not only would **oppose to them the** opinion of **the archdukes and** of the whole **aulic council, but** could **also prove the contrary** by plain and **irrefragable** arguments. **Ungenerous it cannot be,** because he desired **no reward,** and none **was in** question. Ungrateful it cannot be ; for kings and emperors are **exempt by** the nature of things from that odious vice. It is the **duty of** subjects to do their utmost for the advantage of the prince ; nothing is owing to them **for** an act of duty : duty is the payer, not the receiver. **Whatever** is accorded by a sovereign to his vassal is granted by **special indulgence ;** a signification of being pleased, a testimonial of being served, a patent to the person thus gratified that he is at **full liberty to serve and** please again. There can be gratitude only where there are obligations and duties ; and to suppose any in **reciprocity between** prince and people is rank Jacobinism.

Francis. Insurgents talk always of their country ; a term which I would willingly never hear at all, and which no good subject ever utters in the first place. *Emperor and country, king and country,* we **may bear, but** hardly ; although I have been assured that such phrases are uttered by many well-meaning men. But **whoever heard** of *country and emperor, country and king ?* The times are bad enough ; still, the subversion of right principles is not universal and complete.

Metternich. What orders would your Majesty give, relating to this Andrew Hofer ?

Francis. He appears an irreverent, rash, hot-headed man : he could however be kept in order, as I said yesterday, by entering into one of my Austrian regiments, by going into Transylvania, or by lying a few years in the debtors' prison ; and perhaps the French government, after a time, would be satisfied with the arrangement. To deliver him up is, after all, the more conformable to the desires of Bonaparte ; and he can do me more injury than Hofer can do me good.

Metternich. Your Majesty has contemplated the matter in its true political point of view, and is persuaded that those few diamonds, of which I informed your Majesty as usual, have no influence on my sentiments. I would not even offer my opinion ; but hearing your Majesty's, it is my duty to see that your imperial will and pleasure be duly executed.

X. LORD CHESTERFIELD AND LORD CHATHAM.[1]

Chesterfield. It is true, my lord, we have not always been of the same opinion, or, to use a better, truer, and more significant expression, of the same *side* in politics ; yet I never heard a sentence from your lordship which I did not listen to with attention. I understand that you have written some pieces of advice to a young relative : they are mentioned as being excellent. I wish I could have profited by them when I was composing mine on a similar occasion.

Chatham. My lord, you certainly would not have done it, even supposing they contained, which I am far from believing, any topics that could have escaped your penetrating view of

[1 Imag. Convers., ii., 1824; ii., 1826. Works, ii., 1846. Works, iii., 1876.] .

manners and morals : for your lordship and I set out diversely
from the threshold. Let us then rather hope that what we both
have written, with an equally good intention, may produce its due
effect ; which indeed I am afraid may be almost as doubtful, if
we consider how ineffectual were the cares and exhortations, and
even the daily example and high renown, of the most zealous and
prudent men on the life and conduct of their children and
disciples. We will however hope the best rather than fear the
worst, and believe that there never was a right thing done or a
wise one spoken in vain, although the fruit of them may not
spring up in the place designated or at the time expected.

It [1] may be difficult, I fear indeed it is impossible, to give our
young nobility the graces and the amenity of the French ; therefore
I would rather try to cultivate the virtues inherent in them than
engraft such as are uncongenial with the stock. We have indeed
some few among us who far excel in politeness the most polished
of any other nation ; but the generality are as far surpassed, not
merely by one nation, but by almost all. There is in them an
arrogance, a self-sufficiency, an exhibition of defiance, which turn
away from them the attentions they would receive abroad. Hence
they call insincere those who actually did attempt to endure them,
but were unable to keep pace with their professions and intentions.
Yet, my lord, I do not despair of your accomplishing what it
would be hopeless to expect from any other. For, since you were
viceroy of Ireland, I have seen many natives of that country no less
elegant in manners than the most accomplished of French gentlemen.

Chesterfield. I look back with satisfaction to my residence
among them.

Chatham. Well may your lordship. Never since the conquest has Ireland passed so long a time in tranquillity and contentment. In this, my lord, you stand high above the highest
of our kings ; and by those who are right-minded, and who judge
of men by the good they do and the difficulty of doing it, you
will be placed by future historians in an elevated rank among the
rulers of mankind. Pardon me, for to praise a great man in his
presence is no slight presumption.

[¹ First ed. reads : " expected. *Chesterfield.* Pray, if I am not taking
too great a freedom give me the outline of your plan. *Chatham.*
Willingly," &c. (32 lines below).]

Chesterfield. My lord, although I did not come to you for my reward, I receive it at your hands with humble gratitude, and may begin to think I have in part deserved it. And now, if I am not taking too much freedom in requesting it, be pleased to give me the outline of your plan for education.

Chatham. Willingly, my lord ; but since a greater man has laid down a more comprehensive one, containing all I could bring forward, would it not be preferable to consult it ? I differ in nothing from Locke, unless it be that I would recommend the lighter as well as the graver part of the ancient classics, and the constant practice of imitating them in early youth. This is no change in the system, and no larger an addition than a woodbine to a sacred grove.

Chesterfield. I do not admire Mr Locke.

Chatham. Nor I; he is too simply grand for admiration : I contemplate and revere him. Equally deep and clear, he is both philosophically and grammatically one among the most elegant of English writers.

Chesterfield. If I expressed by any motion of limb or feature my surprise at this remark, your lordship I hope will pardon me a slight and involuntary transgression of my own precept.[2] I must entreat you, before we move a step farther in our inquiry, to inform me whether I am really to consider him[3] so exquisite in style.

Chatham. Your lordship is capable of forming an opinion on this point, certainly no less correct than mine.

Chesterfield. Pray, assist me.

Chatham. Education and grammar are surely the two driest of subjects on which a conversation can turn : yet if the ground is not promiscuously sown, if what ought to be clear is not covered, if what ought to be covered is not bare, and above all if the plants are choice ones, we may spend a few moments on it

[2 Machiavelli's saying " volto sciolto e pensieri stretti" was a favourite one of Chesterfield. He writes (vol. ii., p. 90, ed. 1774) " The height of abilities is to have volto sciolto e pensieri stretti." Again (vol. iii., p. 298) " People unused to the world have babbling countenances ; and are unskilful enough to show what they have sense enough not to tell."]

[3 First and 2nd. ed. read : " him in style the most elegant of our prose authors. *Chatham*," &c.]

not unpleasantly. It appears, then, to me that elegance in prose composition is mainly this: a just admission of topics and of words; neither too many nor too few of either; enough of sweetness in the sound to induce us to enter and sit still; enough of illustration and reflection to change the posture of our minds when they would tire; and enough of sound matter in the complex to repay us for our attendance. I could perhaps be more logical in my definition, and more concise; but am I at all erroneous?

Chesterfield. I see not that you are.

Chatham. My ear is well satisfied with Locke; I find nothing idle or redundant in him, and [4] I admire him particularly for his selection of plain and proper words. This I apprehend to be the prime essential of that eloquence which appeals solely to the reasoning faculties.

Chesterfield. But, in the opinion of you graver men, would not some of his principles lead too far?

Chatham. The danger is that few will be led by them far enough: most who begin with him stop short, and, pretending to find pebbles in their shoes, throw themselves down and complain of their guide.

Chesterfield. What then can be the reason why Plato, so much less intelligible, is so much more quoted and applauded?

Chatham. The difficulties we never try are no difficulties to us. They who are upon the summit of a mountain know in some measure its altitude, by comparing it with many objects around; but they who stand at the bottom and never mounted it can compare it with few only, and with those imperfectly. [5] Until a short time ago I could have conversed more fluently about Plato than I can at present: I had read all the titles to the Dialogues and several scraps of commentary; these I have now forgotten, and am indebted to long attacks of the gout for what I have acquired instead.

Chesterfield. A too severe schoolmaster! I hope he allows a long vacation.

Chatham. Severe he is, indeed: yet, although he sets no

[4 From "and" to "faculties" (4 lines) added in 3rd ed.]
[5 First ed. reads: "imperfectly: so fares it with Plato and his readers on one side, and with Plato and his talkers on the other. Until," &c.]

example of regularity, he exacts few observances and teaches many lessons. Without him I should have had less patience, less reading, less reflection, less leisure ; in short, less of every thing but of sleep.

Chesterfield. Locke,[6] from a deficiency of fancy, is not likely to attract so many listeners as Plato.

Chatham. And yet occasionally his language is both metaphorical and rich in images. In fact, all our great philosophers have this property in a wonderful degree. Not to speak of the devotional, in whose writings one might expect it, we find it abundantly in Bacon, not sparingly in Hobbes, the next to him in range of inquiry and potency of intellect. And what would you think, my lord, if you discovered in Newton a sentence in the spirit of Shakspeare ?

Chesterfield. I should look upon it as upon a wonder, not to say a miracle : Newton, like Barrow, had no feeling or respect for poetry.

Chatham. His words are these : " I don't know what I may seem to the world ; but as to myself, I seem to have been only like a boy playing on the seashore, and diverting myself in now and then finding a smoother pebble or a prettier shell than ordinary, whilst the great ocean of Truth lay all undiscovered before me."

Chesterfield. Surely, Nature, who had given him the volumes of her greater mysteries to unseal ; who had bent over him and taken his hand, and taught him to decipher the characters of her sacred language ; who had lifted up her veil before him higher than ever yet for mortal, that she might impress her features and her fondness on his heart,—threw it back wholly at these words, and gazed upon him with as much admiration as ever he had gazed with upon her.

Plato, I see from the Latin version, lies open on the table : the paragraphs marked with pencil, I presume, are fine passages.

Chatham. I have noted those only which appeared reprehensible, and chiefly where he is disingenuous and malicious.

Chesterfield. They indeed ought to be the most remarkable in the works of a philosopher. If the malice is against those who are thought greater or as great, it goes toward the demonstration that they are so ; if on the contrary the objects of it are inferior to

[6 From " Locke " to " her " (26 lines) added in 2nd ed.]

himself, he cannot take them up without raising them : unworthy of notice, they are more unworthy of passion. Surely, no philosopher would turn to an opposite conclusion from that which in the commencement he had designed to prove : as here he must do.

Chatham. He avoids an open hostility to Democritus and Xenophon and Aristoteles ; yet I have detected him in more than one dark passage, with a dagger in his hand and a bitter sneer on his countenance. I know not whether it has been observed before that these words are aimed at the latter, the citizen of another State and the commentator of other laws,—

Οὐδ' ἐπιθυμία σε ἄλλης πόλεως· οὐδ' ἄλλων νόμων ἔλαβεν εἰδέναι, ἀλλ' ἡμεῖς σοι ἱκανοὶ ἦμεν καὶ ἡ ἡμετέρα πόλις.

The compliment is more injurious to Socrates, for whom it was intended, than the insinuation to Aristoteles. But the prime object of his hatred, open here and undissembled, is Prodicus,—author of the beautiful allegory in which Pleasure and Virtue offer themselves to the choice of Hercules. In one place he mentions him with Polus *and many others,*—the least difficult and least clever of malignant expressions, where genius is the subject of calumny and invective. One hardly could imagine that he had the assurance and effrontery to call Epicharmus the chief of comic writers, before a people who that very day perhaps had been at a comedy of Aristophanes. The talent of Epicharmus lay in puns and ribaldry, and Hiero punished him for immodest conversation.

Chesterfield. I have read somewhere that, when Plato was young, it was predicted of him, from his satirical vein, that he would become in time a substitute for Archilochus.

Chatham. Athenæus, I think, has recorded it. I do not find so much wit as I expected ; and, to speak plainly, his wit is the most tiresome and dull part of him ; for who can endure a long series of conversations full of questions to entrap a sophist ? Why not lead us to the trap at once by some unexpected turn ? Yet[7] Plato ought to be more powerful in wit than in argument, for, it is evident, he labors at it more. There is more applicable good-sense, more delicate wit, more urbanity, more gracefulness in a single

[7] From "Yet" to "more" (3 lines) added in 2nd ed. First and 2nd eds. continue : "There is more ingenuity and gracefulness," &c.]

paper of the *Spectator*, than in six or eight among the minor of these Dialogues; in all which, not excepting the *Phædo*, I was disappointed.

Chesterfield. The language is said to be masterly and sonorous.

Chatham. Αὐτὸ καθ᾽ αὑτὸ ὡσαύτως κατὰ ταῦτα ἔχει, καὶ οὐδέποτε οὐδαμῶς ἀλλοίωσιν οὐδεμίαν ἐνδέχεται.* And[8] again are several of the like sounds and words. Σμικρὰ φύσις οὐδὲν μέγα οὐδέποτε οὔτε ἰδιώτην οὔτε πόλιν δρᾷ.

Chesterfield. Come, come, my lord; do not attempt to persuade me that an old woman's charm to cure a corn or remove a wart, or a gypsy-girl's to catch a sixpence, is Plato's Greek.

Chatham. Look yourself.

Chesterfield. I have forgotten the characters pretty nearly: faith! they appear to me, from what I can pick up, to correspond with the sounds you gave them. Jupiter, it is said by the ancients, would have spoken no other language than Plato's. If ever Jupiter uttered such sounds as these, it could be only when he was crossing the Hellespont.

Chatham. What do you thing of this jingle: Πρῶτον εὐλαβηθῶμέν τι πάθος μὴ πάθωμεν.*

Chesterfield. I really thought that his language was harmonious to the last degree.

Chatham. Generally it is so: his language is the best of him. We moderns are still children in our tongues, at least we English. For my own part, I always spoke in Parliament what I considered the most effectual to persuade my hearers, without a care or a thought touching the structure of my sentences; but knowing that the ancient orators and writers laid the first foundation of their glory upon syllables, I was surprised to find no fewer than nine short ones together in this eloquent author,—ἄνδρας ἀποδεδοκιμακότες. The accents which were guides to them, although unwritten, may have taken off somewhat from this peculiarity, and may have been a sort of support to the feebleness of the sound. No modern language can admit the concourse of so many such; and the Latin was so inadequate to the supply of them that it produced, I believe, but one galliambic in the times

---

* Phædo.

[8 From "And" to "δρᾷ" (3 lines) added in 3rd ed.

of its strength and fertility; which poem required them in greater numbers and closer together than any other, but did not receive mine conjointly.

Chesterfield. Cicero was himself a trifler in cadences; and whoever thinks much about them will become so, if indeed the very thought when it enters is not trifling.

Chatham. I am not sure that it is, for an orderly and sweet sentence, by gaining our ear, conciliates our affections; and the voice of a beggar has often more effect upon us than his distress. Your mention of Cicero on this occasion reminds me of his *O fortunatam natam me consule Romam!* Playful as he was in his vanity, I do not believe the verse is his; but Plato wrote, ἀλλὰ παρ' αὐτούς αὖ τούς δεινούς ὄντας ταῦτα, &c. We[9] may be too fastidious and fantastic in sounds and syllables; but a frequent recurrence of the same is offensive to the ear, and particularly in poetry. Nevertheless, he who appears to have had a more delicate one than almost any of the moderns, and indeed whose Latinity surpasses in elegance that of any of the Romans themselves, excepting Cicero and Cæsar, was persuaded that Tibullus was fond and studious of syllabic repetitions. It appears that this poet, says Muretus, thought it elegant to continue them, and that such as the following did not happen by accident, but were produced by application and design. " *Me mea Ipse seram. Poma manu. Multa tabella. Sicca canis.*"

Chesterfield. The Latin of Muretus may be elaborate and elegant, but he, like nearly all the best modern Latinists, was conceited, fantastical, and weakly-minded. And now I remember having been present at a discussion between two scholars on his merits in style. It was doubted whether he or Bembo is the most accurate; the beauties and faults of each were brought forward, and the sentence was given in favor of Bembo, for two or three reasons, of which the only one I can recollect is that Muretus wrote *sinceritas*, never doubting its Latinity, whereas Bembo when he employed it said, " *Si verbo uti liceat.*"

Chatham. I should never have suspected that a word so requisite was wanting to the Latin tongue. Let[10] me turn over

[9 From "We" to "canis" (12 lines) added in 2nd ed.; from "Chesterfield" to "tongue" (10 lines) added in 3rd ed.]

[10 From "Let" to "Plato's" (33 lines) added in 2nd ed.]

my scrap of paper, which however would best perhaps have kept its place between the leaves here.

Chesterfield. No, my Lord; if you thought any thing worth noticing and writing down, surely I may well think it worth knowing.

Chatham. First, then, I find a mark of admiration that this most learned and eloquent man, Ciceronian as he was and enraptured by Virgil, should not have remarked in him or Cicero what he notices as a peculiarity in Tibullus. " *Sin in* processu. *Sin in* sua. Qui*n* i*n*tra portas. Comprende*re* refert. O*re* re*f*erret. Qu*æ*rer*e* regna. Crines effu*s*a *s*acerdos. A fra*tre* recepi. Surge*re* regna. *Æ*r*e* r*e*nidenti. Serva*re* recursus. Sub au*re* r*e*liquit. Mittêr*e* r*e*lictâ. Stringe*re* r*e*mos. Curre*re* remis." In Cicero I found after an evening's reading, " Si plus adipisca*re* re (where certainly it could as easily have been avoided as committed). Neque excludentes ab eju*s* u*s*u suos. Meo jure re*s*pondeo. Observa*re* re*s*tricte. *M*e *m*etu libero. Reli*q*ui *q*ui. Maxim*e* m*e* tuto. Non es*se* *se* *s*enatorem ; " and a few words lower, "illos enim bonos duce*s* e*sse*, *se* jam confectum *s*enectute." Such a concourse of *es* and *se* is perhaps not to be found again in all the books of my library. Our own language is comparatively poor in sibilants, and would refuse the supplies on this occasion. Similar sounds repeated, not indeed consecutively, but closely, are in Homer and Anacreon :—

Οἵοι Τρῶοι ἵπποι ἐπιστάμενοι πεδίοιο.   *Il. E.*
Δέσποινα, σοὶ μὲν ἵπποι.   *Anac. Frag.*

In the former, you have the same six times in six feet ; in the latter, thrice in three. Yet the sound of neither verse is so unpleasant as that of Horace, where the repetition comes but once :—

"Dirus per urbes Afer *it It*alas."[11]

We have slided into Cicero's language from Plato's. As for his wit, what think you of this : "I am ready, O Socrates, to give myself up to the strangers, to flay me worse than they flay me now, if the flaying ends not in a hide, as that of Marsyas did, but in virtue." Or what think you of a project to make a doll and

[11 The line really runs : "Dirus per urbes Afer *ut* Italas" so that Landor's criticism does not touch Horace at all.]

dedicate it to Memory? The stuff that follows is worse still.
Toward the end of the volume, in the *Gorgias*, Polus says to
Socrates, "Do not you see Archeläus, son of Perdiccas, reigning
over the Macedonians?" to which Socrates replies, "If I do not
see him, I hear of him."

In the beginning of the same dialogue, Gorgias, at the request
of Socrates to be brief, assents to his proposition twice, by using
the monosyllable; whereupon Socrates says, "I admire your
replies, Gorgias; they are as short as they can be." If the same
monosyllable had been the answer to several questions in succession, and if those questions had been complicated and intricate,
then, and then only, the remark had been well-placed.

You remember, my lord, the derivations made by Swift of
Agamemnon, Ajax, Achilles, Andromache, and other names
of heroes and heroines. These are hardly more absurd and
ridiculous than almost all made by Plato and attributed with
great complacency to Socrates, of the same and similar; and
are much less literal. It is incredible how erroneous were the
most learned, both among the Greeks and Romans, on the origin
of words.

Chesterfield. I have heard it reported that our own lexi-
cographers are subject, in some degree, to the same animad-
version: but I can judge more adequately of bad reasoning or
bad wit.

Chatham. A little of the latter tires and nauseates, while in
the former there is generally something to exercise the ingenuity.
I have seen persons who could employ a moment or two unreluctantly in straightening a crooked nail: with about the same
labor and interest I would hammer upon an inexact thought.
Here is one which I wonder that Cicero, in mentioning the
dialogue, has failed to remark. Our philosopher divides rhetoric
into the true and the false; as if any part of a definition or description were to be founded on the defects of what is defined or
described. Rhetoric may be turned to good or bad purposes;
but this is no proof or indication that it must be divided into good
and bad. The use of a thing is not the thing itself; how then is
the abuse?

The wit of Plato's Dialogues is altogether of a single kind, and
of that which in a continuance is the least welcome. For irony

is akin to cavil; and cavil, as the best wit is either good-natured
or wears the appearance of good-nature, is nearly its antipode.
Plato has neither the grace of Xenophon nor the gravity of Cicero,
who tempers it admirably with urbanity and facetiousness.   Although [12] he is most celebrated for imagination, and for an eloquence
highly poetical, there are incomparably more, both in quantity and
quality, of poetical thoughts and images in Bacon than in Plato.
The language of Plato is vastly more sonorous; he is called, and
nobody questions that he is, eloquent; but there is no eloquence
which does not agitate the soul: he never does.   Demosthenes
effects it by strong appeals, and through the reason.   Rousseau
effects it sometimes in despite of the reason, and by uniting the
Graces with the Passions.   We often say we hate Rousseau;
but how often does the lover say (or wish to say) he hates the
beloved!   In fact, the moral part of Rousseau was odious, and
much of the intellectual was perverse and depraved; there was,
however, a noble instrument of harmony, sounding along high
and intricately vaulted arches.   The characteristic of Plato is the
dexterity and ease with which he supports and shifts an argument,
and exhibits it in all its phases.   Nevertheless, a series of interro-
gations, long as he draws them out for this purpose, would weary
me in one dialogue: he continues them in twenty, with people
of the same description, on the same subjects.

Chesterfield.   It is rather an idle thing for an old gentleman
in a purple robe to be sticking pins in every chair on which a
sophist is likely to sit down; and rather a tiresome and cheerless
one to follow and stand by him, day after day in the cold, laying
gins for tom-tits.

Chatham.   In general, I own, he did so; but both he and
Aristoteles turned occasionally their irony (of which indeed the
latter had little) where irony is best employed: against false
piety; against that which would be the substitute and not the
support of morality.   When [13] a high sound issues from a high
soul, our ears and hearts are opened to it; otherwise we let "the
wind blow where it listeth."   He jokes on grave subjects, and
such as he himself thinks to be grave; and he is grave on light
ones.   Can any thing be flatter and duller than: "'It seems

[12 **From** "Although" to "arches" (**15** lines) added in 3rd **ed.**]
[13 From "When" to "mine" (14 lines) added in 3rd ed.]

becoming,' said Glauco, ' that we should stay.' ' Then, if it do seem so,' said I, ' we ought to stay.' "

Chesterfield. Here at least is no quibbling.

Chatham. Do you want a little of that? Let me open almost any page whatever, and I can supply abundantly the most capricious customer. Take for specimen a pinch of the *Polity*. Here he carries his quibbles to such an extent as to demonstrate that *Justice is a sort of thief.* These are his very words, positive and express; no mere inference of mine.

The Greek language, more courteous than the Roman or the French or ours, and resembling in this property the Italian, in addressing a person, had ready among other terms, ὦ θαυμάσιε and ὦ βέλτιστε. Socrates meets an orderly good man, who, from respect to' the laws, is going to accuse his own father of a capital crime, as he imagines it to be; and, doubting if he understood him, asks, ὁ σὸς, ὦ βέλτιστε. Aristoteles, in the eighth book of his *Ethics*, gravely says that children ought to see no indecent statue or picture, unless it represents some god committing the obscenity.

Such[14] are the two best pieces of wit in the two authors; and I suspect that Plato was as unaware in this place of being witty as he was in others of not being so.

In regard to their philosophy, and indeed to that of the ancients in general, there was little of sound and salutary which they did not derive from Democritus or from Pythagoras: from the former Aristoteles drew most, from the latter Plato. Cicero says improperly of Socrates, what is repeated every day in schools and colleges, that he first drew down Philosophy into private houses: Pythagoras had done it more systematically and more extensively. Upon his tenets and his discipline were founded many institutions of the earlier and quieter converts to Christianity.

Chesterfield. There is, I remember, a very dangerous doctrine attributed to this Democritus, whom you mentioned before him: he said that governments should have two supporters,— rewards and punishments. Now twelve hangmen, and even twelve judges, may be paid; but Mansfield, I suspect, would commit any man to Bridewell or the pillory, who had broached a declaration so seditious as that people of ordinary business, un-

[14 From " Such " to " so " (3 lines) added in 3rd ed.]

hired for it, should be paid for doing their duty.   National debts,
he would inform the jury, are not to be aggravated by such idle
and superfluous expenditure, increased at any man's option.

Chatham.   I know not what my Lord Mansfield, a worse
enemy to our Constitution than even that degraded and despicable
prince for whose service he was educated, may think or dictate
on the subject; but among all the books I ever read in which
rewards and punishments are mentioned, I never found one where
the words come in any other order than this : rewards first, then
punishments.   A plain evidence and proof to my humble understanding, that in the same succession they present themselves to the
unperverted mind.   We mention them not only in regard to our
polity, but in contemplation of a better state hereafter ; and there
too they occur to us as upon earth.

Chesterfield.   In the pleadings of Mansfield, in his charges,
in his decisions, in his addresses to Parliament, I have heard
nothing so strikingly true as these observations of your Lordship ; and I wish I had heard nothing so novel.

Chatham.   I, in the name of our country, unite with you,
my lord, in this wish.   Let us trace again the more innocent
wanderings of a greater man, I know not whether less prejudiced,
but certainly less profligate and corrupt.

Socrates, in the *Gorgias*, is represented as saying that he
believes the soul and body both to exist in another state, although
separately ; the body just as it was in life, with its infirmities,
wounds, and distortions.   This would be great injustice ; for
hence a long life, rendered so by frugality and temperance, would
acquire, in part of its recompense, the imbecility of age, with
deafness, blindness, and whatever else is most afflictive and
oppressive in that condition.   The soul carries upon its back,
he says, the marks of floggings and bruises and scars, contracted
by perjuries upon earth, and by the delivery *in court* of unjust
sentences ; such, I believe, in this place, is the meaning of ἀδικίαι,
and not merely any common act of injustice.   The utility of ex-
posures in another life, he says, arises from example to others.
But in what manner can they profit by this example ? From
what wickedness can they be deterred by these scenes of terror ?
Ideas as idly fanciful and childishly silly are in his description of
the infernal rivers, which he derived from the poets, and which,
without line or level, he led over places just as unfruitful after-

ward as before. Returning to this strange body of his, it cannot be supposed an inert substance : the words *after death* mean *after this life upon earth*. If he would say that it is inert, he must suppose it to be motionless: when did it become so? Strange that it should have motion to reach Tartarus, and should then lose it! If so, of what use could it be? He does not say it, nor mean it, I imagine.

Chesterfield. On some occasions, it appears, he leaves off meaning very abruptly. Men [15] leap awkwardly in long flowing dressing gowns, and instead of clearing the thorns and stakes, expose God knows what.

Chatham. It is not wonderful nor strange that Aristoteles should ridicule his vagaries. Nothing can be more puerile and contemptible than the ideas he attributes to Socrates on future punishments: among the rest, that the damned appeal by name to those whom they have slain or wronged, and are dragged backward and forward from Tartarus to Cocytus and Pyriphlegethon, until the murdered or injured consent to pardon them. So the crime is punished, not according to its heinousness, but according to the kindness or severity of those who suffered by it. Now the greater crime is committed in having slain or injured the generous and kind man : the greater punishment is inflicted for injuring or slaying the ungenerous and unkind. Plato [16] tells us, in the *Timæus*, that God created time and the heavens at the same moment, in order that, being born together, they should cease together.

Chesterfield. Does he inform us also that the creator in the beginning separated the light from the darkness?—an idea very Platonic.

Chatham. No.

Chesterfield. What other passage amuses your Lordship?

Chatham. Nothing peculiar to this author. Turning over the leaves, I am reminded of what occurs often in the Athenian law-procedures, that, while the *prosecutor* has the same appellation as with us, the *defendant* is called the *flyer*, ὁ φεύγων: a proof, shall I say, that the Athenians were a wiser people, or a less firm one, than we are? They, as we do, say *to give judgment* ; but they really did give it, and gratuitously : we must drop a

[15 From " **Men** " to " what " (3 lines) added in 3rd ed.]
[16 From " **Plato** " to " poetry " (36 lines) added in 2nd ed.]

purse of gold on every step of the judgment-seat, or be kicked down headlong.

It is very amusing to trace the expressions of different nations for the same thing. What we, half a century ago, called to *banter*, and what, if I remember the word, I think I have lately heard called to *quiz*, gives no other idea than of coarseness and inurbanity. The French convey one of buzz and bustle in *persiffler*; the Italians, as naturally, one of singing, and amusing and misleading the judgment, by *canzonare*, or, as Boccaccio speaks, *uccellare*; the Athenians knew that the Graces and childhood had most power of this kind upon the affections, and their expressions were χαριεντίζειν and παιδεύειν. In manifestoes or remonstrances we English say to *draw up*, from our love of conciseness; the Frenchman says *dresser*, very characteristically; and the Italian, the most verbose of men, *stendere*. Many words have degenerated. Who would imagine that a singer or tippler should derive his appellation from Jupiter?—his fellows call him *jovial*. Our northern gods are respected as little. The vilest of prose or poetry is called *balderdash*: now Balder was, among the Scandinavians, the presiding god of poetry.[17] Braga was the goddess of eloquence: and she has left us *brag* and *braggart*.

I am reminded by the mention of poetry, that Plato is offended in the *Iliad* at the undignified grief of Achilles and of Priam. To clasp the knee is going too far; and to roll in the dust is beastly. I am certain that he never was a father or a friend: not that among us the loss of friends is accompanied by such violence of affliction, but because I have observed that grief is less often in proportion to delicacy, and even to tenderness, than to the higher energies of our nature and the impetuosity of our nobler passions. The intemperate and wild resentment of Achilles at the injustice of Agamemnon, and his self-devotion, certain as he was of his fate, prepare us for intensity and extravagance of feeling, and teach us that in such a character diversity is not incongruity. This censure of the philosopher on the poet convinces me that the wisest of his works was the burning of his tragedies. Heroism, as Plato would have had it, would be afraid to soil his robe, and Passion would blush to

[17 Second ed. reads: "poetry and eloquence. I am," &c. From "I" to "contingency" (47 lines) added in 2nd ed. Landor's etymologies in this passage are not superior to Plato's own.]

unfold her handkerchief. He who could censure the two most admirable passages in Homer could indeed feel no reluctance at banishing the poets from his Republic: and we cannot wonder that he strays wide from sound philosophy, who knows so little of the human heart as to be ignorant that the poet is most a poet in the midst of its varieties and its excesses. Only with God can greatness exist without irregularity: that of Achilles was a necessary and essential part of him. Without it,—no resentment at Agamemnon, no abandonment of his cause and of his countrymen, no revenge for Patroclus, no indignity to the body of his bravest enemy, no impatience at the first sight of Priam, no effusion of tears at his paternal sorrows, no agony stronger than his vows or than his vengeance forcing him to deliver up the mangled hero: in short, no *Iliad*, no Homer. We all are little before such men, and principally when we censure or contend with them. Plato on this occasion stands among the ringers of the twelve unchangeable French bells; among the apes who chatter as they pick out the scurf of Shakspeare. These two poets divide the ages of the world between them, and will divide the ages of eternity. Prudent men, who wish to avoid the appearance of pygmies, will reverently keep at some distance, laying aside here their cruet of vinegar and here their cake of honey. Plato is the only one of the ancients who extols the poetry of Solon; of whom he says that, if he had written his poem on the war of the Athenians against the Island of Atalantis, undistracted by the business of the State, he might have rivalled the glory of Hesiod and Homer. No man of sound judgment ever placed these names together unless as contemporaries; and he must possess a very unsound one indeed, who calculates thus on the contingency [18] of Homer's rival in any statesman.

"Poetical expression," Plato tells you, "is a copy of the poet's own conception of things; and things, of the archetype existing in the divine mind: thus the poet's expression is a copy at the third hand." And this argument he adduces to prove that poetry is far distant from truth. It proves no such thing; and,

[18 Second ed. adds and reads: "contingency of rivalling Homer. *Chesterfield.* I myself love genteel poetry, and read Hammond's elegies rather than the Iliad: at the same time I confess I have reason to think my choice a wrong one and that poetry like religion," &c. (27 lines below.)]

if it did, it would not prove that poetry is not delightful,—and
delight, we know, is its aim and end. But that truths also, and
most important ones, are conveyed by poetry is quite as certain as
that fallacies, and the most captious and quibbling fallacies, are
conveyed by Plato : more certain nothing can be. If the poet
has a conception of things as they emanate from the Divine mind,
whether it is at third hand or at thirtieth, so long as nothing
distorts or disturbs them, what matters it ? The image or archetype is God's : he impresses it on things : the poet represents the
things as they are impressed on his mind by the hand of the
Creator. Now, if this is done, the distance from truth is not
remote. But there is a truth, accommodated to our nature, which
poetry best conveys. There is a truth for the reason ; there is a
truth for the passions ; there is a truth for every character of
man. Shakspeare has rendered this clear and luminous, over all
the stumps and stumbling-blocks and lighter brush-wood and
briers thrown across the path by the puerile trickery of Plato.

    Chesterfield. I have reason to think that [19] poetry like relig-
ion levels the intellects of men,—the wise talking on that subject
as absurdly as the ignorant. Great poets are the only judges of
great poets : and their animosities and prejudices I will not say
pervert their judgment, but blot, interline, and corrupt the copies
we receive of it. I have as little faith in Plato's love as you have
in his philosophy.

    Chatham. In his disquisition on love is a receipt to cure the
hiccup. "If you will hold your breath a little, it will go ; if that
should be disagreeable, take a good draught of water ; but if the
hiccup is very vehement, tickle your nose to sneezing, and when
that has happened once or twice, be the hiccup obstinate as it may,
it will be removed."

    Chesterfield. Who would buy a village cookery-book, or a two-
penny almanac, if the author stuffed into it such silliness at this?

    Chatham. In the same dialogue is a piece of sophistry more
trivial than the receipt. "If all pleasures are weaker than love,
they are the conquered, he the conqueror : Love then, *who pre-
dominates over lusts and pleasures*, is temperate to a wonderful
degree." It is fair however to remark that Agatho, here introduced as the speaker, says a part of what is spoken is serious, a
part is joke. I wish Plato had left some indication by which we

    [[19] From " that " to " it " (26 lines) added in 2nd ed.]

might distinguish the one from the other ; but neither he nor the acutest of his commentators has done it. Sound [20] sense, in my opinion, is preferable to bodiless, incomprehensible vagaries : and if ever I become an author and am praised at all, I trust it will be not because I am so sublime an intelligence as to be unreadable without help, or without a controversy of clever and acute men about my meaning.

He has here also given us a sort of dithyrambic, than which, as it appears to me, nothing is more redundantly verbose ; yet Socrates is introduced as praising it to the skies. His knowledge of poetry, I suspect, did not carry him beyond a fable. To stick there is better than to follow (as Plato exhibits him doing) an old woman, and to relate as his own opinion that the business of genii or demons is to carry prayer and sacrifice from men to the gods, and precepts from the gods again to men. I am not so idle as to run far into his theories, and to examine what never has been and never will be brought into use ; which alone is a sufficient proof of utter worthlessness. Nothing can be more absurd than his regulations for the order of succession to property. Even those of a certain Irish lord are more provident, who, about to die childless, ordered that his money should go to the elder son of his brother, and, if he had no elder son, to the second. As for marriages, on the outset he would appoint a judge to examine the males stark-naked, in order to decide on their fitness for that condition ; females, only to a certain point.

Chesterfield. I am astonished at the enormous proportion of fancy to philosophy, of folly to fancy, and of impudence to folly, in this moralist, theologian, and legislator.

Chatham. You are not, then, disposed to look at the other places marked ?

Chesterfield. In truth, no.

Chatham. He was fond of puns, too, and the silliest and commonest, those on names. Ἤρεσεν οὖν μοι καὶ ἐν τῷ μύθῳ ὁ Προμηθεὺς μᾶλλον τοῦ Ἐπιμηθέως ᾧ χρώμενος ἐγὼ καὶ προμηθούμενος, &c. ; and below, ἀλλὰ Καλλίᾳ τῷ καλῷ, &c.

The worst is, that he attributes the vainest of sophistry and the basest of malignity to Socrates. A wise and virtuous man may have the misfortune to be at variance with a single great author

[[20] From " Sound " to " meaning " (6 lines) added in 3rd ed. ; and from " He " to " no " (25 lines) added in 3rd ed.]

among his contemporaries, but neither a virtuous nor a wise one can be drawn into hostilities against all the best : he to whom this happens must be weak or wicked.   Impudence may prompt some to asseverate that, with prodigious manliness and self-devotion, they hazard to cut their feet and break their shins by stemming the current ; that the perilous state of literature calls aloud on them, and that they encounter it equally for the public good and the correction of the faulty writer.   But the public good, in my opinion, is ill promoted by telling men that all their other teachers are worth nothing, and that to be contented is to be dull, to be pleased is to be foolish.   Nor have I remarked or heard of any instance where morals have been improved by scurrility ; diffidence calmed, encouraged, sustained, led forth, by violence ; or genius exalted by contempt.   I am sorry that a great man should have partaken the infirmities of the least, in their worst propensities. This principally has induced me to show you that, within the few pages you see between my fingers, he has committed as grave faults in style and sentiment, not only as Prodicus, but (I must believe) as Polus.   We hear from the unprejudiced that Prodicus, like our Locke, was exact in his definitions ; we know that he arrived at the perfection of style ; and our gratitude is due to him for one of the most beautiful works delivered down to us from antiquity.

Chesterfield.   Your Lordship has proved to me that a divine man, even with a swarm of bees from nose to chin, may cry aloud and labor hard, and lay his quarter-staff about him in every direction, and still be an indifferent buffoon.

Chatham.   Buffoonery is hardly the thing wherein a man of genius would be ambitious to excel ; but, of all failures, to fail in a witticism is the worst, and the mishap is the more calamitous in a drawn out and detailed one.

He [21] often fails in a contrary extreme.   The soundest of those great critics whom we call grammarians, Dionysius of Halicarnassus, censures him for bringing bombast into philosophical disquisitions : and Dr Hurd, neither a severe judge nor an incompetent one, quoting the passage, adds, "The *Phædrus*, though the most remarkable, is not the only example."

Chesterfield.   Better a little idle play with bubbles and bladders,

[21] From "He" to "sophisms" (8 lines) added in 3rd ed. ; **1st ed.** reads : "*Chesterfield*, Plato," &c.]

than cut and dry dogmas and indigestible sophisms. Plato falls over his own sword, not by hanging it negligently or loosely, but by stepping with it awkwardly; and the derision he incurs is proportionate to the gravity of his gait. Half the pleasure in the world arises from malignity; and little of the other half is free from its encroachments. Those who enjoyed his smartness and versatility of attack laugh as heartily at him as with him, demonstrate that a great man upon the ground is lower than a little man upon his legs, and conclude that the light of imagination leads only to gulfs and precipices.

Chatham. We, however, with greater wisdom and higher satisfaction, may survey him calmly and reverentially, as one of lofty, massy, comprehensive mind, whose failings myriads have partaken, whose excellences few; and we may consider him as an example, the more remarkable and striking to those we would instruct, for that very inequality and asperity of character which many would exaggerate, and some conceal. Let us, however, rather trust Locke and Bacon: let us believe the one to be a wiser man, and the other both a wiser and better. There [22] is as much difference between Plato and Bacon as there is between a pliant, luxuriant twig, waving backward and forward on the summit of a tree, and a sound, stiff, well-seasoned walking-stick, with a ferrule that sticks as far as is needful into the ground and makes every step secure. Hearing much of the poetry that is about him, I looked for it in vain: and I defy any man to fill with it, pure and impure, a couple of such pages as are usually meted out, with honest exactness and great marginal liberality, three hundred to the volume. Florid prose writers are never tolerable poets. Jeremy Taylor is an example among many: his poetry is even worse, if possible, than the austere Hobbes's.

Chesterfield. It is generous in you to countenance the persecuted Locke; and to examine the skull of Bacon, undeterred by a heart so putrid.

Chatham. I declare to you, I should have the courage to say the same thing if they were living, and expelled from court and Christchurch.

Chesterfield. We think more advantageously of artificial

[22 From "There" to "Chatham" (16 lines) added in 3rd ed.]

dignities while the bearers are living, more advantageously of
real when they are dead.

Chatham.   The tomb is the pedestal of greatness.   I make a
distinction between God's great and the king's great. [23]

   "**Non** bene conveniunt nec in unâ sede morantur."

Chesterfield.   So much the worse for both parties.   Compliments are in their place only where there is full as much of
weakness as of merit; so that when I express my admiration to
your Lordship, all idea of compliment must vanish.   Permit me,
then, to say that I have always been gratified at this among your
other noble qualities, that, possessing more wit than perhaps any
man living, you have the moderation to use it rarely, and oftener
in friendship than in enmity.

   Chatham.   Profligate men and pernicious follies may fairly and
reasonably be exposed; light peculiarities may also be exhibited,
but only in such a manner that he who gave the prototype would
willingly take the copy.   But, in general, he who pursues another
race of writers is little better than a fox-hunter who rides twenty
miles from home for the sport: what can he do with his game
when he has caught it?   As he is only the servant of the dogs,
so the satirist is only a caterer to the ferocious or false appetites
of the most indiscriminating and brutal minds.   Does he pretend
that no exercise else is good for him?   He confesses, then, an
unsoundness in a vital part.

   Chesterfield.   Reflections such as these induced me long ago
to prefer the wit of Addison and La Fontaine to other kinds: it
is more harmless, more gay, and more insinuating.

   Chatham.   Our own language contains in it a greater quantity
and a greater variety of wit and humor, than all the rest of all
ages and countries; closing only Cervantes, the Homer of irony,
and not only of sharper and better-tempered wit than he who lies
before me, but even of an imagination more vivid and poetical, a
sounder too and shrewder philosopher.   The [24] little volume of
Bacon's *Essays*, in my opinion, exhibits not only more strength
of mind, not only more true philosophy, but more originality,
more fancy, more imagination, than all these volumes of Plato;
supposing even that he drew nothing from others,—whereas we

   [[23] First ed. reads: "great. *Chesterfield.* **Very** rightly.   Non . . .
morantur. So much," &c.]

   [[24] From "The" to "positions" (9 lines) added in 2nd ed.]

must receive the authority of antiquity, and believe that he owed to them the greater part, and almost the whole. Without this authority, we should perceive it in the absence of fixed principles, and in the jarring of contradictory positions. It must be conceded that we moderns are but slovens in composition, or ignorant for the most part of its regulations and laws; yet we may insist that there have been among us those to whom, in all the higher magistratures of intellect, the gravest of the ancients would have risen up, and have placed with proper deference at their side.

Chesterfield.[25] I never have found any one so unprejudiced and so unprepossessed on Plato.

Chatham. My lord, I do not know that I am entirely.

Chesterfield. How! my lord.

Chatham. I know that everything I have said is just and incontrovertible, and that I could add ten times as much and as fairly; but I cannot take to myself a praise that does not belong to me, any more than I could a purse. I dislike, not to say detest, the character of Plato, as I collect it from his works; and the worst part of it I conceive to be his coldness and insincerity in friendship. He pretended to have been sick during the imprisonment of Socrates: was he so very sick that he could not have been carried to receive the last words of his departing friend?—the last counsels of a master so affectionate and impressive? He was never sick when a prince was to be visited on his throne, insolent and tyrannical as that prince might be.

Chesterfield. A throne is to few so frightful a thing as a death-bed.

Chatham. My lord, it is a more frightful thing to any man who knows it well, than the death-couch of Socrates was to himself, or to those who from their hearts could reason as he did on it.

Chesterfield. I am happy, my lord, and grateful to you, that the conversation has taken a different turn from what I had expected. I came to receive some information from you on what might be profitable in the education of the young, and you have given me some which would be greatly so in that of the old. My system, I know, cannot be quite according to your sentiments; but as no man living hath a nobler air or a more dignified demeanor than your Lordship, I shall be flattered by hearing that

[25 From "*Chesterfield*" to "on it" (22 lines) added in 2nd ed.]

what I have written on politeness meets in some degree your approbation.

Chatham. I believe you are right, my lord. What is superficial in politeness, what we see oftenest and what people generally admire most, must be laid upon a cold breast or will not stand : so far we agree ; but whatever is most graceful in it can be produced only by the movements of the heart.

Chesterfield. These movements, I contend, are to be imitated, and as easily as those of the feet ; and that good actors must beware of being moved too much from within. My lord, I do not inquire of you whether that huge quarto is the Bible, for I see the letters on the back. Permit me.

Chatham. I did not imagine your Lordship was such an enthusiast in religion : I am heartily glad to witness your veneration for a book which, to say nothing of its holiness or authority, contains more specimens of genius than any other volume in existence.

Chesterfield. I kissed it from no such motive : I kissed it preparatorily to swearing on it, as your Lordship's power and credit are from this time forward at my mercy, that I never will divulge the knowledge I possess of your reading Greek and philosophy.

[The Platonic references in this Conversation are given in this note. For many of them the editor is indebted to Mr H. M‘L. Innes, Fellow of Trinity College, Cambridge. In those cases in which Landor has correctly understood the passage to which he refers, only the reference is given.

P. 291, l. 12, Crito, 52 B. "Nor had you any curiosity to know other states or other laws; we [*i.e.*, the laws of Athens] were enough for you, we and the state we ruled." There is no reason to suppose that any insinuation against Aristotle is intended here. L. 19, Theages, 127 E., 128 A. The interpretation put upon the passage is absurd. L. 22, Theætetus, 152 E. Plato calls Homer a master of tragic poetry, and Epicharmus a master of comedy. P. 292, l. 6, Phaedo, 78 D. L. 8, Republic VI., 495 B. ; both passages slightly misquoted. L. 20, Phaedo, 89 C. L. 31, Theætetus, 181 B. P. 293, l. 13, Theages, 126 B. P. 294, l. 33, Euthydemus, 285 C. L. 36. Landor would seem to have derived the conception of a doll dedicated to memory from Theætetus, 191 C.D. Θὲς δή μοι λόγου ἕνεκα ἐν ταῖς ψυχαῖς ἡμῶν ἐνὸν κήρινον ἐκμαγεῖον. . . . Δῶρον τοίνυν αὐτὸ φῶμεν εἶναι τῆς τῶν Μουσῶν μητρὸς Μνημοσύνης. "Suppose then, for the sake of argument, a block of wax immanent in our souls. . . . Let us say that it is a gift from Memory, the mother of the Muses." It is difficult to say exactly how many mistakes are involved in Landor's translation. P. 295, l. 3, Gorgias, 470 D.

L. 8, *ibid.*, 449 D.   L. 16, Cratylus passim.   L. 31.   Plato speaks of a true rhetoric in Phaedrus 259 Foll., and in the Gorgias. There is no question of definition there, of course.   P. 296, l. 37, Rep. I., 328 A. P. 297, l. 8, *ibid.*, 334 B.   L. 12.   ὦ θαυμάσιε, oh admirable man, ὦ βέλτιστε, oh best of men.   In the passage quoted, Euthyphro, 4 A., Socrates addressing the son who is bent upon accusing his own father naturally says, "Your own father, oh best of men."   P. 298, l. 24, Gorgias, 524.   The explanation given of ἀδικίαι is absurd.   P. 299, l. 25, Timaeus, 38 B.   But the passage definitely excludes the notion that time or the heavens should ever cease.   P. 300, l. 15.   παιδεύειν does not mean to banter; Landor is thinking of παίζειν.   L. 25.   Plato's criticism on the grief of Achilles and Priam is to be found Rep. III., 388, A. B. P. 301, l. 28, Timaeus, 21 C.   P. 302, l. 1, Rep. X., 601.   L. 31, Symposium, 185 D.   To appreciate the utter absurdity of this criticism it is only necessary to look at the passage.   P. 303, l. 2, *ibid.*, 196 C. L. 20, *ibid.*   The old woman is Diotima.   P. 304, l. 3, Protagoras, 361 D, 362 A.   P. 307, l. 28, Phaedo, 59 B.

The above note comprises all the more important of the Platonic references in the foregoing Conversation. It may be said that in some cases Landor has not understood the Greek, and that in most he has not understood the meaning.]

XI. ROMILLY AND PERCEVAL.[1]

Romilly.   Perceval, I congratulate you on your appointment.

Perceval.   It is an arduous one, Romilly, and the more after such eloquent men as have preceded me.

Romilly.   What! and do you too place eloquence in the first rank among the requisites of a minister?   Pitt, who could speak fluently three hours together, came about us like the tide along

[1 The friendship of Romilly and Perceval dated from a time when both were young men, and both members of the Midland circuit. Romilly's thoughts were early turned to the barbarity of the criminal laws, and the main labour and strength of his life was spent in endeavours to obtain their amelioration. His work in this cause began as early as 1785, but it was not until 1808 that he introduced in the House of Commons the first of a series of Bills to abolish capital punishment for minor offences.   He renewed his efforts in 1810, 1811, and 1813. Several of these Bills passed in the House of Commons, but none survived the Lords.   And yet, though Romilly did not live to see his labours crowned with success, it is to his untiring zeal that the reformation of our infamous criminal code is owing.   Perceval was made Chancellor of the Exchequer in the Duke of Portland's ministry in 1807, and Prime Minister in 1809.   It is on this last appointment that Romilly's congratulations are given.   Writing of the time when Perceval first joined

the Lancashire sands,—always shallow, but always just high enough to drown us.

Perceval. Despise him as you may, he did great things.

Romilly. Indeed he did : he made the richest nation in the world the most wretched, and the poorest the most powerful.

Perceval. He was unfortunate, I acknowledge it, on the Continent.

Romilly. Like the **Apparition** in the *Revelation*, he put the right foot upon the sea, and the left upon the land, but in such a manner that they could not act in concert.

Perceval. He was placed among the immortals while living.

Romilly. And there are clubs expressly formed for the purpose of irrigating this precious plant of immortality with port and claret. They or their fathers sprang up rapidly in their obscurity under the rank litter of the improvident husbandman. He was called *immortal* by those who benefited from him, the word *God* on such occasions being obsolete.

Perceval. I do not go so far as to call him, what some do, heavenly and godlike.

Romilly. I do.

Perceval. How! you ?

Romilly. Yes : men who have much to give are very like God ; and the more so when the sun of their bounty shines on the unworthy no less than on the worthy. However, he was eloquent, if facility in speaking is eloquence.[2] When we were

the Midland circuit in 1786, Romilly thus describes him, ". . . with . . . indeed very little reading, of a conversation barren of instruction, and with strong and invincible prejudices on many subjects ; yet, by his excellent temper, his engaging manners, and his sprightly conversation, he was the delight of all who knew him. I formed a strong and lasting friendship with him." Speaking of a later time, he says : " Perceval, after he had in a manner, which my private friendship for him could never induce me to consider in a favourable point of view, obtained the situation of Prime Minister, and quite to his tragical end, was desirous that our friendship should remain uninterrupted : I could not, however, continue in habits of private intimacy and intercourse with one whom in public I had every day to oppose." (*See* " Life of Sir S. Romilly," vol. i., p. 67.) (Imag. Convers., iii., 1828. Works, i., 1849. Works, iii., 1876.)]

[2 Speaking in the House of Commons, 1811, Romilly says of Pitt : " with all the talents that Mr Pitt possessed and the great influence which he had so long enjoyed, I looked in vain for any acts of his administration by which he had increased the happiness or improved the condition of any portion of his fellow subjects."]

together in the law-courts, it was reasonable enough to consider our tongues are the most valuable parts of us, knowing that their motion or quiescence would be purchased by dignities and emoluments; but the present times require men of business, men of firmness, men of consistency, men of probity; and what is first-rate at the bar is but second-rate on the council-board.

Perceval. I should be glad of your assistance, our opinions being in general alike.

Romilly. We could not take the same side on civil and criminal causes; neither, can we, for the same reason, in the House of Commons. Whichever may win, we will both lead, if you please.

Perceval. I understand you, and cannot but commend your determination. Yet,[3] my dear Romilly, although there have been many Whig oppositions, there never has been and (in the present state of things) never will be a Whig ministry. The post regulates the principles.

Romilly. A ministry of such virtue as to carry Whig principles into the cabinet, I fear there never will be, however much I wish it. Yet on certain points disconnected from party there is no reason why we two should disagree : I will support you in your favorite plan.

Perceval. What is that ?

Romilly. To soften the rigor of the penal statutes.

Perceval. I once thought it necessary, or at least advisable. My colleagues oppose it; feeling, that, if reform is introduced, it may reach at last the Court of Chancery, and tend to diminish the dignity of the first office under the crown.

Romilly. In[4] England there is no dignity but what is constituted by possessions. If you would propose a grant of fifty or sixty thousand pounds a year to the present chancellor, to indemnify him for the losses he would sustain by regulating his court, I am convinced he would not oppose you.

Perceval. The people are turbulent, and might dislike the grant, reasonable as it must appear to any unprejudiced man. But the principal objection is, that an inquiry would exhibit to the

[3 From "Yet" to "principles" (4 lines), and from "A ministry" to "Yet" (3 lines) added in 2nd ed.]
[4 From "In" to "possessions" (2 lines) added in 2nd ed.]

world such a mass of what we have been lately taught to call abuses, as must greatly tend to alienate the affections of the people from the institutions of their country.

Romilly. Fees are ticklish things to meddle with; forms are venerable, and silk gowns are non-conductors of inquiry into courts of chancery. I confine myself to the criminal statutes; and would diminish the number of capital offences, which is greater in England, I imagine, than the light and heavy put together in the tables of Solon or Numa. Nay, I am ready to believe that Draco himself did not punish so many with blood as we do, although he punished with blood every one indiscriminately.

Perceval. You can adduce no proof, or rather no support, of this paradox.

Romilly. A logician will accept many things which a lawyer would reject, and a moralist will attend to some which would be discountenanced by the logician. Let me remark to you, that we punish with death certain offences which Draco did not even note as crimes, and many others had not yet sprung up in society. On the former position, I need not expatiate; on the latter, let me recall to your memory the vast number of laws on various kinds of forgery; and, having brought them before you, let me particularly direct your attention to that severe one on fraudulent bankruptcy.

Perceval. Severe one! there at least we differ. If any crime deserves the punishment of death, surely this does. Is it not enough that a creditor loses the greater part perhaps of his property, by the misfortune or imprudence of another, without losing the last farthing of it by the same man's dishonesty.

Romilly. Enough it is, and more than enough; but lines of distinction are drawn on murder, and even on the wilful and malicious.

Perceval. There indeed they may be drawn correctly. Malice may arise from injury, more or less grievous, more or less recent: revenge may be delayed and meditated a longer time or a shorter, and may be perpetrated with more or less atrocity; but rarely is it brought to maturity in the coolness of judgment. The fraud under consideration not only is aforethought; it is formed and grounded upon calculation. You remember a trial at Warwick, or rather the report of it, the result of which was, that a serjeant-major, an elderly man, of irreproachable character antecedently, as was proved by the testimony of his superior officer, who had known him for twenty years, was condemned to be hanged (and not by Buller) for stabbing a young reprobate who had insulted and struck him. It was proved that he ran upstairs for his sword, in order to commit the crime. This hardly was afore-thought, and certainly was uncalculated.

Romilly. It is probable that if he had run downstairs, instead of upstairs, his life would not have been forfeited ; or even if his counsel had proved that the mounting of the stairs could have been performed in five steps, as I am inclined to think it might by an outraged man. But it appeared to the judge, on the evidence before him, and perhaps on thinking more about his own staircase than about the staircase of an ale-house, that time sufficient had elapsed for his anger to subside and cool.

Perceval. We have seen judges themselves who required a longer time for their anger to subside and cool, though sitting at their ease upon the cushion, to deliberate on matters where, if life was not at stake, property and character were ; and not the property and character of drunkards and reprobates, but of gentlemen in their own profession, their equals in birth and education, in honor and abilities.

Romilly. Dear Perceval, you have forgotten your new dignity ; however, I will nôt betray you.[5] We are treating this matter a little more loosely than we should do in Parliament, but more openly and fairly. After an acquaintance and, I am proud to say it, a friendship of twenty-seven years, I think you will give me credit for some soundness of principle.

Perceval. If any man upon earth possesses it.

Romilly. Then I will offer to you, if not as my opinion, at least as a subject worth reflection and consideration, whether even a virtuous man, about to fall into bankruptcy, may not commit a fraud, such as by our laws and practice is irremissibly capital ?

Perceval. There, my dear Romilly, you go too far. The question (you must pardon me) is not only inconsiderate, but contradictory ; the thing impossible. Your problem, in other

[5 First ed. reads: "you. Come, you must dip one foot in Lethe or the other will have a thorn in it ere long. We are," &c.]

figures, is this; whether a man may not be at once vicious and virtuous, a rogue and honest man: for you do not put a case in this manner, whether one who has hitherto been always honest, may not commit a capital crime, and afterward be honest again. A useless question even thus, among those which a wise man need not, and a scrupulous man would not, discuss. For the limits that separate us from offences ought not to be too closely under our eyes: a large space of neutral ground should be left betwixt. Part of mankind, like boys and hunters, by seeing a hedge before them, are tempted to leap it, only because it is one. Whenever we doubt whether a thing may be done, let us resolve that it may not. I speak as a moralist, by no means as an instructor: in the former capacity all may speak to all; in the latter, none to you. Excuse me, however, my dear Romilly, if in this instance I tell you plainly, that the joints of your logic seem to me to have been relaxed by your philanthropy.

Romilly. There are questions which may be investigated by two friends in private, and which I would on no account lay before the public in their rank freshness and fulness. In like manner, there are substances, the chief nutriment of whole nations, which are poison until prepared. I would appeal to the judgment and the heart together. He is the most mischievous of incendiaries who inflames the heart against the judgment, and he is the most ferocious of schismatics who divides the judgment from the heart. My argument, if it carried such weight with it as to lay the foundation of a law, would render many men more compassionate (which, after all, is the best and greatest thing we can do on earth), and it would render no man fraudulent.

Suppose a young gentleman to have married a girl equal to himself in fortune, and that, in the confidence of early affection, or by the improvidence of her parents, or from any other cause, there is no settlement. A family springs up around them; he is anxious to provide for it more amply than his paternal estate or his wife's property will allow; he enters into business; from unskilfulness, from the infidelity of agents, or from a change in the times and in the channels of commerce, he must become a bankrupt; his creditors are inexorable.

Perceval. That may happen: he is much to be pitied; I see no remedy.

Romilly. Speaking of those things which arise from our civil institutions, whatever is to be pitied is to be remedied. The greatest evils and the most lasting are the perverse fabrications of unwise policy; but neither their magnitude nor their duration are proofs of their immobility. They are proofs only that ignorance and indifference have slept profoundly in the chambers of tyranny, and that many interests have grown up, and seeded, and twisted their roots, in the crevices of many wrongs. The wrongs in all cases may be redressed, the interests may be transplanted. Prudence and patience do the work effectually.

I must proceed, although I see close before me the angle of divergence in our opinions.

I will not attempt to run away with your affections, Perceval; I will not burst into the midst of your little playful family, beginning to number it, and forgetting my intent, at the contemplation of its happiness, its innocence, its beauty. I will remove, on the contrary, every image of grief from the house of my two sufferers; I will suppose the boys and girls too young (just as yours are) for sorrow; I will suppose the mother not expressing it by tears, or wringing of hands, or frantic cries, or dumb desperation, or in any other way that might move you; but so devoted to her husband as for his sake to cover it with smiles, and to engulf it in the abysses of a broken heart. Yet I cannot make him, who is a man as we are, ignorant of her thoughts and feelings, ungrateful to her affection, past and present, or indifferent to her future lot. Obduracy and cruelty press upon him from one side; on the other are conjugal tenderness and parental love. A high and paramount sense of justice, too, supervenes. What he had received with his partner in misfortune, his conscience tells him, is hers: he had received it before he had received any thing from his creditors; he collects the poor remains of it, and places them apart. Unused to fallacy and concealment, the unlawful act is discovered; the criminal is seized, imprisoned, brought out before the judge. Sunday, the day of rest from labor, the day formerly of his innocent projects, of his pleasantest walks, of visits from friends and kindred, of greeting, and union, and hospitality, and gladness,—Sunday, the day on which a man's own little ones are dearer to him, are more his own, than on other days,— Sunday is granted to him. A further act of grace is extended,— his widow may bury him, and his children may learn their letters on his tombstone.

Perceval. What can be done? We are always changing our laws.

Romilly. A proof how inconsiderately we enact them. I verily do believe that a balloon by flying over the House would empty it; so little sense of public good or of national dignity is left among us.

What I would propose is this: I would, in such cases, deduct the widow's third from the bankrupt's property, and place it in the hands of trustees for the benefit of herself and the children by that marriage.

Perceval. The motion would do you honor.

Romilly. I willingly cede the honor to you. We who are out of place are suspected of innovation; or are well-meaning men, but want practice.

XII. PETER THE GREAT AND ALEXIS.[1]

Peter. And so, after flying from thy father's house, thou hast returned again from Vienna. After this affront in the face of Europe, thou darest to appear before me?

Alexis. My emperor and father! I am brought before your Majesty, not at my own desire.

Peter. I believe it well.

Alexis. I would not anger you.

Peter. What hope hadst thou, rebel, in thy flight to Vienna?

Alexis. The hope of peace and privacy; the hope of security; and, above all things, of never more offending you.

Peter. That hope thou hast accomplished.

[1 Landor has in this Conversation given a somewhat harsh picture of Peter the Great, and has adorned Alexis with a halo to which he has no claim. There can be no doubt that the prince and his mother Eudoxa were engaged in a conspiracy to oppose Peter's reforms in Russia, and only awaited his death to entirely upset all his achievements. When Alexis left St Petersburg he went to Vienna and was thence sent to Naples for his security; but his father discovered that he was, and insisted on his return. At St Petersburg he was brutally treated. The exact manner of his death is unknown, but it is probable that while in the presence of his judges he was knouted and that he died under the lash. His mother and the other persons concerned in the conspiracy were severely punished. *See* Ramband's "Russia," vol. ii., p. 58. (**Imag.** Convers., vol. iii., **1828**. Works, i., 1848. Works, iii., 1876.)]

Thou imaginedst, then, that my brother of Austria would maintain thee at his court—speak !

Alexis. No, sir ! I imagined that he would have afforded me a place of refuge.

Peter. Didst thou, then, take money with thee ?

Alexis. A few gold pieces.

Peter. How many ?

Alexis. About sixty.

Peter. He would have given thee promises for half the money ; but the double of it does not purchase a house, ignorant wretch !

Alexis. I knew as much as that : although my birth did not appear to destine me to purchase a house anywhere ; and hitherto your liberality, my father, hath supplied my wants of every kind.

Peter. Not of wisdom, not of duty, not of spirit, not of courage, not of ambition. I have educated thee among my guards and horses, among my drums and trumpets, among my flags and masts. When thou wert a child, and couldst hardly walk, I have taken thee into the arsenal, though children should not enter according to regulations ; I have there rolled cannon-balls before thee over iron plates ; and I have shown thee bright new arms, bayonets and sabres ; and I have pricked the back of my hands until the blood came out in many places ; and I have made thee lick it ; and I have then done the same to thine. Afterward, from thy tenth year, I have mixed gunpowder in thy grog ; I have peppered thy peaches ; I have poured bilge-water (with a little good wholesome tar in it) upon thy melons ; I have brought out girls to mock thee and cocker thee, and talk like mariners, to make thee braver. Nothing would do. Nay, recollect thee ! I have myself led thee forth to the window when fellows were hanged and shot ; and I have shown thee every day the halves and quarters of bodies ; and I have sent an orderly or chamberlain for the heads ; and I have pulled the cap up from over the eyes ; and I have made thee, in spite of thee, look steadfastly upon them, incorrigible coward !

And now another word with thee about thy scandalous flight from the palace ; in time of quiet too ! To the point ! did my brother of Austria invite thee ? Did he, or did he not ?

Alexis. May I answer without doing an injury or disservice to his Imperial Majesty ?

Peter. Thou mayest. What injury canst thou or any one do, by the tongue, to such as he is ?

Alexis. At the moment, no ; he did not. Nor indeed can I assert that he at any time invited me ; but he said he pitied me.

Peter. About what ? hold thy tongue ; let that pass. Princes never pity but when they would make traitors : then their hearts grow tenderer than tripe. He pitied thee, kind soul, when he would throw thee at thy father's head ; but finding thy father too strong for him, he now commiserates the parent, laments the son's rashness and disobedience, and would not make God angry for the world. At first, however, there must have been some overture on his part ; otherwise thou art too shamefaced for intrusion. Come,—thou hast never had wit enough to lie,—tell me the truth, the whole truth.

Alexis. He said that, if ever I wanted an asylum, his court was open to me.

Peter. Open ! so is the tavern ; but folks pay for what they get there. Open truly ! and didst thou find it so ?

Alexis. He received me kindly.

Peter. I see he did.

Alexis. Derision, O my father ! is not the fate I merit.

Peter. True, true ! it was not intended.

Alexis. Kind father ! punish me then as you will.

Peter. Villain ! wouldst thou kiss my hand too ? Art thou ignorant that the Austrian threw thee away from him, with the same indifference as he would the outermost leaf of a sandy sunburnt lettuce ?

Alexis. Alas ! I am not ignorant of this.

Peter. He dismissed thee at my order. If I had demanded from him his daughter, to be the bed-fellow of a Kalmuc, he would have given her, and praised God.

Alexis. O father ! is his baseness my crime ?

Peter. No ; thine is greater. Thy intention, I know, is to subvert the institutions it has been the labor of my lifetime to establish. Thou hast never rejoiced at my victories.

Alexis. I have rejoiced at your happiness and your safety.

Peter. Liar ! coward ! traitor ! when the Polanders and Swedes fell before me, didst thou from thy soul congratulate me ? Didst thou get drunk at home or abroad, or praise the Lord of Hosts and Saint Nicholas ? Wert thou not silent and civil and low-spirited ?

Alexis. I lamented the irretrievable loss of human life ; I

lamented that the bravest and noblest were swept away the first ;
that the gentlest and most domestic were the earliest mourners :
that frugality was supplanted by intemperance ; that order was
succeeded by confusion ; and that your Majesty was destroying
the glorious plans you alone were capable of devising.

Peter. I destroy them ! how ?   Of what plans art thou
speaking ?

Alexis. Of civilizing the Muscovites.   The Polanders in
part were civilized : the Swedes, more than any other nation on
the Continent ; and so excellently versed were they in military
science, and so courageous, that every man you killed cost you
seven or eight.

Peter. Thou liest ; nor six. And civilized, forsooth ! Why,
the robes of the metropolitan, him at Upsal, are not worth three
ducats, between Jew and Livornese.   I have no notion that
Poland and Sweden shall be the only countries that produce great
princes. What right have they to such as Gustavus and Sobieski ?

Europe ought to look to this, before discontent becomes
general, and the people do to us what we have the privilege of
doing to the people.   I am wasting my words : there is no
arguing with positive fools like thee.   So thou wouldst have
desired me to let the Polanders and Swedes lie still and quiet !
Two such powerful nations !

Alexis. For that reason and others I would have gladly seen
them rest, until our own people had increased in numbers and
prosperity.

Peter. And thus thou disputest my right, before my face,
to the exercise of the supreme power.

Alexis. Sir ! God forbid !

Peter. God forbid, indeed !   What care such villains as thou
art what God forbids !   He forbids the son to be disobedient
to the father : he forbids—he forbids—twenty things.   I do not
wish, and will not have, a successor who dreams of dead people.

Alexis. My father ! I have dreamed of none such.

Peter. Thou hast ; and hast talked about them,—Scythians
I think they call 'em.   Now who told thee, Mr Professor, that
the Scythians were a happier people than we are ; that they were
inoffensive ; that they were free ; that they wandered with their
carts from pasture to pasture, from river to river ; that they
traded with good faith ; that they fought with good courage ;

that they injured none, invaded none, and **feared** none? At **this** rate, I have effected nothing.   The great **founder** of Rome, I heard in Holland, slew his brother for despiting the weakness **of** his walls; and shall the founder of this better place spare a degenerate son, who prefers a vagabond life **to a** civilized one, **a** cart to a city, a Scythian to a Muscovite?   **Have** I not shaved **my** people, and breeched them?   Have **I not formed them** into regular armies, with bands of music and **haversacks?   Are bows better than** cannon? shepherds than dragoons, mare's milk **than** brandy, raw **steaks** than broiled?   The are **tenets** that strike **at** the root of politeness and sound government.   Every prince **in** Europe is interested in rooting them out by fire and sword. There is no other way with false doctrines: breath against breath does little.

Alexis.   **Sire, I never have attempted to** disseminate **my opinions.**

Peter.   **How** couldst **thou?** the **seed would fall only on** granite.   Those, however, **who** caught it brought it to me.

Alexis.   Never have **I** undervalued civilization: on the contrary, I regretted whatever impeded it.   In my opinion, the evils that have been attributed to it sprang from its imperfections and voids; **and** no nation has yet acquired it **more** than very scantily.

Peter.   **How** so? give me thy reasons,—thy fancies rather; for reasons thou hast none.

Alexis.   When **I** find the first **of** men, in **rank** and genius, hating one another, and becoming slanderers and **liars** in order to lower and vilify **an** opponent; when I hear the **God** of mercy invoked to massacres, and thanked for furthering what he reprobates and condemns,—I look back in vain on any barbarous people for worse barbarism.[2]   I have expressed my admiration of our forefathers, who, not being Christians, were yet more virtuous than those who are; more temperate, more just, more sincere, more chaste, more peaceable.

Peter.   Malignant atheist!

Alexis.   Indeed, my father, **were** I malignant I must be an

[2 First ed. reads: "barbarism. Soldiers it is said in ancient mythology sprang from dragons' teeth, sown by Cadmus, who introduced letters.   It would appear that these also came from the same sack as the soldiers, and were only the rottenest of **the fangs kept** till the **last.** I have," &c.]

atheist; for malignity is contrary to the command, and inconsistent with the belief, of God.

Peter. Am I Czar of Muscovy, and hear discourses on
reason and religion? from my own son too! No, by the Holy
Trinity! thou art no son of mine. If thou touchest my knee
again, I crack thy knuckles with this tobacco-stopper: I wish it
were a sledge-hammer for thy sake. Off, sycophant! Off, run-
away slave!

Alexis. Father! father! my heart is broken! If I have
offended, forgive me!

Peter. The State requires thy signal punishment.

Alexis. If the State requires it, be it so; but let my father's
anger cease!

Peter. The world shall judge between us. I will brand thee
with infamy.

Alexis. Until now, O father! I never had a proper sense of
glory. Hear me, O Czar! let not a thing so vile as I am stand
between you and the world! Let none accuse you!

Peter. Accuse me, rebel! Accuse me, traitor!

Alexis. Let none speak ill of you, O my father! The public
voice shakes the palace; the public voice penetrates the grave;
it precedes the chariot of Almighty God, and is heard at the
judgment-seat.

Peter. Let it go to the devil! I will have none of it here
in Petersburgh. Our Church says nothing about it; our laws
forbid it. As for thee, unnatural brute, I have no more to do
with thee neither!

Ho there! chancellor! What! come at last! Wert napping, or counting thy ducats?

Chancellor. Your majesty's will and pleasure!

Peter. Is the Senate assembled in that room?

Chancellor. Every member, sire.

Peter. Conduct this youth with thee, and let them judge
him: thou understandest me.

Chancellor. Your Majesty's commands are the breath of our
nostrils.

Peter. If these rascals are remiss, I will try my new cargo of
Livonian hemp upon 'em.

Chancellor (returning). Sire! sire!

Peter. Speak, fellow! Surely they **have not** condemned him to death, without giving themselves time to read the accusation, that thou comest back so quickly.

Chancellor. No, sire! Nor has either been **done.**

Peter. Then thy head quits thy shoulders.

Chancellor. O sire!

Peter. Curse thy silly *sires!* what art thou about?

Chancellor. Alas! he fell.

Peter. Tie him **up to** thy chair, then. Cowardly beast! what made him fall?

Chancellor. The hand of Death; the name of father.

Peter. Thou puzzlest me; prythee speak plainlier.

Chancellor. We **told** him that **his** crime **was proven and** manifest; that his life was forfeited.

Peter. **So** far, well enough.

Chancellor. He smiled.

Peter. He did! did he? Impudence **shall** do him little **good. Who** could have expected it **from that** smock-face! Go on: what then?

Chancellor. He said calmly, but **not without** sighing twice or thrice, "Lead me to the scaffold: I am weary of life; nobody loves me." I condoled with him, and wept upon his hand, holding the paper against my bosom. He took the corner of it between his fingers, and said, "Read me this paper; read **my** death-warrant. Your silence and tears have signified it; yet **the** law has its forms. **Do** not keep me in suspense. My father says, too truly, I am not courageous; **but the** death that leads **me to** my God shall never terrify me."

Peter. I have seen these white-livered knaves die resolutely; I **have seen** them quietly fierce like white ferrets, with their watery **eyes and tiny teeth.** You **read it?**

Chancellor. In part, sire! **When** he heard your Majesty's name accusing **him** of treason and attempts at rebellion and parricide, he fell speechless. We **raised** him up: he was motionless; **he** was dead!

Peter. Inconsiderate and barbarous varlet as thou art, dost thou recite this ill accident to a father! and to one who has not dined! Bring me a glass of brandy.

Chancellor. And **it** please your Majesty, might I call a——a——

Peter.   Away and **bring it**: scamper!   All equally and alike shall **obey** and serve me.

Hark **ye!** bring the bottle with it: **I must** cool myself— and—hark ye! a rasher of bacon on **thy** life! and some **pickled** sturgeon, and some **krout** and **caviar, and** good strong **cheese.**

XIII.   LOUIS XIV. AND **FATHER LA CHAISE.**[1]

Louis.   **Father,** there is one thing which I **never have confessed;** sometimes considering it almost as a light matter, and sometimes **seeing** it in its true colors.   In **my wars** against **the Dutch I** committed an action—

La Chaise.   Sire, the ears of the **Lord** are al **ways open to those** who **confess** their **sins** to their confessor.   **Cruelties and many other** bad deeds are perpetrated in war, **at which we** should shudder **in our houses** at Paris.

Louis.   The people who were then in their **houses did shudder,** poor devils!   It was ludicrous to see how such clumsy figures skipped, **when the bombs** fell among their **villages, in** which **the** lower part of the **habitations** was under water; **and children** looked from the upper **windows, between** the legs **of calves and** lambs, and of the old household **dog,** struggling **to free** himself, as less ignorant of **his** danger.   Loud shrieks were sometimes heard, when the artillery and **other** implements of **war were** silent ; for fevers raged within their insulated **walls, and** wives execrated their husbands, with whom they had lived **in concord and tenderness** many years, **when** the father enforced **the necessity** of throwing **their** dead infant into the lake below.   **Our** young soldiers on **such** occasions exercised their dexterity, **and** took their choice ; **for the whole family** was assembled at the casement, and prayers **were read over the** defunct, accompanied with some firm and with **some faltering responses.**

[1 For **an** account **of** Louis XIV.'s **invasion of** Holland, see Macaulay, Hist. Eng., Chap. ii. and Chap. **viii., and V**oltaire's Siecle de Louis Quatorze, Chap. x., Imag. Convers., **ii., 1824, ii.,** 1826.   Works, i. 1846.   Works, iii., 1876.]

By these terrible examples God punished their heresy.

La Chaise. The Lord of Hosts is merciful: he protected your Majesty in the midst of these horrors.

Louis. He sustained my strength, kept up my spirits, and afforded me every day some fresh amusement, in the country of this rebellious and blasphemous people, who regularly, a quarter before twelve o'clock, knowing that mass was then performed among us, sang their psalms.

La Chaise. I cannot blame a certain degree of severity on such occasions: on much slighter, we read in the Old Testament, nations were smitten with the edge of the sword.

Louis. I have wanted to find that place, but my Testament was not an old one: it was printed at the Louvre in my own time. As for the edge of the sword, it was not always convenient to use that: they are stout fellows; but our numbers enabled us to starve them out, and we had more engineers and better. Beside which, I took peculiar vengeance on some of the principal families, and on some among the most learned of their professors; for if any had a dissolute son, who, as dissolute sons usually are, was the darling of the house, I bribed him, made him drunk, and converted him. This occasionally broke the father's heart,— God's punishment of stubbornness!

La Chaise. Without the especial grace of the Holy Spirit, such conversions are transitory. It is requisite to secure the soul while we have it, by the exertion of a little loving-kindness. I would deliver the poor stray creatures up to their Maker straightway, lest he should call me to account for their backsliding. Heresy is a leprosy, which the whiter it is the worse it is. Those who appear the most innocent and godly, are the very men who do the most mischief and hold the fewest observances. They hardly treat God Almighty like a gentleman, grudge him a clean napkin at his own table, and spend less upon him than upon a Christmas dinner.

Louis. O father La Chaise! you have searched my heart; you have brought to light my hidden offences. Nothing is concealed from your penetration. I come forth like a criminal in his chains.

La Chaise. Confess, sire, confess! I will pour the oil into your wounded spirit, taking due care that the vengeance of Heaven be satisfied by your atonement.

Louis. Intelligence was brought to me that the cook of the English general had prepared a superb dinner, in consequence of what that insolent and vainglorious people are in the habit of calling a success. " We shall soon see," exclaimed I, " who is successful : God protects France." The whole army shouted, and, I verily believe, at that moment would have conquered the world. I deferred it : my designs lie in my own breast. Father, I never heard such a shout in my life : it reminded me of Cherubim and Seraphim and Archangels. The infantry cried with joy ; the horses capered and neighed and ventriloquized right and left, from an excess of animation. Leopard skins, bear-skins, Genoa velvet, Mechlin ruffles, Brussels cravats, feathers and fringes and golden bands, up in the air at once ; pawings and snortings, threats and adjurations, beginnings and ends of songs. I was Henry and Cæsar, Alexander and David, Charlemagne and Agamemnon : I had only to give the word ; they would swim across the Channel, and bring the tyrant of proud Albion back in chains. All my prudence was requisite to repress their ardor.

A letter had been intercepted by my scouts, addressed by the wife of the English general to her husband. She was at Gorcum : she informed him that she would send him a glorious *mince-pie*, for his dinner the following day, in celebration of his victory. " Devil incarnate ! " said I, on reading the despatch, " I will disappoint thy malice." I was so enraged that I went within a mile or two of cannon-shot ; and I should have gone within half a mile, if my dignity had permitted me, or if my resentment had lasted. I liberated the messenger, detaining as hostage his son who accompanied him, and promising that, if the *mince-pie* was secured, I would make him a chevalier on the spot. Providence favored our arms ; but unfortunately there were among my staff-officers some who had fought under Turenne, and who, I suspect, retained the infection of heresy. They presented the *mince-pie* to me on their knees, and I ate. It was Friday. I did not remember the day when I began to eat ; but the sharpness of the weather, the odor of the pie, and something of vengeance springing up again at the sight of it, made me continue after I had recollected ; and, for my greater condemnation, I had inquired that very morning of what materials it was composed. God set

his face against me, and hid from me the light of his countenance.
I lost victory after victory, nobody knows how ; for my generals
were better than the enemy's, my soldiers more numerous, more
brave, more disciplined.   And, extraordinary and awful! even
those who swore to conquer or die, ran back again like whelps
just gelt, crying, " It is the first duty of a soldier to see his king
in safety."   I never heard so many fine sentiments or fewer songs.
My stomach was out of order by the visitation of the Lord.   I
took the sacrament on the Sunday.

La Chaise.   The sacrament on a Friday's *gras !*   I should
have recommended first a *de profundis*, a *miserere*, and an
eructavit cor meum, and lastly a little oil of ricina, which, administered by the holy and taken by the faithful, is almost as efficacious
in its way as that of Rheims.   Penance is to be done : your
Majesty must fast ; your Majesty must wear sackcloth next your
skin, and carry ashes upon your head before the people.

Louis.   Father, I cannot consent to this humiliation : the
people must fear me.   What are you doing with those scissors
and that pill ?   I am sound ; give it Villeroy or Richelieu.

La Chaise.   Sire, no impiety, no levity, I pray.   In this
pill, as your Majesty calls it, are some flakes of ashes from
the incense, which seldom is pure gum ; break it between your
fingers, and scatter it upon your peruke.   Well done !   Now
take this.

Louis.   Faith! I have no sore on groin or limb.   A black
plaster ! what is that for ?

La Chaise.   This is sackcloth.   It is the sack in which
Madame de Maintenon put her knitting, until the pins frayed
it.

Louis.   I should have believed that sackcloth means—

La Chaise.   No interpretations of Scripture, I charge you from
authority, sire.   Put it on your back or bosom.

Louis.   God forgive me, sinner !   It has dropped down into
my pantaloon : will that do ?

La Chaise.   Did it, in descending, touch your back, belly,
ribs, breast, or shoulder, or any part that needs mortification,
and can be mortified without scandal ?

Louis.   I placed it between my frills.

La Chaise.   In such manner as to touch the skin sensibly ?

Louis. It tickled me, by stirring a hair or two.

La Chaise. Be comforted, then; for people have been tickled to death.

Louis. But, father, you remit the standing in presence of the people?

La Chaise. Indeed I do not. Stand at the window, son of St Louis.

Louis. And perform the same ceremonies? no, upon my conscience! My almoner—

La Chaise. They are performed.

Louis. But the people will never know what is on my head or in my pantaloon.

La Chaise. Penance is performed so far: to-morrow is Friday; one more rigid must be enforced. Six dishes alone shall come upon the table; and, although fasting does not extend to wines or *liqueurs,* I order that three kinds only of wine be presented, and three of *liqueur.*

Louis. In the six dishes is soup included?

La Chaise. Soup is not served in a dish; but I forbid more than three kinds of soup.

Louis. Oysters of Cancale?

La Chaise. Those come in barrels; take care they be not dished. Your Majesty must either eat them raw from the barrel, or dressed in scallop, or both; but beware, I say again, of dishing this article, as your soul shall answer for it at the last day. There are those who would prohibit them wholly. I have experienced —I mean in others—strange uncouth effects therefrom, which, unless they shadow forth something mystical, it were better not to provoke.

Louis. Pray, Father, why is that frightful day which you mentioned just now, and which I think I have heard mentioned on other occasions, called the last; when the last in this life is over before it comes, and when the first in the next is not begun?

La Chaise. It is called the last day by the Church, because after that day the Church can do nothing for the sinner. Her saints, martyrs, and confessors can plead at the bar for him the whole of that day until sunset, some say until after *angelus;* then the books are closed, the candles put out, the doors shut, and the key turned. The flames of purgatory then sink into the floor, and would not wither a cistus-leaf full-blown and shed ; there is nothing left but heaven and hell, songs and lamentations.

Louis. Permit me to ask another question of no less importance, and connected with my penance. The Bishop of Aix in Provence has sent me thirty fine quails.

La Chaise. There are naturalists who assert that quails have fallen from heaven, like manna. Externally they bear the appearance of birds, and I have eaten them in that persuasion. If, however, any one from grave authority is convinced of the contrary, or propends to believe so, and eats thereof, the fault is venial. I conferred with Tamburini on this momentous point. He distinguishes between quails taken in the field, or in the air as they descend, and tame quails bred within coops and enclosures, which are begotten in the ordinary way of generation, and of which the substance in that case must be different. I cannot believe that the Bishop of Aix would be the conservator of creatures so given to fighting and wantonness ; but rather opine that his quails alighted somewhere in his diocese, and perhaps as a mark of divine favor to so worthy a member of the Church. It is safer to eat them after twelve o'clock at night ; but, where there is purity and humility of spirit, I see not that they are greatly to be dreaded.

The fiction of the quails will appear extravagant to those only who are in ignorance that such opinions have prevailed among casuists. The Carthusians, to whom animal food is forbidden, whereby they mean solely the flesh of quadrupeds and of birds, may nevertheless eat the otter and the gull ; it may be eaten by Catholics even in Lent. From this permission in regard to the *gull*, do we derive the English verb and noun ?

We often lay most stress on our slightest faults, and have more apprehension from things unessential than from things essential. When Lord Tylney was on his death-bed, and had not been shaved for two days, he burst suddenly into tears, and cried to his valet, "Are not you ashamed to abandon me? would you let me go this figure into the presence of my Maker ? "

He was shaved, and (let us hope) presented.

.   .   .   .   '   .

Louis XIV. is the great exemplar of kingship, the object of worship to declaimers against the **ferocity** of *the people*. The invasion of Holland, the conflagration of the Palatinate, the revocation of the Edict of Nantes, have severally been celebrated by French poets, French historians, French jurists, **and** French bishops, Massillon and Bossuet among them. The **most** unprovoked act of cruelty on record was perpetrated by another **King** of **France.** These are the words of an historian, their defender and **panegyrist,** Bussières. "**Victi** Bulgari, et ex sociis in servitutem rapti, mox eorum plures relictâ **patriâ** exulatum **ultro abierunt.** Ex iis ad *novem millia, uxoribus liberisque* **impliciti,** a Dagoberto sedes petunt—Jussi per hyemem hærere in Bavariâ **dum** amplius rex deliberaret, in plures urbes domosque sparsi sunt; tum novo barbaroque facinore unâ nocte cæsi omnes simul. *Quippe Dagobertus* **immani** *consilio* **Boiarios** *jubet, singulos suis* **hospitibus necem** *inferre, ratione* **nullâ** *ætatis aut sexûs;* et quâ truculentiâ imperatum, obtemperatum eâdem. Condictâ nocte miseri homines in asylo somni obtruncantur, imbelles feminæ, insontes pueri; totque funera hilaritati fuerunt, non luctui." A peculiar feature in the national character, indestructible amid all forms of government. It is amusing to read our Jesuit's words in the sequel. "Ad **beneficiorum** fontem se convertit, multaque dona elargitus templis, *emendabat* **scelera** *liberalitate*—Nec Dagoberto *liberalitas* pia frustra fuit: siquidem **sancti** quos in vivis multum coluerat, Dionysius, Mauritius, et Martinus, oblati sunt Joanni monacho **vigilanti,** regis animam eripientes e potestate **dæmonum sævisque** tormentis, eamque secum in cœli regiam deducentes."

XIV. SOLIMAN AND MUFTI.[1]

Soliman. **Mufti, my** teacher and slave, I say unto thee, Welcome.

Mufti. Welcome, I say unto thee, my master and disciple.

Soliman. God, he is merciful; God, he is God.

Good fortune follow that pious eructation of thine, O leader of true believers, under me the prince of the faithful!

Mufti. O Son of Selim! may the Almighty deliver into thy hands those thou lovest and those thou hatest. Thy servant here awaits thy commands.

Soliman. My commands are, O Mufti! fountain of truth and

[1 Soliman the magnificent was the greatest of all the Ottoman Emperors. Landor has taken his facts from the Biographie Universelle, but he has confused Charles V.'s disaster at Algiers with his conquest of Tunis. Barbarossa was driven from Tunis. The proposition to translate the Koran into other languages is a Landorian fancy. (Imag. Convers., iii., 1828. Works, i., 1846. Works, iii., 1876.)]

wisdom to the preachers of the word! that praises be offered up in every mosque, for our victory over the infidel.

Mufti. If thy slave might request, unblamably, a farther illumination from thy countenance, O mediterranean of light! he would presume to inquire of thy pure intelligence, *what victory?* For verily the Merciful has bestowed on thee such a series of them, that, if any thing after the miracles of our Prophet were wanting to demonstrate God's reprobation of the unbeliever, the years of thy reign, like successive lightnings that open the heavens and strike the earth, would severally declare it. First, the strongest and most beautiful of European cities, Belgrade, abased her towers and threw open her gates before thy scimitar. The following year ran the swifter its celestial course, that it might behold the sunny Rhodes adorn her brow with the crescent, and the flower of Christian chivalry lie dishonored in the dust. Hungary, the richest portion of the unbeliever's heritage, hath cast her fortresses at thy feet, and hath left her king extinct in the midst of them. Barbarossa, at thy order, hath shaken the principalities of Africa, and hath fixed his flag immovably on the citadel of Tunis. The incestuous Charles hath now lost his navy and army on that coast ; hardly a vessel, hardly a soldier, escaping from the wreck.

Soliman. My intention is to enlighten the dim-sighted, by ordering the Koran to be translated into the languages of all nations.

Why dost thou raise thine eyes, Mufti?

Mufti. God is God ; and Mohamet is his Prophet!

Soliman. Very true : that is what I wish to teach the world universally.

Mufti. God is great! God is merciful! God is just!

Soliman. Who the devil doubts it ?

Mufti. God loveth his people! God abases the proud! God exalts the humble!

Soliman. Let him, let him. What is that to the purpose? Are we at prayers? are we in the mosque? that thou utterest these idle fancies—truths I mean ; making thy lips quiver like a pointer's at a partridge. Get the Koran translated well and thoroughly : I have given orders already for the commencement. Let those who believe, believe now the better ; and those who never believed, begin.

Mufti. O son of Selim! if every man reads, one or two in every province will think.

Soliman. Let them, let them: few shall have leisure for that. What harm would it do among the old and lame; the only people left out of the soldiery in wise and good governments.

Mufti. The lame and the old grow stronger in the tongue; as the deaf grow stronger in the sense of feeling, the blind in that of hearing. They will chatter about things holy.

Soliman. Why not!

Mufti. Alas! O son of Selim! the miracles of our Prophet, those gems of our religion, would lose their lustre, handled and turned over by the ungodly.

Soliman. No doubt they would: therefore I will make them godly, and teach them the true word.

Mufti. Serene Highness! let us of the mosque do that. The Clement hath appointed us to his ministry.

Soliman. My resolution is to scatter the good seed in all lands, having now well ploughed and harrowed them.

Mufti. Suppose, O my master and lord! we turn the plough and harrow over them another time or two.

Soliman. God is merciful! we cannot do that, if they embrace the faith.

Mufti. The Koran would lose much of its beauty if we attempted to translate it from the language in which it was delivered to us by our Prophet.

Soliman. Swine do not look for sightly food, but for plentiful. The Koran would bestow on the dogs (dogs indeed no longer when once circumcised) everlasting life, taken in what manner and in what words it may be.

Mufti. Think, O magnificent!—

Soliman. I will think no more about the matter: it shall be done; I see no other way of making good subjects.

Mufti. The waters of Damascus have not lost their virtues in tempering the sabre. Books never made men believers. We must, under that benign influence which Heaven showers upon the son of Selim, preserve the Koran, preserve the book of life, from the vulgar.

Soliman. What! shall we, acknowledged even by our enemies as the most honest and just of men, descend from that high

station, and imitate the impostures of popes? Shall we say at
one moment, " This is the book of life ; " and at the next, " It
is death to touch it ! " Answer me : no evasion !

Mufti. Prince of the faithful ! it behoveth not us to follow
or to countenance the errors of the unbeliever, against whom
God hath so sharply set his face at all times, and lately most portentously ; yet surely that policy must be excellent and admirable
which uniteth so many, in other respects not foolish nor unwary,
under such camel-loads of absurdities, lies, and blasphemies.

Soliman. No proof whatever ; no evidence, no sign, no indication. Sesostris, Semiramis, Alexander, Gengis-Khan, thought
differently and acted alike. Human life is hardly modified in
the least degree by articles of faith, excepting when they are first
promulgated. Heaven is the place for them. There we shall
know at last what are the fruits of each tree : on earth, rarely a
blossom hath expanded. We only know that the leaves of them
all are bitterish, some rather more acrid, some rather less, and
that every man makes a wry face when he tastes his neighbor's,
though habit teaches him to chew his own complacently. Equally
learned men, equally acute men, equally virtuous men, have
followed various religions : philosophers have been idolaters ;
idiots (may the Righteous One forgive me if I speak amiss of
those whom His grace hath sanctified !) have followed our holy
standard ; and madmen (the Prophet help and comfort them !)
have covered their cracked brains with green turbans. He whose
name is the Wonderful hath willed it. Marvellous as this is, no
less marvellous is the certainty that all mankind are, sooner or
later, to embrace our religion, and enter with us into Paradise.
It is our duty to convert the obstinate ; not with fire and sword,
like those who farm out faith, the slaves of sin, the dust of
idolatry ; but, like equitable men, by fairer means and gentler.

Mufti. My advice, if advice may be offered by the worm to
the goshawk, is, that the Koran be kept inviolate in the hands of
the judge and of the preacher ; that, nevertheless, it be expounded
to the people in as many tongues as it can tether ; that it be
served out to them decorously and ceremoniously, like sherbet ;
and that they do not hastily and promiscuously put their hands
into it, as into a *pillau.* Hast thou not seen thy soldiers, O
conqueror of Christianity ! hurry, after a victory, to slake their

thirst at the fountain, and thus render that turbid which was pure and limpid, and which, if distributed by the few, dispassionate and patient, would have sufficed for all, without any contention or animosity? Even so is it with the living stream of our faith. `

Soliman. [2] Its miracles are manifold, its virtues infinite : the corrupt heart alone sickens over it, the froward spirit alone avoids it. Every other is deserted by myriads yearly ; none beside hath seen within the same period so many converts, so few deserters. If we wanted proof of its superiority and divinity, here are they : here Reason and Faith join hands.

Mufti. Surely no rational creature can ever doubt in future of our holy doctrine, when he hears recited the victories of thy right hand, O prince of the strong and faithful ! If his evil genius shall have drawn him into the shadow of death, by confounding him with doubts and delusions, let his father or his preacher come forward and stop him on the declivity, by relating to him how the navies of the Christian powers were twice united against us in thy glorious reign ; how the last was overwhelmed on the Afric shores, by the finger of God directing his storms against it. In this manner did the Almighty punish the pride and obstinacy of the infidel, ignorant or regardless of his warning so short a time before, when a more powerful fleet, united from all Christendom against the true believers, was dissipated in the port of Zealand, without a tempest, without a burst of thunder, without a breath of air from any quarter of the heavens. Let him be taught how the Merciful hath rendered the unbelieving princes the readiest and best instruments of our power and greatness. The firmest ally of Islamism hath been always the most Christian king : the eldest son of the Church is the adopted one of Mahomet. We may employ him hereafter to sweep off and annihilate the multiplying sects of his religion ; as our chamberlains put hedgehogs on the ground-floor, to kill and consume the cockroaches. A little filth must be suffered quietly, in order to preserve us from the encroachments of vermin, more troublesome and more disgusting. While, to pass over the most Christian king, the rest around him crouch, and watch one another, like tigers ; while in their most loving mood they grumble and whine

[2 First ed. reads: " *Soliman.* Nothing should confuse it, nothing should dry it up. Its," &c.]

internally, like enamoured cats; we whip them away from before us, or kick them out of our path amid the riotous writhing of their accouplements, and evince the purity of our faith from the effects of their infidelity.   No belief, how coarse and sordid soever, will not rather be swallowed by the people under them, than one bartered and retailed so scandalously as theirs, after all the scourges, axes, and fagots the wretched fools and their fathers have undergone for it; to say nothing of the hay-stacks and corn-stacks they have been transferring every year for its enjoyment. What then, when our true religion is displayed to them in her purity and freshness and effulgence, by the side of their old cripple, caught in thievery blotched with sores, procuress to her elder daughter, famisher of all her younger, brawling, riotous, calumnious, drunken, maintaining no decency in her own house, and leaving no peace in her neighbor's!   O son of Selim, do we want books for proofs?   Must the people take the Koran into their hands, to inquire if a toad is a toad, if a viper is a viper? We will give them the bread of life, in due portions, as they need it; but we will not permit that the whole mass of it be contaminated by the rancidity of their touch.   Let those who possess the holy volume as an inheritance hold it, and muse upon it.   But the tree newly planted may be loosened by the wind; the rigor of winter may kill it; even the genial sun may be its death.

Soliman.   Tell the linguists and interpreters to stop.   Mufti, we meet again at prayers.   I am going to the bath and to the harem.   Seest thou that vessel, whose sails, although now in the mid-channel, appear as if they were about to be entangled in the cypresses of Scutereh?

Mufti.   Sublime serenity! thy slave descries it.

Soliman.   By that vessel, which at one moment seems as if it danced to music, at another as if it reeled with the inebriety of delight, I expect some thirty young Georgians.

Mufti.   The Holy One guide thee, O son of Selim, and make thee flourish!

XV. MR PITT AND MR CANNING.[1]

Pitt. Dear Canning, my constitution is falling to pieces, as fast as, your old friend Sheridan would tell you, the constitution of the country is, under my management. Of all men living, you are the person I am most desirous to appoint my successor. My ambition is unsatisfied while any doubt of my ability to accomplish it remains upon my mind. Nature has withholden from me the faculty of propagating my species: nor do I at all repine at it, as many would do; since every great man must have some imbecile one very near him, if not next to him, in descent.

Canning. I am much flattered, sir, by your choice of me, there being so many among your relatives who might expect it for themselves. However this is only another instance of your great disinterestedness.

Pitt. You may consider it in that light if you will; but you must remember that those who have exercised power long together, and without control, seldom care much about affinities. The Mamelukes do not look out for brothers and cousins: they have favorite slaves who leap into their saddles when vacant.

Canning. Among the rich families, or the ancient aristocracy of the kingdom—

Pitt. Hold your tongue! prythee, hold your tongue! I hate and always hated these. I do not mean the rich: they served me. I mean the old houses: they overshadowed me. There is hardly one, however, that I have not disgraced or degraded; and I have filled them with smoke and sore eyes, by raising a vassal's[2] hut above them.

I desire to be remembered as the founder of a new system in England: I desire to bequeath my office by will, a verbal one;

[1 See Introduction to vol. i. for some remarks on Landor's antipathy to Canning. The Conversation is supposed to take place shortly before Pitt's death. It was not until some twenty years later that Canning became prime minister. (Imag. Convers., iv., 1829; Works, i., 1846. Works, iii., 1876.)]

[2 First ed. reads: "their neighbour's hut," &c.]

and I intend that you, and those who come after you, shall do the same!

As you are rather more rash than I could wish, and allow your words to betray your intentions; and as sometimes you run counter to them in your hurry to escape from them, having thrown them out foolishly where there was no occasion nor room,—I would advise you never to speak until you have thoroughly learned your sentences. Do not imagine that, because I have the gift of extemporary eloquence, you have the same. No man ever possessed it in the same degree, excepting the two fanatics, Wesley and Whitfield.

Canning. In the same degree, certainly not; but many in some measure.

Pitt. Some measure is not enough.

Canning. Excuse me: Mr Fox possessed it greatly, though not equally with you, and found it enough for his purpose.

Pitt. Fox foresaw, as any man of acuteness may do, the weaker parts of the argument that would be opposed to him, and he always learned his replies:[3] I had not time for it. I owe every thing to the facility and fluency of my speech, excepting the name bequeathed me by my father: and, although I have failed in every thing I undertook, and have cast in solid gold the clay colossus of France, people will consider me after my death as the most extraordinary man of my age.

Canning. Do you groan at this? or does the pain in your bowels grow worse? Shall I lift up the cushion of your other chair yonder?

Pitt. Oh! oh!

Canning. I will make haste, and then soften by manipulation those two or three letters of condolence.

Pitt. Oh! oh!—next to that cursed fellow who foiled me with his broken weapon, and befooled me with his half-wit, Bonaparte.

Canning. Be calmer, sir! be calmer.

Pitt. The gout and stone be in him! Port wine and Cheltenham-water! An Austrian wife, Italian jealousy, his

[3 First ed. reads: "replies more studiously than anything else. I had," &c.]

country's ingratitude, and his own ambition, dwell with him ever-lastingly!

Canning. Amen! let us pray!

Pitt. Upon my soul, we have little else to do. I hardly know where we can turn ourselves.

Canning. Hard indeed, when we cannot do that!

Be comforted, sir! The worse the condition of the country, the greater is the want of us; the more power we shall possess, the more places we shall occupy and distribute.

Pitt. Statesmanlike reflection.

Canning. "Those who have brought us into danger can alone bring us out," has become a maxim of the English people.

Pitt. If they should ever be strong again, they would crush us.

Canning. We have lightened them; and, having less ballast, they sail before the wind at the good pleasure of the pilot.

Pitt. A little while ago I would have made you chancellor or speaker, for composing and singing that capital song of the *Pilot*,[4]—so I thought it: at present I never hear the word but it gives me the sea-sickness, as surely as would a fishing-boat in the Channel. It sounds like ridicule.

Canning. *We* have weathered the storm.

Pitt. I have not. I never believed in any future state; but I have made a very damnable one of the present, both for myself and others. We never were in such danger from without or from within. Money-lenders and money-voters are satisfied: the devil must be in them if they are not; but we have taken the younger children's fortunes from every private gentleman in Great Britain.

Canning. Never think about it.

Pitt. I have formerly been in their houses; I have relatives and connections among them; if you had, you would sympathize. I feel as little as any man can feel for others, you excepted. And this utter indifference, this concentration, which inelegant men call selfishness, is among the reasons why I am disposed to appoint you my successor. You are aware that, should the people recover their senses, they would drive us in a dung-cart to the scaffold. *Me* they cannot: I shall be gone.

[4 See Life of Pitt, vol. iii., p. 380, for Canning's song on Pitt—"The Pilot that weathered the storm."]

Canning. We must prevent the possibility; we must go on weakening them. The viper that has bitten escapes; the viper that lies quiet in the road is cut asunder.

Pitt. Why, Canning! I find in you both more reasoning and more poetry than I ever found before. Go on in this manner, and your glory as a poet will not rest on *pilots* and *pebbles*, nor on a ditchside nettle or two of neglected satire. If you exhibit too much reflection, I may change my mind. You will do for my successor: you must not more than do.

Canning. On the contrary, sir, I feel in your presence my deep inferiority.

Pitt. That, of course.

Canning. Condescend to give me some precepts, which, if your disease should continue, it might be painfuller to deliver at any other time. Do not, however, think that your life is at all in danger, or that the supreme power can remain long together in any hands but yours.

Pitt. Attempt not to flatter me, Canning, with the prospect of much longer life. The doctors of physic have hinted that it is time I should divert my attention from the affairs of Europe to my own; and the doctors of divinity drive oftener to the chancellor's door than to mine. The flight of these sable birds portends a change of season and a fall of bones.

I have warned you against some imprudences of yours; now let me warn you against some of mine. You are soberer than I am; but, when you are rather warm over claret, you prattle childishly. For a successful minister, three things are requisite on occasion: to speak like an honest man, to act like a dishonest one, and to be indifferent which you are called. Talk of God as gravely as if you believed in him. Unless you do this, I will not say, what our Church does, you will be damned; but, what indeed is a politician's true damnation, you will be dismissed. Most very good men are stout partisans of some religion, and nearly all very bad ones. The[a] old women about the prince are as notorious for praying as for prostitution; and, if you lose the old women, you lose him. He is their prophet, he is their champion, and they are his Houris.

[a First ed. reads: "bad ones. Besides, if you lose the old women you lose the Heir Apparent. He is their champion," &c.]

Canning. I shall experience no difficulty in observing this commandment. In our days, only men who have some unsoundness of conscience and some latent fear, reason against religion ; and those only scoff at it who are pushed back and hurt by it.

Pitt. Canning ! you must have brought this with you from Oxford : the sentiment is not yours even by adoption ; it is too profound for you, and too well expressed. You are brilliant by the multitude of flaws, and not by the clearness nor the quantity of light.

Canning. On second thoughts, I am not quite sure, not perfectly satisfied, that it is, as one may say, altogether mine.

Pitt. This avowal suggests another counsel.

Prevaricate as often as you can defend the prevarication, being close pressed ; but, my dear Canning ! never—I would say— come, come, let me speak it plainly : my dear fellow, never lie.

Canning. How, sir ! what, sir ! pardon me, sir ! But, sir ! do you imagine I ever lied in my lifetime ?

Pitt. The certainty that you never did, makes me apprehensive that you would do it awkwardly, if the salvation of the country (the only case in question) should require it.

Canning. I ought to be satisfied ; and yet my feelings—If you profess that you believe me incapable—

Pitt. What is my profession ? what is my belief ? If a man believes a thing of me, how can I prevent or alter his belief ? or what right have I to be angry at it ? Do not play the fool before me. I sent for you to give you good advice. If you apprehend any danger of being thought what it is impossible any man alive should ever think you, I am ready to swear in your favor as solemnly as I swore at Tooke's [6] trial.

[6 See below note on p. 346. Dundas, or Lord Melville as he afterwards became, had already been attacked by Landor in his commentary on Trotter's Life of Fox. See Mr Colvin's Life of Landor, p. 65. The following epigram of Landor's on Melville's denial of the charge of peculation brought against him is worth quoting :

" God's laws declare
        Thou shalt not swear
By ought in heaven above or earth below.
        ' Upon my honour, Melville ! ' cries,
        He swears and lies.
Does Melville then break God's commandment ?   No ! "]

I am presuming that you will become prime minister : you will then have plenty of folks ready to lie for you ; and it would be as ungentlemanly to lie yourself as to powder your own hair or tie your own shoe-string. I usually had Dundas at my elbow, who never lied but upon his honor, or supported the lie but upon his God. As for the more delicate duty of prevarication, take up those letters of inquiry and condolence, whether you have rubbed the seals off or not in your promptitude to serve me, and lay them carefully by ; and, some years hence, when any one exclaims, " What would Mr Pitt have said ? " bring out one from your pocket, and cry, " This is the last letter his hand, stricken by death, could trace." Another time you may open one from Burke, some thirty years after the supposed receipt of it, and say modestly, " Never but on this momentous occasion did that great man write to me. He foretold, in the true spirit of prophecy, all our difficulties." But remember : do not quote him upon finance, else the House will laugh at you. For Burke was as unable to cast up a tailor's bill as Sheridan is to pay it.

I was about to give you another piece of advice, which on recollection I find to be superfluous. Surely my head sympathizes very powerfully with my stomach, which the physicians tell me is always the case, though not so much with us in office as with the honorable gentlemen out. I was on the point of advising you never to neglect the delivery of long speeches : the minister who makes short speeches enjoys short power. Now, although I have constantly been in the habit of saying a great deal more than was requisite to the elucidation of my subject, for the same reason as hares, when pursued, run over more ground than would bring them into their thickets, I would have avoided it with you, principally to save my breath. You can no more stop when you are speaking than a ball can stop on an inclined plane. You bounce at every impediment, and run on ; often with the very thing in your mouth that the most malicious of your adversaries would cast against you ; and showing what you would conceal, and concealing what you would show.[7] This is of no ill conse-

[7 First ed. reads: " show, as Lady D. did at Lady A.'s., while she was arranging the flowers in her bosom, talking to an admirer and forgetting she was on the stairs until she fell down them. This is," &c.]

quence to a minister : it goes for sincerity and plain-dealing.
It would never have done at Christ-Church or Eton ; for boys
dare detect any thing, and laugh with all their hearts. I
think it was my father who told me (if it was not my father
I forget who it was) that a minister must have two gifts ; the
gift of places, and the gift of the gab. Perfectly well do I
remember his defence of this last expression, which somebody
at table, on another occasion, called a vulgarism. At the end
of the debate on it, he asked the gentleman whether all things
ought not to have names ; whether there was any better for
this ; and whether the learning and ingenuity of the company
could invent one. The importance of the faculty was admirably
exhibited, he remarked, by the word *gift*. He then added, with
a smile, " The alliteration itself has its merit : these short sayings
are always the better for it ; a pop-gun must have a pellet at both
ends."

Ah, Canning ! why have I not remembered my father as perfectly in better things ? I have none of his wit, little of his
wisdom ; but all his experience, all his conduct, were before me
and within my reach. I will not think about him now, when it
would vex and plague me.

Canning. It is better to think of ourselves than of others ;
to consider the present as every thing, the past and future as
nothing.

Pitt. In fact, they are nothing : they do not exist ; what
does not exist, is nothing.

Canning. Supposing me to be prime minister—I am delighted
at finding that the very idea has given a fresh serenity to your
countenance.

Pitt. Because it makes me feel my power more intensely than
ever ; or at least makes me fancy I feel it. By my means, by my
authority, you are to become the successor of a Shelburne ; of a
Rockingham, and a Chatham.

Canning. Sir, I request you to consider—

Pitt. Whether I have the right of alluding to what all have
the right of recollecting, and which right all will exercise. I
wish you as well as if, by some miracle in my favor, I had been
enabled to beget you : that which I hope to do is hardly less
miraculous ; and, if I did not bring to my mind what you are, I

should not feel what I am. Do not you partake of the sentiment? Would it be any great marvel or great matter, if the
descendant of some ancient family stepped up to the summit of
power, even with clean boots on? You must take many steps,
and some very indirect ones; all which will only raise you in
your own esteem, if you think like a politician.

You are prone to be confident and overweening. Be cautious
not to treat Parliament as you may fancy it deserves, and not to
believe that you have bought votes when you have paid the
money for them.

Canning. Why, sir?

Pitt. Because it will be expected of you, in addition, to
speak for a given space of time. The people must be made to
believe that their representatives are *persuaded;* and a few plain
words are never thought capable of effecting this. Your zeal and
anxiety to leave no scruple on the mind of any reasonable man
must be demonstrated by protestations and explanations; and
your hatred of those who obscure the glory of England, in their
attempts to throw impediments in your way, must burst forth
vehemently, and stalk abroad, and now and then put on a suit
that smells of gunpowder.

Canning. I have no objection to that.

Pitt. It saves many arguments, and stops more; and, in short,
is the only comprehensible kind of *political economy.*

Whenever the liberty or restriction of the press is in debate,
you will do wisely to sport a few touches of wit, or to draw out
a few sentences of declamation on blasphemy and blasphemers.
I have observed, by the countenances of country gentlemen, that
there is something horrifying in the sound of the word,—something that commands silence.

Canning. I do not well understand the meaning of it.

Pitt. Why should you? Are you to understand the meaning
of every thing you talk about! If you do, you will not be
thought deep. Be fluent, and your audience will be over head
and ears in love with you. Never stop short, and you will never
be doubted. To be out of breath is the only sign of weakness
that is generally understood in a chancellor of the exchequer.
The bets, in that case, are instantly against him, and the sounder
in wind carries off the king's plate.

Canning. I am aware that to talk solemnly of blasphemy gives a man great weight at the time, and leaves it with him. But if a dissenter or a lawyer should ask me for a definition of a blasphemer?

Pitt. Wish the lawyer more prudence, and the dissenter more grace. Appeal to our forefathers.

Canning. To which of them? The elder would call the younger so, and the younger the elder.

Pitt. Idiots! but go on.

Canning. In our own days the Lutheran denounces the Unitarian for it; *he* retorts the denunciation. The Catholic comes between, to reconcile and reclaim them. At first, he simmers; then, he bubbles and boils; at last, inflamed with charity, he damns them both. "To you, adopted heir of the Devil and Perdition," says he to the believer in God's unity, "it would be folly and impiety to listen a moment longer. And you, idle hair-splitter, are ignorant, or pretend to be, that transubstantiation rests upon the same authority as trinitarianism. The one doctrine shocks the senses, the other shocks the reason; both require to be shocked, that faith may be settled."

"Very like your Saint Augustin," interposes the Unitarian: "he should have written this. When Faith enters the school-room, Reason must not whisper; if she might, she would say, perhaps, the question is, whether the senses or arithmetic be the most liable to error."

"Sir! sir!" cries again the Catholic, "you have no right to bring any question into the house of God without his leave, nor to push your sharp stick against the bellies of his sheep, making them shove one another and break the fold."

Pitt. Do not run wild in this way, retailing the merriment of your Oxford doctors in their snug parties. Such, I am sure, it must be: for you have not had time to read any thing since you left Eton; you think but little, and that little but upon yourself; nor has indeed the wing of your wit either such a strength of bone in it, or such a vividness of plumage.

Canning. I don't know that. I must confess, however, I drew a good deal both of my wit and my divinity from our doctors, when they had risen twice or thrice from the bottle, and turned their backs on us from the corner of the room.

Pitt. I hope you will be rather more retentive, and remember at what time you are to lament, as well as at what time you are to joke and banter. On these occasions, lower your voice, assume an air of disdain or pity, bless God that, such is the peculiar happiness of our most favored country, every man may enjoy his opinion in security and peace.

Canning. But some, I shall be reminded, have been forced to enjoy it in solitude and prison.

Pitt. Never push an argument or a remark too far ; and take care to have a fellow behind you who knows when to cry *question! question!* As for reminding, those only whom you forget will remind you of any thing. Others will give you full credit for the wisdom of all your plans, the aptness of all your replies, the vivacity of all your witticisms, and the rectitude of all your intentions.

Canning. Unless it should fatigue you, sir, will you open your views of domestic polity a little wider before me ?

Pitt. Willingly. Never choose colleagues for friendship or wisdom.[8] If friends, they will be importunate ; if wise, they may be rivals. Choose them for two other things quite different : for tractability and connections. A few men of business, quite enough for you, may be picked up any where on the roadside. Be particular in selecting for all places and employments the handsomest young men, and those who have the handsomest wives, mothers, and sisters. Every one of these brings a large party with him ; and it rarely happens that any such is formidable for mental prowess. The man who can bring you three votes is preferable to him who can bring you thrice your own quantity of wisdom. For, although in private life we may profit much by the acquisition of so much more of it than we had ourselves, yet in public we know not what to do with it. Often it stands in

[8 " Lord Mulgrave was named by Mr Pitt Secretary of State for Foreign Affairs, a post which, as some persons thought, would overtask his mental powers. Shortly afterwards Lord Mulgrave came one morning to breakfast with Mr Pitt, and desiring to eat an egg, could find on the table only a broken egg-spoon. 'How can Pitt have such a spoon as this?' he asked of Lady Hester. 'Don't you know,' answered the lively lady, 'have you not yet discovered that Mr Pitt sometimes uses very slight and weak instruments to effect his ends?'"—Stanhope, " Life of Pitt," iv., 87.]

our way; often it hides us; sometimes we are oppressed by it. Oppose in all elections the man, whatever may be his party or principles, who is superior to yourself in attainments, particularly in ratiocination and eloquence. Bring forward, when places are found for all the men of rank who present themselves, those who believe they resemble you: young declaimers, young poets, young critics, young satirists, young journalists, young magazine-men, and young lampooners and libellers; that is, those among them who have never been more than ducked and cudgelled. Every soul of them will hope to succeed you by adoption.

My father made this remark,* in his florid way. When an insect dips into the surface of a stream, it forms a circle round it, which catches a quick radiance from the sun or moon, while the stiller water on every side flows without any; in like manner, a small politician may attract the notice of the king or people, by putting into motion the pliant element about him; while quieter men pass utterly away, leaving not even this weak impression, this momentary sparkle. On which principle Dundas used to say, "Keep shoving, keep shoving!" I do not know whether the injunction was taken by all his acquaintance in the manner and in the direction he intended.

A great deal has been spoken, in the House and out of the House, on parliamentary reform.

Canning. I have repeatedly said that without it there is no salvation for the country: this is embarrassing.

Pitt. Not at all: oppose it; say you have changed your mind,—let that serve for your reason; and do not stumble upon worse by running against an adversary. You will find the country going on just as it has gone on.

Canning. Bad enough, God knows!

Pitt. But only for the country. People will see that the fields and the cattle, the streets and the inhabitants, look as usual. The houses stand, the chimneys smoke, the pavements hold together: this will make them wonder at your genius in keeping them up, after all the prophecies they have heard about their going down. Men draw their ideas from sight and hearing. They do not know that the ruin of a nation is in its probity, its

* Pitt's father never made it; but it was necessary to attribute it to some other person than Pitt himself.

confidence, its comforts. While they see every day the magnificent equipages of contractors **and** brokers, read of sumptuous dinners given by cabinet-ministers and army **agents,** and are invited to golden speculations in the East and in the **West,** they fancy there is **an** abundance of prosperity and wealth ; **whereas,** in fact, it is in these very places that wealth **and** prosperity **are shut** up, accumulated, and devoured.

I deferred from session to session a **reform in Parliament ;** because, having sworn to promote it by all the means in my power, I did not wish to seem perjured to the people. **In** the affair of Maidstone, nobody could **prove** me so : I only swore I had forgotten what nobody but myself could swear that I remembered.[9] It was evident to the whole world that I was a perjured man ; **it was equally** that I was a powerful **one :** and **the** same nation **which would have** sent another **to the** pillory, sent **me to the Privy** Council. **It** is inconceivable to you what pleasure I **felt** in committing it, when **I reflected** on the difference it proved between me and people in general. But beware of fancying you resemble **me.** My father's crutch was my sceptre, and it will fall **into the** grave with **me. There** is no bequeathing **or** devising this part of the inheritance. **I** improved it **not a little.** My adherents **at** Maidstone thought my father would have hesitated **to forget so bravely.** Appearances were against me. **The** main object **of** my early life, what I had repeated every day, what brought **me into** credit and into power, was unlikely to escape my memory in **an** instant ; and in the midst of those who at that time had surrounded me, applauded me, and followed me. **Yet** bishops and chancellors will **drink to me, after my** death, as the most honest man that ever lived.

[9 Pitt was summoned as a witness **for** the defence **at** Horne Tooke's trial in 1794. He was asked if he remembered a meeting held **at** the Thatched House Tavern in 1782, **where** he recommended that an en-**deavour** should be made to-bring **public** opinion to bear **upon** the House **of Commons** on the question of Reform. He answered **that** he could not **charge** his memory, but that his " general recollection was that it was the **sense of** that meeting that means should be taken during the summer to recommend petitions **to** Parliament . . . with a view to Reform." Probably Landor has confused the two trials in his memory. First ed. reads : " remembered ; certainly all appearances were " &c. (11 lines below).]

Canning. What! even when they can get nothing and want nothing from you?

Pitt. They want from me more than you are aware of: they want my example to stand upon. They will take their aim against our country from behind my statue.

Canning. She has fleshier parts about her than the heel, and their old snags will stick tight in them till they rattle in the coffin.

Pitt. Do not disturb them. You may give over your dalliance with' reform whenever you are tired of it. You did not begin as a states-*man* but as a states-*boy :* you are under me ; and you cannot act more wisely than by telling folks that I had seen my error in the latter part of my life.

Canning. Perhaps they will not believe me.

Pitt. Likely enough ! but courtesy and interest will require their acquiescence, and they will act as if they did. The noisiest. of the opposition are the lawyers ; partly from rudeness, partly from rapacity. Lay it down as a rule for your conduct, that the most honest one in Parliament is as indifferent about his party as about his brief: whoever offers him his fee has him. Of these there is hardly an individual who had any more of a qualification than you or I had ; yet they assume it, as well as we. Is there in this no fallacy, no fraud ? Some of them were so wretchedly poor that a borrowed watch-key hung from a broken shoestring at their tattered fob ; and, when they could obtain on credit a yard of damaged muslin for their noses, they begged a pinch of snuff at the next box they saw open, and sneezed that they might reasonably display their acquisition.

Canning. I wonder that these people should cry out so loudly for a fairer representation.

Pitt. Some have really the vanity to believe that they would be chosen, and might choose their colleagues ; others follow orders ; the greater part wish no such thing, and, if they thought it likely to succeed, would never call for it. The fact is this : the most honest and independent members of Parliament are elected by the rotten boroughs. They pay down their own money, and give their own votes : they are not subservient to the aristocracy nor to the treasury. The same cannot be said on any other description of members. I never ventured to make such a remark in Parliament. The people would be alarmed and struck with horror, if you clearly showed that the very best part of their representation is founded on nothing sounder than on rank corruption. Perhaps I am imprudent in suggesting the fact to you, knowing your *diabetes* of mind, and having found that your tongue is as easily set in motion, and as unconsciously, as the head of a mandarin on the chimney-piece at an inn.

Cease to be speculative.

Canning. We cease to be speculative when we touch the object.

Pitt. It is then unnecessary to remind you that you want only a numerical majority. Talents count for talents ; respectability for respectability. The veriest fag that Dundas ever breeched for the South gives as efficient a vote as a Romilly or a Newport.

In the beginning of my career as minister, I sometimes wished that I could have become so and have been consistent. I have since found that inconsistency is taken for a proof of greatness in a politician. "He knows how to manage men ; he sees what the times require ; his great mind bends majestically to the impulse of the world." These things are said, or will be. Certain it is, when a robe is blown out by the wind, showing now the outer side, now the inner, then one color, then another, it seems the more capacious, and the richer.

If at any time you are induced by policy, or impelled by nature, to commit an action more ungenerous or more dishonest than usual ; if at any time you shall have brought the country into worse disgrace or under more imminent danger,—talk and look bravely ; swear, threaten, bluster ; be witty, be pious ; sneer, scoff ; look infirm, look gouty ; appeal to immortal God that you desire to remain in office so long only as you can be beneficial to your king and country ; that, however, at such a time as the present, you should be reluctant to leave the most flourishing of nations a prey to the wild passions of insatiate demagogues ; and that nothing but the commands of your venerable sovereign, and the unequivocal voice of the people that recommended you to his notice, shall ever make you desert the station to which the hand of Providence conducted you. They have keen eyes who can see through all these words : I have never found any such, and have tried thousands. The man who possesses them may read [10] Swedenborg and Kant while he is being tossed in a blanket.

Above all things, keep your friends and dependants in good humor and good condition. If they lose flesh, you lose people's confidence. My cook, two summers ago, led me to this reflection at Walmer. Finding him in the court-yard, and observing that, however round and rosy, he looked melancholy, and struck his hips with his fists very frequently, as he walked along, I called to him, and, when he turned round, inquired of him what had happened to discompose him. He answered that Sam Spack the butcher had failed.

"Well, what then?" said I, "unless you mean that his creditors may come upon me for the last two years' bill?" He shook his head, and told me that he had lent Sam Spack all he was worth, a good five hundred pounds. "The greater fool you!" replied I. "Why, sir!" said he, opening his hand to show the clearness of his demonstration, "who would not have lent him any thing, when he swore and ate like the devil, and drank as if he was in hell, and his dog was fatter than the best calf in Kent?"

It occurs to me that I owe this unfortunate cook several years' wages. Write down his name, William Ruffhead. You must do something to help him. A diversion on the coast of France would be sufficient; order one for him. In six months he may fairly pocket his quiet twenty thousands, and have his paltry three guineas a day for life. Write above the name, "deputy commissary." Ruffhead is so honest a creature, he will only be a dogfish in a shoal of sharks.

Never consent to any reduction in the national expenditure. Consider what is voted by Parliament for public services as your own property. The largest estate in England would go but a little way in procuring you partizans and adherents: these loosely counted millions purchase them. I have smiled when people, in the simplicity of their hearts, applauded me for neglecting the aggrandizement of my fortune. Every rood of land in the British dominions has a mine beneath it, out of which, by a vote of Parliament, I oblige the proprietor to extract as much as I

[10] First ed. reads: "read Adam Smith and Emmanuel Kent, while," &c.]

want, as often as I will. From every tobacco-pipe in England a dependant of mine takes a whiff ; from every salt-vase, a spoonful. I have given more to my family than is possessed by those of Tamerlane and Aurungzebe ; and I distribute to the amount of fifty millions a year in the manner I deem convenient. What is any man's private purse other than that into which he can put his hand at his option ? Neither my pocket nor my house, neither the bank nor the treasury, neither London nor Westminster, neither England nor Europe, are capacious enough for mine : it swings between the Indies, and sweeps the whole ocean.

Canning. I am aware of it. You spend only what you have time and opportunity for spending. No man gives better dinners; few better wine—

Pitt. Canning! Canning! Canning! always blundering into some coarse compliment !

Reminding me of wine, you remind me of my death, and the cause of it. To spite the French and Bonaparte, I would not drink claret : Madeira was too heating ; hock was too light and acid for me.

Canning. Seltzer-water takes off this effect, the Dean of Christ-church tells me.

Pitt. It might have made my speeches windier than was expedient ; and I declined to bring into action a steam-engine of such power, with Mr Speaker in front and the treasury-bench in rear of me. The detestable beverage of Oporto is now burning my entrails.

Canning. Beverage fit for the condemned.

Pitt. If condemned for poisoning.

As you must return to London in the morning, and as I may not be disposed or able to talk much at another time, what remains to be said I will say now.

Never be persuaded to compose a mixed administration of Whigs and Tories ; for, as you cannot please them equally, each will plot eternally to supplant you by some leader of its party.[11]

Employ men of less knowledge and perspicacity than yourself, if you can find them. Do not let any stand too close or

<hr>

[11 First ed. reads: " party. Wellesley has a great deal more acuteness,

too much above ; because in both positions they may look down into your shallows, and see the weeds, at the bottom. Authors may be engaged by you : but never pamper them ; keep them in wind and tractability by hard work. Many of them are trusty while they are needed ; enrich them only with promised lands, enjoying the most extensive prospect and most favorable exposure. For my part, I little respect any living author. The only one, ancient or modern, I ever read with attention, is Bolingbroke, who was recommended to me for a model. His principles, his heart, his style, have formed mine exclusively. Every thing sits easy upon him. Mostly I like him because he supersedes inquiry,—— the thing best to do and to inculcate. We should have been exterminated long ago, if the House of Commons had not thought so, and had not voted us a Bill of Indemnity ; which I was certain I could obtain as often as I should find it neces-sary, be the occasion what it might. Neither free governments nor arbitrary have such security : ours is constituted for evasion. I hope nobody may ever call me the *Pilot of the Escape-boat.* In Turkey, I should have been strangled ; in Algiers, I should have been impaled ; in America, I should have mounted the gallows in the market-place ; in Sweden, I should have been pistoled at a public dinner or court-ball : in England, I am ex-tolled above my father.

Ah, Canning ! how delighted, how exultant was I, when I first heard this acclamation ! When I last heard it, how sorrowful ! how depressed ! He was always thwarted, and always succeeded : I was always seconded, and always failed. He left the country

a great deal more perspicuity than you. **Employ him at** a distance, and gratify his inclination for pleasure and expense. Among the whigs Lord Henry Petty has conciliated many friends by his good manners, his variety of information, his facility of communicating it, and his sincerity. He speaks well ; and though you have the credit of being a good scholar, he is known to be a better. These are the only men in both houses worth noticing ; beware of them. Lord Henry would be the worse neighbour to you from the memory of his father who was liberal in his encourage-ment to the learned, and indeed to men of genius and science in every department. I am afraid the son partakes of this feeling, which will draw many about him, and obtain him friends and supporters even among those who have no literary claims and no want of patronage. For my part I have no respect for any living author or living genius. The only one," &c. (10 lines below).]

flourishing; I leave it impoverished, exhausted, **ruined.** He left many able statesmen ; I leave *you.*

Excuse me : dying men are destined to **feel and** privileged **to** say unpleasant things.

Good-night! I retire to rest.

XVI. ARCHBISHOP BOULTER AND PHILIP SAVAGE.*

Boulter. Heartily **glad am I to** see you, **my** brother, if, in **these** times of calamity **and** desolation, such a sentiment may be expressed or felt. My **wife** is impatient to embrace her sister.

---

* Boulter, primate of Ireland, **and** president **of the** council, saved that kingdom from pestilence and famine in the year 1729, by supplying the poor with bread, medicines, attendance, and every possible comfort and accommodation. Again in 1740 and 1741 two hundred and fifty thousand were fed, twice a day, *principally at his expense,* as we find in *La Biographie Universelle,*—an authority the least liable to suspicion. He built hospitals at Drogheda and Armagh, and endowed them richly. No private man, in any age or country, has contributed so largely to relieve the sufferings of his fellow-creatures; to which object he and his wife devoted their ample fortunes, both during their lives and after their decease.

Boulter was certainly the most disinterested, the most humane, the **most** beneficent man **that** ever guided the councils of Ireland. I am not certain **that I** should have thought of offering this tribute **to** his memory, if his connection with my family by his marriage had not often reminded me of him ; for we do not always bear in mind what is due to others, unless there is something at home to stimulate the recollection.

Philip Savage, Chancellor of the Exchequer, was likewise so irreproachable, that even Swift, the reviler of Somers, could find in him no motive for satire and no room for discontent. [See Lecky's History of England during the Eighteenth Century, vol. ii., 219, for an account of Boulter's charities during the famine of 1729; on page 417 of the same volume is the following passage. "The letters of Primate Boulter, who led the English party, furnish abundant evidence of this antagonism. 'The only way to keep things quiet here,' he wrote, 'is by filling the great places with the natives of England.' 'I must request your grace,' he wrote to the Duke of Newcastle, 'that you would use your influence to

Savage. My lord primate, I did not venture to bring her with me from Dublin, wishing to wait until I had explored the road, and had experienced the temper of the people.

Boulter. I much regret her absence, and yet more the cause of it; let me hope, however, that nothing unexpectedly unpleasant has occurred to you in your journey hither.

Savage. I came on horseback, attended by one servant. Had I been prudent, he would not have worn his livery; for hardly any object is more offensive to the poor, in seasons of distress, than a servant in livery, spruce and at his ease. They attach to it the idea of idleness and comfort, which they contrast with their own hard labor and its ill requital.

Two miles from Armagh, we were met by a multitude of work-people; they asked my groom who I was; he told them my name, and, perhaps in the pride of his heart, my office. Happily they never had heard of the one or the other. They then enclosed me, and insisted on knowing whether I came with orders from the castle to fire upon them, as had been threatened some days before.

"For what? my honest friends!" cried I.

"For wanting bread and asking it," was the answer that ran from mouth to mouth, frequently repeated, and deepening at every repetition, till hoarseness and weakness made it drop and cease. I then assured them that no such orders were given, or would ever be; and that the king and government were deeply afflicted at their condition, which however was only temporary.

Upon this there came forward one from among them; and, laying his hand upon the mane of my horse, he laughed till he

have none but Englishmen put into the great places here for the future.' . . . He watched with an eager cat-like vigilance every sign of decaying health, that made it probable that some great man would soon drop from his post, and sometimes even before the catastrophe, sprang forward to secure the place for an Englishman. Few matters indeed occupy a larger place in his letters." For some amusing verses on Boulter, see Dr S. Madden's "Boulter's monument. A Panegyrical poem sacred to the memory of that great and excellent prelate and patriot the most Reverend Dr Hugh Boulter," etc. The following are perhaps the happiest lines—

"Ha! mark! what gleam is this which paints the air? The blue serene expands! Is Boulter there?"

(Imag. Convers., iv., 1829. Works, i., 1846. Works, iii., 1876.)]

staggered. I looked at him in amaze. When he had recovered himself a little from his transport, he said, " I hope you are honest, my friend! for you talk like a fool, which in people of your sort is a token of it, though sometimes one no weightier than Will Wood's for a halfpenny. [1] But prythee now, my jewel, how can you in your conscience take upon yourself to say, that the king and his ministers care a flea's rotten tooth whether or not we crack with emptiness and thirst, so long as our arms fill their bellies, and drive away troublesome neighbors while they are napping afterward? Deeply afflicted! is it deeply afflicted! O' my soul, one would think there was as much pleasure in deep affliction as in deep drinking, or even more: for many have washed away their lands with claret, and have then given over drinking; but where is the good fellow that has done any thing in this quarter by way of raising his head above such a deep affliction! Has the king or his lord-lieutenant sent us the value of a mangy sow's bristle? I may be mistaken; but I am apt to think that, shallow as we are bound to believe we are in other things, our affliction is as deep as theirs, or near upon it; and yet we never said a word about the matter. We only said we were naked and starving, and quitted our cabins that we may leave to our fathers and mothers our own beds to die on, and that we may hear no longer the cries of our wives and little ones, which, let me tell you, are very different in those who are famishing from any we ever heard before. Deeply afflicted! Now afore God! what miseries have they suffered, or have they seen? I hear of rich people in Dublin with such a relish for deep affliction they will give eighteen-pence for a book to read of it."

Partly in hopes of proceeding, and partly in commiseration, I slipped a guinea into the fellow's hand. He took it, and did not thank me; but continuing to hold it, together with my horse's mane, he said, "Come along with me." I thought it prudent to comply. At the distance of about a mile, on the right hand, is the cabin to which I was conducted. A wretched horse was standing half within it and half without, and exhibiting in his belly and ribs the clearest signs of famine and weariness. " Let us hear," said my guide, "what is going on."

I dismounted and stood with him. Looking round about the

[1 For Wood's half-pence, see Swift's Drapier's Letters.]

tenement, I found no article of furniture; for the inhabitant was lying on the floor, covered with his clothes only. Against the wall of the doorway was hanging from a nail a broken tin tobacco-box, kept open by a ring which had formerly been the ornament of a pig's snout. Its more recent service was to make a hole in a piece of paper, on which I read, "Notice to quit."

There was a priest in the cabin, who spoke, as nearly as I can recollect, these words: "You are the only Catholic in the parish, and ought to set an example to the rest of them about you."

"Father!" said a weak voice, "you told me I might go to the archbishop's when I grew stouter, and get what I could; it being the spoil of an enemy. Such was my hunger on first recovering from the fever, and the worse perhaps from having had nothing to eat for a couple of days, that, when the servants gave me a basin of broth, I swallowed it. None of them had the charity to warn me that it was a piece of beef which was lying at the bottom, or to tell me that (for what they knew) it might be a turnip; so, without thinking at all about it, I just let it take its own way! There was no more of it than the size of a good potato; a healthy man would have made but four bites of it; I had a bitch that would have swallowed it at one, when she had whelps. I have seen a man who would make so little of it, he would let his wife eat it all, at a meal or two: it was next to nothing. In my mind, I have a doubt whether, as there might be some fever left upon me, it was not rather the show of beef rising out of the broth than real beef. For sure enough I might mistake, as I might in thinking I was well again when I had still the fever; which could scarcely come back upon me for eating, when it had come upon me the week before for not eating. Howsoever, I went home and laid myself down and slept, and dreamed of angels with ladles of soup in their hands, some looking ugly enough, and others laughing, and one of them led that very horse of yours into the cabin: I should know him again anywhere. We looked in each other's face for ten minutes; then down he threw himself on me, as though I were no better than ling and fern. There he would have stayed, I warrant, till sunrise, if it had not been Sunday morning."

"How!" cried the priest. "What then! all this iniquity

was committed upon the Saturday!" "This day week," answered the sick man, humbled as much, I suspect, by blundering into the confession, as he was by the reproof.

"And now, by my soul! our Lady calls you to an account, sinner!" said the priest, angrily. "I would not wonder if the arch-heretic you call archbishop gave out so many thousand bowls of soup a day, for the sake of drowning that soul of yours, swiller and swine! Hither have I been riding a matter of thirteen miles, to see that every thing is going on as it ought, and not an ounce of oatmeal or a potato in the house."

The poor inhabitant of the cabin sighed aloud. My conductor strode softly toward the priest, and, twitching him by the sleeve, asked him softly what he thought of the man's health. The poor creature heard the question, and much more distinctly the answer, which was, that he could not live out another day. He requested the holy man to hear his confession. The most grievous part of it had been made already: but now the piece of beef had its real size and weight given to it; he had eaten it with pleasure, with knowledge; he had gone to bed upon it; he had tried to sleep; he had slept; he had said no more *ave-marias* than ordinarily. A soul laboring under such a mountain of sin required (God knows how many) masses for its purgation and acquittance.

"Be aisy!" said my conductor. "He shall sup with our blessed Lord in Paradise by seven o'clock to-morrow night, if masses can mash potatoes, or there is buttermilk above."

On saying this, he pulled open the priest's hand, slapped it with some violence, left the guinea in it, and wished me a pleasant ride. I could not bear to let him quit me so abruptly, glad as I should have been before at his departure. I asked him whether the dying man was his relative. He said, "No." I wished to replace his generosity somewhat more largely.

"Sir!" said he, "I have enough for several days yet; when it is gone, the archbishop will give me what he gives the rest. As for that massmonger, he shall eat this rasher of bacon with me this blessed night, or I'll be damned." So saying, he drew a thin slice from his pocket, neither wrapped in paper nor in bread.

Boulter. I hope soon to find out this worthy man, the warmth of whose heart may well atone for that of his expressions ; but, lest he should be too urgent in his invitation, I will immediately send one to my brother clergyman, entreating him to dine with us. We have always fish on Fridays and Saturdays from the lake near us, in case we may be favored by any Roman Catholic visitor.

This slight displeasure is, I hope, the only one you have met with.

Philip Savage. I must confess it grieved me to see the sheriff's officers erecting the gallows at the entrance of the city : it must exasperate the populace. Men in the extremity of suffering lose sooner the sense of fear than the excitability to indignation : the people of Ireland have endured enough already.

Boulter. Indeed have they. It was thought the excess of hardheartedness, when men asked for bread, to give a stone ; but better a stone than a halter.

Philip Savage. As our country-gentlemen, in this part of Ireland particularly, are rather worse than semi-barbarous, and hear nothing from their cradles but threats and defiance, they may deem it requisite and becoming to erect this formidable signal of regular government against the advances of insurrection.

Boulter. More are made insurgents by firing on them than by feeding them ; and men are more dangerous in the field than in the kitchen.

Philip Savage. In critical times, such as these, some coercion and some intimidation may be necessary. We must be vigilant and resolute against the ill-intentioned.

Boulter. My dear brother! would it not be wiser to give other intentions to the ill-intentioned ? Cruelty is no more the cure of crimes than it is the cure of sufferings : compassion, in the first instance, is good for both. I have known it bring compunction when nothing else would. I forbear to enlarge on the enormous inhumanity of inflicting the punishment of death for small offences ; yet I must remind you to ask yourself, whether, in your belief, ten years ever elapsed in Ireland, or even in England, without some capital sentence wrongfully pronounced. If this be the case, and most men think it is, does it not occur to you that such a penalty should for ever be expunged from our statute-book? Severe as another may be, reparation of some kind may be made, on the detection of its injustice. But what reparation can reach the dead from the living? What reparation can even reach the judge who condemned him? for he too must be almost as much a sufferer. In vain will the jurymen split and subdivide the responsibility; in vain will they lament that nothing now can mitigate the verdict. Release, then, the innocent from this long suffering, if you will not release the guilty from a shorter. What can be expected from the humanity of men, habituated to see death inflicted on their fellow-men, for offences which scarcely bring an inconvenience on the prosecutor? And what can be expected from the judgment of those above them, who denounce vengeance to preserve peace, and take away life to show respect for property? More ferocity hath issued from under English scarlet than from under American ochre. Violent resentments are the natural propensities of untamed man: the protection of our property does not require them.

Philip Savage. The legislator and judge feel none.

Boulter. Why then imitate them in voice and action? Is there any thing lovely or dignified in such an imitation?

Philip Savage. Our judges in these days are not often guilty of the like unseemliness, which was common fifty years ago.

Boulter. Certainly they are less boisterous and blustering than under the first James and the first Charles, and have wiped away much of that rudeness and effrontery which is chastened in other professions by civiller company and more salutary awe: nevertheless, at the commencement of the disturbances which this famine brought about, many poor wretches were condemned to death, after much intemperate language from the judges, who declined to present petitions on their behalf to the lord-lieutenant, as I told you in my letter. Probably they are little pleased that his flexibility of temper hath yielded to our remonstrances and authority. Painful would be my situation as president of the council, and yours as chancellor of the exchequer, if such people as are usually sent hither for lords-lieutenant were as refractory as they are remiss. I trust it will ever be found convenient to appoint men of clemency to the first station, and that I shall never be forced to exercise on them the powers entrusted to me of coercion and control.

It is well when people can believe that their misfortunes are temporary. How can we apply such a term to pestilence and famine ?

Philip Savage. Surely the violence of the evil eats away the substance of it speedily. Pestilence and famine are, and always have been, temporary and brief.

Boulter. Temporary they are, indeed : brief are they, very brief. But why? because life is so under them. To the world they are extremely short ; but can we say they are short to him who bears them? And of such there are thousands, tens of thousands, in this most afflicted, most neglected country. The whole of a life, be it what it may be, is not inconsiderable to him who leaves it ; any more than the whole of a property, be it but an acre, is inconsiderable to him who possesses it. Whether want and wretchedness last for a month or for half a century, if they last as long as the sufferer, they are to him of very long duration. Let us try, then, rather to remove the evils of Ireland, than to persuade those who undergo them that there are none. For, if they could be thus persuaded, we should have brutalized them first to such a degree as would render them more dangerous than they were in the reigns of Elizabeth or Charles.

There will never be a want of money, or a want of confidence, in any well-governed State that has been long at peace, and without the danger of its interruption. But a want of the necessaries of life, in peasants or artisans, when the seasons have been favorable, is a certain sign of defect in the constitution, or of criminality in the administration. It may not be advisable or safe to tell every one this truth : yet it is needful to inculcate it on the minds of governors, and to repeat it until they find the remedy ; else the people, one day or other, will send those out to look for it who may trample down more in the search than suits good husbandry.

God be praised ! we have no such exclamation to make as that of Ecclesiastes : " Woe to thee, O land ! whose king is a child,"—an evil that may afflict a land under the same king, for years indefinite. Our gracious sovereign, ever mindful of his humble origin, and ever grateful to the people who raised him from it to the most exalted throne in the universe,—a throne hung round with the trophies of Cressy, Agincourt, Poitiers, and Blenheim,—has little inclination to imitate the ruinous pride of Louis the Fourteenth ; to expend his revenues, much less those of his people, in the excavation of rivers, the elevation of mountains, and the transplantation of Asia, with all her gauds and vanities, under the gilded domes of fairy palaces.

Philip Savage. Versailles is a monument, raised by the king of one country for the benefit of kings in all others ; warning each in successive generations not to exhaust the labor and patience of his people, by the indulgence of his profusion and sensuality.

Boulter. Let us hope, my brother, that the poverty this structure has entailed on the French may not hereafter serve for the foundation of more extensive evils, and exacerbate a heartless race, ever disposed to wanton cruelties, until they at last strike down the virtuous for standing too near, and for warning them where their blows should fall. In which case they will become even worse slaves than they are, from the beating they must sooner or later undergo.

If I could leave the country in its present state, and if I possessed the same advantage of daily access to the king as when I attended him from Germany, I should take the liberty of representing to him, that his own moderation of expenditure might well be copied in the public, and that some offices and some pensions in this country might be lopped off, without national dishonor or popular discontent.

Philip Savage. There has always been an outcry against places and pensions, whether the country was flourishing or otherwise. We may lop until we cut our fingers and disable ourselves for harder work. Surely a man of your grace's discernment would look well to it first, and remember, that, where the sun is let in, the wind too may let in itself.

Boulter. A want of caution is not among my defects ; nor is an unsteady deference to the clamors of the multitude. It is necessary to ask sometimes even well-dressed men, have not the judges places ? is not every office of trust a place ? and can any government be conducted without its functionaries ? I do not follow the public cry, nor run before it.

Pensions, too, occasionally are just and requisite. What man of either party will deny, that a Marlborough and a Peterborough deserved such a token of esteem from the country they served so gloriously? or that the payment of even a large annuity to such illustrious men is not in the end the best economy? These rewards stimulate exertion and create merit. They likewise display to other nations our justice, our generosity, our power, our wealth, and are the best monuments we can erect to Victory. Do not be alarmed lest the people should insist on too rigorous a defalcation. The British people, and still more the Irish, would resent, as a private wrong, the tearing one leaf from the brow of a brave defender. On the contrary, to say nothing of clerks and commissaries, the grant of pensions to ambassadors and envoys, who cannot act from their own judgment, and who only execute the orders of others, without the necessity of genius, of learning, of discernment, or of courage, is superfluous to a nation in its prosperity, and insulting to one in its distress. They are always chosen out of private friendship; and their stipends, while they act, are only presents made to them by their patrons. To pay them afterward for having taken the trouble to receive these presents, is less needful than to send a Christmas-box to my wig-maker, because I had preferred him already, and had paid him handsomely for making me a wig at midsummer. Should we not think him a foolish man if he expected it, and an impudent one if he asked it?

We are so fortunate as to have few pensions to discharge, and little debt: nevertheless, in times disastrous like these, when many thousands, I might say millions, are starving, and when persons once in affluence have neither bread nor work, it behooves us, who wish security and respectability to the government, to deduct from waste and riot that which was not given originally for distinguished merit, and which may now save the lives of generations, and scarcely take the garnish off one dish in the second courses of a few.

At my table you will find only ordinary fare; and I hardly know whether I am not sinning while I thank my God that it is plentiful.

XVII.　MAHOMET AND SERGIUS.[1]

Mahomet.　Thou knowest, my dear Sergius, that heretofore the bishops of Rome have conferred and counselled on the necessity of depriving the priesthood of marriage, that the brethren may be devoted to them entirely, and insulated from the people.

Sergius.　Such a scheme indeed hath been agitated more than once ; yet I suspect it can never be carried into execution. If the Roman pontiff should succeed in his intentions,[2] would the Greek follow ?

Mahomet.　There hath always been jealousy between them, of each other's weight and authority.

Sergius.　It began about dresses and jewels, then flamed forth again on the comparative number of rich widows and holy virgins in the convents of East and West. As beauty and embroidery, music and mutilation, are matters of taste and opinion, they looked for something to split upon decorously. An iota[3] served ; this iota clove many thousand skulls, and found nothing. Latterly they have fought upon surer ground, over the relics of confessors and martyrs, and, in time of truce, have bidden high against each other for the best odor of sanctity any Jew or Arab would bring them.

[1 On Sergius, see Landor's note at end of Conversation; his view of Mahomet's character is of course entirely unhistoric. It is doubtful whether Mahomet himself ever clearly claimed to have accomplished miracles at all. Gibbon points out, ix., 273 (ed. 1819) that the cleaving of the moon referred to in the Conversation is founded upon a passage in the Koran, which may be translated: " Now had the hour come and the moon was severed in twain," *i.e.*, it was half-moon. (Imag. Convers., iv., 1829. Works, i., 1846. Works, iii., 1876.)]

[2 First ed. reads: " intentions, the Greek would follow. *Mahomet*," &c.]

[3 The Catholic church from the date of the Nicene Synod has maintained the consubstantiality of the Son with the Father, declaring that both are of the same substance ; a doctrine expressed by the word homoousion. One of the opposing sects of Arians, contending that the substance was not the same but only similar, chose to express their views by the word " homoiousion," inserting into the orthodoxy of the Catholics a destructive i.]

Mahomet. I myself keep in reserve the thigh-bone of an honest jade of a mule ; the fellow of which thigh-bone is inclosed in a glass case at Ancona, as belonging to Saint Eufemia. My saint was rather a wincing one. I should not have liked to put my muzzle quite so near her crupper, in her state of probation, as the faithful do now she is canonised. I introduced oil of amomum, a perfume unknown among the Italians, into both bones. The first, like a fool, I sold for three hundred gold pieces : the remaining one shall bring me, with God's help, five hundred ; proving its authenticity by identity of odor, and thus confounding the sceptic and scoffer. If men are wilfully blind, let them remain so : they shall fall into the ditch when there is none to help them. In vain does the cresset shine from the tower, if the perverse will run upon the shoals and rocks. In vain does the crier's voice cry "God is Great," if we hang back and budge, and will not lend him even our little finger to try a portion of his strength thereon. But he saith, "I am a sword to the wicked, and a shield to the good, and a mountain-encampment fed with living waters to him and him only who placeth his trust in me." Thus saith the Strong and Merciful, whose name be praised evermore, through his servant, the dust of his feet. "Did I not," saith he, "hide the prophet Jonas three days and three nights in the whale's belly? But my prophet Mahomet, whom I have chosen to be cover and clasp, pumice-stone and thong, to the book of prophecy, hath lain three times three in a locust's."

Sergius. Quiet! quiet! never say that! The Catholics will think either that thou mockest or that thou surpassest their impudence, and will stone thee.

Mahomet. I will preach where there are no stones big enough.

Sergius. They will crucify thee.

Mahomet. I will preach where there are no trees high enough.

Sergius. They will burn thee alive.

Mahomet. I will preach where they shall be burnt alive themselves if they come near me, and without a fagot, a wisp of straw, or a match. Men are very humane in the desert : it is only where there are meadows and cornfields, and young nuns and choristers, that the gadfly of persecution pricks them.

Sergius. Thou talkest reasonably again, dropping in thy phraseology from the third heaven of Orientalism.

Mahomet. Leave me my third heaven: we agreed upon it.

Sergius. We will pick the mule's thigh-bone together.

Mahomet. My mule, I promise thee, Sergius, shall carry both of us the first stage on our journey.

Again to business.

If my introduction is somewhat long, it is only that I may smoothen the path to arrangements of great advantage to thee, unoffered and unpremeditated in any former conversation. Although[4] the Greeks had the earliest and best claim to supremacy, if indeed the Christian dispensation could admit any (which the first Roman bishops denied), the Emperor Mauritius wished the Patriarch of Constantinople to possess it, that something like order might at length be established in his extensive and loose dominions, and that the lust of ecclesiastical power might be controlled by the presence of the imperial. This cost him his life from the pope, who himself did not live long enough to gather the fruits he had engrafted with so skilful and sharp a knife. Popes trip up one another, like children on the icy streets of Cyzicus. Gregory and Sabinian followed in rapid march: then came Bonifacius, who found on the throne Phocas, the murderer of his emperor and patron. Never were two such men so well met: they upheld one another; and Rome from that time forward hath preserved the authority she usurped. She hath always been an auxiliary of the audacious and the unjust, knowing that they pay best and promise most, and that right and equity, peace and honor, want nothing and expect nothing at her hands. Her thunders are composed from chaos; her light, from the fragments of civilization and the flames of war. We will take advantage of the weakness that wickedness leaves behind it, and of the hatred and contempt in which papal ambition is holden through Greece and Asia.

Sergius.[5] I hope the Roman pontiff may at least order the priests to observe celibacy, if he does not subject them to another ceremony, taken, like the greater part of their worship, from the

[4 Cf. p. 167; see also Gibbon's account of Phocas and Gregory's infamous conduct.]

[5 First ed. reads: "*Sergius.* An excellent," &c. (4 lines below).]

ancient rites of Cybele. An excellent regimen for priests! but it would ruin monachism.

Mahomet. So far is the Greek Church from a desire to imitate the Roman, that I am well convinced she would, for contradiction, instantly order both priests and monks to marry. On this principle, in my institutions I am resolved to allow four wives to every man. In order to strengthen the Oriental Church against the Occidental, and that you never may suppose I would take an undue advantage of you, I recommend that you should prove from the Scriptures how every tenth girl belongs to the religious, as clearly as every tenth lamb and wheat-sheaf, and that monks are more religious than priests.

Sergius. Thou canst not prove the former.

Mahomet. Nor thou.

Sergius. No.

Mahomet. Nor both together.

Sergius. I question it.

Mahomet. O thou infidel! the Scriptures contain every thing.

Sergius. I have no mind, friend Mahomet, they should contain this. I will never have ten wives, nor four, nor any; and, if the Œcumenical bishop orders those under his authority to repudiate theirs, certain I am that our Church will exhort and command every priest, and perhaps every monk, to take one.

Mahomet. Well! what harm?

Sergius. Short-sighted mortal! what harm indeed! If she bids us have wives of our own, she will shortly come to such a pass that she will bid us have none *but* our own,—a grievous detriment to the vital interests of the faith.

Mahomet, thou art the heartiest laugher under heaven. Prythee let thy beard cover thy throat again. There now! thy turban has fallen behind thee. Art thou in fits? By my soul, I will lay this thong across thy loins, if thou tossest and screamest in such a manner, to the scandal of the monastery.

Mahomet. Words are magical. The blindest and tenderest young saintling that ever was whelped could not have whined so pathetically, "A grievous detriment to the vital interests of the faith!"

Sergius. There is a time for all things. Now a serious word with thee.

Mahomet. Let me hear it.

Sergius. Brother Pemphix, a worthy priest, hath espoused a beautiful creature. O the charms of such a friendship as mine with Pemphix! I am the confessor of the fair Anatolis. Ah, Mahomet! Mahomet! The delight of authority! The diviner power of persuasion! The glory of hearing the appeal, " Now ought I, sweet Sergius?"

Mahomet. I discover all her beauty at those words.

Sergius. Perish then those words for ever! · Her beauty ought to rest upon my heart, veiled and sacred : no thought should dwell with it, no idea rise from it, but mine.

Mahomet. Is she so very beauteous? Why sighest thou -and maddenest and starest? Is there any thing strange in the question? I never saw her nor heard of her.

Sergius. Anatolis is a star.

Mahomet. Bad!

Sergius. Heaven itself—

Mahomet. Worse and worse. She must be too much for thee.

Sergius. Peace, profane one! Anatolis is a rose—

Mahomet. Pshaw! they all are. God made the rose out of what was left of woman at the creation. The great difference is, we feel the rose's thorns when we gather it; and the other's, when we have had it some time.

Sergius. The gales of Paradise breathe from this opening bud.

Mahomet. Gales never were given for one only.

Sergius. The mild even-tempered Anatolis is the coyest and most difficult young creature ; and Pemphix complained to me about it, a few days after their union :—

" Canst thou do nothing with her, brother Sergius? Try, for the love of God! Rouse thyself! rouse thyself! Be resolute! be brotherly. Meditation is an excellent thing, but man was also made for action."

Mahomet. In the plains of Damascus I myself am fain to take exercise. Many gales of Paradise blow about these gardens, and over the banks of these little streams. We have some

pleasant spots in Arabia, more in Idumea; but he who possesseth
Syria may hold in contempt the possessors of all the earth beside.
Love, and enjoy for ever, Anatolis; retain to thy last breath the
pleasure of discoursing on her in confidence, and of forbidding
thy friend to think about her! Chide him if he mention her;
hate him if he ask nothing concerning her. If he smile, detest
his impudence; if he look grave, abhor his insensibility.

Sergius! mayest thou long do thus! Earth can afford thee,
Heaven can promise thee, nothing more.

Sergius. Yet, Mahomet, on cooler thoughts, dear to me as is
Anatolis, I am not disposed to resign the power and authority[6]
we should participate, and which I am weary of expecting.

Mahomet. Wait but a little while. Every thing is most
promising in Arabia. It is a difficult matter in my country to
persuade the hearers even of our wildest stories that they are but
fiction. Where there is such a thirst for the marvellous, it is
easier to equip a new religion than a new camel. We must be
daring. In spite of thy advice, I am resolved to prove that I
have been up in heaven.

Sergius. Take heed! take heed! they cannot believe that.

Mahomet. They will not believe a word of truth, until they
believe many a falsehood. I must have witnesses.

Sergius. Here lies the difficulty. Let me send to Rome for
them,—indeed, to any part of Italy: it would ruin thee to
purchase them here, the rogues are so exorbitant.

Mahomet. I will have them unbought, pure, sincere, steadfast.
Heat an Arab, and he keeps hot for life. But, my dear Sergius,
thou hast lived thy early days in Rome: art thou not fond of
that city, so full of allurements?

Sergius. I was very fond of it.

Mahomet. Could nothing induce thee to return?

Sergius. Not now: thou knowest the reason.

Mahomet. The patriarchate of Constantinople is unworthy of
thy ambition now the Roman pontiff takes the precedency.

Sergius. He shall take it no longer when I am patriarch.

Mahomet. I should rather like, if convenient to Sergius, to

[6 First ed. reads: "authority, which thou consentedest to obtain for
me, and which," &c.; and (1 line below) 1st ed. reads: "*Mahomet.*
The Patriarch is not dead. Every thing," &c.]

extend my empire **over** the plains of Damascus ; chiefly because
this empire must be extended **by** the sword, **which** is tempered
nowhere **in** such perfection **as** by the waters **of** Abana and
Pharpar.

Sergius. I demur to this.

Mahomet. I would engage to **give thee in exchange the whole**
of Europe.

Sergius. Mahomet, thou art **ambitious.**

Mahomet. To serve my friend ; otherwise, no mortal **was**
ever so far removed from it. I have many other faults ; none,
however, which a friend can suffer from, or ought to see.

Sergius. Although I little doubt that any plausible **new**
religion would subvert the old rottenness that lies accumulated
around **us,** now that people find the priests of Christ assuming **the**
garb **and** language of despots, with **the** temper and trade **of**
executioners, **yet** it may **be the** labor of years to penetrate **with an**
army from the centre of **Arabia into this country.**

Mahomet. Of two **or three at most.** **I have** had visions that
promise me Syria.

Sergius. Mahomet, the **system** I laid **down for thee contains**
no **visions.**

Mahomet. Many spring from it.

Sergius. Thou wouldst alter it, I see.

Mahomet. It was too **pure :** people have fed upon prodigies ;
they must have them still. Situate the native **of** a watery plain
upon the mountain, and he will regret the warm comfortable fogs
and the low fleeting lights of his marsh.

I **would continue on** the best terms with my adviser and
guide ; **but verily my entrails** yearn for the good people of
Damascus.

Sergius. **Leave them to me ; and, if thy entrails yearn, take**
a goblet of cyprus.

Mahomet. I[7] dare not drink **wine :** it aggravates my malady,
the only one **to** which I am subject. Another inspiration here
comes over me. I will forbid the use of this beverage. Why
should others enjoy what I cannot ?

Sergius. True religionist ! **But, Mahomet ! Mahomet !** will
vision upon vision, revelation **upon** revelation, supersede **this**

[7 From " I " to " world " (**30 lines**) added in 2nd ed.]

delicious habit? Relinquish such an impracticable conceit.
Forbid wine, indeed! God himself, if he descended on
earth, and commanded it in a louder and clearer voice than that
at which the creation sprang forth, unless first he altered the
composition both of body and soul, would utterly fail in this
commandment.

Mahomet. I will order it: I will see it executed; for now
thou urgest me. Yea, Sergius! men shall abstain from wine in
all those regions of the earth where wine hath fragrance and
captivation; and they shall continue to drink it and be damned
where it is nauseous and fiery and Æthiopian in complexion;
and the priests in those regions shall drink the most of it. Thus
saith the Lord.

Sergius. He hath said many things which nobody minds. If
whole nations abstain from wine, by any ordinance, prophetic
or angelic, and from such wine as Syria and Cyprus and Chios
and Crete afford us, there will be a miracle not resembling most
others: no miracle of a moment, witnessed by the ignorant and
run away with by the impostor, a sacrilege to examine; but a
miracle to be touched and interrogated, as long, as attentively, as
intrinsically, as the most incredulous could require, and such as
all the world must acknowledge to be irresistible, and must bend
before its divinity.

Mahomet. I do not desire all the world: let me have but
Asia, if I can win it over to the faith.

Sergius. Win it over and welcome, if thou canst.

Mahomet. Faith is so strong in me, I can do all things.

Sergius. Do them: leave me Anatolis and the patriarchate,
just as they both are now.

Mahomet. I begin to imagine and believe that many of those
things which I would have communicated as visions, are realities.

Sergius. Thou wilt succeed the better for thinking it.

Mahomet. God guides us mysteriously, and changes us
miraculously.

Sergius. He doth indeed, if he hath made a religionist of
thee.

Mahomet. "God, he is God, and Mahomet is his prophet."
By the Eternal! those words are divine.

Sergius. They will be, by the Eternal! if they only win

thee some three or four stout cities in Arabia, and deliver into thy hands, with some rich caravan, about as many (or rather more) unbelieving girls, ready and ripe for conversion and ablution, with faces a whit nearer in color to the snow than to the sands ; such as Paphlagonia and Armenia send us, by the blessing of the Lord.

Mahomet. Hitherto, when I dreamed that thou madest to me any cession of territory for the plantation of the faith, thou didst give me thy blessing and cede it.

Sergius. And thou didst to me in like manner. But now thy dreams cover nation after nation ; let us agree, my friend Mahomet, to dream no more. Lie on thy left side, man, on thy noble camel-hair couch, white and black like a zebra (as thou boastest in thy poetry), and never turn thy face again toward Syria.

Mahomet. This seems, my friend, like a threat.

Sergius. Say rather, like divination.

Mahomet. I can divine better than thou canst.

Sergius. Contentment is better than divination or visions. Thou wert born and educated in Arabia ; and nothing can transcend the description thou hast given me of thy native country.

Mahomet. All native countries are most beautiful ; yet we want something from them which they will not give us. Our first quarrels of any seriousness are with them ; as the first screams and struggles of infants, the first tearing of robes and sobs of anger, are against their mothers.

Delightful is it to bathe in the *moonsea* on the sands, and to listen to tales of genii in the tent ; but then in Arabia the anxious heart is thrown into fierce and desperate commotion, by the accursed veil that separates beauty from us. There we never see the blade of that sweet herbage rise day after day into light and loveliness, never see the blossom expand ; but receive it unselected, unsolicited, and unwon. Happy the land where the youthful are without veils, the aged without suspicion ; where the antelope may look to what resting-place she listeth, and bend her slender foot to the fountain that most invites her.

Odoriferous gales ! whether of Deban or of Dafar, if ye

bring only fragrance with you, carry it to the thoughtless and light-hearted! carry it to the drinker of wine, to the feaster and the dancer at the feast. If ye never have played about the beloved of my youth, if ye bring me no intelligence of her, pass on! away with you!

Sergius. We may be with the girl we love in many places, so many that we lose the recollection.

Mahomet. Is that possible? Then you do not sit very near her.

Sergius. Yes, and touch her.

Mahomet. A young girl? beautiful? affectionate? before marriage? Do not nod, but tell me unequivocally.

Sergius. I say it.

Mahomet. Sergius! thy whole religion, in all its incredibilities, containeth none like this.

Sergius. Believe me; I am not preaching. Certainly we have much the advantage here; but thou mayest order things after our manner.

Mahomet. I shall grow old before this change can take place; besides, I must have a revelation for it.

Sergius. And why not.

Mahomet. Alas! it is not worth my while. However, I am hale enough yet to make another visit to Damascus.

Sergius. As a preacher I hope, not as a prophet.

Mahomet. God's will de done.

Sergius. If thou, in spite of thy faith, shouldst. yet happen to fail in thy enterprise, come into our brotherhood; if, in despite of thy rashness, thou shouldst succeed in it, thy friend Sergius follows thy standard, and brings over to thee nine-tenths of the Church establishment. But do not omit the Houris. Quote Solomon; celebrate his wisdom and concubines; damn his idolatry of wood and stone, when he had flesh and blood to idolize; grant sherbet and coffee, opium and divorces. Remember—

Hark! the bell rings! Put on thy slippers, come along with me. Courtesy to the Virgin, dip thy finger in the font, and chant the litany.

Mahomet. I never sang a note in my whole life.

Sergius. What matters that? Courage! strike up among us.

Mahomet. I hate singing: it is fit only for madmen and drunkards and the weakest and pettiest of the birds. Beside, I tell thee again, I cannot. Are there not reasons enough?

Sergius. By no means. Didst thou not say, faith is so strong in thee thou canst do all things?

Mahomet. Yes, but I must have the will first: even God must will before he does any thing; I am only his Prophet. Why dost thou laugh? why dost thou display thy teeth, lifting and lowering them like unto the dog that biteth off his fleas! No ridicule! I deserve it not. My potency is known to thee, although not in its whole extent. Know, then, I have cut the moon asunder with my scimitar.

Sergius. Who, in the name of the Prophet (this I think is the way we are to speak), will ever believe such an audacious lie?

Mahomet. Universally will the chosen of the Most High believe it, although the grunters and snorers in thy sty eschew it. I have in readiness a miracle so much greater, that every face in Arabia will sink as deep in the sand before it as the tortoise when she is laying her eggs.

Sergius. I do not understand thee.

Mahomet. It is something to cut asunder the moon; but I have already done incalculably more, as thou thyself, O Sergius, shalt acknowledge.

Sergius. Speak, and plainly; for, upon my soul! I know not when thou art in earnest and when otherwise; and almost do I suspect that, in the illusions of hope and in the transports of ambition, thou sometimes givest credence to thine own devices.

Mahomet. Be thou my judge in this matter. Under an oath to secrecy, I have unfolded to Labid the poet, son of Rabiah, what I intend for the first chapter of my Koran; and he cried before me, and is ready to cry before the people, "O Mahomet! son of Abdallah, son of Achem, son of Motalib, thou art a greater poet than I am."

Sergius. Begone upon thy mission this instant! Miracles like others have been performed everywhere; like this, never upon earth. A poet, good or bad, to acknowledge a superior! Methinks I see the pope already in adoration at thy feet, and hear the patriarchs calling thee father. I myself am half a convert. Hie thee homeward: God speed thee!

The story of Sergius the Nestorian monk assisting Mahomet in the compilation of the Koran, is often repeated on the authority of Zonaras. Gibbon has deemed it unworthy of notice. Sergius was only the assistant of Mahomet in the same manner as the rest of the churchmen. The impostor of Rome was the truest ally to the impostor of Mecca; who found more wickedness committed under the garb of Christianity, more ambition, more malice, more poisonings and stabbings, than any other religion had experienced among its leaders, not only in the same period of time, but in the whole course of its existence. So, within two centuries, reckoning from his first appearance as a prophet, half the Christians in the world, and nearly all who were not coerced by the armies of princes in submission to the pope, abandoned their religion and adopted M...

FRA FILIPPO LIPPI AND POPE EUGENIUS THE FOURTH.[1]

Filippo! I am informed by my son Cosimo de' any things relating to thy life and actions, and, among thy throwing off the habit of a friar. Speak to me as Was that well done?

ari, Life of Fra Filippo Lippi. "While upon the coast of was amusing himself on the sea in company with some friends; y they were all carried off together by the Moorish galleys the sea in those parts, and so conveyed to Barbary, where they on the chain and enslaved; and there, with much discomfort, he ghteen months. But one day, having had much familiarity with he took it into his head to make a picture of him; he there- burnt stick from the fire, and made on the white wall a picture full length in Moorish garments. This was told to his master er slaves; and so marvellous a feat did it seem to those people, er draw nor paint, it was the occasion of his being set free from where he had so long been kept. . . . After he had executed le paintings for his master, he was sent safely to Naples." The introduction of Pope Eugenius into the Conversation is an anachronism into which Landor has been led by Vasari, who says, a little lower down, that Fra Filippo was sent to Pope Eugenius the Fourth to present him with some of his pictures, as a gift from Cosimo de Medici, and that he pleased the Pope. See also Browning's poem, Fra Lippo Lippi. (Works, ii., 846. Works, iii., 1876.)]

Filippo. Holy Father! it was done most unadvisedly.

Eugenius. Continue to treat me with the same confidence and ingenuousness; and, beside the remuneration I intend to bestow on thee for the paintings wherewith thou hast adorned my palace, I will remove with my own hand the heavy accumulation of thy sins, and ward off the peril of fresh ones, placing within thy reach every worldly solace and contentment.

Filippo. Infinite thanks, Holy Father, from the innermost heart of your unworthy servant, whose duty and wishes bind him alike and equally to a strict compliance with your paternal commands.

Eugenius. Was it a love of the world and its vanities that induced thee to throw aside the frock?

Filippo. It was indeed, Holy Father! I this I think is courage to mention it in confession am an audacious offences.

Eugenius. Bad! bad! Repentance is of most High be- sinner, unless he pour it from a full and overflow eschew it. I the capacious ear of the confessor. Ye must ne very face in forward and bluntly up to your Maker, startling toise when horrors of your guilty conscience. Order, decency, opportunity, must be observed.

Filippo. I have observed the greater part of them : and opportunity. ; but I

Eugenius. That is much. In consideration of it Sergius, absolve thee.

Filippo. I feel quite easy, quite new-born. now not

Eugenius. I am desirous of hearing what sort of fe st do I experiencest when thou givest loose to thy intractable of am- wishes. Now, this love of the world, what can it m love of music, of dancing, of riding? What, in short, is i n oath

Filippo. Holy Father! I was ever of a hot and abiah, constitution. cried

Eugenius. Well, well! I can guess, within a trifle, w met! leads unto. I very much disapprove of it, whatever it i rt a And then? and then? Prythee go on: I am inflamed ike miraculous zeal to cleanse thee.

Filippo. I have committed many follies, and some sins. on

Eugenius. Let me hear the sins; I do not trouble my

about the follies; the Church has no business with them. The State is founded on follies, the Church on sins. Come, then, unsack them.

Filippo. Concupiscence is both a folly and a sin. I felt more and more of it when I ceased to be a monk, not having (for a time) so ready means of allaying it.

Eugenius. No doubt. Thou shouldst have thought again and again before thou strippedst off the cowl.

Filippo. Ah! Holy Father! I am sore at heart. I thought indeed how often it had held two heads together under it, and that stripping it off was double decapitation. But compensation and contentment came, and we were warm enough without it.

Eugenius. I am minded to reprove thee gravely. No wonder it pleased the Virgin, and the saints about her, to permit that the enemy of our faith should lead thee captive into Barbary.

Filippo. The pleasure was all on their side.

Eugenius. I have heard a great many stories both of males and females who were taken by Tunisians and Algerines; and although there is a sameness in certain parts of them, my especial benevolence toward thee, worthy Filippo, would induce me to lend a vacant ear to thy report. And now, good Filippo, I could sip a small glass of muscatel or Orvieto, and turn over a few bleached almonds, or essay a smart dried apricot at intervals, and listen while thou relatest to me the manners and customs of that country, and particularly as touching thy own adversities. First, how wast thou taken?

Filippo. I was visiting at Pesaro my worshipful friend the canonico Andrea Paccone, who delighted in the guitar, played it skilfully, and was always fond of hearing it well accompanied by the voice. My own instrument I had brought with me, together with many gay Florentine songs, some of which were of such a turn and tendency that the canonico thought they would sound better on the chir, and rather far from shore, than within the walls of the some linicate. He proposed, then, one evening when there was wind stirring, to exercise three young abbates * on their several a little way out of hearing from the water's edge.

Eugenius. I disapprove of exercising young abbates in that pleasanter.

* Little boys, wearing clerical habits, are often called *abbati*.

Filippo. Inadvertently, O Holy Father! I have made the affair seem worse than it really was. In fact, there were only two genuine abbates; the third was Donna Lisetta, the good canonico's pretty niece, who looks so archly at your Holiness when you bend your knees before her at bedtime.

Eugenius. How! where?

Filippo. She is the angel on the right-hand side of the Holy Family, with a tip of amethyst-colored wing over a basket of figs and pomegranates. I painted her from memory: she was then only fifteen, and worthy to be the niece of an archbishop. Alas! she never will be: she plays and sings among the infidels, and perhaps would eat a landrail on a Friday as unreluctantly as she would a roach.

Eugenius. Poor soul! So this is the angel with the amethyst-colored wing? I thought she looked wanton: we must pray for her release—from the bondage of sin. What followed in your excursion?

Filippo. Singing, playing, fresh air, and plashing water stimulated our appetites. We had brought no eatable with us but fruit and thin *marzopane*, of which the sugar and rose-water were inadequate to ward off hunger; and the sight of a fishing-vessel between us and Ancona raised our host's immoderately. "Yonder smack," said he, "is sailing at this moment just over the very best sole bank in the Adriatic. If she continues her course and we run toward her, we may be supplied, I trust in God, with the finest fish in Christendom. Methinks I see already the bellies of those magnificent soles bestar the deck, and emulate the glories of the orient sky." He gave his orders with such a majestic air, that he looked rather like an admiral than a priest.

Eugenius. How now, rogue! Why should not the churchman look majestically and courageously! I myself have found occasion for it, and exerted it.

Filippo. The world knows the prowess of your Holiness.

Eugenius. Not mine, not mine, Filippo! but His who gave me the sword and the keys, and the will and the discretion to use them. I trust the canonico did not misapply his station and power, by taking the fish at any unreasonably low price; and that he gave his blessing to the remainder, and to the poor fishermen and to their nets.

Filippo.   He was angry at observing that the vessel, while he thought it was within hail, stood out again to sea.

Eugenius.   He ought to have borne more manfully so slight a vexation.

Filippo.   On the contrary, he swore bitterly he would have the master's ear between his thumb and forefinger in another half-hour, and regretted that he had cut his nails in the morning lest they should grate on his guitar.   "They may fish well," cried he, " but they can neither sail nor row ; and, when I am in the middle of that tub of theirs, I will teach them more than they look for."   Sure enough he was in the middle of it at the time he fixed ; but it was by aid of a rope about his arms, and the end of another laid lustily on his back and shoulders.   "Mount, lazy, long-chined turnspit, as thou valuest thy life," cried Abdul the corsair, " and away for Tunis." If silence is consent, he had it.   The captain, in the Sicilian dialect, told us we might talk freely, for he had taken his siesta.   " Whose guitars are those ? " said he.   As the canonico raised his eyes to heaven and answered nothing, I replied, "Sir, one is mine ; the other is my worthy friend's there." Next he asked the canonico to what market he was taking those young slaves, pointing to the abbates.   The canonico sobbed, and could not utter one word.   I related the whole story ; at which he laughed.   He then took up the music, and commanded my reverend guest to sing an air peculiarly tender, invoking the compassion of a nymph, and calling her cold as ice.   Never did so many or such profound sighs accompany it.   When it ended, he sang one himself in his own language, on a lady whose eyes were exactly like the scimitars of Damascus, and whose eyebrows met in the middle like the cudgels of prize-fighters.   On the whole, she resembled both sun and moon, with the simple difference that she never allowed herself to be seen, lest all the nations of the . earth should go to war for her, and not a man be left to breathe out his soul before her.   This poem had obtained the prize at the University of Fez, had been translated into the Arabic, the Persian, and the Turkish languages, and was the favorite lay of the corsair.   He invited me, lastly, to try my talent.   I played the same air on the guitar, and apologized for omitting

the words, frqm my utter ignorance of the Moorish. Abdul
was much pleased, and took the trouble to convince me that
the poetry they conveyed, which he translated literally, was
incomparably better than ours. "Cold as ice!" he repeated,
scoffing: anybody might say that who has seen Atlas; but a
genuine poet would rather say, "Cold as a lizard or a lob-
ster." There is no controverting a critic who has twenty stout
rowers and twenty well-knotted rope-ends. Added to which,
he seemed to know as much of the matter as the generality
of those who talk about it. He was gratified by my attention
and edification, and thus continued: "I have remarked in
the songs I have heard, that these wild woodland creatures
of the West, these nymphs, are a strange fantastical race. But
are your poets not ashamed to complain of their inconstancy?
Whose fault is that? If ever it should be my fortune to take
one, I would try whether I could not bring her down to the
level of her sex; and, if her inconstancy caused any complaints,
by Allah! they should be louder and shriller than ever rose
from the throat of Abdul." I still thought it better to be a
disciple than a commentator.

Eugenius. If we could convert this barbarian and detain
him awhile at Rome, he would learn that women and nymphs
(and inconstancy also) are one and the same. These cruel
men have no lenity, no suavity. They who do not as they
would be done by, are done by very much as they do. Women
will glide away from them like water: they can better bear two
masters than half one; and a new metal must be discovered before
any bars are strong enough to confine them. But proceed with
your narrative.

Filippo. Night had now closed upon us. Abdul placed the
younger of the company apart; and, after giving them some boiled
rice, sent them down into his own cabin. The sailors, observing
the consideration and distinction with which their master had
treated me, were civil and obliging. Permission was granted me,
at my request, to sleep on deck.

Eugenius. What became of your canonico?

Filippo. The crew called him a conger, a priest, and a
porpoise.

Eugenius. Foul-mouthed knaves! could not one of these

terms content them? On thy leaving Barbary was he left
behind?

Filippo. Your Holiness consecrated him, the other day,
Bishop of Macerata.

Eugenius. True, true; I remember the name, Saccone.
How did he contrive to get off?

Filippo. He was worth little at any work; and such men are
the quickest both to get off and to get on. Abdul told me he
had received three thousand crowns for his ransom.

Eugenius. He was worth more to him than to me. I received but two first-fruits, and such other things as of right belong
to me by inheritance. The bishopric is passably rich: he may
serve thee.

Filippo. While he was a canonico he was a jolly fellow,—
not very generous, for jolly fellows are seldom that; but he would
give a friend a dinner, a flask of wine or two in preference, and a
piece of advice as readily as either. I waited on Monsignor at
Macerata, soon after his elevation.

Eugenius. He must have been heartily glad to embrace his
companion in captivity, and the more especially as he himself was
the cause of so grievous a misfortune.

Filippo. He sent me word he was so unwell he could not see
me. "What!" said I to his valet, "is Monsignor's complaint
in his eyes?" The fellow shrugged up his shoulders, and walked
away. Not believing that the message was a refusal to admit me,
I went straight upstairs, and finding the door of an ante-chamber
half open, and a chaplain mulling an egg-posset over the fire, I
accosted him. The air of familiarity and satisfaction he observed
in me left no doubt in his mind that I had been invited by his
patron. "Will the man never come?" cried his lordship.
"Yes, Monsignor!" exclaimed I, running in and embracing
him; "behold him here!" He started back, and then I first
discovered the wide difference between an old friend and an egg-
posset.

Eugenius. Son Filippo! thou hast seen but little of the
world, and art but just come from Barbary. Go on.

Filippo. "Fra Filippo!" said he, gravely, "I am glad to see
you. I did not expect you just at present. I am not very
well: I had ordered a medicine, and was impatient to take it.

If you will favor me with the name of your inn, I will send for you when I am in a condition to receive you; perhaps within a day or two." "Monsignor!" said I, "a change of residence often gives a man a cold, and oftener a change of fortune. Whether you caught yours upon deck (where we last saw each other), from being more exposed than usual, or whether the mitre holds wind, is no question for me, and no concern of mine."

Eugenius. A just reproof, if an archbishop had made it. On uttering it, I hope thou kneeledst and kissedst his hand.

Filippo. I did not, indeed.

Eugenius. O! there wert thou greatly in the wrong. Having, it is reported, a good thousand crowns yearly of patrimony, and a cononicate worth six hundred more, he might have attempted to relieve thee from slavery, by assisting thy relatives in thy redemption.

Filippo. The three thousand crowns were the uttermost he could raise, he declared to Abdul; and he asserted that a part of the money was contributed by the inhabitants of Pesaro. "Do they act out of pure mercy?" said he. "Ay, they must; for what else could move them in behalf of such a lazy, unserviceable, street-fed cur?" In the morning, at sunrise, he was sent aboard. And now, the vessel being under-weigh, "I have a letter from my lord Abdul," said the master, "which, being in thy language, two fellow-slaves shall read unto thee publicly." They came forward and began the reading: "Yesterday I purchased these two slaves from a cruel, unrelenting master, under whose lash they have labored for nearly thirty years. I hereby give orders that five ounces of my own gold be weighed out to them." Here one of the slaves fell on his face; the other lifted up his hands, praised God, and blessed his benefactor.

Eugenius. The pirate? the unconverted pirate?

Filippo. Even so. "Here is another slip of paper for thyself to read immediately in my presence," said the master. The words it contained were, "Do thou the same, or there enters thy lips neither food nor water until thou landest in Italy. I permit thee to carry away more than double the sum: I am no sutler; I do not contract for thy sustenance." The canonico asked of the master whether he knew the contents of the letter; he replied, no. "Tell your master, lord Abdul, that I shall take them into consideration." "My lord expected a much plainer answer; and commanded me, in case of any such as thou hast delivered, to break this seal." He pressed it to his forehead, and then broke it. Having perused the characters reverentially, "Christian! dost thou consent?" The canonico fell on his knees, and overthrew the two poor wretches who, saying their prayers, had remained in the same posture before him, quite unnoticed. "Open thy trunk and take out thy money-bag, or I will make room for it in thy bladder." The canonico was prompt in the execution of the command. The master drew out his scales, and desired the canonico to weigh with his own hand five ounces. He groaned and trembled: the balance was un-steady. "Throw in another piece: it will not vitiate the agree-ment," cried the master. It was done. Fear and grief are among the thirsty passions, but add little to the appetite. It seemed, however, as if every sigh had left a vacancy in the stomach of the canonico. At dinner, the cook brought him a salted bonito, half an ell in length; and in five minutes his Reverence was drawing his middle finger along the white back-bone, out of sheer idleness, until were placed before him some as fine dried locusts as ever provisioned the tents of Africa, together with olives the size of eggs and color of bruises, shining in oil and brine. He found them savory and pulpy; and, as the last love supersedes the foregoing, he gave them the preference, even over the delicate locusts. When he had finished them, he modestly requested a can of water. A sailor brought a large flask, and poured forth a plentiful supply. The canonico en-gulfed the whole, and instantly threw himself back in convulsive agony. "How is this!" cried the sailor. The master ran up, and, smelling the water, began to buffet him; exclaiming, as he turned round to all the crew, "How came this flask here?" All were innocent. It appeared, however, that it was a flask of mineral water, strongly sulphureous, taken out of a Neapolitan vessel laden with a great abundance of it for some hospital in the Levant. It had taken the captor by surprise in the same manner as the canonico. He himself brought out instantly a capacious stone jar covered with dew, and invited the sufferer into the cabin. Here he drew forth two richly-cut wine-glasses, and, on filling one of them, the outside of it turned suddenly pale, with a myriad of indivisible drops, and the senses were refreshed with the most delicious fragrance. He held up the glass between himself and his guest, and, looking at it attentively, said, "Here is no appearance of wine : all I can see is water. Nothing is wickeder than too much curiosity : we must take what Allah sends us, and render thanks for it, although it fall far short of our expectations. Beside, our Prophet would rather we should even drink wine than poison." The canonico had not tasted wine for two months,—a longer abstinence than ever canonico endured before. He drooped ; but the master looked still more disconsolate. "I would give whatever I possess on earth rather than die of thirst," cried the canonico. "Who would not?" rejoined the captain, sighing and clasping his fingers. "If it were not contrary to my commands, I could touch at some cove or inlet." "Do, for the love of Christ!" exclaimed the canonico. "Or even sail back," continued the captain. "O Santa Vergine!" cried in anguish the canonico. "Despondency," said the captain, with calm solemnity, "has left many a man to be thrown overboard : it even renders the plague, and many other disorders, more fatal. Thirst, too, has a powerful effect in exasperating them. Overcome such weaknesses, or I must do my duty. The health of the ship's company is placed under my care ; and our lord Abdul, if he suspected the pest, would throw a Jew, or a Christian, or even a bale of silk, into the sea : such is the disinterestedness and magnanimity of my lord Abdul." "He believes in fate, does he not?" said the canonico. "Doubtless ; but he says it is as much fated that he should throw into the sea a fellow who is infected, as that the fellow should have ever been so." "Save me, O save me!" cried the canonico, moist as if the spray had pelted him. "Willingly, if possible," answered calmly the master. "At present I can discover no certain symptoms ; for sweat, unless followed by general prostration, both of muscular strength and animal spirits, may be cured without a hook at the heel." "Giesu-Maria!" ejaculated the canonico.

Eugenius. And the monster could withstand that appeal?

Filippo. It seems so. The renegade who related to me, on my return, these events as they happened, was very circumstantial.

He is a Corsican, and had killed many men in battle, and more out; but is (he gave me his word for it) on the whole an honest man.

Eugenius.   How so? honest? and a renegade?

Filippo.   He declared to me that, although the Mahometan is the best religion to live in, the Christian is the best to die in; and that, when he has made his fortune, he will make his confession, and lie snugly in the bosom of the Church.

Eugenius.   See here the triumphs of our holy faith! The lost sheep will be found again.

Filippo.   Having played the butcher first.

Eugenius.   Return we to that bad man, the master or captain, who evinced no such dispositions.

Filippo.   He added, "The other captives, though older men, have stouter hearts than thine." "Alas! they are longer used to hardships," answered he. "Dost thou believe, in thy conscience," said the captain, "that the water we have aboard would be harmless to them? for we have no other; and wine is costly; and our quantity might be insufficient for those who can afford to pay for it." "I will answer for their lives," replied the canonico. "With thy own?" interrogated sharply the Tunisian. "I must not tempt God," said, in tears, the religious man. "Let us be plain," said the master. "Thou knowest thy money is safe: I myself counted it before thee when I brought it from the scrivener's. Thou hast sixty broad gold pieces: wilt thou be answerable, to the whole amount of them, for the lives of thy two countrymen if they drink this water?" "O Sir!" said the canonico, "I will give it, if, only for these few days of voyage, you vouchsafe me one bottle daily of that restorative wine of Bordeaux. The other two are less liable to the plague: they do not sorrow and sweat as I do. They are spare men. There is enough of me to infect a fleet with it; and I cannot bear to think of being any wise the cause of evil to my fellow-creatures." "The wine is my patron's," cried the Tunisian; "he leaves every thing at my discretion: should I deceive him?" "If he leaves every thing at your discretion," observed the logician of Pesaro, "there is no deceit in disposing of it." The master appeared to be satisfied with the argument. "Thou shalt not find me exacting," said he; "give me the sixty pieces, and the wine shall be thine." At a signal, when the contract was agreed to, the two slaves entered bringing a hamper of jars. "Read the contract before thou signest," cried the master. He read: "How is this? how is this? *Sixty golden ducats to the brothers Antonio and Bernabo Panini, for wine received from them?*" The aged men tottered under the stroke of joy; and Bernabo, who would have embraced his brother, fainted.

On the morrow there was a calm, and the weather was extremely sultry. The canonico sat in his shirt on deck, and was surprised to see, I forget which of the brothers, drink from a goblet a prodigious draught of water. "Hold!" cried he angrily: "you may eat instead; but putrid or sulphureous water, you have heard, may produce the plague, and honest men be the sufferers by your folly and intemperance." They assured him the water was tasteless, and very excellent, and had been kept cool in the same kind of earthen jars as the wine. He tasted it and lost his patience. It was better, he protested, than any wine in the world. They begged his acceptance of the jar containing it. But the master, who had witnessed at a distance the whole proceeding, now advanced; and, placing his hand against it, said sternly, "Let him have his own." Usually, when he had emptied the second bottle, a desire of converting the Mahometans came over him; and they showed themselves much less obstinate and refractory than they are generally thought. He selected those for edification who swore the oftenest and the loudest by the prophet; and he boasted in his heart of having overcome, by precept and example, the stiffest tenet of their abominable creed. . Certainly they drank wine, and somewhat freely. The canonico clapped his hands, and declared that even some of the apostles had been more pertinacious recusants of the faith.

Eugenius. Did he so? Cappari! I would not have made him a bishop for twice the money if I had known it earlier. Could not he have left them alone? Suppose one or other of them did doubt and persecute, was he the man to blab it out among the heathen?

Filippo. A judgment, it appears, fell on him for so doing. A very quiet sailor, who had always declined his invitations, and had always heard his arguments at a distance and in silence, being pressed and urged by him, and reproved somewhat arro-

...es be recoverable!   Even if they should have submitted to
unholy rites, I venture to say they have repented.

ippo.   The devil is in them, if they have not.

ugenius.   They may become again as good Christians as ever.

ippo.   Easily, methinks.

ugenius.   Not so easily; but by aid of Holy Church in the administration of indulgences.

ippo.   They never wanted those, whatever they want.

ugenius.   The corsair, then, is not one of those ferocious creatures which appear to connect our species with the lion and tiger.

ippo.   By no means, Holy Father!   He is an honest man; like many of his countrymen, bating the sacrament.

ugenius.   Bating!   poor beguiled Filippo!   Being unbaptized they are only as the beasts that perish : nay worse ; for, soul being imperishable, it must stick to their bodies at the day, whether they will or no, and must sink with it into the fire and brimstone.

ippo.   Unbaptized!   why, they baptize every morning.

ugenius.   Worse and worse!   I thought they only missed the stirrup; I find they overleap the saddle.   Obstinate, blind reprobates!   of whom it is written—of whom it is written—of whom, I say, it is written—as shall be manifest before men and angels in the day of wrath.

ippo.   More is the pity!   for they are hospitable, frank, courteous.   It is delightful to see their gardens, when one is at the weeding and irrigation of them.   What fruit! what specimens! what trellises! what alcoves! what a contest of rose and of vine for supremacy in odor! of lute and nightingale for supremacy in song!   And how the little bright ripples of the docile brooks, the fresher for their races, leap up against one another, to reach the clove! and how they chirrup and applaud, as if they too had a sense of some importance in these parties of pleasure that are never separate!

ugenius.   Parties of pleasure!   birds, fruits, shallow-running brooks, lute-players, and wantons!   Parties of pleasure! and blasphemies of these!   Tell me now, Filippo, tell me truly, what corrupt, complexion in general have the discreeter females of that hapless country.

Filippo. The color of an orange-flower, on which an over-laden bee has left a slight suffusion of her purest honey.

Eugenius. We must open their eyes.

Filippo. Knowing what excellent hides the slippers of this people are made of, I never once ventured on their less perfect theology, fearing to find it written that I should be abed on my face the next fortnight. My master had expressed his astonishment that a religion so admirable as ours was represented, should be the only one in the world the precepts of which are disregarded by all conditions of men. "Our Prophet," said he, "our Prophet ordered us to go forth and conquer; we did it: yours ordered you to sit quiet and forbear; and, after spitting in his face, you threw the order back into it, and fought like devils."

Eugenius. The barbarians talk of our Holy Scriptures as if they understood them perfectly. The impostor they follow has nothing but fustian and rhodomontade in his impudent lying book from beginning to end. I know it, Filippo, from those who have contrasted it, page by page, paragraph by paragraph, and have given the knave his due.

Filippo. Abdul is by no means deficient in a good opinion of his own capacity and his Prophet's all-sufficiency; but he never took me to task about my faith or his own.

Eugenius. How wert thou mainly occupied?

Filippo. I will give your Holiness a sample both of my employments and of his character. He was going one evening to a country-house, about fifteen miles from Tunis; and he ordered me to accompany him. I found there a spacious garden, overrun with wild-flowers, and most luxuriant grass, in irregular tufts, according to the dryness or the humidity of the spot. The clematis overtopped the lemon and orange trees; and the perennial pea sent forth here a pink blossom, here a purple, here a white one, and, after holding (as it were) a short conversation with the humbler plants, sprang up about an old cypress, played among its branches, and mitigated its gloom. White pigeons, and others in color like the dawn of day, looked down on us and ceased to coo, until some of their companions, in whom they had more confidence, encouraged them loudly from remoter boughs, or alighted on the shoulders of Abdul, at whose side I was standing. A few of them examined me in every position their inquisitive eyes could take ; displaying all the advantages of their versatile necks, and pretending querulous fear in the midst of petulant approaches.

Eugenius. Is it of pigeons thou art talking, O Filippo ? I hope it may be.

Filippo. Of Abdul's pigeons. He was fond of taming all creatures,—men, horses, pigeons, equally ; but he tamed them all by kindness. In this wilderness is an edifice not unlike our Italian chapter-houses built by the Lombards, with long narrow windows, high above the ground. The centre is now a bath, the waters of which, in another part of the enclosure, had supplied a fountain, at present in ruins, and covered by tufted canes, and by every variety of aquatic plants. The structure has no remains of roof ; and, of six windows, one alone is unconcealed by ivy. This had been walled up long ago, and the cement in the inside of it was hard and polished. " Lippi ! " said Abdul to me, after I had long admired the place in silence, " I leave to thy super-intendence this bath and garden. Be sparing of the leaves and branches ; make paths only wide enough for me. Let me see no mark of hatchet or pruning-hook, and tell the laborers that who-ever takes a nest or an egg shall be impaled."

Eugenius. Monster ! so then he would really have impaled a poor wretch for eating a bird's egg ? How disproportionate is the punishment to the offence !

Filippo. He efficiently checked in his slaves the desire of transgressing his command. To spare them as much as possible, I ordered them merely to open a few spaces, and to remove the weaker trees from the stronger. Meanwhile I drew on the smooth blank window the figure of Abdul and of a beautiful girl.

Eugenius. Rather say handmaiden : choicer expression, more decorous.

Filippo. Holy Father ! I have been lately so much out of practice, I take the first that comes in my way. Handmaiden I will use in preference for the future.

Eugenius. On then ! and God speed thee !

Filippo. I drew Abdul with a blooming handmaiden. One

of his feet is resting on her lap, and she is drying the ankle with
a saffron robe, of which the greater part is fallen in doing it.
That she is a bondmaid is discernible, not only by her occupation,
but by her humility and patience, by her loose and flowing brown
hair, and by her eyes expressing the timidity at once of servitude
and of fondness. The countenance was taken from fancy, and
was the loveliest I could imagine ; of the figure I had some idea,
having seen it to advantage in Tunis. After seven days Abdul
returned. He was delighted with the improvement made in the
garden. I requested him to visit the bath. "We can do
nothing to that," answered he, impatiently. "There is no
sudatory, no dormitory, no dressing-room, no couch. Sometimes
I sit an hour there in the summer, because I never found a fly in
it ; the principal curse of hot countries, and against which plague
there is neither prayer nor amulet, nor indeed any human defence."
He went away into the house. At dinner, he sent me from his
table some quails and ortolans, and tomatoes and honey and rice ;
beside a basket of fruit covered with moss and bay-leaves, under
which I found a verdino fig, deliciously ripe, and bearing the impression of several small teeth, but certainly no reptile's.

Eugenius. There might have been poison in them, for all that.

Filippo. About two hours had passed, when I heard a whirr
and a crash in the windows of the bath (where I had dined and
was about to sleep), occasioned by the settling and again the flight
of some pheasants. Abdul entered. "Beard of the Prophet !
what hast thou been doing? That is myself ! No, no, Lippi !
thou never canst have seen her : the face proves it ; but those
limbs ! thou hast divined them aright ; thou hast had sweet
dreams them ! Dreams are large possessions ; in them the possessor may cease to possess his own. To the slave, O Allah ! to
the slave is permitted what is not his !—I burn with anguish to
think how much—yea, at that very hour. I would not another
should, even in a dream—But, Lippi ! thou never canst have
seen above the sandal ?" To which I answered, "I never have
allowed my eyes to look even on that. But if any one of my
lord Abdul's fair slaves resembles, as they surely must all do, in
duty and docility, the figure I have represented, let it express to
him my congratulation on his happiness." "I believe," said he,
"such representations are forbidden by the Koran ; but, as I do

not remember it, I do not sin. There it shall stay, unless the
angel **Gabriel** comes to forbid it." He smiled in saying so.

Eugenius. There is hope of this Abdul. His faith hangs
about him more like oil than pitch.

Filippo. He inquired of me whether I often thought of those
I loved in Italy, and whether I could bring them before my eyes
at will. To remove all suspicion **from** him, I declared I always
could, and that one beautiful object occupied all the cells of my
brain by night and day. He paused and pondered, and then said,
"Thou dost **not** love deeply." I thought I had given the true
signs. "No, Lippi! we who love ardently, we, with **all our**
wishes, all the efforts of our souls, cannot bring before us the
features which, while they were present, we thought it impossible
we ever could forget. Alas! when we most love the absent,
when we most desire to see her, we try in vain to bring her image
back **to us.** The troubled heart shakes and confounds it, even as
ruffled waters do with shadows. Hateful things are more hateful
when they haunt our sleep : the lovely **flee** away, or are changed
into less lovely."

Eugenius. What figures now have these unbelievers?

Filippo. Various **in** their combinations as the letters **or the**
numerals ; but they all, like these, signify something. **Almeida**
(did **I** not inform your Holiness?) has large hazel eyes—

Eugenius. Has she? thou never toldest me that. Well, well!
and what else has she? Mind! be cautious! use decent **terms.**

Filippo. Somewhat pouting lips.

Eugenius. **Ha!** ha! What did they pout at?

Filippo. And she is rather plump than otherwise.

Eugenius. No harm in that.

Filippo. And moreover **is cool, smooth, and firm as** a nectarine
gathered before sunrise.

Eugenius. Ha! ha! do not remind me of nectarines. **I am**
very fond of them ; and this is not the season! Such females as
thou describest are said to be among the likeliest to give reasonable
cause for suspicion. I would not judge harshly, I would not
think uncharitably ; but, unhappily, being at so great a distance from
spiritual aid, peradventure a desire, a suggestion, an inkling—ay?
If she, the lost Almeida, came before thee when her master was
absent—which I trust she never did—But those flowers and shrubs

and odors and alleys and long grass **and alcoves** might strangely hold, perplex, and entangle two incautious young persons—ay?

Filippo. I confessed all I had to confess **in** this matter, the evening **I** landed.

Eugenius. Ho! I am no candidate for **a seat** at the **rehearsal** of confessions; but perhaps my absolution might be somewhat more pleasing and unconditional. **Well**! well! since I am **un**worthy of such confidence, go about thy business—paint! paint!

Filippo. Am I so unfortunate **as** to have offended **your** Beatitude?

Eugenius. Offend *me*, man! who offends *me*? I took **an** interest in thy adventures, and was concerned lest thou mightest **have** sinned; for, by my soul! Filippo! those **are** the women that the devil hath set his mark on.

Filippo. It would do your Holiness's heart good to rub it out again, wherever he may have had the cunning to make it.

Eugenius. Deep! deep!

Filippo. Yet it may be got **at;** she being a Biscayan by birth, as she told me, and not only baptized, but going **by** sea along **the** coast for confirmation, when she was captured.

Engenius. Alas! to what an imposition of **hands was this** tender young thing devoted! Poor soul!

Filippo. I sigh for her myself when I think of her.

Eugenius. Beware lest the sigh be mundane, and lest the thought recur too often. I wish it were presently in my power **to** examine her myself on her condition. What thinkest thou! Speak.

Filippo. Holy Father! she would laugh in your face.

Eugenius. So lost!

Filippo. **She declared to** me she thought she should have died, from the instant she was captured until she was comforted by Abdul; but **that** she was quite sure she should if she were ransomed.

Eugenius. Has the wretch then shaken her faith?

Filippo. The very last thing he would think of doing. Never did I see the virtue of resignation in higher perfection than in the laughing, light-hearted Almeida.

Eugenius. Lamentable! Poor **lost** creature! lost in this world and in the next.

Filippo. What could she do ? how could she help herself?

Eugenius. She might have torn his eyes out, and have died a martyr.

Filippo. Or have been bastinadoed, whipped, and given up to the cooks and scullions for it.

Eugenius. Martyrdom is the more glorious the greater the indignities it endures.

Filippo. Almeida seems unambitious. There are many in our Tuscany who would jump at the crown over those sloughs and briers, rather than perish without them : she never sighs after the like.

Eugenius. Nevertheless, what must she witness! what abominations! what superstitions!

Filippo. Abdul neither practises nor exacts any other superstition than ablutions.

Eugenius. Detestable rites! without our authority. I venture to affirm that, in the whole of Italy and Spain, no convent of monks or nuns contains a bath ; and that the worst inmate of either would shudder at the idea of observing such a practice in common with the unbeliever. For the washing of the feet indeed we have the authority of the earlier Christians ; and it may be done, but solemnly and sparingly. Thy residence among the Mahometans, I am afraid, hath rendered thee more favourable to them than beseems a Catholic, and thy mind, I do suspect, sometimes goes back into Barbary unreluctantly.

Filippo. While I continued in that country, although I was well treated, I often wished myself away, thinking of my friends in Florence,—of music, of painting, of our villegiatura at the vintage-time ; whether in the green and narrow glades of Pratolino, with lofty trees above us, and little rills unseen, and little bells about the necks of sheep and goats, tinkling together ambiguously; or amid the gray quarries, or under the majestic walls of ancient Fiesole ; or down in the woods of the Doccia, where the cypresses are of such girth that, when a youth stands against one of them, and a maiden stands opposite, and they clasp it, their hands at the time do little more than meet. Beautiful scenes, on which Heaven smiles eternally, how often has my heart ached for you ! He who hath lived in this country can enjoy no distant one. He breathes here another air ; he lives more life ; a brighter

sun invigorates his studies, and serener stars influence his repose.
Barbary hath also the blessing of climate ; and, although I do not
desire to be there again, I feel sometimes a kind of regret at
leaving it. A bell warbles the more mellifluously in the air when
the sound of the stroke is over, and when another swims out from
underneath it, and pants upon the element that gave it birth. In
like manner, the recollection of a thing is frequently more pleasing
than the actuality : what is harsh is dropped in the space between.
There is in Abdul a nobility of soul on which I often have
reflected with admiration. I have seen many of the highest rank
and distinction, in whom I could find nothing of the great man,
excepting a fondness for low company, and an aptitude to shy and
start at every spark of genius or virtue that sprang up above or before them. Abdul was solitary, but affable; he was proud, but
patient and complacent. I ventured once to ask him, how the
master of so rich a house in the city, of so many slaves, of so many
horses and mules, of such cornfields, of such pastures, of such gardens, woods, and fountains, should experience any delight or
satisfaction in infesting the open sea, the high-road of nations ?
Instead of answering my question, he asked me in return, whether
I would not respect any relative of mine who avenged his country,
enriched himself by his bravery, and endeared to him his friends
and relatives by his bounty ? · On my reply in the affirmative, he
said that his family had been deprived of possessions in Spain,
much more valuable than all the ships and cargoes he could ever
hope to capture, and that the remains of his nation were threatened
with ruin and expulsion.

"I do not fight," said he, "whenever it suits the convenience,
or gratifies the malignity or the caprice, of two silly, quarrelsome
princes ; drawing my sword in perfectly good-humour, and sheath-
ing it again at word of command, just when I begin to get into a
passion. No : I fight on my own account ; not as a hired assassin,
or still baser journeyman."

Eugenius. It appears, then, really that the infidels have some
semblances of magnanimity and generosity ?

Fillipo. I thought so when I turned over the many changes
of fine linen ; and I was little short of conviction when I found
at the bottom of my chest two hundred Venetian zecchins.

Eugenius. Corpo di Bacco ! Better things, far better things,

I would fain do for thee, not exactly of this description; it would excite many heart-burnings.   Information has been laid before me, Filippo, that thou art attached to a certain young person, by name, Lucrezia, daughter of Francesco Buti, a citizen of Prato.

Filippo.   I acknowledge my attachment: it continues.

Eugenius.   Furthermore, that thou hast offspring by her.

Filippo.   Alas! 'tis undeniable.

Eugenius.   I will not only legitimatize the said offspring by *motu proprio* and rescript to consistory and chancery—

Filippo.   Holy Father! Holy Father!   For the love of the Virgin, not a word to consistory or chancery, of the two hundred zecchins.   As I hope for salvation, I have but forty left; and thirty-nine would not serve them.

Eugenius.   Fear nothing.   Not only will I perform what I have promised, not only will I give the strictest order that no money be demanded by any officer of my courts, but, under the seal of St Peter, I will declare thee and Lucrezia Buti man and wife.

Filippo.   Man and wife!

Eugenius.   Moderate thy transport.

Filippo.   O Holy Father! may I speak?

Eugenius.   Surely, she is not the wife of another?

Filippo.   No indeed.

Eugenius.   Nor within the degrees of consanguinity and affinity?

Filippo.   No, no, no.   But — man and wife!   Consistory and chancery are nothing to this fulmination.

Eugenius.   How so?

Filippo.   It is man and wife the first fortnight, but wife and man ever after.   The two figures change places: the unit is the decimal, and the decimal is the unit.

Eugenius.   What then can I do for thee?

Filippo.   I love Lucrezia: let me love her; let her love me. I can make her at any time what she is not: I could never make her again what she is.

Eugenius.   The only thing I can do, then, is to promise I will forget that I have heard any thing about the matter.   But, to forget it, I must hear it first.

Filippo. In the beautiful little town of Prato, reposing in its idleness against the hill that protects it from the north, and looking over fertile meadows, southward to Poggio Cajano, westward to Pistoja, there is the convent of Santa Margarita. I was invited by the sisters to paint an altar-piece for the chapel. A novice of fifteen, my own sweet Lucrezia, came one day alone to see me work at my Madonna. Her blessed countenance had already looked down on every beholder lower by the knees. I myself, who made her, could almost have worshipped her.

Eugenius. Not while incomplete : no half-virgin will do.

Filippo. But there knelt Lucrezia ! there she knelt ! first looking with devotion at the Madonna, then with admiring wonder and grateful delight at the artist. Could so little a heart be divided ? 'Twere a pity ! There was enough for me : there is never enough for the Madonna. Resolving on a sudden that the object of my love should be the object of adoration to thousands, born and unborn, I swept my brush across the maternal face, and left a blank in heaven. The little girl screamed : I pressed her to my bosom.

Eugenius. In the chapel ?

Filippo. I knew not where I was : I thought I was in Paradise.

Eugenius. If it was not in the chapel, the sin is venial. But a brush against a Madonna's mouth is worse than a beard against her votary's.

Filippo. I thought so too, Holy Father !

Eugenius. Thou sayest thou hast forty zecchins : I will try in due season to add forty more. The fisherman must not venture to measure forces with the pirate. Farewell ! I pray God, my son Filippo, to have thee alway in his holy keeping.

XIX.   WILLIAM WALLACE AND KING EDWARD I.[1]

Edward.   Whom seest thou here?

Wallace.   The King of England.

Edward.   And thou abasest not thy head before the majesty of the sceptre!

Wallace.   I did.

Edward.   I marked it not.

Wallace.   God beheld it when I did it; and he knoweth, as doth king Edward, how devoutly in my heart's strength I fought for it.

Edward.   Robber! for what sceptre?   Who commissioned thee?

Wallace.   My country.

Edward.   Thou liest: there is no country where there is no king.

Wallace.   Sir, it were unbecoming to ask in this palace, why there is no king in my country.

Edward.   To spare thy modesty, then, I will inform thee. Because the kingdom is mine.   Thou hast rebelled against me; thou hast presumed even to carry arms against both of those nobles, Bruce and Cummin, who contended for the Scottish throne, and with somewhat indeed of lawyer's likelihood.

Wallace.   They placed the Scottish throne under the English.

Edward.   Audacious churl! is it not meet?

Wallace.   In Scotland we think otherwise.

Edward.   Rebels do, subverters of order, low ignorant knaves, without any stake in the country.   It hath pleased God to bless

[1 Landor has taken some of the facts of this dialogue from the account given in Hume's history.   Many Scotch historians assert that the colloquy between Bruce and Wallace on the Carronside determined the former to devote himself to the cause of Scotland.   Wallace was betrayed by Menteith in the summer, and was brought to London in August—not in the winter as Landor affirms.   Edward the First in this Conversation is painted unreasonably black. (Imag. Convers., iv.   Works, i., 1846. Works, iii., 1876.)]

my arms; what further manifestation of our just claims demandest thou? Silence becomes thee.

Wallace. Where God is named. What is now to the right bank of a river, is to the left when we have crossed it and look round.

Edward. Thou wouldst be witty truly! Who was wittiest, thou or I, when thy companion Menteith delivered thee into my hands?

Wallace. Unworthy companions are not the peculiar curse of private men. I chose not Menteith for his treachery, nor re-warded him for it. Sir, I have contended with you face to face; but would not here: your glory eclipses mine, if this be glory.

Edward. So, thou wouldst place thyself on a level with princes!

Wallace. Willingly, if they attacked my country; and above them.

Edward. Dost thou remember the Carron-side, when your army was beaten and dispersed?

Wallace. By the defection of Cummin and the arrogance of Stuart.

Edward. Recollectest thou the colloquy that Bruce con-descended to hold with thee across the river?

Wallace. I do, sir. Why would not he, being your soldier, and fighting loyally against his native land, pass the water, and ex-terminate an army so beaten and dispersed? The saddle-skirts had been rather the stiffer on the morrow, but he might have never felt them. Why not finish the business at once?

Edward. He wished to persuade thee, loose reviler, that thy resistance was useless.

Wallace. He might have made himself heard better if he had come across.

Edward. No trifling; no arguing with me; no remarks here, caitiff! Thou canst not any longer be ignorant that he hath slain his competitor, Cummin; that my troops surround him; and that he perhaps may now repent the levity of his reproaches against thee. I may myself have said a hasty word or two; but thou hast nettled me. My anger soon passes. I never punish in an enemy any thing else than obstinacy. I did not counsel the accusations and malignant taunts of Bruce.

Wallace.   Sir, I do not bear them in mind.

Edward.   No?

Wallace.   Indeed, I neither do nor would.

Edward.   Dull wretch! I should never forget such.   I can make allowances; I am a king.   I would flay him alive for half of them, and make him swallow back the other half without his skin.

Wallace.   Few have a right to punish; all to pardon.

Edward.   I perceive thou hast at last some glimmering of shame; and adversity makes thee Christian-like.

Wallace.   Adversity, then, in exercising her power, loses her name and features.   King Edward! thou hast raised me among men.   Without thy banners and bows in array against me, I had sunk into utter forgetfulness.   Thanks to thee for placing me, eternally, where no strength of mine could otherwise have borne me!   Thanks to thee for bathing my spirit in deep thoughts, in refreshing calm, in sacred stillness!   This, O King! is the bath for knighthood: after this it may feast, and hear bold and sweet voices, and mount to its repose.

I thought it hard to be seized and bound and betrayed by those in whom I trusted.   I grieved that a valiant soldier (such is Menteith) should act so.   Unhappily! he must now avoid all men's discourses.   'Twill pierce his heart to hear censures on the disloyal; and praises on the loyal will dry up its innermost drop. Two friends can never more embrace in his presence but he shall curse them in the bitterness of his soul, and his sword shall spring up to cleave them.   "Alas!" will he say to himself, "is it thus? was it thus when I drew it for my country?"

Edward.   Think now of other matters: think, what I suggested, of thy reproaches.[2]

Wallace.   I have none to make myself.

Edward.   Be it so: I did not talk about that any longer.

Wallace.   What others, then, can touch or reach me?

Edward.   Such as Bruce's.

Wallace.   Reproaches they were not; for none were ever cast against me: but taunts they were, not unmingled with invitations.

[2 First ed. reads: "reproaches, which no doubt thou deemest unmerited. *Wallace,*" &c.]

Edward. The same invitations, and much greater, I now repeat. Thou shalt govern Scotland for me.

Wallace. Scotland, sir, shall be governed for none : she is old enough to stand by herself, and to stand upright ; the blows she hath received have not broken her loins.

Edward. Come, come, Wallace ! thou hast sense and spirit : confess to me fairly that, if thou wert at liberty, thou wouldst gladly make Bruce regret his ill-treatment of thee.

Wallace. Well, then, I do confess it.

Edward. Something would I myself hazard,—not too much ; but prudently and handsomely. Tell me now plainly—for I love plain-speaking and every thing free and open—in what manner thou wouldst set about it ; and perhaps, God willing, I may provide the means.

Wallace. Sir, you certainly would not : it little suits your temper and disposition.

Edward. Faith ! not so little as thou supposest. Magnanimity and long-suffering have grown upon me, and well become me ; but they have not produced all the good I might have expected from them. Joyfully as I would try them again, at any proper opportunity, there is nothing I am not bound to do, in dearness to my people, to rid myself of an enemy.

In my mind no expressions could be more insulting than Bruce's, when he accused thee, a low and vulgar man (how canst thou help that ?), of wishing to possess the crown.

Wallace. He was right.

Edward. How ! astonishment ! Thou wouldst then have usurped the sovereignty !

Wallace. I possessed a greater power by war than peace could ever give me ; yet I invited and exhorted the legitimate heir of the throne to fight for it and receive it. If there is any satisfaction or gratification in being the envy of men, I had enough and greatly more than enough of it, when even those I love envied me : what would have been my portion of it, had I possessed that which never should have been mine ?

Edward. Why, then, sayest thou that Bruce was right ?

Wallace. He judged, as most men do, from his own feelings. Many have worn crowns ; some have deserved them : I have done neither.

Edward.   Return to Scotland ; bring me Bruce's head back ; and rule the kingdom as viceroy.

Wallace.   I would rather make him rue his words against me, and hear him.

Edward.   Thou shalt.

Wallace.   Believe me, sir, you would repent of your permission.

Edward.   No, by the saints !

Wallace.   You would indeed, sir.

Edward.   Go, and try me ; do not hesitate : I see thou art half inclined ; I may never make the same offer again.

Wallace.   I will not go.

Edward.   Weak, wavering man ! hath imprisonment in one day or two wrought such a change in thee ?

Wallace.   Slavery soon does it ; but I am, and will ever be, unchanged.

Edward.   It was not well, nor by my order, that thou wert dragged along the road, barefooted and bareheaded, while it snowed throughout all the journey.

Wallace.   Certainly, sir, you did not order it to snow from the latter days of December till the middle of January ; but whatever else was done, if my guard spake the truth—

Edward.   He lied, he lied, he lied—

Wallace.—or the warrant he showed me is authentic, was done according to your royal order.

Edward.   What ! are my officers turned into constables ? base varlets !   It must have seemed hard, Wallace !

Wallace.   Not that, indeed ; for I went barefooted in my youth, and have mostly been bareheaded when I have not been in battle.   But to be thrust and shoven into the courtyard ; to shiver under the pent-house from which the wind had blown the thatch, while the blazing fire within made the snow upon the opposite roof redden like the dawn ; to wax faint, ahungered, and athirst, when, within arm's length of me, men pushed the full cup away, and would drink no more,—to that I had never been accustomed in my country.   The dogs, honester and kinder folks than most, but rather dull in the love of hospitality, unless in the beginning some pains are taken with them by their masters, tore my scant gear ; and then your soldiers felt their contempt more natural and easy. The poor curs had done for them what their betters could not do; and the bolder of the company looked hard in my face, to see if I were really the same man.

Edward. O the rude rogues! that was too bad.

Wallace. The worst was this. Children and women, fathers and sons, came running down the hills—some sinking knee-deep in the incrusted snow, others tripping lightly over it—to celebrate the nativity of our blessed Lord. They entreated, and the good priest likewise, that I might be led forth into the church, and might kneel down amid them. "Off!" cried the guard; "would ye plead for Wallace the traitor?" I saw them tremble, for it was treason in them; and then came my grief upon me, and bore hard. They lifted up their eyes to heaven, and it gave me strength.

Edward. Thou shalt not, I swear to thee, march back in such plight.

Wallace. I will not, I swear to thee, march a traitor.

Edward. Right! right! I can trust thee—more than half already. Bruce is the traitor, the worst of the two: he raises the country against me. Go; encompass him; entrap him, quell him.

Sweetheart! thou hast a rare fancy, a youth's love at first sight, for thy chains: unwilling to barter them for liberty, for country, for revenge, for honor.

Wallace. Honor [3] and revenge, such as I have carried in my bosom, are very dear to me! For liberty and country I have often shed my blood, and, if more is wanting, take it. My heart is no better than a wooden cup, whereof the homely liquor a royal hand would cast away indifferently. There once were those who pledged it! where are they? Forgive my repining, O God! Enough, if they are not here.

Edward. Nay, nay, Wallace! thou wrongest me. Thou art a brave man. I do not like to see those irons about thy wrists: they are too broad and tight; they have bruised thee cruelly.

Wallace. Methinks there was no necessity to have hammered the rivets on quite so hard; and the fellow who did it needed not to look over his shoulder so often while he was about it, telling

[3 For "Honor and revenge," 1st ed. reads: "the two latter"; for "liberty and country," 1st ed. reads: "the two former."]

the people, "This is Wallace." Wrist or iron, he and his hammer cared not.

Edward.   I am mightily taken with the fancy of seeing thee mortify Bruce.   Thou shalt do it : let me have thy plan.[4]

[[4] First ed. reads: "plan. *Wallace.* **Sir, I have none** worthy of your royal participation. *Edward.* **Thou formest** the **best** possible in one moment, and **executest** them in **another.** *Wallace.* Peradventure the only one I could **devise** and execute, **in this** contingency, might not please you. *Edward.* **It** would, beyond measure, I promise thee: **set** about it instantly : I must enjoy it before I rest. Tell it me, tell it me. *Wallace.* Must I? *Edward.* Thou must: I am **faint** with waiting. *Wallace.* I would go unto him bareheaded: I would **kiss** his hand. *Edward.* Nothing can be better: **wary,** provident, deep. . . . *Wallace.* I **would** lead him before the altar, if my entreaty could do it. . . . *Edward.* No, no, no! . . . **unless in case of** necessity. *Wallace.* I would adjure him by the Lord of Hosts, the preserver of Scotland. . . . *Edward.* No harm in that. . . . *Wallace.* . . . to pity his country. . . . *Edward.* Ay; it would vex him to reflect on what a state it is in at present. *Wallace.* . . . and to proclaim a traitor to his king and **God** every Scotchman who abandons or despairs of her. *Edward.* What is **this**? Why would it hurt him? I comprehend not half the stratagem. How! thy limbs swell longer, thy stature higher. . . . **Thou** scornest, thou scoffest, thou defiest me! a prisoner! a bondman! **By** the Holy Ghost! the hurdle shall creak under thee to-morrow. *Wallace.* To-morrow! *Edward.* To-morrow; I repeat it. *Wallace.* So soon? *Edward.* Yea, by the rood! no later. *Wallace.* King Edward, I never thought **to** thank thee. *Edward.* What audacious insurgent pride! what villanous loftiness! By all the saints of heaven! every town in England shall have a fair sight of thee, more or less; hand or foot, brisket or buttock, heart or liver. *Wallace.* They should have seen me, King of England, to greater advantage, if thy sword alone had been against me. *Edward.* To-morrow thy tongue, I trow, shall wag less bravely, tho' it have a good spear to support it. I will render thee a terror to thy riotous gang. The raven shall take a text from thee and preach over thee, and merry Carlisle shall ring the bells after the service. *Wallace.* Thou needest not send branch nor bough nor cutting to Carlisle : that city, from autumn to spring, hath beheld the tree nod in its glory, and feared lest it sweep her walls. *Edward.* Sirrah! where I am, mark me, there is but one greater. *Wallace.* Thou hast endeavoured to **make** another, and **wilt** almost accomplish it. *Edward.* Guards! away with him. . . . A traitor's doom awaits thee. *Wallace.* Because I would not be one. *Edward.* Laughter, too, **and** lewd mockery. Carry him **back to prison**: **cord** him! pinion him! cart him! *Wallace.* Thou **followest me** to death, less willingly, and slower.]

XX. NICOLAS AND MICHEL.[1]

Nicolas.   Well, my brother! you have been among the
frequenters of court and coffee-house more recently than I have ;
pray tell me what is the opinion, or rather, what are the opinions,
of people in general on our march against Constantinople.

Michel.   Brother, we were not educated on the principle of
noticing the ideas of the powerless.   Our policy has ever been
invariable, whether in the hands of the intelligent or of the
ignorant.   The men who surrounded Catharine, who conversed
with her, who corresponded with her, left behind them the mark
of the axe at certain distances in the forest we are penetrating, and
we have only to look over the chart and give directions. ·

Nicolas.   Very true.   Other States enjoy no such advantages :
intrigue runs into intrigue ; duplicity doubles upon duplicity ; the
cable too much twisted cuts itself, and the anchor lies flat along
the sand.   To undo the labours of a predecessor, and to denounce
the fallacy or the folly of his projects, is the chief business of a
prime minister in every other cabinet.   Have you been able to
find out nothing in regard to their sentiments ?[2]

Michel.   If any thing were in them, I might have found it out.
Gravity, honesty, fairness, unreservedness, reciprocity, and a
sincere and disinterested love of peace and order, are in the eyes
and upon the lips of all diplomatists.   The King of England
regards you as his brother ; the King of France embraces you as
his son ; the Emperor of Austria rode side by side with your
illustrious predecessor, whose views were the same as his ; and he
never will believe it possible that your Imperial Majesty, equally
wise and magnanimous, can change one tittle.   There are those
who whisper the contrary, but none heeds them.

[1 Nicolas succeeded his brother Alexander in 1825.   In spite of
Austria's efforts to secure the neutrality of Russia, Nicolas continued his
brother's favourable policy towards the Greeks, who were then in the
midst of their long struggle for liberty.   The Conversation must be supposed to have taken place before Russia joined with England at the time
of the battle of Navarino.   (Imag. Convers., v., 1829.   Works, i., 1846.
iii., 1876.)]

[2 First ed. reads : "sentiments of our neighbours ?"]

Nicolas. Palaces should have no whispering galleries, or they should be left to the women and pages. So Francis says he is resolved not to believe what they tell him, and what he sees: well, I am the last man in the world who would 'shake his belief, seeing it firm and fitting.

Michel. He added, if his majesty the Autocrat of all the Russias had declared war against the Turk to protect the Greek a few years ago, while a million or two were living, such war perhaps might have had its plea and its abettors: but since in the whole of the Morea, in the whole scene of the war, there are not forty thousand adult males surviving, nor the same number of females of an age to reproduce them; since all the boys and girls in the country do not amount to thirty thousand,—it surely requires a second thought whether war should be lighted up in the centre of Europe for so minute an object. His Majesty the Emperor of Austria is himself of a different opinion: he has received positive information from indisputable authority, from eye-witnesses, that such was the wretchedness of the Greeks, brought on them by their rebellion, many who never had fought came forward in the line of march and threw stones or even berries and grass at the Turks, that they might finish their existence less criminally than by suicide, and less miserably than by famine.

Nicolas. Great God! is this true?

Michel. I asked the same question of the traveller: he saw it.

Nicolas. I am ashamed of my supineness. Merciful Father of mankind, forgive me!

Michel. Many were driven mad by thirst and hunger, many by desperation, many by the sight of the last child carried off by the Arabs; and there was one—he was more frantic than the rest, but he was of briefer agony—who yet remembered the name of every hill and mountain he had seen or heard of, and called on each and on all to cover him: for he had caught his infant's breath as it left the body in his house, and had not dared to go forth and bury it with Christian burial.

Nicolas. If these things were false, they would have been said before. Wisdom and Truth are unwinged deities, and are less to be known by their features than by their tardiness and taciturnity. I might have died, and have never known half the justice of my cause. Policy is a jealous and a selfish thing; and Honor is quite as jealous, quite as selfish. Here find we more than state-papers can enwrap, more than manifestoes dare make manifest. A million hearts shall heave these wrongs to God, a million swords shall avenge them. Are there men upon earth who dare commit them, and none to say, "Ye shall not do it"? What! my brother of Austria talks of moderation and forbearance. Let him open the prisons of Mantua a few moments, not for pardon, not for remission, but only that the captive may see, looking close, whether his finger has inscribed on the slippery green wall the right year of our Lord in the right place, or one upon another, ten, eleven, twelve. Let him, in his imperial bounty and apostolic piety, add a mouthful of fresh air from the marsh, and a slip of sunshine that the dogs on the outside have done with; let him, freely and boldly: I will not protest against his encouragement of secret sects and novel opinions. He talks then of the centre of Europe, does he? My torch is in the extremity of it: he may decide whether I shall carry it to the centre. Our brother Alexander grew lazy and fond of pleasure: he deferred the declaration of hostilities too long. I know not whether his delay of them cost him his life or not: certain I am our nation would have risen in arms against him, and against me likewise, had our religion been longer oppressed, our honor insulted, our armies defied, and our treaties violated. Let any potentate in Europe give me an example of so just a war. The strongest of our arguments is the declaration of our enemy that he was deceiving us with pacific protestations, and that he never intended to comply with the arbitration he recently had accepted and long solicited. I regret that it is impossible for a king or emperor to obtain the whole truth from any man, excepting some one perhaps in his own family; and this one is generally on the least friendly terms with him. My regret would, in my own particular case, have been the lighter, if you, my dear Michel, could have carried my wishes into execution, and could have conversed at this crisis on terms of equality and intimacy with intelligent and well-informed strangers.

Michel. While I was at Moscow I met an Englishman, who intended to travel through the empire, and to whom, on his presentation to me, I gave all the facilities I could.

Nicolas. Are you sure he is not a spy?

Michel. If he is, I shall have a better opinion of his government than it ever has deserved in the memory of man. It has employed in no department, from the lowest to the highest, a functionary of equal perspicacity. He had left Constantinople about two months, and he confirmed to me the news that the Duke of Wellington has placed himself at the head of the administration.

Nicolas. I know not whether this event is at all unfavorable to me. It must be regarded in two points of view. During the war, while he held the command of the army, he showed the light of his countenance to those officers only whose families were strong in parliamentary interest : whether he did this according to orders from the ministry, or with private and remoter views, is at present no subject for inquiry. He must now make the fortunes of his military supporters, and not only of those, but of the new generation, their sons and nephews, who were children at the close of hostilities. These must be provided for; and war is the only means : such is the system of government in England. But England, who suffers more by beating than by being beaten, is, relatively to the other States of Europe, less powerful than she ever was ; and nothing but invasion or madness could incite her, for the next half century, to take up arms. The slower the nation is, the readier will be the aristocracy, which must now become all-powerful. Popular power and popular feeling are odious to the Duke of Wellington ; and he has exercised his usual judgment in seizing the moment when both are at the lowest. The few persons in the House of Commons, on whom the country had any reliance, have abandoned the hopeless cause, and have made their patriotism very palatable. We may safely admit them to kiss our hands, when the pages have removed our hats and gloves from the antechamber. I had persuaded Mr Canning to join with France in sending troops against Ibrahim. Every thing was ready : the two nations would have quarrelled within six weeks. England, it must be confessed, never, in these last fifty years, had a minister so prudent and wary in continental politics as Wellington. He foresees the consequences of such a step ; and, not only from hatred of the Greeks and their adherents, but from sound policy, will keep his troops away. The French are impetuous and thoughtless ; they may invade the

Morea, not with the design of aiding the insurgents, nor with the hope of holding the country and thus rendering the Seven Isles of no utility to England, but in order to exchange it for Crete or Cyprus. I was unable to avert the war: I was unwilling to defer it; nor indeed could any time be more favorable for my operations, unless it should be two years hence, when the Duke of Wellington may be called to settle things upon a durable basis. The French government and I must let him have a war: the best plan will be to draw lots which shall gratify him. One or other must do it; else things in England cannot go on quietly, and the aristocracy will be little better than the higher classes of the people.

Michel. The Turks appear to be more angry both with France and England than with us.

Nicolas. A sense of indignity is stronger among the Turks than among any other nation upon earth. From me they expected open war, and have it: from France and England they expected protection, and experience perfidy. To me they would rather open the gates of Constantinople, than to them the harbor of Navarino.

Let me hear the remarks of the traveller.

Michel. Before the troops began to march, he waited on the Governor of Moscow with a plan of operations.

Nicolas. Depend upon it, he is a spy then. How the English are changed! The French Revolution has altered the French but little, the English totally.[3] The Gallic twigs shook and bent and lost some leaves, but rose up again in the same direction, resumed the same form, and displayed the same fruits and foliage. Whatever was light and worthless in France seems to have been blown across the Channel, and to have taken root in England. I do not complain of military government; an excellent thing, temperately used: but I little apprehended that the English would so readily submit to it.

Michel. Something of this occurred to the traveller, who remarked that the condition of England is at present what the

[3 If any person be desirous of having an adequate idea of the mischievous effects which have been produced in this country by the French Revolution and all its attendant horrors, he should attempt some legislative reform on humane and liberal principles." *See* Life of Sir S. Romilly.]

condition of France was at the dissolution of the Directory.
Stock-jobbers ruled; persons of the highest rank visited and
courted them: they were raised to dignities above the de-
fenders of the nation.[4] The only sign of prosperity was the
profusion and waste of public money. Where the taxes are
enormous, said he, nobody cares who rules, or how he rules.
The distress of families, penury, want, are directly and in
themselves but minor evils: worse are the prostration of public honor, the prostitution of private dignity, contempt of old
usages, indifference to improvement, hopelessness at last and
apathy, even in those who would have given their lives to their
country.

Nicolas. Spies often talk in this florid way.

Michel. When your Majesty sees the whole plan, you may
think differently of the author.

Nicolas. Do you recollect it?

Michel. Yes, together with what he said to me politically.

Nicolas. I will not again interrupt you; let me hear it.

Michel. These were nearly his words:—

Ere you attempt to carry a plan into execution, you must
not only look toward the road before you, but sometimes on
each side and behind. Russia no doubt is in good intelligence
with Sweden and Prussia, whose interest it is at all times to be in
harmony with her.

Nicolas. He speaks wisely: if he is not a spy, he ought at
least to be a privy councillor.

Michel. The better to ensure the friendship and co-opera-
tion of Sweden, I would resign to her, said he, that portion of
Finland which was last detached from her, together with the
whole of Lapland, on condition that she supply to me her maritime force during eight months, the Emperor paying the seamen
and provisioning. The King of Sweden is ambitious of possessing the entire peninsula; and what is proposed to be ceded is
worth little to Russia.

I hardly dare mention what he added.

Nicolas. Speak plainly, my dear brother: he appears no
fool.

Michel. He observed that the French nation is in an

[⁴ First ed. reads: "nation, and above her judges. The," &c.]

indescribable degree attached to the Polander; and that not only throughout France, but equally throughout Germany, the sentiment is prevalent and universal. He recommended that, until the capture of Constantinople, no direct answer should be given to foreign ministers; that nothing should be said further than His Imperial Majesty, having shown a forbearance from hostilities unexampled in the history of any powerful nation, is resolved to show a disinterestedness yet more remarkable, and to make such cessions of conquest as will not only satisfy but astonish Europe.

Nicolas. What can he mean?

Michel. That your Majesty will grant to Mehemet Ali the possession of Syria, Arabia, Cyprus, Egypt, and Mauritania, the Euphrates being the boundary on the east in its whole extent. I may now revert to Poland.

Nicolas. Now, indeed, you may.

Michel. He recommends that your Majesty should cede to the King of Prussia, to be governed by his second son and the heirs of that prince, the provinces of Varsavia, Grodno, Minsk, and Volhynia, on condition that Prussia joins to it all her possessions on the right of the Vistula, and whatever she retains of ancient Poland on the left: and furthermore that Austria restores Gallicia. This compact, he says, would be disadvantageous to Prussia, unless you erected in her favor a kingdom of Dalmatia, adding to it Croatia, Bosnia, Servia, and Albania, and bounding it by the river Verdar in Macedonia, and by the ridges of Olympus.

Nicolas. What would Austria say?

Michel. He proposes that the favorite plan of Austria should be executed, though not exactly in her manner. He would allow to the Archdukes of Austria the whole of Italy, which would quietly and gladly submit to them if constitutions were granted. The Duke of Modena is detested for his avarice, his treachery, his cowardice, and his cruelty; the King of Sardinia is unpopular; his heir is distrusted and despised alike by the prince and people, and he would think himself fortunate to possess the island. What the Switzers hold in Lombardy may be recovered by payment of the money for which it was pledged. All that country, all the country from the torrent at Nervi, near Genoa, to the source of the Trebia and to the mouth of the Po, should constitute one kingdom for an archduke : another should possess the kingdom of Adria, from the mouth of the Po to the Gulf of Taranto, bounded by the Apennines on the west. The kingdom of Etruria should extend from the bridge of Nervi to the Tiber, and follow the Teverone to its source. The city of Rome, within the walls, might be the Pope's.

Nicolas. But the kingdom of Naples, must it be ceded to an archduke? Would France and Spain consent to it?

Michel. Sicily is more than enough, he thinks, for kings hardly on a level either in intellect or information with the wretchedest and most sordid on the Atlantic coast of Africa. He supposes that Russia, Prussia, Austria, Sweden, and England, are unanimous. France and Spain have nearer interests, and may be called home if they stir. By these arrangements, the families of the Emperor of Austria and King of France would govern a larger population in Europe than your Majesty, and England a larger in Asia. What right or reason, then, has any one of them to complain of an undue weight in the balance? Russia would be surrounded by States incapable of molesting her; while Prussia would be well indemnified for a narrow and barren coast, easily to be taken from her in the first war with Russia or with France.

Nicolas. I may abstain from seizing all I could seize; but I do not like to give up any thing I possess.

Michel. An objection foreseen by the traveller, who adduced many proofs of shortsightedness in politicians from what he called this distemper.

Nicolas. Will others do it if I do?

Michel. Again his very words! This reflection, he said, throws a damp on nearly all generosity, and stints the higher growth to the standard of the lower. *Will others do it if I do?* blights more good than takes growth : and, *If I do not, others will*, prompts to more evil than is allowed to lie inert.

Nicolas. Plausible! there is something in him. What were his military views?

Michel. Principally, to follow the march of Cesarini ; to secure a strong position or two on the right bank of the Danube ; to be perfectly sure that the Governor of Servia is in your interest, and to render him completely so by granting him the government for life ; by no means to invade that country, or any part of Bosnia, or more of Bulgaria than the frontiers ; to seize or blockade every port and roadstead, and to occupy or observe all the stronger of the positions, from the mouths of the Danube to the canal of Constantinople. For this purpose in particular the Swedish fleet is desirable. The expense, which may appear to be greater than of forces equally numerous that march by land, is much less. The roads of the sea are not to be broken up by the enemy's pioneers ; the cattle, safely stored in the small compass of barrels, are not to be driven off ; ambuscades there are none here ; horses are not left behind for want of provender, for want of shoes, for wounds, or for diseases.* Battering trains do not here consume what would almost be sufficient for the sustenance of the armies ; and the broken carriages of abandoned cannon do not impede the passage of the troops. In attempting to penetrate the mountains of Balkan, in which many thousand soldiers must perish, a part only of the provisions can accompany the army ; and the enemy will have daily opportunities of attacking it with advantage. He may delay it throughout the months of July and August, when the plains are burned up, and neither provender nor water can be procured sufficiently. Fevers too will be prevalent among you ; and certainly not a third of your forces can be brought, after those months and that march, against Constantinople. Coast the Black Sea with successive armies and incessant debarkations. Water and provisions of every kind may partly be found and partly imported ; places may be taken as there are opportunities, without any great care whether in order or not. Perhaps it might be more advantageous to take Sisepoli before Varna, since it would impede the provisioning both of Varna and of Bourgas. Neither Rudshuk nor Silistria need be besieged : every place lower than Silistria should be occupied by gun-boats.

Nicolas. We must go regularly to work : we must take the strong places along the Danube.

Michel. The stranger thinks differently, for this reason : In the strong places great magazines are formed, and they are well garnished with cannon ; but the Turks have few waggons, few tumbrils, few beasts of burden in them ; and those in the country

---

* This was published seventeen months before the passing of the Balkan, and the loss of 10,000 horses and oxen.

will be seized by our **Cossacks**, as well as the grain, the straw, and the hay. So there is no danger of their rising in the rear of you ; and, were it possible, you have always a force equal to theirs, in readiness to occupy the positions.

Nicolas. The distance is greater by the Black Sea.

Michel. Somewhat ; but the march is to be performed in less time. You have always one flank protected ; you have always fresh **food** ; you have always fresh water ; you have wine, brandy, medicines, iron, **wood** ; you have, instead of heat and dust and suffocation, temperate and salubrious breezes ; you have frequent and commodious places for halting, and, what always should be well considered, readier and less painful means of carrying off the sick and wounded. You never need fight, unless where your **fleet** and gunboats can co-operate. Quantities of projectiles to any amount may attend the army. If such as have lately **been** invented are employed by your forces, undiminished and healthy as they would be, Constantinople cannot resist forty hours, and must fall before the end of **August.** The city will blaze in all quarters, partly from your fire against it, partly from the indignation of the janizaries and their adherents, and partly from the revenge of the Armenians and **Greeks.** Your Majesty will then enjoy the opportunity of bestowing a forfeited empire on an inveterate enemy. By the cession of all his European dominions to you, any part of them which may be occupied by another must be evacuated and restored. By your concession of the rest, Barbary will be no longer a scourge and disgrace to the maritime powers of Europe. Mehemet may reign in Damascus or Alexandria, possessing a territory larger than France, Spain, Portugal, **Italy,** and the British Isles, united, and capable with proper management of supporting more inhabitants than the whole number of his present subjects. [5]

Nicolas. In good truth, Michel, I do not fear any power in Europe. Austria may molest me : I can ruin her. One blow,

[5 First ed. reads : "subjects. Your neighbours, said the traveller, are unaware that your possession of Turkey would be highly and instantaneously advantageous to their commerce. If they oppose it, they not only throw more than they can find elsewhere, but must lose their vessels by the shoal of privateers you send out against them. *Nicolas,*" &c.]

one treacherous act, and I cast a firebrand into Italy, and another
into Hungary, which the world upon it could not extinguish.

France here would not oppose me.[6] Who would, then?
The season is hot, the wood dry; a spark is enough: I would
rather not blow it, lest the blaze extend too far, and the wind
carry it back again toward me. There is not a government in
Europe, among the greater, which a touch on the exterior might
not overturn. Some are laden so heavily with debt, they cannot
keep afloat; others swell with gross affronts; and others agonize
with broken promises. Then, between ourselves, the rulers are
fools and scoundrels, and I begin to suspect such characters are
going out of repute.[7]

Did the traveller say any thing of his own country?

Michel. England, he said, is strong in self-defence; but,
added he, if her minister had influence enough to bring about a
war, the people would refuse to pay the taxes. You and she
never need come in contact: you may injure each other's prosperity,
you cannot shake each other's power. Let France play with the
Greeks until she fall asleep upon them; it is the business of
England, who ought to have retained her conquest, to beware
that France does not again take Egypt. Let England watch
her; do you[8] rather encourage and flatter than perplex her.

Such was the opinion of the imaginary spy.

Nicolas. Send him to me; I will give him an audience and
a star, admit him as[9] a privy councillor, and appoint him to a
post on the Caspian.

Michel. I offered him my recommendations: he declined
them gravely and respectfully, giving me his reason.

Nicolas. What was it?

Michel. He said that, having lately been conversant with
Sophocles and Plato, he entertained the best-founded hopes, in
case of a maritime war, he should be nominated, on some vacancy,
as worthy of bearing his Britannic Majesty's commission of purser
to a fire-ship.

[6 First ed. reads: "me: Bavaria would not, certainly. Who!" &c.
Six lines below 1st ed. reads: "swim" for "keep afloat."]

[7 First ed. reads: "repute, for any rank higher than ministers and
masters of ceremonies. Did," &c.]

[8 First ed. reads: "you be courteous, and rather," &c.

[9 From "as" to "councillor" added in 2nd ed.; four lines below from
"Nicolas" to "it?" added in 2nd ed.]

XXI. THE DUKE OF WELLINGTON AND SIR ROBERT INGLIS.[1]

Duke. Good morning, Sir Robert Inglis, I am glad to see you.

Inglis. Your Grace is extremely obliging in fixing so early an hour for the audience I requested.

Duke. We cannot meet too early for business, long or short.

Inglis. The present is most important to the Administration of which your Grace is the main support.

Duke. If you think so, we will despatch it at once. I presume you mean the matter of Lord Ellenborough.

Inglis. Exactly, my lord duke.

Duke. Your objections, I think, rest on something which wounded your feelings on the side of religion?

Inglis. Not mine only, may it please your Grace.

Duke. It neither pleases nor displeases me, Sir Robert Inglis. I am an impartial man; and this is a matter that lies among the bishops.

Inglis. I fear they will not stir in the business.

Duke. The wiser men they.

Inglis. But surely it is most offensive to pay twenty thousand men, and two millions of money, for a pair of sandal-wood gates, which are not of sandal-wood, in order to fix them again to a temple which does not exist: a temple which, while it did exist, was dedicated to the most immoral and impure

[1 Lord Ellenborough's grandiloquent proclamations must have been a little unintelligible to the people of India. The invasion of Afghanistan appeared to him to be a vengeance taken by the Hindoos for the Mahommedan conquest of India, a bit of history some centuries old. "Our victorious army bears the gates of the temple of Somnauth in triumph from Afghanistan, and the despoiled tomb of Sultan Mahmud looks upon the ruins of Ghaznee. The insult of eight hundred years is at last avenged." Unfortunately for Lord Ellenborough, while he insulted the Mahommedans, he offended the religious feelings of the Hindoos, and had finally to admit that the gates of Somnauth were not a genuine relic at all. The name of Sir Robert Inglis is familiar as the pattern of the despairing Tory. (**Works, ii., 1846.** Works, iii., 1876.)]

of worship; which afterward was converted to a mosque, and is now the receptacle of all the filth in the city that is ever removed at all.

Duke. You say the gates are not of sandal-wood; yet Lord Ellenborough is accused by the Radicals of setting up sandal-wood gates. This is frivolous.

Inglis. He made a proclamation in the style of Bonaparte.

Duke. Not he, indeed; he is no more like Bonaparte than you are. Another frivolous objection. I do assure you, Sir Robert Inglis, he always thought Bonaparte a miserably poor creature in comparison with himself; for, even in his best days, or (to use the word well for once) his *palmy* days, Bonaparte had notoriously little hair, and wore it quite flat. Then, after he made a peace, which to many, who pull back the past to overlay the present, seems as glorious as that which Lord Ellenborough has just concluded, what did Bonaparte? Mind! I am speaking now his lordship's sentiments; for I never speak in disparagement of any person I have been in the habit of meeting in society; but what, in his lordship's opinion, did he, which could excite his envy or imitation? Instead of turning his sword into a pruning-hook, which would have been ostentation and folly in one who never left behind him any thing to prune, and scarcely a pruner, he neglected the only use to which Lord Ellenborough might reasonably have expected him to apply it: he overlooked the obvious utility of its conversion into curling-irons. The cannon his lordship has taken from the enemy, no doubt, will be so employed; at least, they may contribute to it, as far as they go. I do not expect it will be thought advisable, in the present state of her Majesty, to discharge them in the park. Really, I see no reason why, after their remounting, they should not enter on another career of conquest. And where better than against the artillery on the crested heights of Almack's? Do not look so grave, my good Sir Robert Inglis. We are both of us on half-pay in the same department, and our laurels grow rigidly cold upon us.

Inglis. I protest, my lord duke, I do not comprehend your Grace.

Duke. Then we will converse no longer on a subject of such intricacy, in which only one of us has had any practice.

Inglis. He was desirous of ingratiating himself with the Hindoos.

Duke. So he should be. A third frivolous objection.

Inglis. But at the danger of alienating the Mahometans.

Duke. They hate us as you hate the devil; therefore they are not to be alienated. A fourth frivolous objection.

Inglis. My lord duke, I pretend to no knowledge of the parties in India, or their inclinations.

Duke. Then why talk about them?

Inglis. My zeal for the religion of my country.

Duke. What have they to do with the religion of our country, or we with theirs?

Inglis. We, as Englishmen and Christians, have very much to do with theirs.

Duke. Are they, then, Christians and Englishmen? We may worry those who are near us for believing this and disbelieving that; but, until there are none to worry at home, let the people of India fight and work for us, and live contentedly. You live contentedly. But you are too grave and of too high standing to be bottle-holder to conflicting religions. I am sure, Sir Robert Inglis, I would wish fair play and no favor.

Inglis. I trust, my lord duke, I never wish anything unfair.

Duke. And if I have any reputation in the world, it is for loving all that is most fair.

Inglis. Such is your Grace's character.

Duke. Well, then, let Somnauth and Juggernauth share and share alike.

Inglis. In the bottomless pit?

Duke. Wherever is most convenient to the parties. Juggernauth, I must confess to you, has been taken most into consideration by us, being an old ally, in a manner; and our Government has always paid six thousand a year toward his maintenance.

Inglis. I deplore it.

Duke. Every man is at liberty to deplore what he likes, but really I do not see why you should hit upon this in particular. Not a bishop or archbishop rose from his seat in Parliament to denounce or censure or discommend it; therefore I am bound in conscience as a member of the Church of England, in duty as a peer, and in honor as a gentleman, to believe it all right.

Inglis. Surely not, my lord duke. I yield to no man in veneration for the Church as by law established, or for those descendants of the Apostles, nevertheless.

Duke. Better that I should be wrong in my theology than they; but I cannot well be wrong when I agree with lords so learned, particularly now you remind me of their unbroken descent from the Apostles. They are the fairest and most impartial men in the world; they let all religions thrive that do not come too near their own. They never cry "stand back" on slight occasions; and I firmly believe you could never engage more than a couple of them to lend a hand at the car of Juggernauth, even in cool weather. Some of them, whose skirts the reformers have been clipping, would be readier than the rest; but they must have a very high minister in view before they would let you buckle on the harness.

Inglis. I respect their motives. In like manner they abstained from voting on the question of the slave-trade. It behoves them to avoid all discussion and disquisition on the policy of ministers.

Duke. So it does you and me. I lean to neither of the contending gods in particular: they are both well enough in their way; if they are quiet with us, let them do as they like with their own people, who certainly would not have worshipped them so long if they had misbehaved. Do not encourage men, ignorant men particularly, to throw off any restraint you find upon them: it is no easy matter to put another in the place, well-looking as it may be, and clever as you may think yourself in cutting it out and fitting it to the wearer.

Inglis. These wretched men have souls, my lord duke, to be saved from the flames of hell.

Duke. I hope so; but I am no fireman. I know what good, meanwhile, may be done with them in the hands of the priests, if you let the priests have their own way; but if you stop their feeds, what work can you expect out of them?

Inglis. So long as they have their way, Christianity will never be established in Hindostan.

Duke. Bad news, indeed! Upon my life, I am sorry to hear it; especially when other most religious men have taken the trouble to assure me that it would prevail against the devil and all his works. We must not be hasty, Sir Robert Inglis. There are some things at which we may make a dash ; others require wary circumspection and slow approaches. I would curtail the foraging ground of an enemy, never of an ally. We must wink upon some little excesses of theirs, while we keep our own men strictly to duty.   Beside, we are hard driven, and cannot give up patronage.

Inglis.   If your Grace's conscience is quite satisfied that the service of Government requires a certain relaxation in what we consider vital essentials, we must submit.

Duke.   Our consciences may not be quite so easy as one could wish, nor are our places ; but we must take into consideration the necessity of collecting the revenue of Hindostan ; and the priests in all countries can make it difficult or easy. Lord Ellenborough is affable, and I trust he will hang a religion in each ear, so that neither shall hang higher than the other.

Inglis.   We are taught and commanded to judge not hastily. Now, I would not judge hastily my Lord Ellenborough ; but certainly it does bear hard on tender consciences to believe he entertains that lively faith which—

Duke.   Pooh, pooh ! If he has any faith at all, I will answer for him it is as lively as a turtle; which, you know, is proverbial : no advertisement calls the thing otherwise. You may call Ellenborough a silly fellow, but never a dull one, unless when wit and humor are required ; and business wants none of their flashes to show its path.

Inglis.   Belief in his Creator—

Duke.   He believes in all of these, better than they believe in him, from those who created him Secretary of State to those who created him Governor-General.

Inglis.   I meant to signify his religion.

Duke.   He might ask you what that signifies.

Inglis.   We require from all the servants of her Majesty, from all who are in authority under her, as our Church service most beautifully expresses it—

Duke.   Well, well ! what would you have ? I will speak from my own knowledge of him : I know he believes in a deity; I heard him use the very name in swearing at his groom ; and, on the same occasion, he cried aloud, " The devil take the fellow ! " Can you doubt, after this, that his religion is secure on both flanks ?

Inglis. God has, from the beginning, set his face against idolatry.

Duke. I don't wonder. I am persuaded you are correct in your statement, Sir Robert Inglis.

Inglis. He reproved it, in his wrath, as one among the most crying sins of the Jews.

Duke. They have a good many of that description; but they must have been fine soldiers formerly. Do you think, Sir Robert Inglis, they are likely, at last, to get into the Houses of Parliament?

Inglis. God forbid!

Duke. For my own part, I have no voice on the occasion. Other rich folks, quite as crying and craving and importunate,—lawyers more especially,—crowd both yours and ours. But I think a sprinkling of Jews might help you prodigiously just at present; for, by what I hear about them, there are nowhere such stiff sticklers against idolatry, at the present day, as those gentlemen! We both are connected, to a certain extent, with the University of Oxford. Now, people do tell me that many of those who voted for us, as well as many of those who did not, are inclined to a spice of it.

Inglis. They deny the charge.

Duke. Of course they do; so do the people of Hindostan, even those among them who possess no pluralities, no preferment. They all tell you there is something at the bottom of it which you do not see, because you are blind and stupid and unbelieving. They all, both here and there, tell you that, to learn things rightly, you must become a child once more. Now, against the child's doctrine I have nothing to say, but I have a serious objection, in my own person, to certain parts of the discipline.

Inglis. Your Grace is grave, apparently, which could not surely be the case if such abomination were about to be tolerated in our principal seats of learning.

Duke. In truth, I was not thinking about the seats of learning; nor, indeed, do I see any danger in pious men erecting the Cross to elevate their devotion. I fear more the fagot than the solid timber; and, when I know they came out of the same wood, I am suspicious they may be travelling the same road.

But, until an evil intention is manifest, I would let people have their own way, both in Oxfordshire and Hindostan. In regard to giving them money, I leave that matter entirely to the discretion of their votaries.

Inglis. I grieve for this lukewarmness in your Grace.

Duke. It is high time for me to be lukewarm, and hardly that.

Inglis. I did not enter upon politics, or question an officer —a high, a very high functionary of her Majesty—in regard to the expediency of favoring one religion of the Hindoos against the other, and that professed by the more warlike and powerful.

Duke. Did not you? Then what can you question?

Inglis. I question, and more than question, the correctness of his views in winking at impurity; for the worship of the Lingam is most impure.

Duke. We do wink at such things, Sir Robert; we do not openly countenance them. I am no worshipper of the Lingam. I speak as an unprejudiced man; and, depend upon it, if Lord Ellenborough had any tendency to that worship, the priests would make him undergo a rigorous examination, and probably would reject him after all. Nothing in his past life lays him open to such an imputation.

Inglis. God forbid I should imply such an obscenity!

Duke. Do not embarrass by this implication, or any other, the march of a ministry which not only has pointed stakes at every ten yards, but a toll-bar at every twenty. I tell you from my own knowledge, that Ellenborough is only a coxcomb. Respect him, for he is the greatest in the world: and the head of every profession should be respected. What would you have? Whom would you have? You are an aristocrat; you have your title, and, no doubt, your landed estate. Would you send to govern India, as was done formerly, such men as Clive and Hastings? They could conquer and govern empires. What then? Could they keep Ministers and the friends of Ministers in their places? No such thing. Therefore, my good worthy Sir Robert Inglis, do not let us talk any more nonsense together. Our time is valuable; we have not too much left.

Inglis. Whatever, by God's providence, we may still look forward to, let us devote to his service, repressing to the utmost of our power all attempts to aid or comfort a false and most impure religion.

Duke. A bargain! we will; that is, you and I. Let us enter into a compact, this very hour, never to worship the Lingam in word or deed. We will neither bow down to it nor worship it, nor do any thing in word or deed which may point to such a conclusion. I promise, furthermore, to use all my interest with her Majesty's Ministers, that they will immediately send a despatch to Lord Ellenborough, ordering him not to set up the gates again in a temple which has ceased to exist for many centuries; but that, as the gates have been carried about a thousand miles, and as we have lost about as many men (to say nothing of field-pieces) in conveying them back, his Excellency do issue another proclamation, empowering six of the Generals and six of the Supreme Council, to leave India forthwith, bearing with them, to show the devotion both of Mahometans and Hindoos to her Majesty, a toothpick-case and twelve tooth-picks, made therefrom, for the use of her Majesty and her successors. Do you ride, Sir Robert Inglis?

Inglis. I have no horses in town.

Duke. My horse is waiting for me in the court-yard, and I think it proper to set my servants an example of punctuality. Perhaps I may have the pleasure of meeting you in the park.

Inglis. I have occupied too much of your Grace's time?

Duke. Very little.

Inglis. I would only beg of your Grace that you prevail on Ministers to hesitate before—

Duke. I never tell any man to hesitate. Right or wrong, to hesitate is imbecility. How the deuce can a man fall while he is going on? If Peel stops suddenly, the Whigs will run in and cut his brush off.

Inglis. God forbid!

Duke. They don't mind what God forbids, not they. A man is never quagmired till he stops; and the rider who looks back has never a firm seat. We must cast our eyes not at all behind, nor too much before, but steadily just where we are. Politicians are neither lovers nor penitents. I see, Sir Robert Inglis, you are in haste. I will lay before Peel, and the rest of them, all your suggestions. In the meantime, be a little patient; Juggernauth is not coming down St James's Street.

XXII. BISHOP SHIPLEY AND BENJAMIN FRANKLIN.[1]

Shipley. There are very few men, even in the bushes and the wildernesses, who delight in the commission of cruelty; but nearly all, throughout the earth, are censurable for the admission. When we see a blow struck, we go on and think no more about it; yet every blow aimed at the most distant of our fellow-creatures is sure to come back, some time or other, to our families and descendants. He who lights a fire in one quarter is ignorant to what other the winds may carry it, and whether what is kindled in the wood may not break out again in the corn-field.

Franklin. If we could restrain but one generation from deeds of violence, the foundation for a new and a more graceful edifice of society would not only have been laid, but would have been consolidated.

Shipley. We already are horrified at the bare mention of religious wars; we should then be horrified at the mention of political. Why should they who, when they are affronted or offended, abstain from inflicting blows—some from a sense of

[1 Landor probably supposed this Conversation to take place in the year 1775, soon after the Declaration of American Independence. Landor supposes Bishop Shipley and his son William to have accompanied Franklin on his way to the ship in which he was to sail for America. Jonathan Shipley, bishop of St Asaph, was an intimate friend of Franklin's, and a strong opponent of the American War. Franklin frequently visited him, but there is no reason to suppose that the friends were ever mobbed or attacked in any way, though they were doubtless unpopular. The Bishop is frequently mentioned in Boswell's " Life of Johnson "; see index to Dr Birkbeck Hill's edition. The Doctor describes him as " knowing and conversible," and remarks that " he went everywhere." His daughter married Sir William Jones. His son, William Shipley, was Dean of St Asaph. He was a strong Whig. In 1784 he was prosecuted for publishing a pamphlet, entitled " A dialogue between a Gentleman and a Farmer." It was at this trial that Lord Mansfield laid down the doctrine that Juries had no power to find whether the pamphlet was or was not a libel, but only as to publication. (Works, ii., 1846. Works. iii., 1876.)]

decorousness and others from a sense of religion—be forward to instigate the infliction of ten thousand, all irremediable, all murderous? Every chief magistrate should be arbitrator and umpire in all differences between any two, forbidding war. Much would be added to the dignity of the most powerful king by rendering him an efficient member of such a grand Amphictyonic council. Unhappily they are persuaded in childhood that a reign is made glorious by a successful war. What school-master ever taught a boy to question it? or, indeed, any point of political morality, or any incredible thing in history? Cæsar and Alexander are uniformly clement; Themistocles died by a draught of bull's blood; Portia, by swallowing red-hot pieces of charcoal.

Franklin. Certainly no woman or man could perform either of these feats. In my opinion it lies beyond a doubt that Portia suffocated herself by the fumes of charcoal; and that the Athenian, whose stomach must have been formed on the model of other stomachs, and must therefore have rejected a much less quantity of blood than would have poisoned him, died by some chemical preparation, of which a bull's blood might, or might not, have been part. School-masters who thus betray their trust ought to be scourged by their scholars, like him of their pro-fession who underwent the just indignation of the Roman Consul. You shut up those who are infected with the plague: why do you lay no coercion on those who are incurably possessed by the legion-devil of carnage? When a creature is of intellect so per-verted that he can discern no difference between a review and a battle, between the animating bugle and the dying groan, it were expedient to remove him, as quietly as may be, from his devasta-tion of God's earth and his usurpation of God's authority. Compassion points out the cell for him at the bottom of the hospital, and listens to hear the key turned in the ward : until then, the house is insecure.

Shipley. God grant our rulers wisdom, and our brethren peace !

Franklin. Here are but indifferent specimens and tokens. Those fellows throw stones pretty well; if they practise much longer, they will hit us. Let me entreat you, my lord, to leave me here. So long as the good people were contented with hoot-

ing and shouting at us, no great harm was either done or apprehended; but, now they are beginning to throw stones, perhaps
they may prove themselves more dexterous in action than their
rulers have done latterly in council.

Shipley.   Take care, Doctor Franklin !   *That* was very near
being the philosopher's stone.

' *Franklin.*   Let me pick it up, then, and send it to London by
the diligence.   But I am afraid your ministers, and the nation at
large, are as little in the way of wealth as of wisdom, in the
experiment they are making.

Shipley.   While I was attending to you, William had started.
Look ! he has reached them : they are listening to him.   Believe
me, he has all the courage of an Englishman and of a Christian ;
and, if the stoutest of them force him to throw off his new black
coat, the blusterer would soon think it better to have listened to
less polemical doctrine.

Franklin.   Meantime a few of the town-boys are come nearer,
and begin to grow troublesome.   I am sorry to requite your
hospitality with such hard fare.

Shipley.   True, these young bakers make their bread very
gritty, but we must partake of it together so long as you are with
us.

Franklin.   Be pleased, my lord, to give us grace ; our repast
is over : this is my boat.

Shipley.   We will accompany you as far as to the ship.
Thank God ! we are now upon the water, and all safe.   Give
me your hand, my good Doctor Franklin ! and although you
have failed in the object of your mission, yet the intention will
authorize me to say, in the holy words of our Divine Redeemer,
" Blessed are the peacemakers ! "

Franklin.   My dear lord ! if God ever blessed a man at the
intercession of another, I may reasonably and confidently hope in
such a benediction.   Never did one arise from a warmer, a
tenderer, or a purer heart.

Shipley.   Infatuation ! that England should sacrifice to her
king so many thousands of her bravest men, and ruin so many
thousands of her most industrious, in a vain attempt to destroy
the very principles on which her strength and her glory are
founded !   The weakest prince that ever sat upon a throne, and

the most needy and sordid parliament that ever pandered to distempered power, are thrusting our blindfold nation from the pinnacle of prosperity.

Franklin. I believe *your* king (from this moment it is permitted me to call him *ours* no longer) to be as honest and as wise a man as any of those about him ; but unhappily he can see no difference between a review and a battle. Such are the optics of most kings and rulers. His parliament, in both houses, acts upon calculation. There is hardly a family in either that does not anticipate the clear profit of several thousands a year, to itself and its connections. Appointments to regiments and frigates raise the price of papers ; and forfeited estates fly confusedly about and darken the air from the Thames to the Atlantic.

Shipley. It is lamentable to think that war, bringing with it every species of human misery, should become a commercial speculation. Bad enough when it arises from revenge,—another word for honor.

Franklin. A strange one, indeed! but not more strange than fifty others that come under the same title. Wherever there is nothing of religion, nothing of reason, nothing of truth, we come at once to honor ; and here we draw the sword, dispense with what little of civilization we ever pretended to, and murder or get murdered as may happen. But these ceremonials both begin and end with an appeal to God, who, before we appealed to him, plainly told us we should do no such thing, and that he would punish us most severely if we did. And yet, my lord, even the gentlemen upon your bench turn a deaf ear to him on these occasions ; nay, they go further : they pray to him for success in that which he has forbidden so strictly, and, when they have broken his commandment, thank him. Upon seeing these mockeries and impieties age after age repeated, I have asked myself whether the depositaries and expounders of religion have really any whatever of their own ; or rather, like the lawyers, whether they do not defend professionally a cause that otherwise does not interest them in the least. Surely, if these holy men really believed in a just, retributive God, they would never dare to utter the word *war*, without horror and deprecation.

Shipley. Let us attribute to infirmity what we must else attribute to wickedness.

Franklin. Willingly would I ; but children are whipped severely for inobservance of things less evident, for disobedience of commands less audible and less awful.   I am loath to attribute cruelty to your order : men so entirely at their ease have seldom any.   Certain I am that several of the bishops would not have patted Cain upon the back while he was about to kill Abel ; and my wonder is that the very same holy men encourage their brothers in England to kill their brothers in America ; not one, not two nor three, but thousands, many thousands.

Shipley. I am grieved at the blindness with which God has afflicted us for our sins.   These unhappy men are little aware what combustibles they are storing under the Church, and how soon they may explode.   Even the wisest do not reflect on the most important and the most certain of things, which is that every act of inhumanity and injustice goes far beyond what is apparent at the time of its commission ; that these, and all other things, have their consequences ; and that the consequences are infinite and eternal.   If this one truth alone could be deeply impressed upon the hearts of men, it would regenerate the whole human race.

Franklin. In regard to politics, I am not quite certain whether a politician may not be too far-sighted ; but I am quite certain that, if it be a fault, it is one into which few have fallen.   The policy of the Romans in the time of the republic seems to have been prospective.   Some of the Dutch also, and of the Venetians, used the telescope.   But in monarchies the prince, not the people, is consulted by the minister of the day ; and what pleases the weakest supersedes what is approved by the wisest.

Shipley. We have had great statesmen,—Burleigh, Cromwell, Marlborough, Somers ; and, whatever may have been in the eyes of a moralist the vices of Walpole, none ever understood more perfectly, or pursued more steadily, the direct and palpable interests of the country.   Since his administration, our affairs have never been managed by men of business ; and it was more than could have been expected that, in our war against the French in Canada, the appointment fell on an able commander.

Franklin. Such an anomaly is unlikely to recur.   You have in the English Parliament (I speak of both houses) only two great men ; only two considerate and clear-sighted politicians,—

Chatham and Burke.   Three or four can say clever things;
several have sonorous voices; many vibrate sharp comminations
from the embrasures of portentously slit sleeves; and there are
those to be found who deliver their oracles out of wigs as worshipful as the curls of Jupiter, however they may be grumbled at
by the flour-mills they have laid under such heavy contribution :
yet nearly all of all parties want alike the sagacity to discover
that in striking America you shake Europe ; that kings will come
out of the war either to be victims or to be despots ; and that
within a quarter of a century they will be hunted down like
vermin by the most servile nations, or slain in their palaces by
their own courtiers.   In a peace of twenty years you might have
paid off the greater part of your national debt, indeed as much of
it as it would be expedient to discharge, and you would have
left your old enemy France laboring and writhing under the
intolerable and increasing weight of hers.   This is the only
way in which you can ever quite subdue her ; and in this you
subdue her without a blow, without a menace, and without a
wrong.   As matters now stand, you are calling her from attending
to the corruptions of her court, and inviting her from bankruptcy
to glory.

Shipley.   I see not how bankruptcy can be averted by the
expenditure of war.

Franklin.   It cannot.   But war and glory are the same thing
to France, and she sings as shrilly and as gaily after a beating as
before.   With a subsidy to a less amount than she has lately been
accustomed to squander in six weeks, and with no more troops
than would garrison a single fortress, she will enable us to set you
at defiance, and to do you a heavier injury in two campaigns than
she has been able to do in two centuries, although your king was in
her pay against you.   She will instantly be our ally, and soon our
scholar.   Afterward she will sell her crown-jewels and her church-
jewels, which cover the whole kingdom, and will derive unnatural
strength from her vices and her profligacy.   You ought to have conciliated us as your ally, and to have had no other, excepting Holland
and Denmark.   England could never have, unless by her own
folly, more than one enemy.   Only one is near enough to strike
her ; and that one is down.   All her wars for six hundred years
have not done this ; and the first trumpet will untrance her.   You

leave your house open to incendiaries while you are running after a refractory. child.   Had you laid down the rod, the child would have come back.   And because he runs away from the rod, you take up the poker.   Seriously, what means do you possess of enforcing your unjust claims and insolent authority ?   Never since the Norman Conquest had you an army so utterly inefficient, or generals so notoriously unskilful : no, not even in the reign of that venal traitor, that French stipendiary, the second Charles. Those were yet living who had fought bravely for his father, and those also who had vanquished him ; and Victory still hovered over the mast that had borne the banners of our Commonwealth : *ours, ours,* my lord ! the word is the right word here.

Shipley.   I am depressed in spirit, and can sympathize but little in your exultation.   All the crimes of Nero and Caligula are less afflicting to humanity, and consequently we may suppose will bring down on the offenders a less severe retribution, than an unnecessary and unjust war.   And yet the authors and abettors of this most grievous among our earthly calamities, the enactors and applauders (on how vast a theatre !) of the first and greatest crime committed upon earth, are quiet, complacent creatures, jovial at dinner, hearty at breakfast, and refreshed with sleep ! Nay, the prime movers in it are called most religious and most gracious ; and the hand that signs in cold-blood the death-warrant of nations is kissed by the kind-hearted, and confers distinction upon the brave !   The prolongation of a life that shortens so many others is prayed for by the conscientious and the pious !   Learning is inquisitive in the research of phrases to celebrate him who has conferred such blessings, and the eagle of genius holds the thunderbolt by his throne !   Philosophy, O my friend, has hitherto done little for the social State ; and Religion has nearly all her work to do !   She too hath but recently washed her hands from blood, and stands neutrally by, yes worse than neutrally, while others shed it.   I am convinced that no day of my life will be so censured by my own clergy as this, the day on which the last hopes of peace have abandoned us, and the only true minister of it is pelted from our shores.   Farewell, until better times !   May the next generation be wiser !   And wiser it surely will be, for the lessons of Calamity are far more impressive than those which repudiated Wisdom would have taught.

Franklin.   Folly hath often the same results as Wisdom : but Wisdom would not engage in her school-room so expensive an assistant as Calamity.   There are, however, some noisy and unruly children whom she alone has the method of rendering tame and tractable : perhaps it may be by setting them to their tasks both sore and supperless.   The ship is getting under weigh. Adieu once more, my most revered and noble friend !   Before me in imagination do I see America, beautiful as Leda in her infant smiles, when her father Jove first raised her from the earth ; and behind me I leave England, hollow, unsubstantial, and broken, as the shell she burst from.

Shipley.   Oh, worst of miseries, when it is impiety to pray that our country may be successful !   Farewell ! may every good attend you ; with as little of evil to endure or to inflict, as national sins can expect from the Almighty !

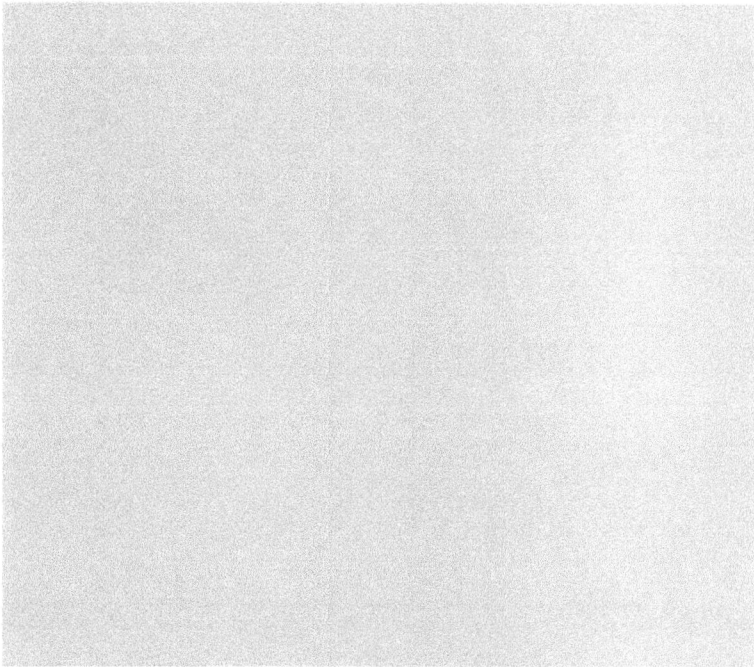

TURNBULL AND SPEARS, PRINTERS, EDINBURGH.

www.ingramcontent.com/pod-product-compliance
Lightning Source LLC
Chambersburg PA
CBHW032306280326
41932CB00009B/722